Advance Praise for Thunder at the Gates

"We have long known of the history of the pioneering black Massachusetts regiments of the Civil War—the Fifty-fourth and Fifty-fifth Infantry and Fifth Cavalry—and their impact on the military and political battlefields. In this deeply researched and stunningly narrated new study of their exploits, Egerton, by focusing our attention squarely on the men, both the enlisted and officers, has found a new and exciting way to retell the story of those whose actions had a profound impact on the outcome of the struggles against slavery and racial oppression."

—RICHARD J. BLACKETT,
Professor of History, Vanderbilt University

"'None were braver in the fight' wrote the poet Paul Laurence Dunbar about Massachusetts' black regiments, and Douglas Egerton takes up that refrain, chronicling with nuance and insight the heroic struggle for freedom and justice of soldiers such as Lewis and Charles Douglass, William Carney, and Stephen A. Swails. Egerton brilliantly interweaves personal stories and political context, evoking the battlefields of Fort Wagner and Olustee, and the profound legacy of what happened there. This is a great book, worthy of the men who inspired it."

—ELIZABETH R. VARON,
author of *Appomattox: Victory, Defeat,
and Freedom at the End of the Civil War*

Also by Douglas R. Egerton

The Wars of Reconstruction:
The Brief, Violent History of America's Most Progressive Era

Year of Meteors: Stephen Douglas, Abraham Lincoln,
and the Election That Brought on the Civil War

Death or Liberty:
African Americans and Revolutionary America

Rebels, Reformers, and Revolutionaries:
Collected Essays and Second Thoughts

He Shall Go Out Free: The Lives of Denmark Vesey

Gabriel's Rebellion:
The Virginia Slave Conspiracies of 1800 and 1802

Charles Fenton Mercer and the Trial of National Conservatism

The Denmark Vesey Affair:
A Documentary History (with Robert L. Paquette)

The Atlantic World: A History, 1400–1888
(with Alison Games, Kris Lane, and Donald R. Wright)

THUNDER AT
THE GATES

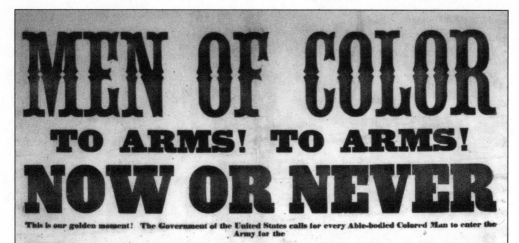

MEN OF COLOR

TO ARMS! TO ARMS!

NOW OR NEVER

This is our golden moment! The Government of the United States calls for every Able-bodied Colored Man to enter the Army for the

Three Years' Service!

And join in Fighting the Battles of Liberty and the Union. A new era is open to us. For generations we have suffered under the horrors of slavery, outrage and wrong; our manhood has been denied, our citizenship blotted out, our souls seared and burned, our spirits cowed and crushed, and the hopes of the future of our race involved in doubt and darkness. But now our relations to the white race are changed. Now, therefore, is our most precious moment. Let us rush to arms!

FAIL NOW, & OUR RACE IS DOOMED

On this the soil of our birth. We must now awake, arise, or be forever fallen. If we value liberty, if we wish to be free in this land, if we love our country, if we love our families, our children, our home, we must strike now while the country calls; we must rise up in the dignity of our manhood, and show by our own right arms that we are worthy to be freemen. Our enemies have made the country believe that we are craven cowards, without soul, without manhood, without the spirit of soldiers. Shall we die with this stigma resting upon our graves? Shall we leave this inheritance of Shame to our Children? No! a thousand times NO! We WILL Rise! The alternative is upon us. Let us rather die freemen than live to be slaves. What is life without liberty? We say that we have manhood; now is the time to prove it. A nation or a people that cannot fight may be pitied, but cannot be respected. If we would be regarded men, if we would forever silence the tongue of Calumny, of Prejudice and Hate, let us Rise Now and Fly to Arms! We have seen what Valor and Heroism our Brothers displayed at Port Hudson and Milliken's Bend, though they are just from the galling, poisoning grasp of Slavery, they have startled the World by the most exalted heroism. If they have proved themselves heroes, cannot WE PROVE OURSELVES MEN?

ARE FREEMEN LESS BRAVE THAN SLAVES

More than a Million White Men have left Comfortable Homes and joined the Armies of the Union to save their Country. Cannot we leave ours, and swell the Hosts of the Union, to save our liberties, vindicate our manhood, and deserve well of our Country. MEN OF COLOR! the Englishman, the Irishman, the Frenchman, the German, the American, have been called to assert their claim to freedom and a manly character, by an appeal to the sword. The day that has seen an enslaved race in arms has, in all history, seen their last trial. We now see that our last opportunity has come. If we are not lower in the scale of humanity than Englishmen, Irishmen, White Americans and other Races, we can show it now. Men of Color, Brothers and Fathers, we appeal to you, by all your concern for yourselves and your liberties, by all your regard for God and humanity, by all your desire for Citizenship and Equality before the law, by all your love for the Country, to stop at no subterfuge, listen to nothing that shall deter you from rallying for the Army. Come Forward, and at once Enroll your Names for the Three Years' Service. Strike now, and you are henceforth and forever Freemen!

E. D. Bassett,	Rev. J. Underdue,	P. J. Armstrong,	Rev. J. C. Gibbs,	Elijah J. Davis,
William D. Forten.	John W. Price,	J. W. Simpson,	Daniel George,	John P. Burr,
Frederick Douglass,	Augustus Dorsey,	Rev. J. B. Trusty,	Robert M. Adger,	Robert Jones,
Wm. Whipper,	Rev. Stephen Smith,	S. Morgan Smith,	Henry M. Cropper,	O. V. Catto,
D. D. Turner,	N. W. Depee,	William E. Gipson,	Rev. J. B. Reeve,	Thos. J. Dorsey,
Jas. McCrummell,	Dr. J. H. Wilson,	Rev. J. Boulden,	Rev. J. A. Williams,	I. D. Cliff,
A. S. Cassey,	J. W. Cassey,	Rev. J. Asher,	Rev. A. L. Stanford,	Jacob C. White,
A. M. Green,	James Needham,	Rev. Elisha Weaver,	Thomas J. Bowers,	Morris Hall,
J. W. Page,	Ebenezer Black,	David B. Bowser,	J. C. White, Jr.,	J. P. Johnson,
L. R. Seymour,	James R. Gordon,	Henry Minton,	Rev. J. P. Campbell,	Franklin Turner,
Rev. William T. Catto,	Samuel Stewart,	Daniel Colley,	Rev. W. J. Alston,	Jesse E. Glasgow.

A Meeting in furtherance of the above named object will be held

And will be Addressed by

U. S. Steam-Power Book and Job Printing Establishment, Ledger Buildings, Third and Chestnut Streets, Philadelphia.

THUNDER AT THE GATES

The Black Civil War Regiments
That Redeemed America

Douglas R. Egerton

BASIC BOOKS
NEW YORK

Designed by Linda Mark

Library of Congress Cataloging-in-Publication Data
Names: Egerton, Douglas R., author.
Title: Thunder at the gates : the black Civil War regiments that redeemed America / Douglas R. Egerton.
Description: Philadelphia, PA : Basic Books, 2016. | Includes bibliographical references and index.
Identifiers: LCCN 2016032057| ISBN 9780465096640 (hardcover) | ISBN 9780465096657 (ebook)
Subjects: LCSH: United States—History—Civil War, 1861–1865—Participation, African American. | Massachusetts—History—Civil War, 1861–1865—Participation, African American. | United States. Army. Massachusetts Infantry Regiment, 54th (1863–1865) | United States. Army. Massachusetts Infantry Regiment, 55th (1863–1865) | United States. Army. Massachusetts Cavalry Regiment, 5th (1864–1865) | United States. Army—African American troops—History—19th century. | African American soldiers—Massachusetts—History—19th century. | United States—History—Civil War, 1861–1865—Campaigns.
Classification: LCC E492.9 .E35 2016 | DDC 973.7/415—dc23 LC record available at https://lccn.loc.gov/2016032057

10 9 8 7 6 5 4 3 2 1

Once again, for Leigh

Contents

"ROBERT GOULD SHAW"

Why was it that the thunder voice of Fate
Should call thee, studious, from the classic groves,
Where calm-eyed Pallas with still footstep roves,
And charge thee seek the turmoil of the state?
What bade thee hear the voice and rise elate,
Leave home and kindred and thy spicy loaves,
To lead th' unlettered and despised droves
To manhood's home and thunder at the gate?
Far better the slow blaze of Learning's light,
The cool and quiet of her dearer fane,
Than this hot terror of a hopeless fight,
This cold endurance of the final pain,—
Since thou and those who with thee died for right
Have died, the Present teaches, but in vain!

   —PAUL LAURENCE DUNBAR, 1913
   (son of a veteran of the Fifty-fifth)

"THE ADVANTAGES OF LIVING
IN TIMES CALLED CALAMITOUS"

A nation does not know its strength until tested by a calamity. Then it is, that its power of endurance and capacity to invent are developed. Its latent energy, unknown in times of peace and plenty, is forced into action. Listlessness gives way to caution; *dormancy* to untiring watchfulness; in a word it proves its power to exist, and thus commands respect from all.

Misfortunes awake all the better feelings of our nature. In the hour of adversity we feel drawn closer to each other, and the common cord running through all humanity vibrates in sympathy for mutual suffering. We extend the narrow home circle till it includes the entire human family, and around a common cause we work with a common will. Our pride is humbled, and we are reminded of our dependence on a higher power. The gloom passes, the sun shines out. We walk stronger, better, freer!

—Norwood Penrose Hallowell,
Harvard College essay, March 22, 1860

Prologue

WEARY AFTER THE LONG MARCH, THE BLACK INFANTRYMEN FELL to their knees, dropping their muskets and pulling off their heavy gear. Their white colonel, twenty-eight-year-old Alfred Hartwell, a Massachusetts native and a Harvard man, consulted his hand-drawn map and guessed them to be on the outskirts of Pineville, a South Carolina village of roughly 100 buildings. That morning, April 3, 1865, Hartwell had received orders to take a detachment of the Massachusetts Fifty-fifth Volunteer Infantry Regiment and head upland toward Lake Moultrie in search of Confederate cavalry. After firing a few shots at a mounted party riding in advance of Hartwell's infantry, the Confederates vanished, but not before lynching a number of runaway slaves they found hiding in a swamp. The discovery of the bodies brought the soldiers to their feet, and by the time they reached the gates of a plantation owned by Charles Porcher, the company was in no mood to be charitable to those yet loyal to the collapsing Confederacy. A former captain in his regiment's sister unit, the Fifty-fourth, Hartwell was experienced enough to appease his revenge-minded soldiers by arresting the sixty-three-year-old Porcher, whom he denounced as "an original and most decided rebel," while his

1

men fanned out to inform Porcher's human property of their freedom. One officer demanded to know whether Porcher was hiding "any wine in his cellars," and after the unrepentant slaveholder lied to the unit—the wines were found in his attic—the soldiers and Porcher's newly freed slaves helped themselves to the bottles; "one or the other" group, Lieutenant Colonel Charles Fox later admitted, "while in liquor," set fire to Porcher's house and outbuildings.[1]

Although Hartwell's orders merely called for the Fifty-fifth to search for remaining Confederate forces in the interior, the black soldiers gloried in serving the cause of liberation. Months before, Sergeant James Monroe Trotter had observed that "we found the old system of slavery in full operations as it had always been." As they overran Carolina plantations Hartwell demanded that soon-to-be former masters "blow their horns, to summon the slaves from their work up to the house." An officer—typically a black sergeant—then made a speech, "informing them they were free." There was "joy on those plantations, I need not tell you," Lieutenant George Garrison informed his father, abolitionist William Lloyd Garrison. Trotter would explain to the freedpeople that they could leave for Charleston if they wished, but that if they planned to remain on the estate, the army would assist in drawing up "a written agreement to compensate for labor done." A former slave himself, Trotter remarked that "the former slaveholders wince under this new order of things. It seems to hurt them sorely—having to treat as intelligent free men and women [those whom] they have tyrannized over with impunity." Trotter was not much surprised that the planters he dealt with were respectful "and were very skillful in concealing whatever bitterness they may have felt when seeing a 'nigger' with shoulder straps." The black sergeant could laugh at this, but only because he wore "a good Colt revolver" on his hip.[2]

Having taught school in the Midwest before the war, Trotter understood all too well that it was not just Southern whites who despised the idea of a black man with stripes on his uniform, or even a black man in uniform. For two years, the Fifty-fourth and Fifty-fifth—and now the first Northern black cavalry regiment, the Massachusetts Fifth—had battled Northern racism when not assaulting impregnable Confederate fortifications. The nearly 5,000 men who served in the three regiments recognized that the problems facing the nation were not all the result of secession.

Most of the recruits hailed from states that denied them the right to vote, banned their children from public schools, and allowed thugs to beat them when they boarded streetcars and trains. Trotter and his fellows had signed on to crush the Confederacy and put an end to the enslavement of 4 million blacks, but also to win for themselves the full rights and privileges of American citizens.

THOSE WHO ENLISTED IN EARLY 1863 UNDERSTOOD THAT IT WAS BY no means certain that their sacrifice would convince white Americans to accept their claims. A good many Northern freemen had fathers or uncles who had served in previous wars. Roughly 5,000 black men had joined the Patriots during the Revolution, but significantly, those soldiers disproportionately hailed from those New England states that were home to few African Americans overall. (Another 15,000 Africans and African Americans, mostly from the South, sided with the Loyalists as the best path to freedom.) Only Massachusetts permitted slaves to volunteer in exchange for their freedom, and many, such as Peter Salem, fought at both Concord and Bunker Hill. Several other Northern states allowed bondmen to enlist as substitutes for their masters, which typically resulted in freedom—provided they survived the fighting. Black veterans had prayed that the Revolution might offer not merely new opportunities for freedom but also full participation in the new political order. When Massachusetts crafted its new state constitution in 1780—even before slavery was abolished in the state—it rewarded black veterans by allowing all freedmen the right to vote. Slavery in the North collapsed fastest in those states that had lower proportions of blacks, but also in those that had high numbers of black veterans, who often returned from the war armed and prepared to liberate wives and children and to sue for political rights when necessary. Now their sons hoped to force an unwilling nation to finally recognize those rights.[3]

Because of that recent history, from the moment the first black man enlisted, Northern Democrats feared the obvious connection between military service and future demands for federal citizenship. "The only motive for adopting the black soldier system was the fanatical idea of negro equality," fumed a New York publisher, "and the determination of the radicals to

do everything possible to raise the negro to the social and political level of
the white." Despite disastrous setbacks for the U.S. Army at both battles of
Bull Run, the Peninsula Campaign, and again in December 1862 at Fredericksburg, most Democrats appeared to prefer an endless bloodbath to the
prospect of black voting rights. So worried was the Lincoln administration
about appeasing Northern racists that it was not until the Emancipation
Proclamation went into effect in January 1863 that his War Department
permitted Massachusetts governor John A. Andrew to begin raising black
regiments. As abolitionist Frederick Douglass spoke across the North in
favor of Andrew's proposal, the vitriol reached ugly new lows. "Fred Douglass sounds the war cry to the darkeys of New York," sneered a Cleveland
editor. "Let us imagine Fred standing on an eminence near Rochester, a
perfume bottle in one hand," speaking to the black recruits, as "the swords
of the charcoal officers protrude between their legs like monkey's tails."
That Douglass, born a slave in Maryland, had become a respected, elegantly dressed, and eloquent antislavery orator clearly outraged the Ohio
publisher, but perhaps his real fear was that black soldiers would aim "their
muskets North, South, East and West" and not merely at the Confederate
military.[4]

The theory that black soldiers and veterans could not be adequately
controlled by white officers was also raised on Capitol Hill, especially by
politicians from the border slave states that had not seceded. "You put one
white man to command a thousand negroes at the South," charged Kentucky congressman John J. Crittenden, but "will he restrain them? Will
it not result in servile war?" The aged Crittenden, a former senator and
attorney general who had condemned the Emancipation Proclamation,
had sons fighting for both the U.S. and the Confederacy. His son Thomas
Crittenden, despite remaining loyal to the Union, had owned eleven slaves
in 1860, and the congressman hoped to end the war with the smallest possible modification of white supremacy.[5]

In contradiction with the notion that black males, if provided with a
rifle, would wage a war of racial extermination against all whites regardless
of region, other critics insisted that African Americans were too cowardly
to make effective soldiers. When James Grace, a recruiting officer for the
Fifty-fourth Infantry, attempted to promote the regiment in New Bedford, the city's "rougher element" jeered him, laughing that "he thinks the

negroes will fight!" The whaling town was renowned as a safe haven for runaway slaves, yet even there whites assured Grace that "they will turn and run at the first sight of the enemy." One Manhattan journalist added that while black soldiers would respond when faced with Confederate bayonets, just "as the most timid animal might fight in a corner," all "sensible" people agreed that "fifty thousand white men are worth more to any army than five hundred thousand negroes." Even many Southern whites, despite long memories of Nat Turner's fiery 1831 rebellion, claimed—or at least pretended to claim—that they had nothing to fear from black soldiers. "Cuffee won't fight," North Carolina's Catherine Edmondston maintained. "He is afraid of cold iron & shot terrifies him." Such bravado conceivably reflected efforts to bury fears that their own bondmen yearned to take up arms against them, but in early 1863 it was widespread enough to suggest that most Southern whites were unconcerned about the prospect. When told that the North was considering black recruits, Confederate War Department clerk John B. Jones merely shrugged, confident that black men would promptly flee the battlefield and "we shall get their arms."[6]

Still other Northerners feared that the morale of white soldiers, already low after the failed invasions of the South in the fall and winter, would suffer further from having to serve beside black men. Speaking before the House of Representatives in early February 1863, Congressman William Allen of Ohio worried that "no negroes in the free States will offer their services to these new regiments," and so the Lincoln administration would be forced to rely on the fugitive slaves already crowding into Washington and Baltimore. The "soldiers now in the Army will never submit to this," Allen warned. "They will leave the Army as rats desert a sinking ship." Certainly no "high-minded" whites would consent to serve as officers of black units, he sneered; the entire proposition was "absurd and ridiculous." No less than General John A. Dix, a New York free-soiler, cautioned Governor Andrew that white soldiers might regard black regiments as insulting to their manhood. If "the twenty millions of white males" in the North could not subdue a far smaller number of Confederates, he counseled, then the rebellion "would never be suppressed," and the use of Northern freemen or Southern runaways "would prove utterly fallacious."[7]

Initially, at least, such fears proved justified. A good number of soldiers complained to their officers, their parents, and their congressmen about what they regarded as the radical transformation taking place in the Union's war aims. Previously, Lincoln had waged a war for reunion only, but as of the first day of 1863 the administration championed black freedom as well. "I can tell you we don't think mutch of [the Proclamation] hear in the army," groused Ohio private Chauncey Welton, "for we did not enlist to fight for the negro." Now that the War Department had taken the next logical step and was considering Governor Andrew's request, Welton reported, "men are deserting evry day from our regment." Private James Brewer, although he endorsed emancipation as a military tactic, wrote that he was "awfull mad about Negroe arming," which he dismissed as "a burlesk on the white man's Soldiering." Quite possibly, Welton's and Brewer's grammatical shortcomings hinted at the concern of many middle- and working-class whites that liberation might lead to an African American exodus out of the South and so pose economic competition for white veterans across the North. "Is there a member here who dare say that Ohio troops will fight successfully or fight at all," Congressman Samuel Cox queried the House, "if the result shall be the flight and movement of the black race by millions northward to their own State?"[8]

On occasion, the racist fears of Northern Democrats were founded on even less convincing rationales. The *Chicago Times* charged that with Congress preparing to institute a draft, Andrew's request to raise black regiments was merely a way for its white residents to avoid military service. Massachusetts "mainly provoked the war," the *Times* alleged, and was "instrumental in converting it into a negro emancipation crusade," yet now Andrew planned to entice black men from the free states to complete "her quota" while its wealthy white men "will purchase their exemptions." Not to be outdone, Kentucky's Garrett Davis rose in the Senate to suggest that as New England was home to so few black men, it would have to resort to reopening the Atlantic slave trade to fill the regiments. The strangest allegations appeared in the pages of the *Detroit Free Press*. Fearful that Lincoln might lose his reelection bid in 1864, its editor insisted, Republicans in Congress contrived to "surround [Lincoln] with nigger soldiers; to take control of the militia from the States, and confer it absolutely upon him." Once the black soldiers supported Lincoln's dictatorship with "bayonets," the president intended to "clothe him[self] with power to suspend *habeas corpus* whenever he pleases" and to "subjugate and eliminate the local banks."[9]

Fearing that their moment of opportunity might be lost, black activists and abolitionists picked up their pens in response to the lengthy list of white fears and accusations. Among the most eloquent was twenty-four-year-old James Henry Gooding, a North Carolina–born slave turned Massachusetts mariner. President Lincoln had called for the end of slavery in his Proclamation, Gooding wrote in the *New Bedford Mercury* in the spring of 1863, but it "depends on the free black men of the North, whether it will die or not." Without the help of African Americans, Gooding feared, the war might well be lost. But even if the United States proved victorious and only white men served, "language cannot depict the indignity, the scorn, and perhaps violence, that will be heaped upon us." Black men had to take the lead in killing slavery. "Now is the time to act," he concluded. Gooding would be among the first to enlist in the Fifty-fourth.[10]

In early 1863, virtually all Americans—white and black, Confederate and Unionist, Republican and Democrat—understood that the three black regiments were to serve as a test case. Irregular efforts were then under way in Kansas and along the Carolina coast to arm blacks, but those actions were far from the public's gaze and largely unwelcome to the War Department. Instead, the eyes of the United States were on Massachusetts. Should its soldiers succeed and fight brilliantly, that would open the door for other Northern states to begin recruiting African Americans and for the federal government to place blue uniforms on runaways and refugees in Washington and the border states. Should they live down to the dismal expectations of conservative Democrats, white soldiers, and more than a few moderate Republicans, that performance would not only put an end to the experiment but set off repercussions for American society for generations to come.

THE STORY OF THE FIFTY-FOURTH, OR AT LEAST THE FIRST FEW months of its history, has appeared in fiction and film, from Louisa May Alcott's "My Contraband," a short story first published in late 1863, to the 1989 movie *Glory*. Because Bob, Alcott's fictional former slave, dies at Fort Wagner on July 18, 1863, in the regiment's second battle, her story concludes just as later recruits such as Trotter were arriving at Readville, Massachusetts, the site of the regiment's training. Alcott's tale might have formed the basis for the pervasive misconception that the saga of the earliest black troops ended only six months after enlistments first began. *Glory* adheres to that truncated narrative, suggesting that the history of the Fifty-fourth concluded that July night on the parapets of Fort Wagner. Of the six main characters in the film, only Robert Gould Shaw actually existed. The other five are either composite characters or are so loosely based on real soldiers that the screenwriter gave them fictional names. Men who played central roles in the regiments, such as Frederick Douglass's sons Lewis and Charles, earn not so much as a cameo appearance. In reality, while the assault on Wagner was a defining moment, a majority of the regiment fought on until the end of the war and even served as an occupying force in Charleston until the fall of 1865. Having enlisted less to preserve the Union than to win the peace, the men of the Fifty-fourth fought on in the years after Appomattox, either by renewing their prewar activism or by going into politics and serving in Southern state assemblies.

Curiously, although black soldiers in the Union army have been the subject of numerous studies, no complete history of the three Massachusetts regiments exists. There are two accounts of the months leading up to the battle on Morris Island, where Fort Wagner stood, but both are outdated, in more senses than one. Above all, both focus on Robert Gould Shaw at the expense of the black men who served under him. Neither book says anything about the volunteers who later transferred into or enlisted in its sister infantry and cavalry regiments. Many other books have chronicled why soldiers fought in this conflict, but they invariably focus on the white combatants; for white Northern soldiers, at least, their most powerful motivation was the salvation of the Union. By comparison, the soldiers described in this volume enlisted to assert their claim, and that of their race, to state and federal citizenship. Others sought to demonstrate their manhood and sense of self-worth, while still others—especially those in the Fifth Cavalry—hoped to march back into their native South and liberate those loved ones they had left behind.

This book tells the story of these three interconnected regiments by following the lives and careers of a small number of soldiers. Some had been born into slavery, and others were sons of privilege. Most survived the conflict, and some did not. Although no account set during the turbulent Civil War era can ignore decisions made by presidents and congressmen and generals, my focus is on these individual officers, infantrymen, and cavalrymen. Their saga began well before the guns of Sumter, continued into the battles of the Reconstruction era, and even stretched into the first decades of the twentieth century. History told from the top down tells us much about why the Civil War came to be. But the story of these fourteen men tells us instead just what the war was like, particularly for those soldiers who embraced black liberation as their paramount goal, sought to transform a white man's war into a revolutionary struggle for freedom, and then ventured their lives on the battlefield in pursuit of that dream.

CHAPTER ONE

The Travelers

THE YOUNG HARVARD STUDENT HAD ONCE DREAMED OF LIVING "in times called calamitous," and now he understood that this was no moment for those who harbored any doubts about their cause, or about their courage. Aboard the steamers *Williams, Maple Leaf,* and *Recruit,* on the morning of August 3, 1863, the soldiers of the Fifty-fifth Massachusetts Volunteer Infantry Regiment prepared to debark on Morris Island, just south of Charleston Harbor. The skies shone "clear and beautiful," but the regiment had recently learned of the disastrous assault on Battery Wagner and the heavy losses incurred by their sister unit, the Fifty-fourth Infantry. The news was particularly heartrending for the Fifty-fifth's commander, Colonel Norwood Penrose Hallowell, as his older brother, Edward Needles Hallowell, had been badly wounded in the fight. "If we succeed in taking Charleston," vowed Lieutenant George Garrison, "the intention is, I think, not to leave one stone upon another, but to level it to the ground." Also watching Morris Island and the U.S. blockading fleet heave into view were two former slaves turned schoolteachers, Nicholas Said and James Monroe Trotter. Two other soldiers were still in transit from Boston. One of them, Henry Jarvis, born a slave on Virginia's Eastern Shore, had stolen a small craft in 1861 and sailed thirty-five miles across the Chesapeake Bay to Fort Monroe and freedom. The other, John M. Smith, a peddler and stove-maker from Maine, had deserted the Fifty-fifth from Camp Readville in Massachusetts. Captured in Boston, Smith was given the choice of trial and possible execution or rejoining his unit in the South. Rather to the dismay of his fellows, Smith opted for the latter.[1]

Observing the arrival of the transport steamers from the dock on Morris Island were the bloodied but unbroken survivors of Wagner. Peter Vogelsang Jr., a forty-five-year-old hotel clerk and porter from Manhattan, Edward Hallowell, and Lewis Douglass (like Lieutenant Garrison, a son of a great abolitionist) were all on sick leave after July's fighting. Stephen Swails, a light-skinned boatman from Elmira who had joined the army to escape a troubled, reckless youth in upstate New York, stood on the wharf to welcome the Fifty-fifth, as did two friends lately of New Bedford, Massachusetts. William Carney, a Virginia runaway, and James Henry Gooding, born a slave in North Carolina but legally freed by his white father, had rallied the black community in their seaport town and marched its men north to Boston to join the Fifty-fourth. "The men appear to be in splendid physical condition, and take the two regiments in the aggregate, I think the 55th is superior in material to the 54th," Gooding mused. "But the hardships incident to a soldier's life may equalize them in a month or two."[2]

Of all the men who were to serve in the state's three black units, none hailed from more distant shores than Nicholas Said. In later years, he listed his place of residence as "traveler," and that was an understatement. At a time when most white Americans resided near the place of their birth—or at best, had relocated one state due west in search of fresher farmland—Said, before taking part in his adoptive country's great civil war, had passed through dozens of nations in Africa and Europe and nearly as many states in North America. First known as Mohammed Ali bin Said, he was born in Kouka (now Kukawa), the capital of the Kingdom of Bornou, "on or about the year 1836, of the Christian era," as he later recalled. Even by Central African standards, his family was a large one. As allowed under his Muslim faith, his father kept four wives, and Mohammed was the thirteenth of nineteen children born to his mother, Dalia. The family was prosperous, but while Said was still young, his father and three brothers died in battle.[3]

By the time of Said's birth, the ancient kingdom (located in the north-eastern section of modern Nigeria) was in a state of decline, engulfed by internal turmoil and warfare with neighboring states. Amid the upheaval, the regional traffic in slaves and weapons only intensified. Although both the United States and Britain had banned the importation of Africans by 1808, the Ottoman Empire continued to purchase roughly 10,000 slaves each year for domestic service. Buyers preferred African women, but for most of the century a small number of men were captured and shipped north as well. Said's mother warned him about the dangers posed by the Kindils, desert pastoralists, who earned their livelihood by providing traders with captives. When he was about fifteen, Said joined a number of boys in gathering eggs and fowl in a nearby wood. Suddenly the cry of "Kindil! Kindil!" went up, and the boys scattered. Said tripped and fell, and then all went black. When he awoke, Said found himself "on horseback behind a man, and tied to him with a rope." After walking for ten days, the group reached the town of Katchna, a commercial center on one of the main northern trading routes that crossed the Sahara en route to Tripoli.[4]

Said's captors put the boys up for sale, and within a few days he was purchased by Abd-Al-Qadir, an Arab merchant. The boy's price was a burnoose and a rusty blunderbuss, which Said later guessed to be worth about $10 in American currency. Said's new master planned to sell the boy, together with some ivory, in the north. Upon reaching Murzuq, a walled trading outpost (in modern Libya), Al-Qadir set the boy to work on his farm. Said was unaccustomed to hard labor, and after several weeks in the fields he begged his master to sell him "to some Turk or Egyptian." At length, Al-Qadir acceded. Said's newest buyer was Abdy Agra, a young Turkish officer who was in need of a servant for his father. Said had all but resigned himself to life with the officer when, after several months, Agra announced that the time had arrived for Said to be shipped to his father in Tripoli. Since Al-Qadir was again moving north with a load of goods, Agra entrusted the boy's care to his former owner.[5]

And so it was that at the age of sixteen Said began life in Tripoli with a third owner. Hadji Daoud, an old man with three wives and a long, flowing white beard, peddled tobacco in his shop and proved to be a kind master. Said "learned to speak the Turkish language tolerably." He later boasted that he had always possessed "an extraordinary aptitude for the

acquirement of languages," and as his extraordinary life was to demonstrate, that claim had the virtue of accuracy. During Daoud's third pilgrim-
age to Mecca, much of the Turkish marketplace burned, and with it his
business. Destitute, Daoud informed Said that he would have to be sold to
cover his debts. "I began, this time to think that it was my fate to pass from
hand to hand, with never a sure and definite resting place," Said worried.
In search of the best possible price, Daoud's agent carried Said across the
Mediterranean to Smyrna, where he was sold to a Turkish officer named
Yusuf, the brother-in-law of Reşid Pasha, the pro-Western minister of foreign affairs. Reşid had once served as the Ottoman ambassador to France,
and his household was so secular that Said fretted that Reşid "was not truly
Islam." But Said enjoyed the silk clothes he wore as Yusuf's manservant
and relished the ice cream he tasted for the first time, and so he learned
to ignore Reşid's habit of dining with Christians, shaking their hands, and
sipping their champagne. His "blood boiled with anger," however, when he
witnessed the family's enslaved concubines "cuffed and beaten" by Reşid's
eunuch custodians. "I never could be reconciled to it," he sighed.[6]

Reşid counted foreign ministers and ambassadors among his intimates,
and he was especially close to Admiral Alexander Menshikov, the Russian
envoy to Constantinople. The tall, sixty-six-year-old nobleman "took a
great fancy" to Said the first time he laid eyes upon him, and "after that,"
Said remarked, "he would not allow Reşid Pasha any rest" until he agreed
to sell the boy. For a boy who had once been sold for a robe and a rusty
musket, Menshikov, in search of an exotic toy, "offered a large price," and
at length Yusuf and Reşid consented. By this time, Said had grown into a
slender, attractive young man of medium height. An American journalist
later described him as having "pleasing features," with a "complexion perfectly black." The tattoos imprinted upon his forehead as a child gave him a
mysterious quality, and he practiced a "quiet and unassuming address" that
was perhaps the result of a lifetime of domestic service.[7]

As tensions between Russia and the Ottoman Empire escalated, Menshikov increased Russia's demands, until Sultan Abdülmecid I, backed
by the British ambassador, finally rejected what he regarded as an assault
on Turkish sovereignty. A furious Czar Nicholas II recalled his envoy in
early May, and Said "accompanied him on the journey" to Russia. They
boarded the warship *Vladimir* and in two days reached the Black Sea port

Although most of the men who served in the three pioneering regiments lived outside of Massachusetts in 1863—thirty men of the Fifty-fourth listed Canada as their home—none came from farther away than Nicholas Said. Said spent so much of his life as an enslaved domestic that he disliked command and declined promotion in the ranks. *Courtesy Massachusetts Historical Society.*

of Odessa, where Menshikov kept one of his many estates. Unfree labor, in the guise of serfdom, still existed in Russia, and Said was given to understand that his master owned 56,000 serfs. The two traveled on to St. Petersburg, where the admiral found orders from the czar commanding him to hasten to the Crimea and take command of the Russian forces. Menshikov decided to leave his manservant behind and loaned the boy to Prince Nicholas Troubetzkoy. Twenty-five years old, the single prince lived near the theater district, and when Said and his temporary proprietor were not prowling the city's "societies, theaters, mansions of the rich and noble," the prince tutored Said in both French and Russian, his fourth and fifth languages. The Americans Said would come into contact with during the following decade had no way to assess his Russian or Turkish, but the white officers he served under—Harvard graduates all—praised his "French [as] quite Parisian and his Italian correct." Grateful for the prince's enormous "kindness" and friendship, Said agreed to convert to a Christian faith that he little understood. On November 12, 1855—Said's first inclusion of a precise date in his autobiography—the nineteen-year-old was baptized and dropped his birth name for that of Nicholas Said. The prince presented Said with a solid gold cross to wear on his breast; in coming years Said would find good cause to keep the crucifix tucked under his uniform.[8]

Muslim or Christian, Said remained manservant to Troubetzkoy, although that legal technicality did not stop them from becoming close friends—and perhaps much more. The prince longed to travel, and so the two Nicholases set out for Moscow, then made their way north to Archangel. Warsaw and Vienna followed, as did Prague, Dresden, and Paris. From there they journeyed to Venice and Florence, and Said put his time to good use by beginning to learn Italian, although the former Muslim also discovered the pleasures of wine, "sometimes drinking too much." To demonstrate his wealth, the prince dressed elegantly, with Said, in a conscious display of Orientalism, beside him "in a Turkish costume, embroidered with gold" as they strode down the city's boulevards. A chance encounter while dining in Venice with an African manservant born not far from Kouka prompted in Said a longing to return home.[9]

When the two journeyed to London in late 1859, Said opted to part ways. Perhaps he learned that slavery was illegal in Britain, or possibly he knew that his friend and traveling companion would not attempt to restrain him. Certainly, for the past several years, Said had experienced a very loose sort of domestic servitude, quite different from what he would later encounter in South Carolina. As recompense for years of service and comradery, the prince handed Said two £50 notes, and the two parted in tears. Said booked a modest room at the Strangers' Home for Asiatics, Africans, and South Sea Islanders located at the docks on West India Street.[10]

Said hoped to book a steamer for Malta, go on to Tripoli, and then finally go back to Bornou by caravan, but his money began to run low. The proprietor of the hotel encouraged Said to visit Isaac Jacob Rochussen, a Dutch businessman recently arrived from Suriname. Rochussen was about to marry, and he and his bride Catherine intended to travel throughout the Caribbean and North America. He required a manservant for the tour, and he assured Said that after the trip of twelve months, he would bring him back to London and assist with his return to Africa. They settled upon compensation of £3.11 each month, plus travel, board, and clothing expenses. Two days later they purchased tickets for Liverpool, where they booked passage aboard the *Bohemian,* due to sail for Portland, Maine, on December 21, 1860. The shipping clerk scribbled down his name, age, and country of origin: Nicholas Said, twenty-three, "Africa."[11]

The steamer made good time, arriving in Maine just before noon on January 5. Said and the Rochussens tarried only a few hours in Portland before sailing down the coast for Boston, and then, after two days, for Manhattan, where Said had his first encounter with American racism. On their first Sabbath in New York City, Rochussen thought to attend services at the Dutch Reformed Church on Lafayette Place. Three years before, its minister, Dr. George Cheever, had published an influential abolitionist pamphlet entitled *God Against Slavery*. Rochussen, who regarded himself as a sound antislavery man, had read the essay and assumed that "such odious distinctions" as the special balcony pews for Americans of color he had heard of would not exist in Cheever's congregation. The three arrived early, and Rochussen and his wife found empty seats in the main chapel; Said, nicely dressed in "livery," instinctively found a pew directly behind them. Rochussen was praying silently when he heard whispering and turned to find a white congregant urging Said to move to the balcony. Said's employer rose and complained that he was shocked to discover that Cheever's church was not "in harmony with the views he professed," and the three swept out of the church. Having lived as a slave for eight years, Said well understood the prerogatives of class, but this was the first time he witnessed the conflation of class and race. It was also his first warning that, even in the free states, men such as Cheever flattered themselves to be antislavery reformers without showing the slightest desire to have anything to do with those of a darker skin.[12]

Said and his employers boarded the *Karnak*, owned by the Cunard line, and departed for the Caribbean. Among the passengers were wealthy abolitionists Frank and Sarah Shaw, whose son Rob was to play an important role in Said's life. Said was more interested in their brief detour to Cap Haitian and the memories that evoked of black victories. "I found myself exceedingly delighted to be in the country where the heroes [of] the 'Haitian Independence' contended with the armies of Napoleon," he remembered. "I had always admired the exploits of Toussaint Louverture, Dessalines, Christophe, and other negro leaders, whose heroism and military talents are an honor to the African race." Said and his employers concluded their tour with a large, circular swing through western New York and into Canada, where the Rochussens left him near Montreal, leaving all of their luggage behind. Said began to suspect that he had been tricked, and he "had a strange presentiment that [he] would never see them again." He waited at the hotel for several more weeks, but the manager finally concluded that the couple had absconded, leaving a debt of $2,000. The hotel seized all of the Rochussens' baggage. Taken was all of Said's clothing, his "four Turkish costumes, three full suits," and "dozens of linen and fine English flannel shirts." Gone too were Said's dreams of returning to Bornou, as he had but $380 left in his pocket.[13]

While awaiting his employer's return, Said had become friendly with the Reverend D. T. Johnson. The minister advised Said to return to the United States and to consider living in either Buffalo or Detroit, "where there were a great number of colored people." Evidently Buffalo failed to suit him, as upon reaching the city he took passage aboard the *Concord* as a deckhand. Said had not endured hard labor for years, however, and his "strength failed." After crossing Lake Erie and landing in Detroit, Said again sought employment as a manservant. In a strange coincidence, in a life full of curious turns, the African was recognized by the Reverend George Duffield, who had first met Said several years earlier on the ship *Egitto,* at which time Said was owned by Menshikov. Duffield introduced the traveler to "the principal colored people" of Detroit, a city of 45,000, and Said began a new life as a French tutor. He was still in Detroit that fall when Abraham Lincoln captured Michigan's six electoral votes, to the dismay of Duffield, who supported John Bell's Constitutional Union Party. Said had not resided in his new country for the five years required for citizenship, but in any case, the 1857 *Dred Scott* decision denied federal citizenship to even free African Americans and the state of Michigan restricted voting rights to white men. Nevertheless, as a former slave, Said took a keen interest in Southern secession and the coming fury.[14]

ALTHOUGH SAID COULD NOT HAVE KNOWN IT WHEN THE *BOHEMIAN* steamed into Maine in January 1861, just ten miles to the north of his embarkation, in the small coastal town of Yarmouth, lived a young man of about his age. Born in Old Town, Maine, around 1842, John M. Smith barely survived a troubled childhood. Although his parents, John Dennis Smith, a free black, and Cynthia Ann Downing, a white woman, claimed to have married in 1838, by the time the boy was eight his father was either dead or had abandoned his family and the child was one of twenty-five inmates in the Brunswick "Poor House." The light-skinned John was the only person of color in the institution; his mother lived nearby in the home of a white farmer, helping the older couple with their newborn daughter. By 1860, Smith eked out a meager income as a "pedler," though he occasionally listed his occupation as "stove maker." Fate would unite the traveler and the peddler within three years, although fortune planned very different destinies for the two men.[15]

When Nicholas Said exited the segregated church in Manhattan, had he walked but a few blocks toward the Bowery, he would have reached Stanton Street and the rented home of Peter Vogelsang Jr., a forty-three-year-old hotel clerk and porter. Peter's father, Peter Vogelsang Sr., was a native of St. Croix, and his mother was from Manhattan. Little explanation exists for the porter's German surname, as the Province of Brandenburg had lost its leasing rights in the Danish West Indies nearly a century before. But despite hair and facial features that betrayed an African lineage, Peter's complexion was such that army recruiters variously described him as "white" or "light" or "colored." The elder Vogelsang had done well for himself, and prior to his death in 1844 he managed steamers on the Albany line. The family remained well connected to other socially prominent black families along the Hudson. Peter's brother Thomas found employment in Albany as a merchant sailor, while his sister Jane wed James Forten Jr., the son of one of the wealthiest men in Philadelphia. At some point in the late 1830s, Peter also married well. His bride was Theodosia Burr De-Grasse, whose prosperous family was connected to the late vice president and whose sister married George T. Downing, a restaurateur and activist two years Peter's elder. They had three children—George Peter, Maria, and John—before Theodosia died young of tuberculosis in May 1854. Such a tragic loss, together with the demands of a busy job and a young family to care for, would probably have led most men to watch the growing sectional divide of the late 1850s with some detachment; in addition, Vogelsang's status as a renter did not allow him to meet the $250 property requirement New York State imposed on black voters. Yet whatever contempt Vogelsang had for Northern racism, he hated slavery more.[16]

When Said journeyed through central New York with the Rochussens, he had passed above Elmira, home to the Swails family. In 1860, Peter Swails was sixty, his wife Joanna forty-eight. Both had been born in Maryland, perhaps into slavery, and they had resided for a time in Lancaster County, Pennsylvania, where their six children were born. Southern Pennsylvania was also home to gangs of professional slave catchers, and as the Fugitive Slave Act of 1850 granted accused blacks no rights of attorney—technically, runaways had broken no law and were nothing more than errant property—freedpeople had relocated farther north over the course of the decade. Census takers recorded that Peter was mixed-race and employed as a "boatman." As was typical of most struggling black families new to freedom, almost all of the children pitched in to help the household survive. Stephen Atkins Swails, at twenty-eight the eldest, found employment roughly 140 miles to the east in Cooperstown as a waiter in the elegant "three story hotel" owned by Daniel Keyes.[17]

Joanna was as light-skinned as her husband—census takers listed both as "mulatto" in 1860—and Stephen Swails was so fair that later journalists often described him as "white" or "a light quadroon." Confident in his good looks, Swails sported a thick mustache and brushed his straight hair back away from his forehead. Cooperstown was far from his father's gaze, and he soon took notice of a twenty-one-year-old servant named Sarah Thompson. Soon Stephen and Sarah were seen together about Cooperstown, but his reputation was not a good one. Keyes finally fired the waiter "for habitual drunkenness and dishonesty." With his standing in tatters in the small town, Swails returned home to Elmira. Sarah Thompson, who was pregnant, remained behind.[18]

The first months of 1863 found Swails working in Elmira as a "boatman" and living on Jay Street, just blocks from the estate of coal magnate Jervas Langdon, whose then-eighteen-year-old daughter would one day marry writer Samuel Clemens. By that time, Sarah had given birth to a boy, Stephen Jr., and in spite of the lack of a marriage certificate she gave the child the surname of Swails rather than Thompson. Despite Swails's obvious lack of desire to legalize their relationship, Sarah continued to see him, and in 1863 or 1864 she bore him another child, a daughter named Minnie Swails.[19]

SAID HAD ALSO UNKNOWINGLY PASSED CLOSE BY THE HOME OF JAMES Monroe Trotter. Born a slave in Grand Gulf, Mississippi, about twenty-five miles south of Vicksburg, the light-skinned James was the son of Letitia, a bondwoman, and her master, Richard Trotter. While the precise nature of their relationship remains lost to history, James's early life suggests that however coercive or unequal the union may have been, it was not the violent rape experienced by so many black women. Unlike most children born into slavery, James was later able to tell an army clerk his precise birthdate—February 8, 1842—and by the time he was ten, if not before, he and his mother and sister Sally were living in Cincinnati, Ohio. Escape from the lower South was far from easy, even along the Mississippi River, and mothers rarely succeeded in fleeing with young children. Most likely, Richard Trotter ferried his black family north and left them in the care of Hiram Gilmore, an English clergyman who ran a school for freed blacks in Cincinnati. When James was about twelve, his mother passed away, and he and his sister were taken in by Robert Thomas, a fifty-five-year-old black carpenter. James was able to continue his education at the Gilmore School, an institution for freed slaves, and after moving to nearby Hamilton, Ohio, he studied music. By 1860, eighteen-year-old James Trotter, who continued to regard Thomas as his "guardian," had taken a job teaching school in Chillicothe, and his sister Sally remained with the Thomas family.[20]

ALSO BORN INTO SLAVERY WAS JAMES HENRY GOODING. ALTHOUGH most of the men he was to serve with could boast of unusual backgrounds, Gooding's own journeys were almost as far-flung as those of Said. As was the case with Trotter, Gooding's mother, Sarah Tucker, was a slave and his father, James M. Gooding, was white. What made their relationship unique was that Gooding was not Sarah's owner, but rather a white man who loved her. Born in 1813, he was a country "merchant" in New Bern, North Carolina, living with his parents, when he first met Sarah. On August 28, 1838, Sarah gave birth to their son. No record indicates who Sarah's owner was, but in 1846, one month after the child turned eight, the "boy Henry had his freedom purchased by James M. Gooding," who then "brought him to N.Y. and gave him his Manumission papers." The elder Gooding entrusted the deed to the Pearl Street law office of White and

Baines, together with $30 for the first year's room and board at Manhattan's Colored Orphan Asylum, though James Henry remained in contact with his parents. By 1851, Gooding had put cash enough aside to also purchase Sarah, and in January they were wed in North Carolina. Twelve years after that, when James Henry himself took a bride, he listed "James & Sarah" under the "names of parents," although they were surely not present at the ceremony.[21]

Built in 1837 on Forty-third Street and Fifth Avenue, the Colored Orphan Asylum enjoyed the patronage of a number of wealthy abolitionists. Cassius Clay, the antislavery cousin of Kentucky senator Henry Clay, held fund-raising speeches at the institution, as did John Jay, the son of the late Supreme Court chief justice. By the time Gooding's father left him in its care, 262 black children had passed through the orphanage's doors. The children performed most of the orphanage's housework, which both kept costs low and trained the female inmates for domestic service. As Gooding's later love of reading indicated, the institution's school was serviceable, although its teachers emphasized the basic skills necessary for black tradesmen rather than the sort of education required for universities or the professions.[22]

The standard of care improved immeasurably the year Gooding arrived in the person of black physician James McCune Smith. Born in Manhattan and educated at the city's African Free School, McCune was rejected by Columbia College because of his color. He instead sailed for Scotland and enrolled at the University of Glasgow, where he graduated first in his class. By the time he accepted the position as the head physician at the orphanage, McCune was engaged in a private practice that treated white as well as black patients. The social circle of prominent black families in Manhattan being a small one, Peter Vogelsang was a friend. The doctor somehow also found time for activism, which brought him into contact with abolitionist Frederick Douglass. McCune was soon to care for wounded African American soldiers being shipped home through Manhattan.[23]

Young James Henry Gooding, often known simply as Henry, spent three years at the orphanage. When he turned thirteen—and so of age to make his way in the world—the institution's directors apprenticed him to Albert Westlake, a dentist in the process of relocating from Manhattan to Woodbridge, New Jersey. The prospect of a lifetime of yanking decaying teeth out of rotting jaws held little appeal; by the summer of 1856, Gooding was renting a room in New Bedford, Massachusetts.[24]

Owing to the whaling industry, New Bedford had exploded in size during the previous three decades, expanding from 3,000 residents in 1830 to 22,300 in 1860. Freedpeople and runaway slaves flocked to the port, which by the time of Lincoln's election boasted over 1,500 persons of color. The transient nature of the community, together with the large number of African Americans, made New Bedford a safe haven for blacks, who hailed it as "the fugitive's Gibraltar." Gooding arrived in the city during the peak of its whaling years, when 329 whale ships—approximately half of the republic's entire whaling fleet—claimed the city as their homeport. Some of the nation's wealthiest merchants resided in New Bedford along Union Street, while black mariners and artisans lived beside working-class whites on South Water. Black barbers, grocers, and clothiers crowded into the junction of Bedford and Allen Streets, commonly dubbed "Dog Corner," where, one abolitionist fretted, they "crammed into lofts, garrets and cellars, blind alleys and narrow courts."[25]

As Gooding tramped the streets of New Bedford, he could hardly help noting the large number of aged, destitute watermen. The city's Overseers of the Poor kept records on "sick & destitute" black seamen, but for young James Henry, seventeen and physically fit, a whaling voyage offered a black man equal pay for equal work. On the high seas, as one mariner put it, "a colored man is only known and looked upon as a man, and is promoted in rank according to his ability and skill to perform the same duties as a white man." On July 18, 1856, Gooding stepped into the city's courthouse to obtain his Seamen's Protection Certificate, a passport of sorts issued by the federal government to mariners, proclaiming them to be "citizens" of the United States. Despite being freed by his father, Gooding took no chances in the wake of the Fugitive Slave Act, and both he and a new friend, mariner Sylvanus Holt, swore that he "was born in Troy in the State of N.Y." One month shy of his eighteenth birthday, Gooding also thought it prudent to add a year to his age, insisting that he was nineteen. The clerk scrutinized the young man before picking up his pen: "Henry Gooding. Height 5, 5½. Complexion, Mulatto. Hair, Curley. Eyes, black."[26]

Three days later, Holt and Gooding signed on with the *Sunbeam*, a 360-ton ship of three masts, with its foremast rigged square. Gooding, listed as a "greenhand"—a sailor new to the trade—was one of thirty men aboard. New England captains and their mates tended to descend from old Yankee stock, but the men who crowded below decks were a mixture of white and black, European and American, from every corner of the world. The only other American of color aboard was sixteen-year-old Albert Seals of Alexandria, Virginia, but the *Sunbeam* was also temporary home to three Pacific Islanders, George, Jim, and Joe Kanacka. Herman Melville, who knew the town well, once marveled that New Bedford bested every other Atlantic seaport in its polyglot mixture of humanity: "Actual cannibals stand chatting at street corners; savages outright; many of whom yet carry on their bones unholy flesh. It makes a stranger stare." Perhaps Gooding did too.[27]

When they had a choice, Massachusetts seamen preferred either a quick voyage to the Caribbean or the slightly longer six-week Atlantic crossing to European shores. But Gooding had no cause to remain in a republic that was increasingly hostile to black claims of citizenship and equality. The *Sunbeam*'s voyage promised to be a long one: New Bedford newspapers described a departure for both "the Atlantic and Pacific Oceans." In fact, by the time Gooding next stepped foot in New Bedford, more than three years had passed, and the divisive election of 1860 was well under way.[28]

The *Sunbeam* sailed south and east, rounding the Cape of Good Hope and docking in June at St. Mary's Island off India's west coast. Only one month into the voyage, both the fourth mate and the ship's cook were taken "of[f] duty with the veneral," a malady they undoubtedly picked up while docked in New Bedford. When the cook failed to convalesce, Captain Samuel Cromwell put Gooding to work in the galley. Evidently the captain instinctively thought of putting one of his two black crewmen into service, or perhaps as the least experienced mariner onboard, Gooding was the expendable choice. For his part, Gooding welcomed the task, as it afforded him much of the day to read before the time came to prepare the crew's supper. September of 1858 found the ship near Australia, and finally, as they cruised back by Indonesia, they killed five whales. "Took in Sail and got ready for cutting," the captain scribbled into the log. "At daylight commenced cutting [and] had the head of[f] and body cut in Latter." By then, Gooding had celebrated two birthdays aboard the *Sunbeam*. When not reading or cooking, he found time enough to try his hand at

Whaling voyages often lasted for years, and so for former slaves like James Henry Gooding, the *Sunbeam* (above) promised refuge from an unfriendly American republic. *Courtesy New Bedford Whaling Museum.*

verse, composing "The Sailor's Thoughts of Home," a poem rendered all the more poignant by the fact that he did not really have one. "To think of the dear loved, as I roam from shore to shore," he mused. "And think that three long years must pass, / E're I shall see them more."[29]

In early September 1859, the ship passed Mauritius, a British colony off the coast of Madagascar, and by the dawn of the new decade word arrived in New Bedford that the *Sunbeam* was headed home, carrying at least 1,450 barrels of oil. After taking several more whales on the return voyage, the *Sunbeam* sailed into port on April 13, 1860, carrying "1650 b[arre]ls sp[erm]" whale oil—the second-highest haul of any New Bedford–based whaler that year. After more than three years at sea, a wobbly Gooding stepped onto dry land, with $360.61 in his pocket.[30]

Within five weeks, the now-seasoned mariner signed on with another whaler, the *Black Eagle,* whose skipper, Charles Allen, was black, a rare but not unheard-of phenomenon in New England. (Born around 1803 in Maryland, Allen had either moved or escaped to New England.) This voyage would be shorter and was aimed north for the Cumberland Inlet near the Labrador Sea, in search of Beluga whales. But once they arrived, the weather turned frigid, even by the bleak Arctic norms of Baffin Bay. The whalers in the bay became trapped as the waters froze around them, and Captain Allen used the "team of dogs" brought aboard to trade across the ice with other ships. The worst days came in February 1861 as the men endured a low of –44 degrees, and snow banked up against the side of the *Black Eagle.* On March 20, however, the crew was greeted with "clear weather [and] light winds," and the men took to the ice and were "employed playing ball." Eight months later, on November 3, 1861, the ship returned to New Bedford, laden with 1,222 barrels of oil and 17,800 pounds of whalebone, the latter destined for the corsets of New England's ladies.[31]

One of those ladies was Ellen Louisa Allen, the twenty-five-year-old daughter of Gooding's employer. Upon returning to port, James Henry boarded with the skipper, and there he met Ellen. A proposal of marriage required one final voyage's wages. Allen was hired to captain the *Richard Mitchell* and sail it to Argentina in search of hides and wool, a lengthy voyage indicative of the black skipper's growing reputation in New Bedford. Allen in turn hired Gooding as a cook and steward at the impressive salary of $20 a month, equal to the pay of the second mate. In early February 1862, the *Richard Mitchell* docked first in Manhattan to purchase merchandise for trade; the city's residents were optimistic that General George B. McClellan, who had spent the winter building the Army of the Potomac, would soon capture the Confederate capital of Richmond. By the time the vessel returned from Buenos Aires on August 14, New England talked only of the timid McClellan's disastrous Peninsula Campaign, and before the month was out worse news yet arrived: Confederate general Robert E. Lee had devastated the forces of Major General John Pope at the Second Battle of Bull Run.[32]

With the savings from three voyages put aside, Gooding had more personal matters on his mind. Six weeks after his return, on September 28, James Henry and Ellen were married by the Reverend James Butler at the

Seamen's Bethel Church. The sanctuary, already famous for its somewhat fictionalized appearance in the 1851 novel *Moby Dick, or, The Whale*, welcomed seamen of all races. Although Butler was himself a former mariner, his pulpit did not actually resemble a "ship's bluff bows," as Melville described it. The groom had just turned twenty-four, but he continued to add a year to his age. The state's "Registry of Marriages" required couples to list their race if "other than White." City clerk Henry Leward scribbled a large "M" for "mulatto" next to Gooding's name, and a capital "A" denoting African descent next to Louisa's name.[33]

At about the time of his marriage, Gooding became acquainted with William Henry Carney Jr., a black Virginian two years his junior. Born a slave in Norfolk in 1840, Carney was raised just across the Elizabeth River in the Portsmouth home of Major Richard Carney. His father, William Carney Sr., an enslaved oysterman, knew mariners who could smuggle him north. That would mean abandoning his wife, Ann, and their seven children, but after learning that the Carney estate was soon to be divided and sold, he decided to flee with another young bondman, promising to send for his family when he could afford to do so. The elder Carney and his fellow escapee soon appeared in New Bedford.[34]

By his early teens, William Jr. had labored beside his father as an oysterman. He later assured an army officer that in his will Major Carney had freed his mother, together with all of his slaves, but that claim, rather like Gooding's creation of a Troy birthplace, was devised for his own protection. In his spare moments in Norfolk, William "attended a private and secret school" run by the Reverend George Bain, a white preacher who watched over the city's black community. Like many runaways, Carney was reluctant to explain just how he had escaped the South, for fear of retribution against those left behind. He said only that he "left the sea for a time" in 1856, the year of his father's flight, and "confiscated himself." By the fall of 1859, he was reunited with his father in New Bedford. There he found employment as "a jobber of work for stores" and began to prepare himself "for the ministry." William Sr. was finally able to send Reverend Bain the $300 required for his wife's purchase, but the rest of their children did not reach Massachusetts until 1863, two years after U.S. forces occupied Portsmouth.[35]

WORD OF THE APRIL 12, 1861, CONFEDERATE BOMBARDMENT OF
Fort Sumter found Nicholas Said and James Monroe Trotter teaching
school in Detroit and Chillicothe, respectively; Stephen Swails waiting tables in Cooperstown; Peter Vogelsang porting luggage in the Bowery; John
M. Smith tramping Maine's byways as a peddler; James Henry Gooding
chopping potatoes in the galley of the *Black Eagle;* and William Carney Jr.
pondering a life as a churchman. If the former slave Said wished to serve in
his adopted nation's military in hopes of securing the liberation of 4 million black Americans, and Vogelsang wanted to join up in hopes of forcing
his New York to recognize his claims of citizenship, for Smith and Swails
the war presented the opportunity to begin again. New Yorkers regarded
Swails, now twenty-nine, as little more than "a drunken vagabond," yet
the army offered him the chance to redeem himself, perhaps even one day
to hear himself praised as a hero and applauded as a rising politician. One
wonders, however, whether Sarah Thompson and her children would ever
come to see him in such a flattering light.

"The rebels are doing a hundred times more to abolish Slavery than
all the Abolitionists combined," editorialized one Albany journalist. "The
attack upon Fort Sumter gave it a blow from which it can never recover."
Reading the news across half a continent, the seven may have hoped that
prediction would prove true, but if they planned to assist in slavery's demise, they were sorely disappointed. Two years before, Massachusetts governor Nathaniel P. Banks vetoed legislation that would have allowed black
men to join the state militia, deciding it would be unconstitutional in light
of the *Dred Scott* decision. After Fort Sumter, young African Americans
from Rochester to Syracuse, and from Boston to Manhattan, attempted
to form all-black militia units. "It now remains for the [federal] Government to accept their services," Frederick Douglass remarked, adding that
he thought it "very doubtful." For the time being, as one black minister
lamented to his Whitestown, New York, congregation, the fighting was in
the hands of the "white fellers."[36]

CHAPTER TWO

The Brahmins

"HIS MILITARY RECORD WAS AS GOOD AS ANY FIGHTING QUAKER could desire," a journalist later said. But the journey of Edward Needles Hallowell—simply Ned to friends and family—from a nonviolent, apolitical son of Philadelphia privilege to the fierce officer who led his men in torching South Carolina plantations was not a simple one.[1]

Born on November 3, 1836, at the Walnut Street home of his parents, Morris and Hannah Penrose Hallowell, Ned was raised in a large, loving Quaker family whose members bestowed pet names on one another yet retained the formal address of "thee" and "thou" in all of their correspondence. Morris was a surgeon, but also part heir to Hallowell & Company, a family-owned firm that imported silks from China and India. After a childhood of private tutors, Ned briefly studied at Haverford College, a nearby Quaker school, before accepting a position as a stockbroker on Philadelphia's aptly named Gold Street. But the dashing young man who sported an elegant mustache could hardly avoid the political winds of the late 1850s. By the off-year elections of 1858, he had puzzled his way out of his faith's nonpolitical stance. "Perhaps thee wold like to know how I 'get over' the nonvoting question," he wrote to Norwood Penrose Hallowell, his younger brother by almost three years. "We pay our taxes," he reasoned to Pen, as his brother, then a student at Harvard College, preferred to be called. Doing so was not really voluntary, since failure to do so meant prison and Quakers felt "bound to protect our lives." So if his purse contributed to the Buchanan administration, which he loathed, he was thereby "bound to vote to protect whole classes," and especially enslaved Americans. "I can't see that it is nonsense, I stick to it," Ned insisted, although honesty compelled him to add that if he had not "made this very clear to thee," that was because he had not yet "got it very clear" to himself.[2]

It would take brother Pen a few years more to reconcile himself to casting a ballot, but all members of the family were united in abolitionism. Quakers had long stood against slavery, and both Morris and Hannah were dedicated to the cause. On one occasion some of Morris's Southern customers inquired about his views on slavery, and he angrily turned them out of his office, swearing that while he "sold Goods, not principles," he "would [have] no further dealings with them." Ned had been named for Edward Needles, the president of the Pennsylvania Abolition Society and a close friend to Hannah's mother. In 1859, Ned was himself elected a member of the society. The entire family worked to oppose the Fugitive Slave Act of 1850, which forced private citizens to comply with federal marshals and slave catchers; that law especially, Pen later admitted, "made an Abolitionist of me." Although only eleven at the time, Pen found it inconceivable that "any one born and bred at the North could have avoided being an Abolitionist."[3]

Pen was less a model youth than his three older brothers—William was the eldest, followed by Richard and Ned—and he was briefly suspended from Harvard for hazing a first-year student. But Pen's less-than-pacific nature and robust physique—he was just over six feet tall—proved useful on those occasions when fugitive slaves arrived on the Hallowells' doorstep. In April 1859, the brothers assisted Virginia runaway Daniel Dangerfield, who had been freed by a Philadelphia court but faced a proslavery mob that hoped to return him to his master. The Hallowells hid Dangerfield inside an old tomb in southern Philadelphia until night fell and then spirited him out of the city in Hannah's carriage. Pen drove the team, while Ned, who was "quite ready to use his five-shooter," guarded from the rear box. Just months before, their brother Richard, who was married to the granddaughter of abolitionist and feminist Lucretia Mott, had traveled to Virginia to retrieve John Brown's body and return it north for burial.[4]

Pen had another occasion to pack his pistol when abolitionist Wendell Phillips was invited to speak at Boston's Music Hall. Twice during the previous six weeks, anti-abolitionist mobs had rioted at his lectures, threatening the speaker and wounding members of the audience. To provide protection, Harvard student Oliver Wendell Holmes Jr. recruited his college friends, including Hallowell, to form a human cordon around Phillips. The student bodyguards smuggled Phillips into the hall, but as he left through a side entrance the group was confronted with what Hallowell described as "a howling mob." As the gang rushed at Phillips, Hallowell and the others closed ranks around him. "We fought our way down the little alleyway to Winter Street," he wrote. "A great crowd followed, hooting and howling." They got Phillips safely home, where the orator spent the remainder of the evening guarding his house with one of John Brown's pikes. Quaker pacifism was not long for such a world.[5]

WHILE AT HARVARD, PEN BECAME ACQUAINTED WITH ANOTHER young man of privilege who shared his antislavery convictions. Born in Boston in October 1837, Robert Gould Shaw was one year younger than Ned and two years older than Pen. The Hallowells were more than comfortable, but Shaw hailed from one of the richest families in Massachusetts. The young man's two grandfathers had earned millions by importing goods from China; one ancestor was prominent enough to have had three portraits of himself painted by Gilbert Stuart. Shaw's parents, Francis George Shaw and Sarah Sturgis, were married in 1835, after Frank completed three years of study at Harvard. Rob, as he preferred to be called, was one of five children and the only boy. Anna was his only older sibling; Rob grew particularly close to his younger sister Josephine, known to her family as Effie. The boy grew up under the watchful eye of his grandfather, Robert Gould, after whom he was named. Just before he died, the old man summoned Rob to his bed. Fixing him with a stare, he warned: "I am leaving the stage of action and you are entering upon it. I exhort you to use your example and influence against intemperance and slavery."[6]

So of course antislavery was a conviction that Rob's father had learned at an early age. Although most Brahmins—as the Boston upper class styled themselves—tended toward the social conservatism of the Whig Party, Frank and Sarah passionately believed that the gift of wealth should be put to good use. When Rob was five, his parents purchased an estate adjacent to Brook Farm, a utopian experiment in communitarian life. Henry Sturgis, Sarah's brother, helped to support the commune until its financial demise in 1849. In exchange, the family came into contact with the host of reformers and radicals who visited the Transcendentalist community just west of Boston. There the Shaws met William Lloyd Garrison, editor of the *Liberator,* and Garrison's friend John A. Andrew, an antislavery attorney and rising free-soil politician. Sarah also became close friends with reformer Lydia Maria Child and feminist intellectual Margaret Fuller.[7]

After private tutors, Rob enrolled at St. John's College, a Jesuit institution in Fordham, New York, where he earned average grades. In early 1851, while Frank began construction of an $80,000 house on Staten Island, the family, having decided to undertake a grand tour of Europe, booked first-class rooms for the Continent. The family visited France and Switzerland, then settled for a time near Neuchâtel, on the edge of the Jura Mountains. During the summer of 1853, they rented a house in Sorrento, just south of Naples. There they played host to Frances Anne Kemble, the British actress who had recently returned to the stage following the collapse of her marriage to Pierce Butler, the richest planter in Georgia. Kemble horrified the family—including Rob, who had recently read *Uncle Tom's Cabin,* published the previous year—with tales of her brief stay along the Rice Coast. Most of the family sailed for home in 1855, but Rob remained in the Kingdom of Hanover for additional study so that he might enter Harvard College as a sophomore or junior. The indifferent pupil admitted to his worried parents that he had "no taste for anything except amusing myself." At length he returned to the United States and spent three years at Harvard, withdrawing from the college in 1859. He then accepted a position in his uncle's Manhattan shipping firm. But he was as uninspired a businessman as he had been a student, and at a time when his old college acquaintances were facing down proslavery mobs, Rob resisted his mother's pleas to devote himself to the antislavery movement. "I don't want to become a reformer, Apostle, or anything of that kind," he confessed. "[T]here is no use in doing disagreeable things for nothing."[8]

If his former classmate Pen Hallowell had doubts about a moral man casting a political ballot, Shaw did not; in November 1860, the twenty-three-year-old proudly stepped forward in support of Lincoln. Rob's parents' friend Garrison refused to vote, because he had for years denounced the Constitution as a proslavery document, and some of those abolitionists who did, such as Frederick Douglass, stood with Gerrit Smith and the Liberty Party. But Shaw regarded himself as a realist. Although no abolitionist, the Republican candidate was a lifelong critic of slavery and a dedicated free-soiler; even Garrison publicly conceded that "the election of Abraham Lincoln will be a great and encouraging triumph." Shortly thereafter, Rob saw his parents off as they sailed aboard the *Karnak* for the Bahamas. Sarah, whose health was always poor, found Manhattan's winters difficult, and their kinsman John Shaw had recently opened a hotel in Nassau. One wonders if Rob noticed the African manservant traveling on the *Karnak* with two Europeans. Certainly the election season had turned his attention to slavery and sectionalism. When his uncle tasked him with finding a renter for his house, Rob turned down one applicant on the grounds that a brother-in-law from New Orleans would be living with the family. "We don't want any secessionists about," Rob vowed.[9]

By early April 1861, Northern newspapers spoke of nothing besides the situation in Fort Sumter at the mouth of Charleston Harbor. An attempt three months before to send supplies to the beleaguered fort had failed, and Sumter's commander, Major Robert Anderson, had alerted Washington to his dwindling supply of food. Worried about what war would do to their businesses, many Manhattan shippers hoped that newly elected president Abraham Lincoln would give in to Confederate demands to evacuate the fort. Rob thought otherwise. "Lincoln is going to re-inforce the United States forts," Shaw wrote to his sister Susanna, "and in that case the Southerners will surely resist." Given the demands placed on the president by the Constitution, Shaw reasoned, he had no choice "but to collect the [tariff] revenue and re-take, by force of arms, the United States property which they have stolen." Several years before, Shaw had favored letting the South secede, a position embraced by a good number of white abolitionists who felt morally tainted by living in the same nation as slave-holders. But as there now was "no way of making a peaceable separation without giving up everything," Shaw was "glad, for the credit of the country," that Lincoln planned to "act now with some firmness." Seven days later, just before dawn on April 12, shore batteries opened fire on Sumter, and the war was on.[10]

LINCOLN IMMEDIATELY ISSUED THE CALL FOR 75,000 VOLUNTEERS TO serve for three months, but the question of service divided Northern reformers, particularly since the president's administration insisted that the war was to be waged only for reunion, not for abolition. In keeping with that pledge, the War Department decreed that free blacks who sought to enlist would be turned away. Garrison continued to preach that just as abolitionists should not vote, neither should those "Peace men" who believed in "total abstinence from war, as a Christian duty," don a uniform. Garrison's sons William and Wendell agreed with their father's position, despite the fact that many of Wendell's Harvard classmates promptly enlisted. (George Garrison thought otherwise and after the Emancipation Proclamation transformed the conflict into an abolition war would go in search of a black regiment to lead.) Wendell was almost the only student to remain in class. Within days of the fall of Sumter, the university ceased to function. "The college is full of the spirit of war & indignant at the treatment of the country's flag," the college's librarian remarked. "Very little studying [was] going on." John A. Andrew, now governor, summoned the students to join their local militia companies. Within eight days of the attack on Sumter, 120 young men met to organize the Fourth Battalion of Infantry, a militia unit that dated to the War of 1812. Among them stood Holmes, Pen Hallowell, and Ned Hallowell, who had hastened north to join the regiment "in whose ranks," its commander bragged to Andrew, "are found men of the best classes in our community."[11]

Having quit Harvard two years before, Shaw chose instead to enlist in New York's Seventh Regiment. On April 18, his untrained unit sailed from its camp on Staten Island to protect Washington from secessionists in Virginia and Maryland. Time was of the essence, and Rob was unable to say his farewells to his parents. He confided to his mother that he could not "help crying a little" when he thought of home and family. But he assured himself that she "wouldn't have me stay, when it is so clearly my duty to go." The Seventh hoped to march into the capital by Saturday, April 20, and if they arrived before "Virginia begins to make trouble," he assumed that there would be no fighting. For a young man who had seen so much of Europe, Rob had never been south of New York State, and he looked forward to meeting soldiers from across the North. "Won't it be grand to meet the men from all the States, East and West, down there," he marveled, "ready to fight for the country, as the old fellows did in the Revolution."[12]

Following a very rough day at sea, the Seventh disembarked at Annapolis. Travel to Washington was delayed because the rail lines had "been torn up by the Secessionists." The young man of privilege grumbled about the food, complaining to his father that "the rations we had with us were pretty old, and the meat furnished on board was very horsey." After marching for several miles, they located an operational train and at length pulled into Washington. Although "covered with dust," they marched through the White House grounds to pay tribute to the president. Lincoln walked out to greet them, "looking as pleasant and kind as possible" and holding "his two little boys by the hand." After the Seventh presented arms, the president "took off his hat in the most awkward way, putting it on again with his hand on the back of the rim, country fashion." But if the young patrician was little impressed by the Kentucky-born president's manners, he assured his sister that "Lincoln knows what he is about" and told her that the rude slurs on the president's appearance were unfair. "I have seen many uglier men," he wrote.[13]

One of the privates in Shaw's company was Rufus King, the son of the president of Columbia College and the grandson of the former New York senator. Private King's family was close to Secretary of State William H. Seward, and on April 30, King invited Shaw to accompany him to the secretary's office. Seward was so burdened by affairs of state that he rarely ventured out to eat, instead snacking over the course of the day on crackers, cheese, and cold tea supplied by his daughter-in-law, but he spared a few minutes for "a little talk" with the two soldiers. Although Shaw thought Seward "really didn't look as if he could have written those great speeches," he nonetheless suspected the secretary "of being a pretty sly old fellow." Hoping to bring their chat to a quick end, Seward suggested that the two young men walk over to see the president, and he handed them a note of introduction. The two found Lincoln sitting behind his desk, which was "perfectly covered with letters & papers of every description." They spoke for five minutes, and once again Shaw was oddly drawn to the president's appearance. "It is really too bad to call him one of the ugliest men in the country," Rob lectured his mother, "for I have seldom seen a pleasanter or more kind hearted looking one." Lincoln inquired about their regiment, as well as their education, as his son Robert was then enrolled at Harvard. Nobody else from the regiment had yet enjoyed access to such high office, and King and Shaw strolled back to the Capitol, thinking they "had done a pretty good afternoon's work in calling on the President & Secretary of State both."[14]

Two weeks later, word arrived that Andrew had commissioned Shaw a second lieutenant in the newly created Second Massachusetts Infantry. Rob hastened north to Camp Andrew, named for the state's new governor, in West Roxbury, once home to Brook Farm. Life as a junior officer suited Shaw just fine. The army paid privates $13.00 each month, with an additional clothing allowance of $3.50. But the second lieutenant drew $150 as "part of two months pay." Other benefits included having "cots to sleep on, much better fare, and servants in abundance from among the men." By mid-May, the company was not yet full, so while he awaited deployment, Shaw had ample time to "lie round, & smoke, read or sleep." Boston was not far away, and most evenings he and the other young officers found ways "to have a great deal of fun in one way and another."[15]

By mid-June, the Second was ready to ship southward to Maryland, where it was to guard the upper Potomac River. Shaw was briefly reunited with his family as they passed through Manhattan. Evidently Sarah took his parting hard, for Rob implored her not to "lie awake much dear Mother thinking of me." A second missive reminded her that a good "many Mothers & Fathers & sisters" felt just as badly as she did, and he assured his mother that "there is not much more danger in war than in peace at least for officers." Rob was also a bit embarrassed about the way his mother peppered their friends with his photograph, especially one of him as an officer. Elizabeth Haggerty's daughter Annie, however, was quite another story. Shaw had met Annie in the months just before Sumter, when his sister Susanna arranged a night at the opera. Rob beseeched Susanna to let Annie know that he "had nothing to do with" sending her family so many photographs, but he also hoped that his sister might obtain an image of Annie, provided she could do so without letting Annie know he wanted one.[16]

JUST AS SHAW WAS SAYING HIS FAREWELLS TO HIS FAMILY, PEN HALlowell's Massachusetts Fourth Battalion of Infantry was reorganized as the Twentieth Massachusetts Volunteers. While Ned was briefly dispatched to Missouri to serve on the staff of General John C. Frémont, who had been given command of the Department of the West, Pen was commissioned a first lieutenant on July 1. His Harvard chum Oliver Wendell Holmes Jr. also received his straps as a first lieutenant, with William Raymond Lee, a West Pointer and a distant kinsman to the Virginia general, as the regiment's colonel and Paul Revere, the great-grandson of the silversmith, as its major; other venerable surnames—Whittier, Lowell, Cabot, Milton, and Abbott—staffed its officer corps. The Hallowells headed to Readville, Massachusetts, and Camp Meigs, just as American forces clashed with Confederate armies under General P. G. T. Beauregard at the Battle of Bull Run. The July 21 encounter proved a debacle for the United States. One month before, Shaw had promised his mother that "comparatively few men" would ever die in battle, but now he read reports of nearly 5,000 casualties—killed, wounded, and missing—with Union men roughly three-fifths of that figure. Lincoln had requested volunteers for ninety days only, but Bull Run forced leaders and soldiers on both sides to confront the possibility of a protracted, bloody conflict.[17]

Upon arriving at Readville, the soldiers of the Twentieth were examined by surgeons, who gauged their fitness to serve. Those who passed muster were handed a uniform and a complete suit of underclothing and instructed to head to the camp bathhouse for a warm soaking, an essential order given the unhygienic habits of even wealthy men in the 1860s. On August 19, Colonel Lee received orders to prepare for departure for the nation's capital. Finally, on September 4, the regiment left Readville for Manhattan, where the soldiers were given a lavish send-off and toasted by Governor Andrew, who accompanied them that far. Pen Hallowell dined that evening with family friends "and one of their kid daughters," Sarah Wharton Haydock. Before departing, Pen "gave her [his] photograph."

After a parade down Broadway, the unit boarded ship for Philadelphia and then on to Baltimore. As had Shaw nearly five months before, the Twentieth marched through Maryland with their state flag unfurled and their rifles loaded, but this time, as one officer remarked, "not a hiss or reproach was audible." After commandeering a train pulling cattle cars, the dusty soldiers reached Washington and pitched their tents near Camp Kalorama on the Georgetown heights. Colonel Lee reported to General Ambrose Burnside, who folded the regiment, together with the First Massachusetts Sharpshooters and a Pennsylvania company, into his Fourth Brigade.[18]

Within the month, the Twentieth was to see far more action than they desired. In the days following Bull Run, General George B. McClellan began to build up the Army of the Potomac in preparation for an invasion of Virginia. In mid-October, he instructed General George McCall to march his division toward Leesburg, some thirty-five miles south of Washington, in hopes of discovering Confederate strength in the region; at the same time, he ordered General Charles Stone, whose division was guarding the Maryland banks of the Potomac River, to "make a slight demonstration" in hopes of driving Confederate forces farther south. Traveling with Stone was Colonel Edward Baker, a former Illinois congressman turned U.S. senator from Oregon. Believing he had troops enough at his disposal, Stone told McCall to pull back toward Washington, while he sent raiders, including the Massachusetts Twentieth and Fifteenth, across the Potomac in reconnaissance of a rebel encampment. They found no camp, so on the morning of October 21 the soldiers dispatched a rider in search of Stone and new orders. Instead of having the men recross the river, Baker brought up his troops to assist in the withdrawal, but the small number of boats at their disposal slowed the retreat.[19]

With McCall's troops gone, the Confederates had numbers enough to deal with any American soldiers on their side of the Potomac. Virginia and Mississippi soldiers arrived by early afternoon, forcing the Massachusetts regiments to fan out just within the tree line, the steep drop-off known as Ball's Bluff to their rear. By three o'clock, the fighting was fierce. "Come on, Harvard!" an officer shouted just as Oliver Wendell Holmes Jr. took a bullet to the chest. Only too late did Captain John Putnam see a red-shirted Confederate taking aim, and he fell, his arm shattered, leaving his lieutenant, Pen Hallowell, in charge of his company. Baker dashed back and forth behind the Twentieth's line, shouting for them to hold fast. "It made me wince to see the colonel, so handsome, brave, and cool, expose himself with such noble disdain," Hallowell admitted. "He asked me whether I could stand off the rebels from working through the woods," and after making "some cheery remarks," the senator ran off into the smoke to shore up the faltering line. "You want a fight, don't you?" he roared to others in the Twentieth, and they answered with a cheer. Pen was not with Baker when the lawmaker-turned-officer was hit by six balls, one of them entering his skull just above his left ear, making him the only sitting senator ever to die in battle.[20]

As their numbers dwindled, the men of the Twentieth peeled off their scarlet-lined gray coats. Many hung their new jackets from nearby branches, and Confederates, spying the shapes through the din, fired on the coats. Attempting to hold the end of the line, Hallowell noticed Confederates circling his flank and preparing to fire directly into the regiment's side. Grabbing his rifle, the twenty-two-year-old lieutenant led six men to within range of the Virginians, posting each man behind a tree. The move proved to be "quite effective," and the Confederates retreated. After the fact, Hallowell wished he had thought to ask Colonel Lee to rush "two or three companies" to his position, as he might have wiped "out anything opposed to it." But with Baker killed, the soldiers began to retreat toward the bluff, reported one officer, "throwing away their arms [and] deserting their killed and wounded." As they raced down the hill they discovered that most of the boats were either swamped or already pulling away for the other shore. Many threw off their gear as they plunged into the Potomac, while Confederates knelt at the crest and poured a steady fire down into the terrified men. "The river now seemed covered with heads and was as white as a great hail-storm where the rebel bullets struck," a Massachusetts soldier recalled.[21]

Pen remained cool, methodically loading and firing as he slowly inched toward the river. He later chided himself for doing so, admitting that he was "green and foolish" at the bluff and that he instead should have been "looking after the men." In truth, he did that too, but it was never the Quaker way to boast. Hallowell was still trying to hold his position when he heard Colonel Lee warn the fleeing men that he had done all he could do: "You are at liberty now to care for yourselves." Captain William

Bartlett of Company I raised his sword and bawled: "Those who desire to surrender will follow me." Pen judged that "a perfectly rational thing" to do, yet he was not one of the eighty who tailed Bartlett. Those who opted to stay with Hallowell took cover until it grew dark. Most of the Massachusetts men knew how to swim, and around eight that night they set out for Harrison Island, which divided the Potomac at that point. The occasional shot slapped the water as the soldiers waded in. Pen was the last to do so, stripping off his heavy clothes, then swimming with his sword in one hand and his watch about his neck. Cold and weary, Hallowell and his company reached Maryland shores and located a temporary hospital, where a surgeon found him "a shirt and a pair of drawers."[22]

McClellan denounced the last moments of the battle as a butchery. Union casualties—both killed and wounded—numbered 921, with another 700 missing, most of whom probably drowned as they swam for safety. Downstream, bodies washed ashore at Mount Vernon and at Washington for days. Lee and Revere were reported missing and presumed captured, and Confederates picked up as many as 1,500 abandoned weapons from the field. Confederate losses amounted to a mere 136 killed, with 117 wounded. Holmes survived, as did a young private in Hallowell's company who had a ball completely pass through his body. Pen later saw him walking about camp, but only after writing a letter of condolence to the boy's mother. "One is always startled when he meets a man who he thought was dead," Hallowell reflected. The tragedy marked yet another loss for the United States, but at least one Boston editor remarked that while others fled, the Twentieth had behaved with "admirable discipline and soldierly conduct," fighting "and firing with the precision of veteran soldiers."[23]

IN THE AFTERMATH OF BALL'S BLUFF, THE EXHAUSTED UNION SURVIvors witnessed a growing number of runaway slaves passing by, attempting to reach Washington or Baltimore. The exodus of enslaved Southerners had begun on May 23, 1861, just one month into the conflict, when three bondmen being used by the Confederate military to construct fortifications escaped and reached the gates of Fort Monroe, an enormous citadel at the southern tip of the Virginia peninsula that remained under federal control. In command of the fort was General Benjamin F. Butler, a Massachusetts Democrat who had arrived only the previous day. By late July, an overwhelmed Butler reported that approximately 900 refugees had reached Monroe and were living under his protection. Only 300 were "able-bodied men," he informed the War Department, while the rest were women, children, and the aged, "substantially past hard labor." With "many more coming in" daily, Butler requested clarity from Washington. "Are these men, women, and children slaves?" he wondered. The Fugitive Slave Act of 1850 yet remained in force, but with Virginia's secession, had "all property relations ceased?" Since the first three runaways to reach the fort had been digging Confederate trenches, Butler, an attorney and politician before the war, thought it proper to consider the liberated a critical element of the war effort, and so "contraband of war." The general's idea accorded with traditional war-power theory, and on August 6, 1861, just one week after the receipt of Butler's inquiry, Lincoln signed the Confiscation Act, which effectively ratified Butler's suggestion by allowing for the seizure of all property, including bondmen, being used to support the Confederate military.[24]

Among the first runaways to reach the fort's gates was Henry Jarvis. Born in Northampton County around 1836, Jarvis, commonly known as Harry, labored as an oysterman on Virginia's Eastern Shore. Jarvis's owner was regarded as one of the meanest men in the region, and one day after he shot at Harry to scare him into working harder, the enslaved waterman decided he had "stood it 'bouts long" as he could and ran for the woods. Jarvis hid in the swamps for three weeks, evading the search parties and hunting dogs by crossing and then recrossing streams. One of Jarvis's closest friends, Peter Drummond, whom he had known since he was six, smuggled him food when he could. Jarvis waited until his master threw a fancy ball, knowing the whites would be "drinkin' an' carousin' night an' day," before slipping down to his owner's dock to steal his canoe. Jarvis rigged up a small sail and set out for Monroe, thirty-five miles across the bay. A sudden storm tore his sail and nearly carried it away. But it was "death behind" him, so Harry prayed for God's help and "made fas' de sheet." By morning, he had reached Fort Monroe.[25]

Upon arriving, the self-liberated, twenty-five-year-old oysterman asked to see General Butler and proudly announced himself to be "contraband." He then asked to enlist. A startled Butler replied that the war was for

The youngest son of devout Quakers and militant abolitionists, "Pen" Hallowell briefly served as lieutenant colonel in the Fifty-fourth before agreeing to lead the Fifty-fifth. *Courtesy Massachusetts Historical Society.*

reunion only, and that it was not a "black man's war." Jarvis glared down at the diminutive officer. "It would be a black man's war 'fore dey got fru," he snapped. Jarvis had sailed alone, not wishing to put his wife in danger, although he hoped to send for her before too long. Shortly thereafter, Drummond somehow arrived. Despite offers of employment at Monroe, the two signed on as laborers on a ship sailing for Cuba and Haiti, and then on to Africa. Having no interest in settling in Liberia, they took jobs with another ship heading for Boston, hoping that by the time they returned to the States it would have "got to be a black man's war fo' suah." Both would get their wish.[26]

During the months when Jarvis and Drummond were at sea, the nation continued to wrestle with the thorny questions of race and refugees. On November 24, two other black men arrived in Camp Benton, near Poolesville, Maryland, where the Twentieth was stationed. The two sold "cakes, pies, &c. to the Soldiers," and appearing to be hungry themselves, a German-born soldier invited them to breakfast. As a loyal border state, Maryland was not subject to the Confiscation Act. When a slaveholder

Three years older than Pen, and more politically minded, "Ned" Hallowell transferred from the Massachusetts Twentieth to the Fifty-fourth when black Americans were finally allowed to enlist, initially serving as lieutenant colonel. Hallowell commanded the unit from fall 1863 until the end of the war. *Courtesy Massachusetts Historical Society.*

arrived at the camp, demanding that the army "deliver them up," General Stone agreed and instructed Lieutenant George Nelson Macy to seize the alleged runaways and "escort the prisoners to their supposed owners." Pen Hallowell, catching word of the incident, stormed into Macy's tent and demanded to know by "what authority do you make New England soldiers do such work?" Macy retorted that he was merely carrying out Stone's orders. "I didn't think that any New England Gentlemen would do such dirty work," Hallowell shot back. A true blue blood, Macy declared himself "insulted" at having his honor questioned in such a fashion, and a fuming Hallowell stamped away. A number of Massachusetts papers picked up the story, all of them denouncing the slave-catching "blood-hounds" of the Twentieth. That in turn led to a congressional inquiry as to whether Stone had given "aid and comfort to the rebels," especially after it was discovered that the master in question resided in Leesburg, Virginia, and was not a loyal Maryland man.[27]

The affair at least had the virtue of elevating Hallowell in rank. The regiment's Company D largely comprised German nationals, the vast majority of whom were resolutely antislavery. Most of the company had joined "with the understanding that they, as Massachusetts men, would never be called upon to act against the colored people," one soldier assured

Governor Andrew. Lieutenant Macy, in their view, had performed the slaveholders' "dirty work," and they implored the governor "to let them have an officer who will not violate their consciences, principles & force them to escort slaves." Anxious to protect himself politically, Andrew assured Wendell Phillips and Senator Charles Sumner that he was "greatly pained" by Macy's actions and publicly denounced him as "unworthy of any position of honor, trust or responsibility." (The governor did not mention that the orders originated with Stone, whom he had recently promoted and who enjoyed the patronage of the equally conservative General McClellan.) When Andrew promoted Pen to captain on November 26, it would be the first time the men of Company D agreed to serve under an American-born officer. A few months later, Congress prohibited the army from returning runaways.[28]

THAT SAME MONTH, YET ANOTHER CHILD OF PRIVILEGE DECIDED TO enter the fray. Members of the Adams family had never been warriors. Generation after generation had served their country as politicians and diplomats, but never by picking up a sword. Charles Francis Adams Jr., the grandson and great-grandson of presidents, was the third of seven children born to Charles Francis Adams Sr., a former Massachusetts state assemblyman and the Free Soil Party's 1848 vice presidential nominee. In 1858 the elder Adams won election to the U.S. House of Representatives; after only two years in Washington, Lincoln nominated him to fill the critical role of minister to Great Britain. The diplomat took his fourth child, Henry, with him to London to serve as his secretary, leaving Charles behind to mind the family's business affairs. Having graduated from Harvard in 1856, Charles was quite capable of doing so. But as an antislavery Republican, Charles began to fear that he was shirking his duty to country and cause by wasting the war in a Boston countinghouse. The previous July, he had gone to the train station to say his farewells to those college friends who had joined together with Shaw in the Second Massachusetts Infantry, and he confided to his mother that he "certainly env[ied] them very much." Off to war they went, he lamented, "in good spirits and full of life and hope," abandoning him to trudge slowly back to his books and ledgers.[29]

The July disaster at Bull Run helped clarify matters for Adams. He "began to realize," he admitted later, "the mistake [he] had made in not going earlier." He had missed both Shaw and Hallowell at Harvard, having graduated the year Rob arrived in Cambridge, but many young men his own age were risking their lives for their country too. In his many moments of self-examination, he acknowledged that his father had entrusted him "with the care of the bulk of his property, and never was property so difficult to manage" as during a civil war. Neither did Adams flatter himself a natural-born fighter. Although bored with the law, to join the army was to "give up a profession for which [he was] little adapted for one to which [he was] adapted even less." Yet it was not simply patriotism, or a sense of missing out on a grand endeavor, that inclined him to serve. Charles resented the untenable position his father had placed him in, and his intense dislike of his father made his enlistment a spirited act of youthful rebellion. Adams later described his father as "rigid" and "narrow" and "even less companionable" than his grandfather John Quincy Adams. "The fact was that my father," he remarked, "with the coldness of temperament natural to him, took a wholly wrong view of the subject" and "did not believe in any one taking a hand in [an] actual fight." The elder Adams's disdain for the military was not born of a Garrisonian pacifism, but from a patrician's contempt for common soldiers. Charles Sr., his son feared, "wholly failed to realize that it would have been an actual disgrace had his family, of all possible families American, been wholly unrepresented in the field." With Henry abroad, he himself "was the one to go."[30]

Realizing he could never win his father's approval, in mid-November Adams enlisted in the First Massachusetts Cavalry and only then picked up his pen to alert the U.S. minister to Britain. "I don't know whether you will be surprised or disgusted or annoyed or distressed by the information," Charles Jr. wrote to his father, sadly aware that "proud" would not be one of the adjectives the diplomat would use when he discovered that his son had joined up. "You know it now and I am glad of it!" Adams confessed. "I do not think it right that our family," he lectured, "so prominent in this matter while it is a contest of words, should be wholly unrepresented when it has grown to be a conflict of blows." The senior Adams responded to the news by refusing to respond, but Henry wrote back with a mixed blessing. "I do not think it my duty to express any regrets at the act," Henry observed, owing to the "strange madness of the times," although he prayed that his brother was not "throwing [his life] away." If Henry could not bring himself to defy his father and congratulate his older brother for his courage, he did at least conclude his missive by promising to "be always ready to stand by you with what aid" he might provide.[31]

Being a Boston Brahmin, of course, had its advantages. Adams was enrolled as a first lieutenant. Not only was he not "a soldier by nature" but he admitted with the brutal honesty typical of his forebears that he was also "utterly lack[ing in] a nice, ingratiating tact in [his] dealings with other men." Yet he thought the regiment a fine group and immediately regarded them as "kith and kin." Hardly "popular or adored by" his men, Adams was a capable rider, athletic, and clearly bright and able, and so they respected him. Not so their colonel, Robert Williams. A West Point graduate and a Virginian by birth, Williams was the wrong choice to lead a unit of antislavery New Englanders. "He had a set of us young Harvard fellows for officers," Adams mused, and as "he did not understand our Massachusetts men," his discipline was brutal. In moments of crisis, the colonel was also "invariably drunk" and would prove to be "an utter failure."[32]

As 1862 DAWNED, THE MEN OF MASSACHUSETTS FOUND THEMSELVES scattered across the eastern half of the republic. Shaw and the Second were placed under the command of General Nathaniel Banks (the previous governor of Massachusetts) and deployed against General Thomas J. "Stonewall" Jackson in Virginia's Shenandoah Valley. After Frémont issued a proclamation of emancipation in the West, which Lincoln feared would drive Missouri into the Confederacy, the president relieved the general of his command. Needing a new posting, Ned returned east, securing a commission as second lieutenant in the Twentieth on January 11. The Hallowell brothers and the Twentieth were transferred to the command of McClellan, who planned to ship his army down the Chesapeake Bay to Fort Monroe and then march northwest up the peninsula to capture the Confederate capital of Richmond.

Adams and the First Cavalry sailed even farther southward, landing between Charleston and Savannah, Georgia, in Port Royal Sound, South Carolina, which had been captured by the U.S. Navy the previous November. Both the trip and the landing were "pandemonium," Adams reported to his brother. The unit's major was drunk both before and after their passage, and the guns terrified the horses. "We are all green, officers, men and horses, and long practice is absolutely necessary," he admitted. But as did all American soldiers, Adams hoped to take part in the capture of Charleston, long a hotbed of secession. "Ah," he laughed, "wouldn't I like to ride into Charleston!"[33]

As was the case for many Northern boys, the war provided Adams with his first view of the South and plantation slavery. On February 2, he rode out with the regiment's advance guard to inspect an abandoned plantation on Barnwell Island. The once-elegant estate was littered with smashed furniture and "the remains of a library of fine books." Even though Carolina planters "had brought all this on themselves," he could not help regretting the damage. Adams revealed far less pity for the roughly 7,000 black "contrabands" who flooded into Beaufort, and his letters to his family betrayed the first hints that he would never truly come to understand the black men he would one day lead into battle. He thought the refugees "lazy [and] submissive," although those were traits he at least attributed to their former masters as well. Otherwise, his stereotypical views of African Americans reflected not only the worst of biases but also an inability to understand the slaves' survival mechanisms. The freedmen were "intelligent enough," he assured his father, "but their intelligence too often takes the form of low cunning." Adams believed them to be dishonest, a prejudice he never revised, and he complained to his father that most former slaves were "dreadful hypocrites," as they "would say to their masters, as a rule, what today they would say to us." Apart from the Confiscation Act of the previous July, the federal government had taken no steps against slavery, yet Adams could not grasp that black Carolinians were hedging their bets. Unable to formulate a consistent, rational assessment of black characteristics, he described the freedmen again and again as "lazy," even as he observed that "they will work for money and indeed are anxious to get work."[34]

Like all devout Republicans, Adams was confident that the war would be the undoing of slavery. "Not by any legal quibble of contrabands or

doubtful theory of confiscation," he argued, "but by stimulating free trade."
Northern travelers invariably remarked on Southern poverty, and as he
rode along Carolina's shore Adams thought himself "amid the institutions
and implementations of the middle ages." Coerced slave labor, he believed,
was "awkward, cumbrous, expensive and behind the age," and so the liberation of its working class "will be the greatest blessing which could happen
to the South." But what of the former slaves—or as Adams indelicately
put it, how to resolve "the 'nigger' question?" Although "good tempered
[and] patient," blacks were too "docile" to survive in a tough world gov-
erned by "the operation of economic laws over which Government has no
control." Africans might once have been fierce, he theorized, but centuries
of enslavement had "deprived the African of their capacity for freedom,"
and so any attempt by the Lincoln administration to free or arm African
Americans "would be a terrible calamity to the blacks as a race." Wars often
changed people, but it was not, evidently, in an Adams to evolve.[35]

Adams was right enough, at least, in his objections to the tactics of
General David Hunter, a career soldier who had leveraged his friendship
with Lincoln into being given command of the Department of the South
(comprising Georgia, South Carolina, and Florida). The New York–born
abolitionist found himself on the South Carolina coast, and in April 1862
he requested that the War Department send him 50,000 rifles and an equal
number of "scarlet pantaloons" with which to arm and clothe "such loyal
men as [he] could find in the country." Although he did not say so directly,
Hunter intended to free and enlist Carolina slaves well in advance of any
initiative from Congress or the president. Some male refugees enthusiastically signed on, but as Adams noted, others had good cause to distrust
all white men, and Hunter finally resorted to conscripting men from the
Sea Islands into his unit. Adams suspected that Hunter's great sin was to
engage in a good cause but to do it badly. The general, Adams warned
his father, had "gone crazy" and was inadvertently "doing the blacks all
the harm" he could. When Hunter tried to encourage enlistments by declaring free all slaves in the three states of his department, an exasperated
Lincoln overruled his decree and finally, in late September, removed him
as commander. Adams felt "a strong regret at seeing the red-legged darkies
march off." Instead of provoking conservative Democrats in Congress and

infuriating the commander-in-chief, Hunter might have waited for both black Southerners and white Northerners to get accustomed to the idea of African American military service. "The slaves would have moved when the day came," he assured his father.[36]

WHILE ADAMS AND THE FIRST CAVALRY DRILLED ALONG THE SOUTH Carolina coast, the Hallowell brothers and the Twentieth inched their way toward Richmond as part of McClellan's 120,000-strong army for the Peninsula Campaign. Although he had a vast numerical advantage over the Confederate forces, McClellan sought to avoid a full-scale engagement, hoping his superior host might somehow scare President Jefferson Davis into surrendering. The odds in favor of the Confederacy shifted considerably on May 31, however, when General Joseph E. Johnston launched an assault on the Army of the Potomac while it was divided by the Chickahominy River. In the subsequent battle of Seven Pines, Johnston was badly wounded and General Robert E. Lee became the new commander. Rechristening his forces the Army of Northern Virginia, the aggressive Lee abandoned Johnston's strategy of retreat. In a series of clashes known as the Seven Days, the Confederates launched a sequence of punishing strikes against the timid McClellan.

Although nearly bedridden by illness, Ned Hallowell rejoined the Twentieth in time for the June 29 battle of Savage's Station, the fourth of the Seven Days skirmishes. For the first time in the war, the two brothers found themselves fighting side by side. Although hoping to be part of a broad counterattack, Hallowell realized they were on their own; nevertheless, he vowed "to retard the advance of the enemy to the utmost." Casualties were high on both sides, and buckshot caught Pen on his left side, "perforating [his] clothes and redden[ing his] skin." Moments later, a ball scraped across his stomach; "the shock was as though some one had struck a blow on that part," he remembered. A cannonball mowed down a column of men immediately to his right, soaring so close that it scorched Pen's beard and burned off his eyebrows. Convinced that he would not survive the attack, Hallowell promised himself that if he ever "got out of this hole [he] should never again be scared." Once again responsible for leading an orderly retreat, Pen hurried his company into dense woods, coming out after night fell only long enough to retrieve their wounded. Company D finally caught up with the bulk of the retreating U.S. Army, but only after abandoning several badly wounded officers at a nearby farmhouse, hoping that Confederate surgeons might save them.[37]

Ironically, by failing to press on toward Richmond, the conservative McClellan bettered the odds of the war evolving into a crusade against slavery. Had the Confederacy collapsed that spring, slavery across the defeated South might have survived intact. The New Jersey general had hectored his commander about not confiscating human property from white Southerners, and for that reason some Northern abolitionists grudgingly welcomed Lee's victory. If the South was "overthrown in one great battle and totally scattered they will surrender at once to save their slaves," one New York soldier remarked. "If the war be protracted we shall be driven gradually to emancipate the slaves." Despite almost losing her son Oliver, Amelia Holmes held similarly tough-minded views, informing Pen's and Ned's sister that she prayed "that the war will go on till every slave is free, and that my child will always be ready to defend & struggle for humanity." Amelia "hate[d] bloodshed," but she "hate[d] slavery more." Lydia Maria Child made much the same point to Sarah Shaw. "I pray to God that the victories may not come too fast, and that we may be castigated till we do the right thing," she admitted. But then, reflecting that she was writing to the mother of a young officer in harm's way, she added that her "own prayer gives me a pang, as if it were something wicked and monstrous."[38]

The failure of the Peninsula Campaign also destroyed the initial operation against Charleston, as Adams and 10,000 soldiers were hurried north to protect the capital and reinforce the battered Army of the Potomac. The thought of a long, if not endless, war had begun to trouble Adams. Not that he doubted that the South would one day be defeated; he feared instead that it would become necessary to hold "down by force" the "savage and ignorant" Southern white population and that, in doing so, "a spirit of blind, revengeful fanaticism" could take hold in the North. Never fond of his state's senior senator, Adams worried that Charles Sumner might "bankrupt the nation" to fund "immense standing armies," all in hopes of bringing about the immediate destruction of slavery.[39]

WHILE GENERALLY OPEN TO THE GRADUAL EMPLOYMENT OF BLACK Southerners by the army, the highly educated Adams could be strangely obtuse when it came to the fundamental connection between slavery and secession, or the more immediate linkage of a protracted conflict with emancipation and black military service. Republicans in Congress were quicker to understand what was required. Although roughly 5,000 African Americans had served in New England state militias and the Continental Army during the Revolution, Congress flatly banned blacks from further service in either type of unit in 1792. As McClellan's invasion wilted and soldiers returned north with stories of Confederate fortifications built by conscripted bondmen, some congressmen began to openly discuss amending earlier laws so as to allow Lincoln to employ runaway slaves. Even if no congressmen yet openly embraced the idea of black Americans serving in combat, Republicans at least insisted that families of bondmen who enlisted as laborers should become free too, a powerful motivation for those fortunate enough to have a choice.[40]

In the summer of 1862, unwilling to wait for the commander-in-chief to act, Illinois senator Lyman Trumbull introduced his latest bill regarding the confiscation of rebel property. While his earlier Confiscation Act of 1861 had merely allowed for the appropriation of bondmen being used by the Confederate military, Trumbull's "An Act to Suppress Insurrection, to Punish Treason and Rebellion, to Seize and Confiscate the Property of Rebels," commonly dubbed the Second Confiscation Act and passed on July 17, 1862, expanded considerably upon the first. Under this law, individuals known to be in rebellion against the United States were liable to have their "property, money, stocks, credit," or human chattel commandeered, regardless of whether that property was being used to aid the Confederacy. Betraying the conflicted mind of Northern Republicans, the law empowered the president "to employ as many persons of African descent as he may deem necessary" and to "organize and use them in such manner as he may judge best"—but also to settle outside of the country any slave liberated by the act. Since Lincoln continued publicly to endorse the voluntary emigration of blacks, Trumbull's statute concluded with the contrary provisions that the president could either employ former bondmen in "the suppression of this rebellion" or "make provisions for the transportation, colonization, and settlement, in some tropical country," of the black men and women who reached Union lines.[41]

In part to clarify the bill, on that same hot July afternoon Congress also passed an updated Militia Act. Drafted by Senator Henry Wilson of Massachusetts and championed in the lower chamber by Congressman Thaddeus Stevens of Pennsylvania, the revision of the 1792 Militia Act authorized President Lincoln to call up another 300,000 men, ages eighteen to forty-five, with quotas based on state populations. Going a step further than the Second Confiscation Act, Wilson's bill allowed African Americans—free or contraband—to enlist in the military, where they might perform "camp service, or any other labor." Provided their master was in rebellion, both the recruit and his "mother, wife and children" would become free upon his enlistment. But if the clause permitting black men into "any military or naval service" indicated that congressional Republicans at long last intended to admit them into the army, the wording of the law and a segregated pay scale suggested that they were not to be combatants. White privates were paid $13 each month, but section 15 of the Militia Act—thirty-one words destined to cause anger and division within black units—stipulated that black recruits would receive $10 per month, with $3 of that deducted to cover the cost of uniforms (a fee not charged to white soldiers). Given that Democrats on Capitol Hill denounced even the quietest overtures about black enlistments and proposed that freedmen serve without pay, a racially based pay scale was designed in part to assuage Northern concerns about black equality within the army. It also hinted that many in Congress doubted that black recruits would ever see actual combat.[42]

Because the Militia Act applied only to runaways fleeing disloyal Confederate masters, not to Northern-born freemen, Frederick Douglass blasted the laws as designed "to shield and protect slavery." Instead of allowing black men from New York and Massachusetts to serve their country, Douglass charged in an incendiary editorial, Lincoln inconsistently permitted only rebel chattel to join up, and even then "he merely authorized the military commanders to use them as laborers." Douglass and other Northern activists would have been more incensed yet had they been privy to the correspondence of Governor Samuel Kirkwood of Iowa. Although an antislavery Republican, Kirkwood assured General Henry Halleck that he required no "contrabands" to fill his state quota. But if the administration might send him some freedmen to do "negro work," such as chopping wood, clearing roads, or general "police camp" labor—the term given to latrine duty and trash removal—Kirkwood would be obliged. Privately, the governor added that he had no objections to black men fighting too, for when "this war is over & we have summed up the entire loss of life," he would "not have any serious regrets if it is found that a part of the dead are *niggers* and that *all* are not white men."[43]

IN FACT, BY JULY 1862, IF NOT BEFORE, LINCOLN HAD ALREADY DE-cided to expand upon the Confiscation Acts with a decree of emancipation for those areas still in rebellion. Frustrated by McClellan's refusal to advance, the president had reached the conclusion that emancipation was "a military necessity, absolutely essential to the preservation of the Union." At Seward's urging, Lincoln locked his draft document on black liberty in his desk and awaited the proper moment. That opportunity arrived in September, when General Lee led his Army of Northern Virginia, 55,000 men strong, across the Potomac into Maryland in his first invasion of the United States. The Confederate incursion found the Second Massachusetts in northern Virginia and the Twentieth near Frederick, Maryland. Shaw's regiment had just taken nearly 200 casualties at the Battle of Cedar Mountain. Rob survived the action "without a scratch," but he neglected to inform his family that his luck was due to the fact that his pocket watch had stopped a ball. As McClellan and General "Fighting Joe" Hooker hurried north from Washington to intercept Lee's forces, the Second received orders to pull back and defend Maryland. By then, the Twentieth was already in the thick of it. During the night of September 14, Pen Hallowell, aware that Confederates were nearby, led his company on an eight-mile march to Middletown. "The night was made beautiful by the camp-fires of two hostile armies blazing in all directions," he marveled.[44]

Stopping near the town of Sharpsburg the following day, Lee deployed his forces along a low ridge just behind Antietam Creek. Although Washington would have to be evacuated if Maryland fell, McClellan's habitual timidity and overestimation of the Confederate numbers kept him from approaching Lee's lines until the evening of September 16.

The battle commenced at dawn that day. Having tasted combat for the first time at Cedar Mountain, Shaw was surprised at how cool he remained as his company began to advance. He had not previously felt "the excitement which makes a man want to rush into the fight," he admitted to his father several days later, yet he "did that day." The morning air was thick with smoke and sizzling fragments of metal, and men on either side of Shaw were "wounded by shell, which were flying about loosely." Shaw himself was struck in the neck by a spent minié ball, but it merely bruised the skin.[45]

Far to Shaw's left, Ned Hallowell, who had been dispatched to make contact with General Napoleon J. T. Dana, galloped by his brother, "waving his sword in recognition" of the Twentieth. Ned was not by nature "a contentious man," Pen mused, "but he was one of the few men who really seemed to enjoy a fight" and charged into the fray "with grim delight."[46]

Adams was on the far edge of the battle. The cavalry arrived just as a furious artillery duel erupted, and with each passing moment he expected "to be ordered to advance on the Confederate batteries." But owing in part to McClellan's ill-planned assault, no orders came. At length, the men dismounted and the weary Adams "dropped quietly asleep," waking only long enough to look after his terrified horse.[47]

Elsewhere on the field, chaos and panic took hold as thick smoke obscured battle flags and uniforms. The Fifty-Ninth New York was fresh from camp and so terrified that they fired a volley into the backs of the Fifteenth Massachusetts. Captain Holmes, only recently returned to the Twentieth after being shot at Ball's Bluff, swatted a private in his company with the flat of his sword for firing into the rear before realizing that the Confederates had shifted behind him. Just as he bellowed for his company to face about he took a ball through his neck. The colors of the Twentieth went down four times in as many minutes, and of the five men who sought to raise the flag, four were wounded. Their efforts ceased only when a ball snapped the flagstaff. Amid the thunder, Pen Hallowell suddenly noticed two horses trying to comfort each other, "the one cribbing the neck of the other in a friendly way." With Confederates pouring in a killing fire from three directions, the Twentieth, one sergeant wrote, "melted away, like frost in the sunshine." A bullet shattered Pen's left arm. As soldiers on both sides reloaded and fired as rapidly as they could, nobody paid Pen any attention as he stumbled through Confederate lines. As luck had it, his captain's uniform had remained behind with his company's baggage, and so on that day he wore his old private's blouse. Cradling his fractured, bleeding arm, Pen covered several hundred yards before reaching the Nicodemus farm, which the U.S. Army had converted into a battlefield hospital.[48]

Hallowell lay down on the floor of the parlor, which was littered with men. Because the farm lay behind Confederate positions, Pen took care "to remove his shoulder-straps" and conceal his officer's sword beneath a blanket. Holmes staggered in, holding the back of his neck; miraculously, the ball had barely missed his spine and arteries. A shell landed just outside the farmhouse, shattering the windows and killing several wounded soldiers lying in the yard. After twenty minutes, Union ambulances arrived to carry the most seriously wounded to Keedysville. Pen passed out several times; when he awoke his arm was "much swollen," and he feared the doctors would amputate. Instead, Thomas Antisell, the medical director at the hospital, was called to examine him by a soldier from Philadelphia who thought the wounded man looked familiar. When Hallowell named his father, the stunned cavalryman exclaimed, "Why, I know him!" Antisell performed an exsection, an operation that removed the damaged bone and left Pen's left arm nearly one inch shorter than the right. As Hallowell emerged from his stupor, he heard somebody remark, "He will hardly pull through." But the next morning Hallowell was alive enough to see his brother gazing down at him. "They told me thee was dead," Ned murmured after a long moment. Although himself coming down with typhoid fever, Ned had spent the previous night wandering the battlefield, turning over dead men in search of his brother. Pen shouted for an attendant, who persuaded Ned to lie down on the next cot.[49]

"The next surprise" for the Hallowell brothers was the unexpected appearance of Morris Hallowell. A skilled doctor, the elder Hallowell wanted his sons as far away as possible from the Maryland hospital, and he intended to transport them home to Philadelphia, which lay 170 miles away. He packed both Ned and Pen into a rented carriage and drove the fifteen miles to Hagerstown. There they found an empty freight car headed for Philadelphia; favoring speed over luxury, the Hallowells climbed aboard and tried to make themselves as comfortable as possible. Just as the train pulled away from the station, a young slave appeared at the car's open door

After initially declining the offer to lead the Fifty-fourth, Robert Gould Shaw, prompted by his mother's anguish over his refusal, finally accepted Governor John A. Andrew's offer. *Courtesy Library of Congress.*

and "begged to be taken along." Morris reached down and "yanked him into a dark corner of the car." The lurching of the train made the trip a painful one for Pen and Ned, but the ordeal was soon over when the party arrived in Philadelphia the next afternoon.[50]

Unlike in later conflicts, the army employed neither chaplains nor officers to inform families of their losses, so it fell to newspapers to print the names of those who had been killed or wounded. Pennsylvania newspapers reported that "Captain Norwood Hallowell has a severe wound in the left arm" and that his brother "Edward Hallowell is suffering from an attack of the typhoid fever." But both, the *Inquirer* added, were resting in their father's home. They were among the lucky. The Union wounded numbered a ghastly 9,540, with another 2,108 men killed. Although the U.S. losses slightly outnumbered the Confederate casualties of 10,316—marking Antietam as the single bloodiest day of the conflict—Lee's invaders had been forced to retreat into Virginia, and so, by default, the Hallowells, as did the rest of the North, counted the day as a victory. Colonel Norman Hall of the Seventh Massachusetts praised Ned for serving as General Dana's galloper

Charles Francis Adams Jr., who was expected to care for his family's estate while his father and brother Henry served in Britain, enlisted in part as an act of rebellion against his father. Adams eventually served as colonel in the Massachusetts Fifth, but never learned to respect the black men under his command and later denounced Reconstruction-era reforms in the South. *Courtesy Massachusetts Historical Society.*

despite being "scarcely able to stand," and the general himself commended his aide for his "coolness, bravery, and activity" under fire.[51]

Shaw was luckier still. In the space of a month, a minié ball had smashed only his watch and a spent ball at Antietam had left him with nothing more than a bruise. But in the five weeks from Cedar Mountain to Antietam Creek, the war had claimed the lives of eighty men from the Second. "It seems almost as if nothing could justify a battle like that," he confided to his sister Susanna, "and the horrors inseparable from it." Shaw was disappointed that McClellan did not pursue Lee's army across the Potomac. "We remained in possession of the field, and the enemy drew off undisturbed," he lamented. "Whether that is all we wanted I don't know; but I should think not." In hopes of finding out how the other men from Massachusetts had fared, Shaw rode over to the Twentieth's encampment. He found them much diminished in number. Holmes, he discovered, "has received his second ball," and Pen Hallowell had been "badly hit in the arm." Hallowell "is one of the No. 1 sort," Rob assured his sister.[52]

Shaw also found time to write to Annie Haggerty, taking care to remind her of their trip to the opera nine months before. Rob had not seen her since, but his two close encounters with Confederate rifles had reminded him of his mortality and life outside, and after, the war. As a devoted son,

Rob confessed that he had always loved his mother "more than anyone else in the world," and so he thought himself "wicked" when he realized that he wanted to see Annie "even more." By November, Shaw had not received a firm commitment from the young woman he had met only on several occasions, but her letters hinted of an attachment on her part. He knew his parents would think their distant courtship unwise, yet he assured his mother that if he "ever [got] home" alive, his hope was to "marry Annie," and he wished that Sarah and his father "will be pleased with it."[53]

BY THE TIME SHAW POSTED HIS MISSIVES, HIS WAR HAD BECOME A war for abolition. Five days after Antietam, Lincoln summoned his cabinet and reminded them of the proclamation he had drafted the previous summer. While the July 1862 Confiscation Acts liberated only those slaves owned by known rebels, Lincoln's preliminary proclamation, issued on September 22, freed all enslaved Americans held within Confederate lines. Because Lincoln warned Confederates that they had 100 days to surrender before their human property was liberated (a deadline the president had no expectations that white Southerners would accept), and because most already captured portions of the South were exempted from the proclamation, some abolitionists were dismayed by the decree and its legalistic tone.

Even some moderate Northerners felt the same. Failing to comprehend how the actions of Lincoln and congressional Republicans had yoked the freedom of black Americans to the survival of the republic, or what impact word of the proclamation would have on black Southerners, Shaw did not "see what *practical* good" it would do. "Wherever our army has been, there remain no slaves, and the Proclamation will not free them where we can't go." Shaw little realized how the decree encouraged runaways such as Henry Jarvis to instead come to *them*. He was right enough, however, in fearing that "Jeff Davis will soon issue a proclamation threatening to hang every prisoner they take."[54]

With the Militia Act and the Confiscation Acts on the books, and with the proclamation soon to go into effect, Northern whites at last began to perceive a drift toward the use of black troops. Both congressional Republicans and the president had taken their time arriving at this juncture. The previous January, when Edwin M. Stanton had replaced the hapless Simon

Cameron in the War Department, he was surprised to discover that of all the cabinet members, only Treasury Secretary Salmon Chase believed it foolish to fight Confederate slaveholders without destroying the underlying cause of the rebellion. As early as August 1861, Shaw thought it "extraordinary" that the administration refused to "make use of the instrument that would finish the war sooner than anything else,—viz. the slaves." If nothing else, runaway slaves amounted to "a line of spies right into their camp." Shaw suspected that former slaves "would probably make a fine army after a little drill," since pliable blacks "could certainly be kept under better discipline than our independent Yankees." A year later, on the eve of Antietam, Shaw returned to the issue in a letter that revealed a change of heart on abolitionism. "I think the men would object to it very strongly at first," he admitted to his father, "but they would get accustomed to it in time." And indeed, a good many white soldiers increasingly embraced Shaw's opinions. "Many a man who sneered at her 'abolitionism' now wishes he was a Mass. man," one soldier recorded. "Their prejudice melts away and they begin to acknowledge that Mass. was right."[55]

If nothing else, Northern moderates hoped that emancipation would strip the Confederacy of its enslaved supply corps and the men who dug trenches and constructed rebel fortifications. The "negroes employed to dig those entrenchments," the Chicago *Tribune* insisted, "were worth to the rebels as much as that number of soldiers; and they would be worth as much to us." The president's decree also helped sway public opinion in Britain toward the Union cause. The *London Spectator* commented that, as the proclamation should draw "a great number of negroes Northwards," where they might incite "the greatest jealousy" of white laborers, the obvious solution was to create "a large auxiliary negro army." Unlike Shaw and Adams, however, the *Spectator*'s editor had every confidence that black heroism would pose "by far the most effective check on slavery propagandism" and the theory of African American inferiority. "But if the Northern statesmen will never look beyond the hour, what can save them?"[56]

Northern Democrats, who detested emancipation as an impediment to reconciliation with the South, were vociferous in denouncing plans for black enlistments. Congressional Democrats instinctively grasped the implications of the decree when combined with the Militia Act, and conservative politicians, publishers, and soldiers vented their rage against a campaign they feared they were powerless to halt. One Illinois soldier vowed that the day "the sole issue of the war [became] the 'Nigger Question'" would be the moment that "the war spirit of the West will be virtually dead." The majority of Western troops, he added, *will never strike a blow to free a negro.*" Upon receiving his party's nomination for governor that fall, New York's Horatio Seymour tore into the president for shifting the war's objectives from reunion to antislavery. As did Southern whites, Seymour warned that the inevitable consequence of "arming the slaves" would be "the butchery of women and children for scenes of lust and rapine, or arson and murder unparalleled in the history of the world." Other critics simply thought the entire notion absurd. When former New York congressman James Brooks cautioned an audience that the enlistment of black men would elevate them as "fellow citizens," his listeners erupted in laughter.[57]

Black activists, of course, had precisely such hopes. When African Americans met in an antislavery convention in Ypsilanti, Michigan, they not only promised to "stand ready to obey our country's call, in a summons to arms," but appointed a committee to call on the legislature and demand that it erase the word "white" from the state constitution. Some Northern blacks, however, doubted that lawmakers would reward them with equal rights and citizenship even if they served with distinction. Lincoln's Illinois restricted the franchise to white males, as did Indiana, Ohio, and Michigan. Even after Republicans captured the Indiana statehouse, few assemblymen championed the repeal of the state's "black laws," in part because Democrats hoped to turn the issue of black soldiers to their advantage in 1864.[58]

Some white abolitionists were skeptical from the start, believing that Republicans began to consider black troops only because of the Union's inability to best Confederate forces. Once there was "any real fighting to be done—any Bunker Hill battles to win," one editor wrote, Northern politicians "would doubtless be then willing enough to have [black men] shot at or bayonetted." Whether that service would then lead to a reversal of the *Dred Scott* decision was quite another matter.[59]

Inspired by Congress's tentative moves toward black enlistments, a handful of whites surreptitiously sought to organize black units. As early as 1861, Kansas senator James Henry Lane, previously a free-soil partisan during "Bleeding Kansas," had called for the use of Indian troops in the West, a request met with silence from the War Department. In the days after Lincoln's proclamation, Lane began to enlist men into a black regiment. Writing to Secretary Stanton on August 5, Lane announced that he was "receiving negroes under the late act of Congress," and he wondered whether the White House had "any objections." Stanton replied that while the Militia and Confiscation Acts empowered the president to employ black men in the military, Lincoln had not yet "given authority to raise such troops in Kansas." The old radical continued to quietly do so anyway, dubbing his unit the First Kansas Colored Volunteer Infantry, although he thought it prudent to "keep [the soldiers] from public view."[60]

FOR THE BRAHMINS, AS FOR MUCH OF THE NORTH, CHRISTMAS ARrived with mixed news. The Hallowell brothers continued to convalesce in their parents' Philadelphia home, in the midst of a large number of loving Quaker friends and relatives and, much to Ned's liking, good food and wine. Following the Antietam campaign, Adams and the First Cavalry settled into winter camp at Aquia Creek, Virginia. On December 1, just shy of twelve months after enlisting, news reached Adams that the War Department had promoted him to captain, and for once the dour officer was pleased. "I took great pride in it," he admitted to his diary, "and devoted myself to my duties and improvement." But for Shaw, some fifty miles north of Adams at Fairfax Station, the news was not good: he received word on Christmas Day that his cousin Theodore Parkman had died on December 16, one day after the Union debacle at Fredericksburg, Virginia, which took the lives of 1,284 U.S. soldiers; another 11,369 men were wounded, captured, or reported missing. "I think it's the saddest death we have had yet," Rob told his father. "I never knew a fellow like him for sticking to his principles." With the Army of the Potomac retreating toward Washington, and rumor hinting that an aggrieved president might soon relieve General Ambrose Burnside of his command, the Harvard men all understood that their labors were far from over.[61]

The year 1862 also ended in considerable disquiet for African Americans, some of whom anxiously awaited January 1 and with it the reading of the final Emancipation Declaration. Others continued to doubt that the country of their birth would ever afford them equal rights, or even that the United States could successfully subdue the Confederacy or liberate its millions of enslaved subjects. On occasion, hope and fear divided African American families. As New Year's Day approached, the black community of Boston prepared to celebrate it "as a day of jubilee" at the Tremont Temple, with Frederick Douglass to deliver the keynote oration. In December, Douglass had given speeches across New York and New England, each with the same refrain. "All we ask," he promised his audiences, "is that you treat us as you treat others. Protect us in our rights, and if we cannot sustain ourselves, let us go down." Douglass had long denounced the Republicans for their support of black emigration to Liberia, hints of which had crept into Lincoln's preliminary decree. But Lewis Douglass, Frederick's eldest son, was among those who placed little hope in the republic's future, and that October he considered traveling to the Colombian province of Panama with Senator Samuel Pomeroy, an advocate of colonization. The venture came to nothing when Secretary Seward refused to fund the project, but Lewis and his younger brother Charles continued in their doubts. Yet everything might change, they believed, if the president and his cabinet dropped their misgivings and agreed to the formation of a black regiment.[62]

CHAPTER THREE

Readville

W HEN WILLIAM LLOYD GARRISON FAILED TO APPEAR, THE ABO-
litionists huddled within the Tremont Temple on the morning of
January 1 were not long disappointed. William Wells Brown, a Kentucky-
born runaway turned novelist who was then living in Cambridge, rose to
speak, as did Wendell Phillips and Frederick Douglass. Yet another speaker
promised those in the audience that once they "got through with the enemies of the black man in Dixie," they would carry the fight for equal rights
across the North. Shortly before three o'clock, a messenger arrived at the
temple's doors with news that "the President's Proclamation was coming
over the wires." The chamber erupted with shouts of "Glory to God!"
Some activists had worried that the president would retreat from his
promise following his party's setbacks in the fall elections, but Abraham
Lincoln held true to his pledge: "I have issued the emancipation proclamation, and I can not retract it." Not only did the January decree drop
any references to black emigration, it included the assurance that "such
persons of suitable [physical] condition, will be received into the armed
services of the United States to garrison forts, positions, stations, and other
places, and to man vessels of all sorts." As the last words were read, the

Boston Journal reported, "cheers were proposed for the President and for the proclamation, the whole audience rising to their feet and shouting at the tops of their voices."[1]

The mood was less celebratory in Confederate Richmond. The intimations that the American government intended to liberate and arm Southern bondmen evoked memories of Nat Turner's bloody 1831 revolt and John Brown's failed raid on Harpers Ferry just four years before. Confederate president Jefferson Davis condemned the proclamation as "the most execrable measure recorded in the history of guilty man" and denounced Lincoln's efforts to transform "several millions of human beings of an inferior race, peaceful and contented laborers," into brutes "encouraged to a general assassination of their masters." Ironically, although many Northern whites could not imagine black soldiers as anything but manual laborers, Southern whites feared the worst. With Lincoln's government preparing to arm "the negroes to fight us," one Southern soldier warned his wife, the Confederacy now expected "the blood[iest] year of the war." In expectations of Lincoln's move, Davis had issued a proclamation on Christmas Eve, declaring that "all negro slaves captured in arms be at once delivered over to the executive authorities of the respective States to which they belong to be dealt with" as rebels and runaways. Moreover, and confirming Robert Shaw's fears, those "commissioned officers of the United States" who were "found serving in company with armed slaves" would not be regarded as "soldiers engaged in honorable warfare" but as "criminals deserving death." Officers of black regiments, in short, were to be considered as John Browns, and "whenever captured reserved for execution."[2]

Black Americans and their progressive allies in Washington remained undeterred. Kansas senator James Henry Lane, who had been stealthily enlisting black soldiers since the previous summer, rose in the Senate on December 28 to give notice that he planned to draft legislation authorizing Lincoln to raise 200 regiments "composed of persons of African descent." But Pennsylvania's Thaddeus Stevens, renowned as the "radical of radicals," got his bill done first. Introduced into the House on January 12, 1863, Stevens's handiwork was only a bit more modest than Lane's vision; he called for the creation of 150 black regiments, or 150,000 soldiers. Although the 1862 Militia Act had alluded to black service, Stevens wished to clarify that African Americans would be soldiers, not laborers. His bill also stipulated that the men would draw the same pay as white soldiers, and that its "company officers may be either white or black." An astute politician, Stevens was aware of the level of opposition to black troops, but he hoped the reality of expiring enlistments would silence most critics. Large numbers of white soldiers had signed on in the spring of 1861 for two-year deployments, and the July Militia Act had raised additional white troops for three months only. If Stevens's bill passed, New York attorney George Templeton Strong remarked, "we need not be uneasy about the regiments to be mustered out," as there "will be 300,000 Ethiop[ian]s to fill the gap."[3]

The response of Democratic editors and politicians was fierce, especially among conservatives who continued to insist that only demands for black freedom blocked the path to a negotiated peace. One Detroit publisher alleged that Congress intended to "surround" the president with a permanent palace guard of "nigger soldiers" who would then assist him in "strip[ping] the States of all their Constitutional power." The House debate dragged on over a long seven days. Charles Wickliffe of Kentucky alternated between ridiculing the very notion of black soldiers and fretting about the impact of such legislation on white troops. Deriding black men as "poor, deluded, uninformed creatures [who] will not stand the firing of a gun" before running, Wickliffe thought it unfathomable that the United States could defeat the Confederacy only by "employ[ing] the negro slave and put[ting] Sambo, or some other man meaner than Sambo, in command." Stevens, still feisty and dangerous in debate at age seventy-one, shredded Wickliffe's insinuations that black officers might soon bark orders at white privates. "I do not expect to live to see the day when, in this Christian land, merit shall counter-balance the crime of color," he snapped. "The only place where they can find equality is the grave. There all God's children are equal."[4]

Much to Stevens's dismay, the bill that passed the House on February 3 by a vote of 83 to 54 did so only after substantial revisions. The final version banned the enlistment of bondmen who belonged to loyal masters in border states, and it even prohibited the establishment of recruiting stations for already-free blacks in the loyal slave states. Worse yet, when the bill reached the Senate, it was referred to the Committee on Military Affairs, where Senator Henry Wilson of Massachusetts, the architect of the previous year's Militia Act, ordered the bill withdrawn, ostensibly on the grounds that it unnecessarily replicated his earlier handiwork. Quite possibly, Wilson feared that Stevens's more progressive bill would perish in the Senate. But he also allowed section 15 of his 1862 act to survive, together with its racially based pay inequality, a decision that was to haunt his state over the next two years. Even so, the president pronounced himself happy to work from Wilson's earlier legislation. Despite the "great aversion to the Negro Soldier Bill" on the part of Democrats, Lincoln remarked, he planned to forge ahead with the enlistment of black soldiers, and African Americans now began to be included on the draft rolls of Northern states.[5]

Massachusetts governor John A. Andrew did not share Wilson's qualms about Stevens's lavish plan; while the Senate focused on recruiting runaways as laborers, Andrew was prepared to enlist Northern freemen. Even before Stevens introduced his bill, the governor had contacted Secretary of War Edwin Stanton about raising a black regiment in his state. Although a committed antislavery man, Andrew was also a shrewd politician, and he played on Lincoln's fear of a court challenge to the Emancipation Proclamation. Recruiting black troops, one of the governor's advisers observed, would "silence all doubts as to the legality of the *Act* of Emancipation by taking it out of the *civil* acts & making it a purely military one." On January 26, Stanton replied, authorizing Andrew to recruit "persons of African descent, organized into separate corps" for "three years, or until sooner discharged." Because the Stevens bill had just passed the House, Andrew wrote again for clarification regarding black officers. Since the bill, which Andrew expected to become law, did "not prohibit colored officers in colored Regiments," the governor urged Stanton to "withdraw [his] prohibition so far as concerns line officers, assistant surgeons & chaplain[s]." The secretary replied that the War Department awaited Senate action on the bill. When Wilson buried Stevens's act, the ban on black commissioned officers remained, at least for the foreseeable future.[6]

EVEN HAD THE WAR DEPARTMENT AGREED TO BLACK OFFICERS, THE proposed regiment's first colonel and captains had to be men of experience. A unit led by inexperienced officers could meet with disaster in combat, dooming the entire experiment with black soldiers. Despite being a kinsman of the Shaws, Andrew's adviser, entrepreneur John Murray Forbes, advanced the name of Ned Hallowell, praising him as "a top man [and] a regular Negrophile." If the elder brother served as colonel, Forbes reasoned, "his [younger] Brother" Pen might consent to serve in some supporting capacity in "the Black Regt." Without waiting for a reply, Forbes dashed off a letter to Ned to gauge his interest. When Hallowell was slow to respond, Forbes contacted the governor yet again, assuring him that Ned was "a born leader" who had "showed himself brave and full of resources as a soldier." Most of all, Forbes thought, Ned had "conviction": he may have had aspirations to win higher rank, but more importantly, he was "ambitious in a larger way" in his desire to reform his country.[7]

The governor had other thoughts. His "mind [was] drawn towards Captain Shaw by many considerations," he admitted. Like the Hallowell brothers, Shaw had distinguished himself in combat, and Andrew required "young men of military experience." Since this was to be "the first colored regiment to be raised in the free States," its "success or its failure" would have enormous bearing on other black regiments, and so it was imperative that the men be trained correctly. But Andrew also had politics and practicalities in mind. As a mainstream Republican who lacked the abolitionist fervor of his parents, Shaw could "attract the support, sympathy and active cooperation of many besides his immediate family and friends," while the reputation of Frank and Sarah Shaw might appease those abolitionists who thought the son too moderate. And as the state would have to raise considerable funds for the regiment, their affluence played a role in his choice as well. Ned Hallowell's father was but "a quaker gentleman of Philadelphia," of modest wealth and limited connections, and so the governor regarded Ned as more appropriate for a lieutenant colonelcy.[8]

On January 30, Governor Andrew mailed two letters, a lengthy one to Frank Shaw and a second, shorter missive to Rob. As the regiment was "perhaps the most important corps to be organized during the whole war," as well as a "model for all future colored regiments," Andrew emphasized to Frank, its officers "must necessarily be gentlemen of the highest tone and honor." As such, he intended to nominate as colonel "your son," and "the Lt. Colonelcy to Capt. Hallowell." Andrew revealed that two officers, one from New York and one from Connecticut, had already written to express their interest, but he did not wish to "start the regiment under a stranger to Massachusetts." Should Rob decline the offer, Andrew preferred "its being kept reasonably quiet." The governor's brief memo to Rob simply noted that he had written to his father, "expressing to him my sense of the importance of his undertaking," while urging the young captain "to reply to this offer at the earliest day" possible.[9]

The dual letters, together with the reference to the father in the note to the son, suggest that the governor expected parental pressure to come down on Rob. If so, Frank Shaw did all that and more. Rather than merely forwarding the governor's letter, as Andrew requested, Frank Shaw boarded a train for Washington and then journeyed on to Stafford Courthouse in northern Virginia, where the Second Massachusetts was encamped. Although Frank sought to impress upon his son that both he and the governor considered "it a most important command [and] a great honour," Rob's first inclination was to turn down the post. Having "seen the elephant" together, as soldiers dubbed their first experience in battle, Shaw regarded the men of the Second as his brothers. Rob understood that his mother would especially be disappointed in his refusal to lead black troops, but had he accepted, he confided to his beloved Annie, "it would only have been from a sense of duty." Frank Shaw left, distraught, with a letter in hand from Rob declining the commission.[10]

Within days, Rob "began to think [he] had made a mistake in refusing Governor Andrew's offer." After the Emancipation Proclamation, he reasoned, "the undertaking will not meet with so much opposition as was at first supposed," although he still hoped that Annie would not "care if it is made fun of." On February 5, Rob cabled his father: "Please Destroy My Letter and Telegraph to the Governor that I Accept." Three days later, he wrote again to his father that he was reconciled to the task, and that he required a furlough from Governor Andrew to return home to Massachusetts. "Tell Mother I have not wavered at all, since my final decision," he promised. "I feel that if we can get the men, all will go right."[11]

What caused Shaw's change of heart? Certainly his parents played a role. When she heard of her son's refusal, Sarah dashed off a blunt letter to Andrew. "This decision has caused me the bitterest disappointment I have ever experienced," she confessed. "It would have been the proudest moment of my life and I could have died satisfied that I have not lived in vain." If Rob was not privy to that missive, he certainly knew his mother's mind and could guess, as she assured Andrew, that she "shed bitter tears over his refusal." Sarah also rushed a cable to her son indicating that Annie did not "disapprove" of his appointment, and that mattered greatly. He had always believed, he assured Annie, that it was important "to prove that a negro can be made a good soldier." Most of all, the memory of his old friend James Savage nudged him to reconsider. A proud Republican, Savage had once remarked that the only job that could persuade him to abandon the Second would be to serve with a black regiment. Savage had died the previous October from wounds received at Cedar Mountain, and Shaw mourned him as a man of "purity [and] conscientiousness." The best one could do in life, Rob swore, was to "resemble James Savage." And so he accepted.[12]

While Frank Shaw hurried Rob's latest response to the governor, Andrew urged Ned Hallowell, who needed far less convincing, into accepting a position in the regiment. As Andrew explained it to Frank Shaw, he "wish[ed] both gentlemen" to be part of his state's experiment, and "their relative rank" was of secondary consideration. Fearing that Rob's reluctance was due to fear of command, as the potential failure of the regiment was a very real consideration, Andrew was willing to name Shaw the "Lieut. Colonel, if desired," with Hallowell as the regiment's colonel. Morris Hallowell had already written from Philadelphia to say that both of his sons were "anxious to be useful and would gladly accept a position" in the proposed "Coloured Regiments." But late in the evening of February 7, Governor Andrew received word of Shaw's telegram. In response, Andrew notified Shaw that he had been "designated as Colonel" and should hasten to Boston "as soon as possible to assist in the organization of the regiment."[13]

Civil War regiments comprised ten companies, each with precisely 100 men, an arrangement explicated in General Joseph William Hardee's popular 1855 manual, *Rifle and Light Infantry Tactics for the Exercise and Manoeuvres of Troops*. Governors of each state selected their regiments' senior officers with the approval of the War Department, and then the units were folded into the U.S. Army. Because there were already fifty-three infantry regiments from Massachusetts, Andrew's experiment was christened the Fifty-fourth. On February 9, Andrew penned a note to Secretary Stanton, informing him of Shaw's appointment. By the month's end, William Lloyd Garrison was able to proudly publish the "complete roster" of officers. At the last moment, Andrew inexplicably chose to reshuffle the Hallowell brothers, so that the younger Pen advanced to the rank of lieutenant colonel and Ned was assigned the lower rank of major. To appease Stanton, the governor selected a white doctor, Lincoln Stone, as the unit's head surgeon, but he insisted on John DeGrasse, "a colored physician in Boston, to be Assistant Surgeon." Andrew had also requested that Colonel William Lee forward him names for junior positions, and among those on the list were Garth Wilkinson James—Wilkie, to his friends—son of the wealthy theologian Henry James Sr., and Cabot Russell, a soldier in the Twentieth. Edward Waldo Emerson, the nineteen-year-old son of essayist and poet Ralph Waldo Emerson, repeatedly attempted to sign on, but the sickly youth failed every physical examination. Even so, as Wilkie's brother Henry James Jr. marveled, the Fifty-fourth's officer corps "bristled with Boston genealogies."[14]

The roster of Brahmin officers went a long way in appeasing public opinion in Massachusetts. "Now that it is decided that coloured troops shall be raised," Shaw assured Annie, "people seem to look upon it as a matter of course." The shift had much to do, as Andrew had planned, with Rob. As Effie Shaw's fiancé Charles Russell Lowell bluntly observed, the first black regiment from the North had to be "soberly [run] and not spoilt by too much fanaticism," by which he meant militant abolitionism. And "Bob Shaw," Lowell added, "is not a fanatic." As was the case with many antislavery New Englanders of privilege, Shaw knew few black men intimately, and his discourse indicated as much. In two letters from late February, Shaw felt comfortable using the term "darkey" with his mother, and he laughed to his cousin Elizabeth Russell Lyman that he had become "a Nigger Col." Some white women who traveled with the army to the Carolina coast to work with freedpeople embraced the epithet "Nigger Teachers," in part to lessen its sting, but in the late winter of 1863 that appears not to have been the case with Shaw, who wrote to Lyman's husband Theodore, then in Europe, to say that if he returned home he might serve "as chaplain if he would like to go into a good nigger concern."[15]

GOVERNOR ANDREW HAD HIS OFFICERS; NOW HE NEEDED RECRUITS. The 1860 census had indicated that only 1,973 African American males of military age resided in Massachusetts, and according to the superintendent of the census, if black men volunteered in the same ratio as whites, that would amount to only 394 soldiers. That left the proposed regiment short by at least 600, assuming that all 394 men could pass their physicals. On top of this, Congress was about to pass a new conscription act—it did so on March 3—and with Wilson's Militia Act now interpreted to include African Americans, another round of enlistments would further drain the state of young blacks, who would serve in the army as laborers. The obvious if unprecedented answer, Forbes counseled, was to recruit beyond the borders of the Bay State.[16]

To coordinate the recruitment effort, Andrew pieced together a "Committee of Consultation," commonly dubbed the "Black Committee." He persuaded wealthy abolitionist George Luther Stearns to chair the group. As an industrialist who had amassed a fortune in manufacturing lead pipe, Stearns could appeal to such fellow capitalists as Forbes and Amos Lawrence, who also joined the committee. Yet as a militant abolitionist and one of the "Secret Six" benefactors of Brown's raid at Harpers Ferry, Stearns also enjoyed the credentials to charm what one officer described as "those advanced thinkers and workers who had striven to help and free the slave." As Andrew had always assumed, Frank Shaw joined the committee as well, promising to raise subscriptions from his New York associates for up to $2,500, while Richard Price Hallowell, the second-oldest of the four brothers, consented to serve as the group's treasurer. With the committee in such "good hands," a skeptical Charles Russell Lowell remarked, "this is likely to be a success, if any black regiment can be a success."[17]

For all of its wealth and prestige, the main flaw in a recruitment committee drawn exclusively from white businessmen was that, Stearns aside, it lacked influence in the black community. At one of its earliest meetings, Richard Hallowell suggested—at least as reported by Rob, once again revealing his racial prejudices—that it might "please the coloured population" they intended to contact to have "some influential darkey on the committee." Stearns was friendly with black activist Lewis Hayden, a member of Boston's vigilance committee who had spent the previous decades assisting runaways, and Hayden vowed to promote the committee's cause in the city's African Meeting House.[18]

But as promising as that was, Stearns understood that what was required was a campaign to the west of Massachusetts. Stearns traveled through New

York State as far as Buffalo, meeting with black leaders as he journeyed along the Erie Canal. Upon reaching Buffalo, Stearns hired John Mercer Langston, a Virginia-born freeman who had attended Oberlin College before being admitted to the Ohio bar in 1854. After Stearns and Langston opened an office in Buffalo, Andrew's committee promised to pay New York State operatives $2 for each recruit, give each soldier a bounty of $50, and cover the costs of transportation to Readville. New York's black community put scant trust in white Republicans, however, since they had refused to endorse the failed 1860 ballot initiative removing the property restriction imposed on black voters, and so even when Stearns was present at a recruitment site, he wisely "insisted that [Langston] do the speaking."[19]

Following the establishment of the Buffalo recruiting office, Langston turned his attentions to his adoptive state of Ohio. Home to 8,000 black men, Ohio had the largest pool of potential African American soldiers after New York and Pennsylvania, and Langston enjoyed the support of the state's urbanized black leaders, village shopkeepers, rural farmers, and teachers, including one James Monroe Trotter. As in all of the Midwestern states, Ohio's "Black Laws" restricted the franchise to white males, and Governor David Tod, a Democrat, warned Langston "that this is a white man's government [and] that white men are able to defend and protect it." But because Andrew promised to organize any Ohio recruits "into separate companies" within the Fifty-fourth, Tod could count "the colored men of Ohio" as part of his state's quota allotment under the new conscription act. If nothing else, Langston's efforts reduced the number of black males in Tod's state while easing the draft's burden on its white farmers.[20]

In the Empire State, meanwhile, the obvious choice to raise further awareness for the regiment was Frederick Douglass. Stearns had known the Rochester abolitionist for many years through mutual friends John Brown and Gerrit Smith, and in June he contacted Douglass to work on behalf of the Fifty-fourth both along the canal and in Washington. "Four or five weeks ago this regiment was a thing of speculation and doubt," the black activist announced in his *Douglass' Monthly*, but thanks to "the zeal, industry, and efficiency of Mr. George L. Stearns," a "network of influence has rapidly spread over the whole West." Writing privately to Smith, Douglass admitted that convincing black audiences of the wisdom of dying for a country that refused to recognize them as citizens was often "not to

[his] taste." Yet he had only admiration for Stearns, who regarded "the whole United States as his field for recruiting purposes." Whatever doubts Douglass had regarding the Lincoln administration, he believed that "to arrest, overwhelm, and annihilate the rebellion [was] our first and highest duty." Douglass assured Smith that he "shall probably go soon into the work again," a pledge that revealed how deeply connected the formation of the regiment was with black and abolitionist aspirations.[21]

Douglass was perhaps being overly cautious. For those young black Northerners who had tried to enlist as early as 1861, no public relations campaign was necessary. Black abolitionists recognized Governor Andrew as their ally, yet they also wished to make it clear that their churches and vigilance committees were not subordinate to Stearns's agency. On February 18, even before Stearns took to the hustings, black activists convened in New Bedford's Liberty Hall for a massive "war meeting." Nearly 1,500 people thronged into the building on the corner of Purchase and William Streets. The Reverend William Jackson gaveled the meeting to order before turning the podium over to William Wells Brown. Concerned that some in the audience were reluctant to serve a country that denied them civil equality, Brown counseled that the "prejudice against the race must be overcome by degrees." In any event, "it was a false principle," Brown shouted, to equate moderate Republicans with the proslavery administration in Richmond. "Once armed," he promised, black men "would fight till freedom was established in every State." Every young man in the auditorium should sign up immediately, Brown urged, as "one Massachusetts colored regiment in South Carolina would make the Confederate Government quake with fear." Several dozen men shoved to the front to inscribe their "names on the roll." The first to do so was sea cook James Henry Gooding; somewhat farther back in line was the Virginia runaway then considering a life in the ministry, William H. Carney Jr. Either he was not superstitious or merely too enthusiastic to notice, but Carney was the thirteenth New Bedford man to go for a soldier.[22]

As the abolitionist and black press spread the word, activists convened meetings at various locales in Philadelphia. The first was held at the Oak Street Baptist Church in the western part of the city. There, Pennsylvania-born mariner turned cabinet-maker George Stephens told of his near-enslavement after docking in Charleston five years before; his hatred of slavery, he promised, would lead him to enlist in Boston at the meeting's end. By comparison, the conference held one week later on a frigid February evening in Franklin Hall turned acrimonious after Robert Purvis introduced a resolution praising Massachusetts as "the first in freeing her slaves [and] the first in awarding black men the acknowledgement of citizenship." Born free in Charleston, the light-skinned Purvis had attended Amherst College before marrying into money after his courtship of Harriet Forten, the daughter of black merchant James Forten Sr. and kinswoman to Peter Vogelsang. Leaping from his seat in the audience, David Bustill Bowser, a portraitist who had once painted John Brown, denounced Purvis "in strong terms" as a pawn of white politicians he doubted would ever do justice to black Americans. "He thought that the colored people had no rights whatever under the Constitution of Pennsylvania," he yelled, "and the government doesn't mean to give them rights." As the raucous meeting drew to a close, Purvis pushed through a weaker resolution calling for the appointment of a committee "for the further consideration of this subject." In the end, Bowser relented.[23]

The biggest crowds in New York were reserved for Frederick Douglass. As a former slave who regarded his youthful fistfight with a slave-breaker as the defining moment in his life, he understood the desire for vengeance on the part of Northern blacks, many of whom were just one generation out of slavery. More than any other advocate of the Fifty-fourth, Douglass fused patriotic oratory with a rage against Confederate officials. Since the dawn of the war, Douglass had publicly argued that "Uncle Sam had been fighting with his soft white hand, and had his black hand tied behind him." Determined to use the conflict to overturn the hated *Dred Scott* decision, Douglass believed that once a black man could "get an eagle on [his] button and a musket on [his] shoulder," all of "the devils in Jeff Davis' dominions cannot keep [him] out of citizenship." Although twenty-five years away from slavery, Douglass understood that many of his listeners had scores to settle. For too long, he assured one audience, a series of presidents had been their enemy. "Now the government has given authority" to black men, Douglass thundered, "to shoulder a musket and go down and kill white rebels." Serving in their country's military could earn them political rights even as it allowed blacks to achieve "retribution [against] slaveholders."[24]

Speaking in small towns and hamlets across the Empire State was all to the good, but larger audiences awaited. In February, Douglass traveled to Manhattan to speak at Cooper Union, the East Village venue where Lincoln had given a famous speech that secured his reputation in early 1860. Employing his usual blend of emotionalism, sarcastic humor, and fury, Douglass filled the institute's Great Hall with his rich baritone. Since the emancipation proclamation, Douglass said, with great irony, he felt more like a citizen "and felt whiter, and comb[ed his] hair with much less difficulty." He also drew "laughter and applause" for mocking Northern whites who maintained "that the negroes would not make good soldiers" while at the same time complaining "that perhaps they would fight so well that they would have to be promoted above white men." He then turned serious. Although the governors of New York and Ohio refused to recruit black soldiers, Massachusetts was ready to do so. "Away with prejudice," he demanded, "and in this struggle for liberty [and] country," let the "black iron hand of the colored man fall heavily on the head of the slaveholding traitors and rebels." Stop calling black men "'nigger', and call them soldiers," Douglass concluded. "Give them a chance! Give them a chance!"[25]

For Douglass, the pen had always been as important as the podium. On March 2, he published an 1,100-word manifesto that he correctly assumed would be reprinted across the North. Entitled, "Men of Color, to Arms," Douglass pulled together all of the arguments he had been making since "the Rebel cannon shattered the walls of Sumter." Confronting black antigovernment critics of military service, he repeated his fears that should black men not sign on after Massachusetts "welcomes you to arms as her soldiers," they would "justify the past contempt of the Government towards you." Rather than dwell upon historical wrongs, black Americans needed to remember "that every negro hater and slavery-lover in the land regards the arming of negroes as a calamity." Four million enslaved Americans awaited their arrival in the South, "and the chance is now given you to end in a day the bondage of centuries." Drawing links between black men in blue and those who in the past had sacrificed their lives for freedom, Douglass urged: "Remember Denmark Vesey, of Charleston. Remember Nathaniel Turner, of South Hampton" and those "who followed noble John Brown, and fell as glorious martyrs." Young men were already marching toward "this first regiment at Readville," Douglass wrote, and he promised to "forward to Boston all persons adjudged fit to be mustered."[26]

As expected in a day of cut-and-paste journalism, not only was the essay reprinted in black-owned newspapers such as Robert Hamilton's Manhattan-based *Weekly Anglo-African,* abolitionist journals such as Garrison's *Liberator,* and even friendly Republican journals such as Horace Greeley's *New-York Tribune,* but an abridged version of it even appeared in the Baltimore *Sun.* Other papers, particularly in the lower North and Midwest, declined to reprint the essay but commented on it nonetheless. One journalist sneered that "Fred Douglass is calling on the colored men of the north to come to rescue—but they don't see it." A Harrisburg, Pennsylvania, newspaper denounced black service as "mad fanaticism" and an attempt "to reverse the decrees of God!" The "Rochester darkey has been among us," noted a third, adding that despite his pleas, "the experiment seems now to be mourned by these fanatics as a melancholy failure." Although Langston had succeeded in recruiting a large number of men from Ohio, the Cleveland *Plain Dealer* deplored one of his "war meetings" as "*galvanized* with pretended patriotism" and an abject failure, "dead and forgotten already."[27]

In truth, a good many black leaders continued in their doubts, not so much because of past injuries as to current rumors that black soldiers would not draw equal pay, or that they could not rise to become commissioned officers. Reverend Henry Highland Garnet, born a slave in Maryland and so mistrustful of the federal government that he routinely spoke in favor of black emigration to Mexico or Liberia, publicly wondered, "[W]hat have black men to fight for in this war?" Others noted that men of color had fought at "Bunker Hill and under Washington," yet even after the 1815 Battle of New Orleans, white Americans took it "for granted that 'the niggers couldn't be made to fight.'" But more thought as did Jermain Matthews, who volunteered for the Fifty-fourth despite his fiancée's distress that he could die fighting "for the white man's country." After fleeing the South and becoming "a free man," Matthews wrote, "I solemnly vowed to devote my whole life to best serving my people." James Henry Gooding agreed. "Our people must know that if they are ever to attain any position in the eyes of the civilized world, they must forgo comfort, home, fear, and fight for it," he wrote in an open letter to the *New Bedford Mercury,* and "make up their minds to become something more than hewers of wood and drawers of water all their lives."[28]

After the War Department appointed Stearns as a permanent recruiter and awarded him the rank of major, one of those who briefly considered a similar position was Frederick Douglass himself. At forty-four, Douglass remained vigorous, and Secretary Stanton briefly considered sending him to those parts of the South already under U.S. control. But Douglass's insistence on a rank equal to that held by Stearns, a white man, posed a problem, as did the obvious dangers of working in the occupied Confederacy. "Do not *take any commission* that leads you, *personally,* into the fighting ranks," implored his old friend Julia Griffiths Crofts. "Write as you please, but *never go south,* or killed you *most assuredly* will be," she warned. "You are, in many respects, a *marked man.*"[29]

DOUGLASS TOOK ENORMOUS SATISFACTION, HOWEVER, IN THE FACT, as he informed Gerrit Smith, that "Charlie my youngest Son was the first to put his name down as one of the Company." The elder Douglass had just completed a tour of Buffalo, Auburn, Syracuse, Ithaca, Troy, and Albany, and he had recruited nearly 100 men. That the signature of nineteen-year-old Charles Remond Douglass was the first ascribed on the roster filled his father with pride. Born in Lynn, Massachusetts, Charles worked for his father as a printer. Slightly shorter than Frederick at approximately five feet, nine inches tall, Charles reached Camp Meigs on March 25 and signed on for three years. Owing to both Charles's famous father and his flawless penmanship, Shaw ordered him promoted to lance corporal within the month and assigned to writing up the endless paperwork for the arriving recruits.[30]

Arriving at Readville on the same day was the great abolitionist's eldest son, twenty-two-year-old Lewis Henry Douglass. The tall, athletic Lewis was then employed in the uneventful occupation of "grocer," and so, as with Charles, it took no persuasion to encourage the enthusiastic young man to enlist. After first traveling to Syracuse, Lewis and seventeen other recruits detoured south to Binghamton, amusing themselves "by singing John Brown['s Body] and other songs to the delight of the white passengers in the car." When Lewis's group reached Binghamton, they were joined

by Charles and six others calling themselves "the Loguen guard," after the
Reverend Jermain Loguen, the Tennessee runaway turned Syracuse minister. As Lewis was betrothed to the minister's daughter, Helen Amelia
Loguen—or simply Amelia, as she preferred—he hurried this cheery news
to his beloved. Loguen himself had been recruiting black employees of
the New York and Erie Railroad, "and putting them into the hands of the
young Douglass boys," as he told one reporter. If Charles was a natural
clerk, the popular Lewis was a born leader of men, and by April 1, Private
Douglass of Company F was promoted to sergeant major, the highest noncommissioned rank then possible for a black soldier.[31]

On the morning of Wednesday, March 4, James Henry Gooding bade
farewell to Ellen, his wife of just over five months, and set off with his
friend William Carney and twenty-two other recruits from New Bedford.
Of those traveling north to Readville, ten were married and fourteen were
single. More than half were laborers who left behind no skilled occupation,
while Gooding was one of three mariners. They arrived that afternoon and
met their commanding officer for the first time. Shaw was only ten months
Gooding's senior, but the new private praised him as solicitous, "doing all
he can for the comfort of those now in camp." The recruits marched to
their barracks, where they "found a nice warm fire and a good supper in
readiness." Constructed two years before for white regiments, the barracks,
in the words of one officer, "were great barn-like structures of wood with
sleeping-bunks on either side." Having spent the last several years telling
authorities—including the minister who married him to Ellen—that he
was born in Troy, Gooding opted for yet another fiction and assured several army clerks that New Bedford was his birthplace. The army listed him
as five feet, seven inches tall, slightly more than was noted in his seaman's
papers, and characterized his complexion as "light." Gooding, Carney, and
all of the New Bedford men were assigned to Company C. That evening
Gooding's fellows were all handed new uniforms, "and now," he enthused,
"they are looking quite like soldiers." Since many of the recruits arrived
"poor and ragged," their old clothing was symbolically burned. Dressed in
their Union blues, Pen Hallowell thought, the men "straightened up [and]
grew inches taller."[32]

From New York State arrived Stephen Swails, weary of waiting tables in
Cooperstown and eager to open a new chapter in his troubled life. At age

thirty, he was older than most privates, and on April 8 Shaw ordered the light-skinned soldier promoted to first sergeant. Far younger but no less eager was James Caldwell, the grandson of abolitionist Sojourner Truth, from Auburn, New York. Caldwell was "full of enthusiasm when he heard that colored men" could finally join the military, Truth boasted. "Now is our time Grandmother," he swore, "to prove that we are men." Far older was hotel clerk Peter Vogelsang, who enrolled as a private on April 17. Vogelsang evidently either knew Frank Shaw before the conflict or had met him at a "war meeting" earlier that spring, as Shaw recommended the recruit to his son. Initially, Rob thought Vogelsang, who was twenty-one years his elder, far too old to serve, claiming that "no man of 46 would pass." But after only seven days Shaw admitted his mistake, promoted Vogelsang to sergeant, and assured his father "that your man Vogelsang was accepted" and had proved "very efficient."[33]

Others came from farther away still. Toussaint L'Ouverture Delany, the son of journalist and physician Martin Delany, caught a train from Pittsburgh. Joseph Barge, a North Carolina freeman who regarded himself as "a yankee by cultivation, education, and thinking principles," had fled the South in early 1861 and moved to Massachusetts; from there he "went from Boston as a soldier." Eighteen-year-old George Alexander, a free-born farmer from Charleston, South Carolina, joined in late April, as did two George Washingtons—one of them a Virginian, the other from Syracuse—and no less than three William Henry Harrisons, one a native of Missouri who had been living in Chicago, with the other two from Pennsylvania and Michigan. (Yet a fourth William Henry Harrison, from Maine, would enlist in December 1863.)[34]

Recruits arrived at the rate of about ten each day. By March 12, Shaw reported, they had "near 250 men in camp," and he thought the growing regiment was "getting on swimmingly." A visiting Connecticut reporter counted "about three hundred" men just a few days later, and with the arrival of another fifty from Albany and the Buffalo area, Sergeant Major Lewis Douglass tallied 548 by early April. A number of men in Lewis's company were from Syracuse, and he urged Amelia to send him some Syracuse newspapers. "The young men from Boston and New Bedford receive many little niceties from their friends," he hinted, "which keeps them in cheerful spirits." Also keeping count was Gooding, whose weekly letter to

The eldest son of Frederick and Anna Douglass, Lewis Henry Douglass, with a natural flair for command, was beloved by his men and quickly rose to the rank of sergeant major. Governor Andrew would consider using Douglass as a test case to press the War Department to promote blacks into the commissioned ranks, but the wounds he received atop the walls of Wagner ended that plan. *Courtesy Howard University.*

the *New Bedford Mercury* on April 18 listed the number of recruits as 674. "But they do not come fast enough for the boys here," Gooding insisted. "We want the regiment full, and show that we are men." Hoping to encourage others to sign on, Gooding tried to shame New England readers by pointing to the number of blacks who had arrived from Pennsylvania. "This regiment should be filled now," and all it needed was "326 more men, from Massachusetts." Those already present, however, took to the drills with enthusiasm; when a group of skeptical white officers stopped at Readville to monitor the unit's progress, Shaw was delighted that his men erased any of their "doubts of negroes making good soldiers."[35]

One complicating factor was the rigorous medical examination each recruit faced immediately upon arriving at Readville. Poor nutrition and a lack of protein took their toll on antebellum children, especially those from working-class households. At five feet, seven inches tall, Vogelsang was among the bigger soldiers in the regiment. Lincoln Stone and his team

Charles Remond Douglass was anxious to please his famous father but lacked the capacity for military leadership. His persistent ill health and elegant handwriting kept him at Camp Meigs as a regimental clerk, though he saw action in Virginia after transferring to the Fifth Cavalry in March 1864. *Courtesy Howard University.*

of doctors rejected nearly one-third of all the volunteers. "The first thing I did was to be examined by the surgeon to see if I was in any manner deformed," Lewis wrote to Amelia, "after which I was told to go to an officer whose business it is to take a description of my looks, and then swear me into the service." After promising to "obey all orders from the President of the United States," Lewis collected his uniform. "My badge of office is three stripes placed on my coat in the shape of a half diamond," he added, dutifully drawing an image for Amelia to appreciate.[36]

As the regiment at last filled, its officers took stock of the men and their backgrounds. For a contingent that carried the flag of Massachusetts, only 133 men, or 13 percent, were residents of the state at the war's start. Counting Gooding and Carney, thirty-nine soldiers had arrived from New Bedford, which was two more than provided by Boston. Those present at Camp Meigs by late May hailed from fifteen Northern states, four loyal border states, five Confederate states, Canada, the Caribbean, and, allegedly, the

Arizona Territory. The largest group, or 294 men, had marched north from Pennsylvania. Vogelsang, Swails, and the Douglass brothers were four of the 183 New Yorkers present, while Ohio, with 155 men, delivered the third-largest state delegation. Approximately one-quarter of the soldiers identified themselves as farmers—by comparison to the 50 percent of white Union soldiers who were yeomen—while one-third listed themselves simply as "laborers." Gooding was one of thirty-eight mariners, with Swails listed as one of thirty-four waiters. Swails himself had also once labored as a boatman, and there were twenty-seven of those. Their average age was 24.3 years, while the white officers who led them averaged a slightly younger 24.1 years. Twenty boys ages sixteen and seventeen volunteered as drummers; one of them, Eli Biddle, would be wounded during the fighting but live until 1940. At fifty-seven, America Tabb was briefly the oldest soldier. Allowed to enlist as recompense for his recruitment efforts in Boston, Tabb was soon judged "unfit for duty" and discharged, leaving the far more robust Vogelsang as the regiment's senior soldier.[37]

In part because doctors had rejected so many men, those who passed muster bragged of the unit's physical prowess. "It makes one's heart pulsate with pride as he looks upon those stout and brawny men," Gooding marveled. A correspondent for the *Weekly Anglo-African* agreed, reporting that the soldiers at Camp Meigs, "with very few exceptions, [were] our best young men." George Stephens, the Pennsylvania cabinet-maker who had brought a contingent of black Philadelphians to Readville, insisted that he did not "exaggerate when I say there is no regiment superior, if equal to this in physique and aptitude of men." Four hundred men, he observed, had "been rejected because they did not come up to the highest standard of mental and physical proficiency." Those who remained drilled long hours on the camp's muddy parade grounds, and those men, Stephens swore, could survive "the severest rigors of a campaign in the field." Thin-chested and only five feet, five inches tall himself, Shaw conceded that some of his men appeared "as big as all creation—and look really very well" in their blue uniforms.[38]

The young colonel's assessment of their intellectual ability, however, did not match that of Stephens, and in the early months of 1863 his remarks on what he habitually dubbed his "darkey concern" betrayed a privileged young Brahmin wrestling with previously unexamined attitudes toward

Stephen Atkins Swails joined the Fifty-fourth in part to escape a dissolute youth and a pregnant girlfriend. Utterly courageous under fire, he was shot in the head at Olustee, Florida, but survived to become the first black commissioned officer in the U.S. Army. *Courtesy Massachusetts Historical Society.*

race and class. Writing to his father in late February, Shaw lamented that the recruits who had arrived were "not of the best class of nigs," adding that if the rest of the North would match Massachusetts's bounty of $50, "we should be able to get a much better set from the other states." Shaw's sentiments spoke to class, however, as much as they did to race. Considering that he was less comfortable with dark-skinned, undereducated, rural freemen from Ohio than he was with cultured urbanites such as the Douglass brothers and the light-complexioned Swails and Vogelsang, it was surely no accident that the men he promptly promoted were middle class. In later years, Pen Hallowell implicitly admitted this bias, bragging that while the term "colored soldier" often conjured up images of "the thick-lipped negro of Congo," the men of the Fifty-fourth were "people in whose veins [was] an admixture of the blood of every nationality that is represented on this continent." Clearly, however, leading a black regiment changed these Brahmins. One month to the day after Shaw had complained about the low class of recruits, he confessed a change of heart, writing that he was "perfectly astonished at the general intelligence these darkeys display."

Moreover, for all of Hallowell's theories about the genetic background of his men, Pen always treated them with respect and demanded that those white officers who served with the regiment deport themselves as "gentlemen who understood the correct orthography and pronunciation of the word 'negro.'"[39]

Morning came early at Readville. Drummers beat reveille each day at six o'clock. The soldiers poured out of their bunks and made haste with their morning meal and a quick prayer. "We have every morning for breakfast one third of a six-cent loaf of bread," Lewis reported, "nearly a quart of coffee, and a large piece of fresh or corn beef or ham." For many of the working-class soldiers, the repast was a banquet. Squad drills began at eight-thirty and continued until eleven, and company drills began at the same hour but stretched until five o'clock. Late February turned unusually glacial, even for New England, and Shaw ordered the men "drilled as much as possible in-doors, for it is too cold out there to keep them in the open air for any length of time." But even as spring arrived the weather remained "so stormy" that the men churned the parade grounds into muddy furrows. All were nonetheless "anxious to perfect themselves in drill that they may the sooner meet the Rebs," Gooding noted, "and they all feel determined to fight." A quick break at midday allowed them a meal of "beef and potatoes and the same quantity of bread," and after a long day of drills they were fed again, Douglass informed Amelia, sometimes with "bean soup," but "constantly rice and molasses." As the exhausted men fell into their bunks, the evening ended as it had begun, with a prayer, and "the great degree of fervor exhibited," Gooding swore, could do the Bethel Church in New Bedford proud.[40]

The first to arrive trained only with Harpers Ferry Model 1841 rifles, heavy smoothbore percussion muskets manufactured between 1844 and 1855. By late April, however, the entire regiment was outfitted with 1853 Pattern Enfields, a British-manufactured rifled musket favored by soldiers on both sides of the conflict. The muzzle-loaded weapon fired a .577 caliber minié ball, and its 39-inch barrel could be fitted with a bayonet long enough to be effective against attacking cavalry. "The men can be seen everywhere going through the manual of arms," George Stephens assured the *Weekly Anglo-African,* "in which they are already quite proficient." Having twice experienced the chaos of battle, Shaw relentlessly drilled the recruits, who, as an infantry regiment, had to be prepared to carry out a variety of complicated maneuvers while under fire. Nevertheless, some observers, even white abolitionists, could not refrain from patronizing the soldiers with benign racism. By comparison to white soldiers, the unsigned essay in the *Liberator* maintained, the men of the Fifty-fourth "are in some respects manifestly superior; especially for their aptness in drill, because of their imitativeness and love of music [and] docility in discipline."[41]

"Colonel Robert Gould Shaw was not a sentimentalist," Pen Hallowell acknowledged, and he imposed rigorous discipline at Camp Meigs. Having but a few months during which to mold his army of farmhands and day laborers into a cohesive unit, he adopted the same "methods of coercion" used on white soldiers in what Shaw regarded as the most "well-disciplined regiments." Privates deemed "unruly," Hallowell wrote, were forced to stand on "barrels, bucked, gagged and, if need be, shot." White officers were not exempt from this regimen, for Shaw wanted his men to know that correction was not racially based. One captain complained to his wife that he had never served in "a Regiment where the officers were under as strict discipline as [in] the 54th." General Edward Pierce, the commandant of Meigs, who had witnessed two years of training at the post, finally admonished Shaw to refrain from further "severe and unusual punishments not laid down by regulations." Yet Shaw's approach was effective, if only judging by the results. There were few reported incidents of drunkenness, and the guardhouse was "seldom occupied." Both Shaw and the recruits understood that the eyes of the North were upon them, and nobody at Readville wished the experiment to fail. When one officer sought to test a soldier standing post late one night, the guard barked out, "Who goes there?" and demanded the countersign. When the officer instead responded with, "I will give it directly," the private sliced his bayonet up "through the officer's coat, and into his flesh."[42]

So thoroughly did the soldiers appreciate what was at stake that even when they believed that the entire regiment had been wronged, they maintained order. The promised state bounty of $50, which the recruits expected to receive at the moment of their enlistments, had not yet been paid by the end of March. Two soldiers from Company B deserted, claiming that Massachusetts had failed to keep its part of the bargain. The pair, whom Gooding derided as the sort of men "to be satisfied with nothing," were promptly captured and returned to camp—by black guards, he added, who let them taste "a bayonet in the rear." Shaw had the men fall to and delivered a stern lecture about "the 'guard house,' wearing patent bracelets, and sundry other terrors in store" for those men disgruntled over pay issues. Gooding had scant sympathy for the two, yet he also wanted the editor of New Bedford's *Mercury* to remember that most black soldiers had "nothing to depend upon but their daily labor," and so their "homes are left destitute" in their absence. Questions of pay inequity would haunt the regiment, as well as its companion unit, the Fifty-fifth, until mid-1864, but even so, Gooding believed that most of his company were "determined to act like men, and fight, money or not."[43]

In their rare off hours, the barracks were converted into classrooms. As did Frederick Douglass, the volunteers anticipated that their service would translate into citizenship, which conferred both rewards and responsibilities. It surely did not escape the notice of the unlettered soldiers that the first to be promoted to corporal or sergeant were men of education. Although the camp had no formally organized school, Reverend William Jackson, the black minister who had recruited in New Bedford and now served as the regiment's chaplain, shared his "fine library" with the soldiers, ran Sabbath schools each Sunday, and devoted most evenings to teaching literacy, with the Bible as a text. "Quite a number were remarkably well informed and well educated men," he reported, but those who had spent part of their lives enslaved were a different matter. Jackson and Shaw were not the only ones who noticed the cultural gulf that often divided the working-class soldiers from those of more advantaged backgrounds. Some of the volunteers "amuse themselves by fighting each other," a puzzled Lewis Douglass observed. The bookish Gooding also complained that he was given "nothing to read," although, unlike Douglass, he was at least amused by "some of the odd capers" the men practiced on one another. The patriotic oratory of the working-class soldiers, however, Gooding judged "ludicrous," if typical "to some of our class of people."[44]

The regiment's progress was a group effort, of course, from the colonel to the captains to the newest private. But Gooding thought it important to give Shaw his due. He had accepted the posting when not a "dozen [other] men in the North" would have done so, knowing that failure could forever taint their career. But Shaw "put his hands, his head, his heart to the task," and as a result of his "discipline the regiment was perfect," not owing to "a slavish fear, but obedience enacted by the evidence of a superior and directing mind."[45]

SHAW'S COMBINATION OF FAST-PACED DRILLING AND STERN DISCI-pline was also founded on the knowledge that with spring, large numbers of visitors, politicians, and journalists would descend on Readville, and the men had best be prepared. Not surprisingly, Shaw's friends and family thought that he had performed admirably. Charles Russell Lowell, stationed in Washington, wrote to say that rumors in the capital held that the Fifty-fourth showed "good promise of taking a very high place among our Massachusetts regiments." Rather more surprising was the fact that the relentless training won over cynics as well. One officer, a native of Virginia, toured Readville and made it clear that he regarded it "a great joke to try and make soldiers of 'niggers.'" By day's end, the officer, who had mustered in nearly 20,000 recruits, confessed that the Fifty-fourth appeared "so fine a set of men." The "skeptics need only come out here now, to be converted," a pleased Shaw reported.[46]

Warmer weather, as predicted, brought curious guests of all sorts. The "Ladies' Committee," the female auxiliary of the Black Committee, arrived on April 21. Led by Eliza Andrew, the governor's wife, the group toured the camp, anxious, as one harried officer sighed, "to witness the novel sight of colored soldiers in quarters and on the drill ground." Each weekend saw a "large number of visitors" line up at the main gate. A far larger contingent arrived on April 30, when Governor Andrew squired William Lloyd Garrison and Treasury Secretary Salmon Chase into the camp for a formal review. With the exception of those too ill to drill, the entire regiment donned their "evening dress parades." Andrew presented the noncommissioned officers with swords, which the Douglass brothers accepted with pride. Privately, however, Lewis fretted that his younger brother was "a little green" and had "not learned yet to boss his men around, which is very necessary."[47]

Family members and the abolitionist rank and file—who were often one and the same—crowded into the camp each Sunday. Frederick Douglass paid several visits in early May, on the second occasion accompanied by his wife, Anna, and their daughter Rosetta. The elder Douglass was pleased to see Lewis "looking so well," but as Readville was low in elevation and could be damp and marshy after rains, Charles was sick in the camp infirmary with "a severe cold." The Douglasses brought "a bag of niceties from home," but not what Lewis really desired, which was a visit from the Loguens, or at least a photograph or note from Amelia. Perhaps fearing that her fiancé might not return from the war, Amelia had drawn back from their relationship, and her letters grew scarce. In his numerous missives, Lewis balanced reminders that his service was "in the glorious work of bursting loose those chains" that degraded "millions of human beings to a level scarcely on footing with a brute" with professions that she was "ever dear" to him. Lewis knew that Amelia wished "it were not necessary" for him to enlist, but he trusted that her "love of her happiness of your race and my race reconciles you to our separation." After that failed to elicit the expected response, Lewis at one point reminded Amelia that he was a "privileged character being an officer of the staff" and that he was "thought a good deal of here," a boast that had the virtue of being true.[48]

The sobering prospect of not surviving the war also led Shaw to think of marriage. Rob had fallen for Annie Haggerty shortly after meeting her in the spring of 1861, assuring his friend Elizabeth Russell Lyman that Annie would one day be his "young woman." About the time he agreed to serve with the Fifty-fourth, he asked Annie to marry him and not to wait for the war's end. Neither her parents nor the Shaws thought the timing propitious, since the Fifty-fourth would soon be marching south. "I can't help feeling that, if we are not married before I go," Shaw fretted, "I shall feel very much dissatisfied and discontented." He surely knew that his proposal placed Annie in a most difficult position, and not merely with her parents. Should he die, she would be a widow while still in her twenties; were he to die with them unwed, he would forever be the fallen martyr, against whom other men could never measure up. Without waiting for her parents' approval, Annie agreed. Rob and Annie decided to wed on May 2, as the army was willing to grant him one week's leave at that time. They married in Manhattan before spending their brief honeymoon in the Lenox, Massachusetts, home of Annie's parents. By May 9, the couple was back in Boston, and while Shaw had to return to the regiment, he rode over to see Annie most nights. "Domestic bliss is the thing," he marveled.[49]

While the young couple was still in Lenox, yet more recruits arrived in Readville, and with the Fifty-fourth already filled, Andrew made the decision to employ the new arrivals as the nucleus of a second regiment. The governor offered the colonelcy to both Hallowells—as ever, Andrew regarded the brothers as interchangeable cogs in his military apparatus— but when each expressed the desire to remain with the regiment they had devoted so much energy to forming, he simply ordered the twenty-four-year-old Pen to "stay and help organize it, whether he wishes to or not." Pen relented, Shaw reported, "as the Governor wouldn't let him" ship south, "at any rate." Andrew so notified the War Department, and the chief mustering officer for Massachusetts duly processed the paperwork to "muster out of the service, Lieut. Col. Norwood P. Hallowell, of the 54th Mass. Vols., and muster him in as Colonel of the 55th Regt. Mass. Vols." Shaw had grown very fond of Pen Hallowell and took the transfer hard, especially as he feared that Andrew would next promote Ned to second-in-command of the new unit. "If I lose the Major too, I don't know what I *shall* do," Rob groaned. As it turned out, Governor Andrew did have a promotion in mind, but not for the Fifty-fifth. Much to Shaw's delight, he instead transferred Captain Alfred Hartwell, an attorney and Harvard classmate of Shaw and Ned Hallowell, into the Fifty-fifth and elevated Ned into the vacant position in the Fifty-fourth, ordering him "promoted to be Lt. Col. [on] May 31."[50]

With the new regiment forming and so many white officers shifting units, William Lloyd Garrison's son George decided that the time had at last arrived for him to sign on. Though he promoted the black regiment in the pages of the *Liberator,* both his pacifism and his fear for George's life led the elder Garrison to oppose his son's decision; he even went so far as to warn that his enlistment would injure "the health and happiness of your mother." But some members of Garrison's circle applauded George's enlistment. "So, after all, Norwood Hallowell has accepted the colonelcy of the 55th. I am glad of it," abolitionist Lucy McKim observed to Wendell Garrison. "And your brother George is advertised as one of the lieutenants. Will you give him my warm regards and congratulations?" McKim had remained loyal to pacifism for the first two years of the war, but the Emancipation Proclamation clarified matters for her. "When a brawling nation thrusts our reason & gentleness back in our faces, I undertake to say that one cannot hinder her from worse than murdering four millions of helpless beings," she lectured an unpersuaded Wendell.[51]

WITH THE CREATION OF THE FIFTY-FIFTH, WASHINGTON BELATEDLY moved to nationalize the effort. Congress created a new agency, the Bureau for Colored Troops, and on May 22 Stanton's War Department issued General Order No. 143, placing the bureau under the authority of the adjutant general. Under the order, all black regiments in the process of being mustered by states were elevated to the federal level and assigned a new number as one of the United States Colored Troops, or USCT. Although white soldiers remained organized by state regiments, the USCT was forged in recognition of the reality that African American men felt no loyalty to Northern states that denied them civil rights and instead sought to serve, as one politician noted, "the United States—the government [that] had promised them freedom." Senator James Henry Lane's First Kansas Colored Volunteer Infantry became the Seventy-ninth Infantry USCT, and Thomas Wentworth Higginson's First South Carolina Volunteers, an irregular unit of runaway Carolinians, became the Thirty-third USCT. But to maintain their pride of place as the first Northern regiments to be approved by Washington, the Fifty-fourth and Fifty-fifth (and later the Fifth Cavalry) retained their original designations and took their marching orders from Boston.[52]

As Northern recruiters made it clear that they intended to enlist black men in those parts of the South already under American control, the Confederate Congress moved to endorse Jefferson Davis's proclamation of the previous December. On May 1, in a joint resolution, the Congress authorized the president to "cause full and ample retaliation to be made" for what white Southerners regarded as any violations of the usual rules of war by the United States. As had Davis's Christmas Eve order, the joint resolution required white officers leading black troops to "be put to death or otherwise punished at the discretion" of a military tribunal. All black men taken under arms were to "be delivered to the authorities of the State or States in which they shall be captured" and returned to slavery. Although that clause was more apt for Higginson's unit than for the freemen in the

Fifty-fourth, a few soldiers in the Fifty-fourth, such as William Carney, were runaways; if taken alive, Carney was in danger of being reenslaved in Virginia.[53]

Andrew hurried to Washington in hopes of securing a firm promise from somebody in authority that Confederate retribution would be met with Union reprisals. Although Lincoln was not yet prepared to issue any precise promises of vengeance, Andrew found a sympathetic ally in Stanton. The secretary "stated in the most emphatic manner" that the administration "was prepared to guarantee and defend to these men, all the rights, privileges and immunities that are given, by the laws of civilized warfare, to other soldiers." Although Stanton's statement was reported across the North by the abolitionist press, Andrew was more alarmed by the Confederate policies than were the men of the Fifty-fourth. The common soldiers understood the risks being taken by the white men who led them, and so the May resolution helped to bridge the cultural gulf between the working-class privates and the privileged officers. Pen Hallowell was outraged, but Shaw took it with fatalistic humor. He had always understood that "the officers of colored regiments" would be in a rather "ticklish situation, if caught by the Rebels," he shrugged. If Confederates executed him, they would have to face the wrath of Ned Hallowell, who then "will be in command." Black soldiers were defiant. Camp Meigs was "cropping out corporals and sergeants" fast enough, one proudly insisted, to face down "the rebel President" and his "friends in the North."[54]

They would soon have their chance, since by May the Fifty-fourth was ready for deployment. Worrisome reports appeared in the Northern press that the War Department intended to ship the regiment to Fort Monroe in Virginia. There was a logic to that plan. With nearby Norfolk having surrendered in May 1862, a black unit could not only hold the garrison but help recruit black Virginians for the USCT. Thanks to General Benjamin Butler's "contraband" decree, an enormous "freedman's colony" had emerged in Roanoke, and the Fifty-fourth might protect the growing refugee camp. Troubling, however, was the assumption that black troops would "remain there to man the fort, and thus allow the white troops to go into the field." Other rumors hinted that the Fifty-fourth might "be sent away piece-meal," with some companies sailing for Fort Monroe while others performed guard duty elsewhere. This possibility especially Shaw regarded as destructive to the unit's cohesion and morale. Should the War Department do so, Shaw warned the governor, he intended to "respectfully suggest" that his commission be withdrawn, "and that Captain E. N. Hallowell be commissioned & mustered in" as his replacement. In fact, Andrew complained to Stanton that his soldiers had been "raised and officered, for active [and] not for fatigue duty." General David Hunter, recently reappointed commander of the Department of the South, was clamoring for help along the Carolina coast. "Under Genl. Hunter negro troops will be appreciated and allowed a place in onward and honorable movements of active war," Andrew argued.[55]

Like Charles Francis Adams Jr. the previous year, Shaw and the Fifty-fourth were hopeful for a chance to take part in the capture of Charleston. If there was to be an assault on the city, Shaw admitted, "I trust we shall have a share in it." Sergeant Major Lewis Douglass was even more passionate. To engage South Carolina was "to fight for Liberty & Union," he assured Amelia. "Our regiment is a fine one and no doubt will accomplish much," he added. Not a man in his company wished to give Governor Andrew "occasion to regret the steps he has taken in raising the regiment." Soon, Douglass hoped, Washington would allow for black commissioned officers, and if so, he could be promoted and granted considerable leave to "come home and stay" for a time. In the meantime, he begged his fiancée not to worry or "think of me in pain [or] of me enduring hardships." Most of all, he urged, "[r]emember that if I fall that it is in the cause of humanity, that I am striking a blow for the welfare of the most abused and despised race on earth."[56]

Upon receiving confirmation from the War Department that the Fifty-fourth would be deployed in South Carolina, Andrew wished to give the troops the news himself. For May 18, the governor's office proposed an impressive ceremony for the presentation of flags and banners, one inspiring enough, an aide to Andrew laughed, "to convert all but the most incorrigible Hunkers," as Republicans had dubbed conservative Democrats. Anticipating a crowd, Andrew scheduled extra trains for the ten-mile journey from Boston to Readville, and journalists counted as many as 2,000 spectators, a majority of them African American. The day was beautiful and sunny, but what excited the men most was that Massachusetts paymasters arrived with the long-promised bounty, which, as Gooding remarked, they "had almost despaired of ever getting." Shaw marched his regiment into a tight square surrounding the speaker's podium, after which "the colored ladies of Boston" presented him with an American flag. Other banners followed, from the state flag to a white silk banner emblazoned with the words LIBERTY, LOYALTY, AND UNITY. Then Andrew handed Shaw a telegram from Secretary Stanton, reading: "*The Fifty-fourth Massachusetts will report to General Hunter; make requisitions for transportation, so that they may go at once.*" Gooding was overjoyed. "We have received marching orders," he cheered, adding that he was proud that there was "not a man in the regiment" who was unaware of the dangers as well as the "ignoble death that [may await] him, if captured by the foe, and they will die upon the field rather than be hanged like a dog." Give the Fifty-fourth a chance, Gooding believed, and the "greatest difficulty will be to stop them."[57]

Prayers and speeches dedicated to manhood, nation, Christianity, and home followed, with Andrew assuring the black sons of Massachusetts, as well as those "of surrounding States who have now made themselves citizens" of the Bay State, that their blue uniforms conferred citizenship upon them, regardless of the still-binding *Dred Scott* decision. Pointing to the soldiers, Andrew promised that the American flag was "*their* country's flag now as well as ours," and that they should go forth to "rend the last shackle which binds the limb of the bondman in the rebel States." In a far shorter reply, Shaw thanked the governor for providing the regiment with the "opportunity to show that you have not made a mistake in entrusting the honor of the State to a colored regiment—the first State that has sent one to the war!" From somewhere in the crowd, Frank Shaw joined in the applause as the afternoon concluded with a battalion drill. Sarah Shaw, often unwell, remained at home, but Rob assured her that while the "Governor made a beautiful speech," his own "response was *small potatoes.*"[58]

HUNTER SENT WORD TO PREPARE FOR A DEPARTURE ON MAY 28, which left the regiment but ten days to pack and, for those from the Boston area, say their farewells to loved ones. Northern troops often shipped south out of Manhattan, and Andrew initially planned for a parade down

Broadway. "All America looks on at a Broadway procession," one of his advisers remarked. But New York City was a Democratic stronghold, filled with Irish immigrants fearful of what black liberty and postwar migrations north might mean for their own precarious economic situation. In the event, it was decided that the regiment would retrace the steps of Thomas Sims and Anthony Burns, runaways who had been captured in Boston and marched to the docks by federal marshals and U.S. Marines in 1851 and 1854.[59]

The troops broke camp at an early hour and reached Boston by nine o'clock. A "large crowd" met them at the depot and followed as they strode into the city. One hundred policemen attempted to clear a path toward the parade ground on the Common, and unknown but to Andrew and a few officers, "reserves of police were held in readiness, under cover, to repress any riotous proceedings." Journalists reported that the streets were lined with observers; "men cheered and women waved their handkerchiefs," while the inquisitive crowded the sidewalks to witness the curious sight. As the formation turned onto Essex Street, a young woman rushed out to present Shaw "with a handsome bouquet," and the young colonel paused to thank her. On several occasions, the streets grew so clogged with on-lookers that the soldiers had to pause. "The men grounded arms, and were receiving the parting salutes of their kindred and friends," one reporter ob-served, when three African American women, perhaps the "mother, wife, and sister," ran out to kiss a soldier. One handed him a handkerchief, and as they moved back to the sidewalk the private "leaned his head upon his musket, and wept like a child."[60]

A few observers were determined to show their disfavor, although most wisely did so from upstairs windows. Pen Hallowell spied "certain mem-bers of a prominent club" hissing in disgust as the Fifty-fourth marched by, and Wilkie James heard a few "groans" from those "of the rankest sort." One tough shouted an insult, only to be knocked to the ground by an-other observer. But these were exceptions. Businessmen who stood on the steps of the Exchange cheered the troops, and black entrepreneur George Downing, who came to say his farewells to Vogelsang, his brother-in-law, was thrilled to see "ladies of all complexions," many of them Irish, pass-ing out "ice-water or lemonade" to the soldiers. William Lloyd Garrison watched from the terrace of Wendell Phillips's Essex Street home; somebody thought to drag a bust of John Brown out onto the balcony, and Garrison, quietly sobbing, rested his hand upon it. Poet John Greenleaf Whittier was also moved to tears by the sight. As Shaw "rode at the head of his troops," he wrote Lydia Maria Child, "the very flower of grace and chivalry, he seemed to me beautiful and awful as an Angel of God, come down to lead the host of freedom to victory." Rob's sister Ellen Shaw had nearly the same thought. Watching the procession from a balcony with her mother, Rob's wife Annie, and her other sisters, seventeen-year-old Ellen was both touched and startled by what she witnessed. Knowing where his family would be standing, Shaw paused as he rode by and "looked up and kissed his sword, [and] his face was as the face of an angel." Yet at that moment Ellen had an awful premonition, and "felt perfectly sure he would never come back."[61]

Upon reaching the State House, the Fifty-fourth was joined by Andrew, Senator Charles Sumner, and members of the Black Committee recruiting group. Together they marched through the Common and then down State Street toward the Battery Wharf. A band preceded them, playing "the stirring music of John Brown's hymns." Just before one o'clock, the regiment arrived at the *DeMolay*, their transport ship. Frederick Douglass had come to say good-bye to Lewis (Charles still being unwell and in the hospital at Readville), and he "passed round among the different companies, bidding the soldiers farewell, and giving them words of encouragement." It took three hours to store the guns in watertight boxes, load the men, and walk the officers' nervous horses aboard. Finally, at four, the *DeMolay* steamed out of the harbor, bound for South Carolina.[62]

How "grandly the 54th went off to their work," Douglass marveled to Gerrit Smith, choosing to remember the glory of the afternoon rather than the dangers facing his son outside of Charleston. Rob Shaw thought so too, writing one old friend from the Second Massachusetts that "the passage of the 54th Mass. through Boston was a great success" and remarking that he had never seen "such a heavy turn-out there before." As the *DeMolay* slowly chugged south, Shaw thought back to his initial reluctance to accept Andrew's offer. "Just remember our own doubts and fears, and other people's sneering and pitying remarks, when we began last winter," he wrote Annie on his third day at sea, "and then look at the perfect triumph of last Thursday." Never as devout, or as devoutly abolitionist, as his parents, Shaw told Annie that he was truly "thankful for all my happiness, and my success in life so far." If the Fifty-fourth proved to be "a benefit to the country, and to the blacks, as many people think it will, I shall thank God a thousand times that I was led to take my share in it."[63]

CHAPTER FOUR

The Sea Islands

MANY OF THE OHIO FARMERS ABOARD THE *DeMOLAY* HAD NEVER even seen an ocean, let alone sailed upon one. Fortunately, the first night at sea was smooth, and the following morning broke calm, if foggy. Rob Shaw grumbled that the steamer was "a very slow one," but otherwise he conceded that it was "perfectly clean and well-ventilated." Just after midnight, however, the steamer ran into a strong headwind, and the seas turned rough. The ship "was tossed and pitched about by the waves like a play thing in the hands of a child," Lewis Douglass wrote, "now away up up up, then down, down now on this side, now on that." The same men who had relished the thought of combat in South Carolina looked "as though Death would be a welcome visitor," with many "wishing they never had gone for a soldier." As for himself, Douglass assured Amelia, he "stood it first rate [and] was sick only a half hour." Less lucky was Ned Hallowell's mare. It died and was consigned to the deep. The storm passed on June 1, allowing the "seasick to take some interest in life." Having survived far worse, former sea cook James Henry Gooding made no mention of the tempest in his weekly letter to the *New Bedford Mercury*. The landlubbers, for their part, were fascinated by the porpoises and the shark or two that followed the ship.[1]

On the morning of June 3, the steamer chugged past Charleston Harbor, and in the distance Shaw spied the U.S. naval blockade, and then beyond the ships, "the top of Fort Sumter" and what he guessed to be "the turrets of the iron-clads" supporting the siege. But Charleston was not yet their objective. General David Hunter sent conflicting orders on June 6. The first, a telegraph, instructed Shaw to debark at his headquarters on Hilton Head Island, and the second ordered Captain John Moore, the *DeMolay*'s skipper, to instead "immediately" sail another fifteen miles up the Beaufort River to the town of the same name on Port Royal Island. There, "Col. Shaw 54 Mass. Vols. [should wait] for orders."[2]

Responding to the second order, the *DeMolay* passed the wharf at Hilton Head on the afternoon of June 3, sailing by roughly seventy ships in the harbor. That evening they docked at Beaufort. Anxious to again tread on dry land, the men were stirring by five the next morning. The regiment left the steamer and marched through town toward their camp on an abandoned cotton plantation, where they joined the Fifty-fifth Pennsylvania. Despite the early hour, black Southerners quickly caught word of their arrival. "Our reception was almost as enthusiastic here in Beaufort, as our departure from Boston was," Gooding marveled. The refugees who crowded the small town had doubted that the regiment actually existed, and as the soldiers marched through the streets one man ran up to Gooding, crying, "I nebber bleeve black Yankee comee here help culeer men." Despite his years aboard a whaler, feeding men from around the globe, Gooding found the Sea Islands dialect hard to comprehend, but he suspected that former slaves understood "the *causes* of the war better than a great many Northern editors." Black Carolinians knew what was at stake in the conflict, Gooding supposed, and "they think the kingdom is coming sure enough."[3]

Those white Northerners who had come south as teachers and doctors were equally ecstatic. "Where *did* you get these men?" A. D. Smith wondered to Governor Andrew. "Could you have witnessed the feeling on the arrival of the 'DeMolay' with the Colored Regt. and heard the 'God bless you,' you would have cried too." A number of Massachusetts reformers, most of them funded by the American Missionary Association, had traveled to the Sea Islands to help resettle the "contrabands" flooding into the region. One of those recent arrivals financed by the governor himself was former slave Harriet Tubman, a longtime Douglass family friend. Years before, Tubman had moved to Auburn, New York, not far from Rochester, and Lewis was pleased to see his father's old ally. Andrew had expected Tubman to help distribute clothing and food, but typical of the resolute activist, Lewis noted, she had instead become "captain of a gang of men who pilot the Union forces into the enemy's country." Douglass was also introduced to Robert Smalls, a Beaufort-born slave of about his own age. Trained as a ship's pilot, Smalls had stolen a Confederate military transport, the *CSS Planter,* the year before and successfully sailed it out of Charleston Harbor before turning it over to the U.S. Navy. As a sergeant, Stephen Swails probably also met Smalls that day, although neither could then have imagined what kind of impact the two would have on South Carolina state politics after the war.[4]

The person Shaw wanted to meet was Thomas Wentworth Higginson, colonel of the First South Carolina Volunteers and uncle to Francis Higginson, a twenty-one-year-old lieutenant in the Fifty-fourth. Born in Cambridge and educated at Harvard some fifteen years before Shaw, the minister-turned-activist had long put his principles into practice. Together with George Luther Stearns, Higginson was one of John Brown's "secret six" benefactors. He had also been in the forefront of those who tried to batter their way into the Boston courthouse in an unsuccessful attempt to liberate captured runaway Anthony Burns, and he still carried a saber scar on his chin for the effort. On the day of their arrival, Shaw sent a bottle of champagne to Higginson's camp, and that evening Higginson rode over to see his nephew and to meet Shaw and Hallowell. The three hit if off immediately, with the elder man later remarking that he "was delighted with the officers—the best style of Boston." Shaw returned the favor, telling his mother that he had never met "any one who puts his whole soul into his work," and that he was "very much impressed with his open-heartedness & purity of character." The conversation inevitably turned to the use of black troops. Shaw bluntly admitted that while Higginson's former slaves had proven "effective in bush-fighting," he still wondered "how they would fight in line of battle." Higginson assured Shaw that he had no doubts that they would fare perfectly, and he guessed that Shaw felt the same way. Even so, Shaw mused that it might be prudent to place white soldiers to their rear, "and so cutting off their retreat." The older officer was stunned by the remark, thinking he would "never have dreamed of being tempted to such a step."[5]

WHAT NOBODY IN THE FIFTY-FOURTH COULD GUESS WAS HOW THEIR superiors planned to fit them into the army's strategy along the southern coast, or indeed who exactly would be making that decision. Having already seized Hilton Head and Tybee Islands, as well as the Florida coastal towns of Fernandina and St. Augustine, American forces hoped to expand their domination of the coastline. Charleston was the prize. The first attempt to take the port had come on the afternoon of April 7, when Admiral Samuel Francis Du Pont ordered nine ironclads to steam into the harbor and fire on Fort Sumter. Gunners inside Sumter and to their north in Fort Moultrie on Sullivan's Island poured 2,200 shells into the ships, crippling five and forcing the rest to withdraw. The "army found that they could do nothing," reported one officer, as they were "unable to make a landing until the naval force have silenced the Forts." In the aftermath of the debacle, the War Department instead decided on a combined naval and infantry operation against the city, starting with assaults on James Island and Morris Island's Battery Wagner. Once the outer barriers to the south of Charleston Harbor were in the hands of the army, Morris Island could be used to shell nearby Sumter. After that citadel had crumbled, the navy planned to stage another incursion.[6]

With a new strategy came a new commander. The previous January, Hunter had again been appointed Commander of the South, but the high hopes had not been sustained. Hunter was a sound antislavery man, but even his supporters thought him weak and easily controlled by others. Shaw had been in South Carolina only days before concluding that the general was hardly "a great man," and he immediately heard "some talk of his being relieved." As had Charles Francis Adams Jr., Pen Hallowell considered Hunter's earlier effort to raise "contraband" troops doomed to failure by his heavy-handed tactic of ordering white soldiers to round up and enlist black men as if they were "prisoners," an approach that allowed for "no mutual confidence between officers and men." Edward Pierce, a correspondent for the *New-York Tribune,* warned Andrew that General Truman Seymour, Hunter's chief of staff, was "a strong proslavery man, against arming negroes," and was actively working against abolitionist general Rufus Saxton, the department's military governor. Seymour had "set himself against Saxton's work and [did] all that he could to thwart it," Pierce complained. Since Washington expected to employ black troops, both Northern free blacks and freedmen, in the campaign against Charleston, Seymour's overt racism was more than a mere character flaw; it threatened the entire operation.[7]

Some abolitionists hoped that Higginson would take Hunter's post should he be removed, and in Beaufort speculation was rife that Andrew had sent the Fifty-fourth to South Carolina so that they might serve under his command. Higginson himself doubted the rumors, although he thought it "evil" to ship a black regiment to the Sea Islands before it was decided "who shall be Brigadier General." In hopes of keeping the position in antislavery hands, most of Hunter's staff overruled Seymour and lobbied for Colonel James Montgomery, but Edwin Stanton was savvy enough to recognize that the veteran of "Bleeding Kansas" had little standing among senior officers. On June 12, the War Department tapped thirty-eight-year-old engineer Quincy Adams Gillmore, who had gained fame the previous April by designing the successful bombardment of Georgia's Fort Pulaski. Shaw worried that the new commander was "not a friend to black troops," but having lost confidence in Hunter, he was nonetheless "very glad" to hear the news.[8]

Most of the Fifty-fourth had never experienced anything like a summer on the Southern coast. The weather, one soldier complained, was "intensely hot," and their tents made poor barriers against the large army of insects. Their wool uniforms, so welcome during the early spring in Readville, added to their discomfort. Worse yet, having expected to soon see combat, on June 6 Shaw instead received orders tasking three of his companies with "fatigue work." To the dismay of all, Shaw was forced to dispatch Sergeant Peter Vogelsang and Companies A, D, and H out to "the shell road to work on fortifications."[9]

The men of the Fifty-fourth did soon have the opportunity, however, to band with Montgomery and his Second South Carolina on a brief foray to Darien, Georgia. "These little miserable expeditions are of no

Former hotel clerk Peter Vogelsang was both the oldest soldier and one of the 183 New Yorkers in the Fifty-Fourth. Although severely injured early on, Vogelsang served until the end of the war, rising to the rank of first lieutenant, then returned to Manhattan, where he remained active in the black community until his death in 1887. *Courtesy Massachusetts Historical Society.*

account at all," Shaw sighed, but it was preferable to manual labor and served "to keep up the spirits of our men." Those more dedicated to the cause of liberation thought less about overall military strategy and more about what such incursions meant to black Southerners. "When a slave sees the white soldier approach, he dares not trust him," Gooding suspected, owing to a lifetime of racial animosity. "But if the slave sees a black soldier, he knows he has got a friend," and then once that bondman is liberated, he can himself "be made a soldier, to fight for his own liberty." Teacher A. D. Smith agreed, assuring Andrew that the mere arrival of Shaw's forces "had shaken more trees in rebeldom than any other event that could have happened."[10]

Montgomery's Second South Carolina were preparing to sail for St. Simons Island on the Georgia coast, and Shaw, despite his reservations about what he thought would be a "miserable expedition," wasted little time in requesting that the Fifty-fourth be allowed to join them. As General Gillmore had not yet arrived, Hunter consented to the assignment. The regiment struck camp at sunrise on June 8 after a night of heavy rains, stowed their wet tents aboard the *DeMolay*, and endured another "rough voyage of some eighty miles," arriving at St. Simons the following morning. While the men set to work "pitching camp and clearing the ground," Shaw awaited Montgomery's arrival. Born in Ohio in 1814, the forty-eight-year-old schoolteacher had fought beside John Brown in Kansas, and in some ways Montgomery resembled his old comrade. Captain Luis Emilio described the heavily bearded colonel as "tall, spare, rather bowed, with gentle voice and quiet manner." Shaw had briefly encountered Montgomery in Beaufort and immediately thought him "a strange compound." As a devout Christian, Montgomery "allows no swearing or drinking in his regiment & is anti tobacco." But he was a "bush-whacker," Shaw informed his mother, who "burns & destroys wherever he goes with great gusto, & looks as if he had quite a taste for hanging people & throat cutting." Like all men who had no doubts about their cause, Montgomery was "a perfect fanatic" who believed "that praying, shooting, burning, & hanging are the true means to put down the rebellion." Yet Shaw was confident that Montgomery was a competent commander. Had Montgomery attended West Point and "been educated as a military man," Shaw mused, "he would accomplish a great deal, & he may yet."[11]

As the sun began to set on June 10 the combined regiments boarded the transports *Sentinel* and *Harriet A. Weed*, supported by the gunboat *John Adams*. Montgomery brought five companies from his regiment, and Shaw brought eight, leaving Companies C and F behind—and with them, Douglass and Swails—to guard the camp. Both transports promptly grounded on shoals, and so the raiders had to await high tide. The vessels finally reached the Altamaha River, some 100 miles south of Beaufort, with the *John Adams*, a bemused Captain Emilio noting, "occasionally shelling houses and clumps of woods" along its banks. They reached Darien around three in the afternoon. The town appeared to be nearly deserted, but the gunboat launched a few shells into the heart of the village anyway. Peering over the railing of the *Sentinel*, James Henry Gooding could see no more than about twenty people. There had been reports of a large Confederate force, he knew, but Gooding guessed that they had abandoned the coast given the concentration of U.S. forces on St. Simons Island. Shaw ordered his men ashore, instructing them to post pickets and form in the public square. He counted only "two white women and two negroes."[12]

Traditional rules of war allowed for the confiscation of materials or foodstuffs that aided either combatant, and Darien's waterfront storehouses and mills held large quantities of rice, resin, and cotton, the last of which, smuggled through the American naval blockade, helped keep the wilting Confederate economy afloat. Gooding assisted in loading a number of bales, as well as "about a dozen cows, [and] 50 or 60 sheep," aboard the transports. But Montgomery had more in mind than confiscation. Hunter had encouraged him to engage in "a system of operations which will rapidly compel the rebels either to lay down their arms and sue for restoration of the Union or to withdraw their slaves into the interior." Whether Montgomery would have arrived at the same decision regardless of his orders, after the town "was pretty thoroughly disemboweled" of movable property, he turned to Shaw and, with his customary low voice and "sweet smile," said simply: "I shall burn this town." Shaw was momentarily speechless, finally responding that he "did not want the responsibility of it." Montgomery was "only too happy" to do it himself, lecturing Shaw that white Southerners "must be made to feel that this was a real war, and that they were to be swept away by the hand of God, like the Jews of old." Because Shaw had been assigned to Montgomery's command, he had to allow one of his companies to assist in the arson, although Montgomery cheerfully fired the last building himself. "We are outlawed" by President Davis, Montgomery added; since they could be summarily executed if captured, they were "therefore not bound by the rules of regular warfare." Gooding later reported that the men remaining in camp on St. Simons Island could see the flames from fifteen miles away.[13]

Shaw was disgusted by the affair, denouncing it "as abominable a job" as he had ever had to perform. His soldiers had "met with no resistance there," and the town "was never known to be a refuge for guerrillas." Until that moment, Shaw believed, he had survived the war with his honor intact, and neither he nor any other officer in his regiment wished "to degenerate into a plunderer and robber." For Shaw, the destruction was both a violation of his personal code of honor and an assault on the integrity of his men. As the pioneering Northern regiment, the Fifty-fourth wished to prove to the nation that black men could be effective combatants, and if the regiment spent the remainder of the war burning and looting alongside Montgomery's "contraband" unit, their chance to prove themselves would be lost. The previous October, Confederate general J. E. B. Stuart had raided into Pennsylvania, and as Shaw pointedly observed to Governor Andrew, Montgomery's actions stood in "singular contrast to that of Stuart," who had avoided destroying civilian property. Shaw and Hallowell had consented to serve in a noble experiment designed to vindicate the ideals of New England abolitionism, not to live down to the low expectations of racists in both sections of the nation.[14]

As Shaw expected, Southern whites condemned the act. Even George Luther Stearns scorned the raid as "dirty work" and "unwanton vandalism." Yet not everyone agreed. Frederick Douglass endorsed Montgomery's theory that since the Confederate government was violating the rules of civilized warfare by threatening to summarily execute white officers, they had lost any right to insist that the U.S. Army adhere to a code of conduct they had themselves abandoned. Although Lewis Douglass, as a freeborn Northern soldier, was not subject to Confederate threats against white officers or former slaves, the Rochester abolitionist regarded Davis's edict as highly personal. Harriet Tubman also refused to condemn the raid, since her work under Montgomery as a scout and spy invariably led to the liberation of enslaved Carolinians. The black press was largely silent, but George Stephens published a lengthy defense in the *Weekly Anglo-African*. The Pennsylvania cabinet-maker, who had been promoted to first sergeant on April 30, praised Montgomery as an "active and brave leader [who] gives none under his command time to rot, sicken and die in camp." Although Stephens conceded that the town was "almost entirely deserted" when they arrived, he reminded his readers that Confederate cavalry had been active in the area. Without apology, Stephens defended the burning of Darien as a method of "spreading terror to the hearts of the rebels throughout this region."[15]

Corporal Gooding also saw no cause for regret. A voracious reader, he consumed every account of the affair he could lay his hands on, and he was infuriated by what he found in Manhattan and London newspapers. In a series of letters to the *New Bedford Mercury*, Gooding attacked those "gouty conservatives" who condemned the raid as an "act of Vandalism" by "Nigger guerillas." Their accounts, he fumed, were designed to convince "credulous people that Darien was a place rivaling New York, in commercial importance, and the peer of Rome or Athens, in historical value."

Would Confederate sailors, he wondered, had they the ability to do so, "have any scruples about burning New York with Greek fire?" As for complaints lodged in the London *Times,* the historically conscious Gooding thought it incongruous for British imperialists to describe the raid as an act of "inhuman barbarity." When, he questioned—in a reference to British tactics in putting down the Indian rebellion of 1857—had American soldiers "lashed a rebel to a gun and blown him to pieces?"[16]

Unaware of Shaw's missives to Andrew and the War Department, Montgomery returned to Hilton Head, leaving Shaw temporarily in charge of the camp on St. Simon's. Gillmore had finally arrived to take control of the Department of the South, and prodded by politicians in both Massachusetts and Washington, he consented to withdraw the Fifty-fourth from Montgomery's command. Gillmore ordered the Second South Carolina to relocate to Folly Island, just south of Charleston Harbor, to help construct fortifications. The Massachusetts press was overjoyed. Montgomery's "negro brigade" had been reassigned "to handle the shovel," the Worcester *National Aegis* gloated. "Their disgraceful raids are probably at an end."[17]

GILLMORE GAVE SHAW UNTIL JUNE 24 TO RETURN HIS REGIMENT TO Hilton Head, so the men had nearly two weeks to rest and explore St. Simons. One officer enjoyed the "subtle languor in the hum of insects, the song of birds, and the splash of warm green water upon the shore," while Gooding simply regarded the summer heat as "enough to make a fellow contemplate the place prepared for the ungodly." Gooding had endured a winter in Baffin Bay, but at least the Artic lacked "stink weed, sand, rattlesnakes, and alligators." Shaw discovered that Pierce Butler's abandoned plantation stood nearby, and having met Butler's former wife, actress Frances Anne Kemble, ten years before in Switzerland, he rode over to see it. The estate was deserted but for "about ten of his slaves," all of them "sixty or seventy years old." Some of them remembered Kemble and "looked much pleased" when Shaw mentioned her. One aged slave named John made Shaw promise that if he ever saw her again, he would tell "Miss Fanny" that he sent his regards. "The darkeys here are an interesting study," Shaw commented to an old friend. "You have no conception of the degraded condition they were allowed to live in by their masters." Yet it was not merely the patrician colonel who found the Gullah people of the Low-country exotic. New Bedford–born Lewis Douglass had much the same reaction, calling the refugees he encountered in South Carolina "natives" and describing as almost quaint their habit of "singing and praying nearly every night in their prayer meetings." Whatever else, "they are a happy people," he assured Amelia.[18]

The men spent a long night on June 24 stowing their gear aboard the *Ben Deford,* finally sailing at six the next morning. They made camp across the bay from Hilton Head on St. Helena Island, about fifteen miles southeast of Beaufort. Beyond those basic orders, Shaw received no details. "Whether we go with [Gillmore] and make an attack on Morris Island and Fort Sumter," or remain in "garrison at Beaufort, or on some detached expedition," Rob told his mother, "I can't say." At the very least, most officers regarded Gillmore as "much more active and energetic than Hunter," and that pleased Shaw. His wish was that the Fifty-fourth might get into the fight and, together with Gillmore's forces, put an early end to the conflict, so that he could return home to Annie. "I shan't realize until about two years after the war is over, that I am married," he remarked to his sister Effie's fiancé, Charles Russell Lowell, who had recently been promoted to colonel in the Second Massachusetts Cavalry. Rob was pleased to hear of their engagement, assuring Russell that "there are not many girls like Effie." The two men were only twenty-five and twenty-seven, but the war had altered them both, and Boston seemed very far away. "I hope this war will not finish one or both of us," Shaw added, "and that we shall live to know each other very well."[19]

Shaw's melancholy reflections were interrupted by the arrival of the army's paymaster, bearing the Fifty-fourth's first disbursements. To Shaw's dismay, on orders from the War Department, the regiment had been classified "with the contraband regiments," and so instead of the expected $13 each month, the paymaster offered only $10. This was a great "injustice," Shaw complained to Andrew. His men "were enlisted on the express understanding that they were to be on precisely the same footing as all other Massachusetts troops." The paymaster, whose orders were unambiguous, refused to reconsider. "If he does not change his mind," Shaw assured both his father and the governor, "I shall refuse to have the regiment paid until I hear from you on the subject." Should the federal government fail to maintain its end of the bargain, Shaw believed, the Fifty-fourth ought to "be mustered out of service" and returned to Massachusetts."[20]

The fault, ironically, lay with Massachusetts senator Henry Wilson, a Republican and an ally of Andrew's. By ordering the withdrawal of Thaddeus Stevens's bill to recruit black soldiers, Wilson had permitted section 15 of his July 1862 Militia Act to survive, and so too its proposal to pay blacks on fatigue duty lower wages than white soldiers in active service. Following the May 1863 creation of the Bureau for Colored Troops, Secretary Stanton asked William Whiting, solicitor of the War Department, to provide him with a decision regarding the pay of "persons of African descent." On June 4, Whiting submitted his findings. Both the Second Confiscation Act and the Militia Act authorized the enlistment of blacks as manual workers, although the former made no mention of payment. Wilson's Militia Act, however, stipulated that African American laborers would receive $10 each month, from which $3 would be deducted for clothing. Congress, Whiting added, essentially confirmed this policy in March 1863 by passing legislation paying black cooks $10 each month. After the clothing deduction (the uniform was required, even for those who would not fight), black laborers would receive only $7, or about half of the wages paid to white privates. The assumption was that only white soldiers engaged in combat, and their higher pay reflected the greater risks they faced. A furious Andrew fired off complaints to Stanton, and on the advice of the state assembly, he requested that William Schouler, the adjutant general of Massachusetts, immediately report what remedy he "would advise." Stanton replied only that his hands were tied, as cabinet members lacked the authority to overrule an act of Congress. "For any additional pay or bounty colored troops must trust to State contributions and the justice of Congress at the next session," he responded.[21]

While Shaw awaited word from Boston, the officers found time to enjoy the Fourth of July celebrations. On July 2, Shaw and Hallowell accepted an invitation to tea at a nearby plantation, which had been transformed into a freedmen's school. The two met "four ladies and the same number of gentlemen," but the one who fascinated Rob was Charlotte Forten of Philadelphia. "She is quite pretty, remarkably well-educated, and a very interesting woman," Shaw told his mother. At twenty-five, Forten was exactly his age and "decidedly the belle here." Despite his five months among black troops, Shaw remained very much the Boston Brahmin, and notwithstanding her family's wealth, what made Forten's accomplishments most surprising to him, he admitted, was that she was a mixed-race "quadroon." After a pleasant afternoon on the piazza, the group walked over to the plantation's church to watch a service. The praying, Forten scribbled into her diary, was some "of the very best and most spirited" she had ever heard, and she was pleased that Shaw "listened with the deepest interest." In fact, Rob was merely being polite. "The praying was done by an old blind fellow, who made believe, all the time, that he was reading out of a book," he grumbled. "Their singing, when there are a great many voices, is fine, but otherwise I don't like it at all. The women's voices are so shrill, that I can't listen to them with comfort."[22]

Shaw was far more enthusiastic about the celebration that he, Hallowell, and Saxton witnessed on the Fourth. Held in a grove near a Baptist Church about seven miles from their camp, the festivities began with two speeches by black ministers. Next, one black student stepped forward to read the Declaration of Independence and then, together with other pupils, lined up to sing "My Country, 'Tis of Thee." The freedwomen donned "gay dresses & turbans," which Shaw thought "made the sight very brilliant." If Shaw ever had any doubts about their mission, the celebration helped put them to rest. "Can you imagine anything more wonderful than a coloured-Abolitionist meeting on a South Carolina plantation," Rob asked rhetorically. "Here were collected all the freed slaves on this Island listening to the most ultra abolition speeches," thanks to the arrival of the army. "Now they own a little themselves, go to school, to church, and work for wages." Never the most pious of men, the day nonetheless led Shaw to "believe that God isn't very far off."[23]

The next morning Shaw and Hallowell found there was yet more to celebrate. Two days before, on July 3, Confederate general Robert E. Lee's invasion of Pennsylvania had met with disaster when a charge of 12,000 men was repulsed by heavy U.S. artillery and rifle fire. The Second and Twenty-second Massachusetts had both been in the thick of fighting, the latter suffering a casualty rate of 60 percent. Among the fifteen dead in the regiment was Shaw's old Harvard classmate Charles Mudge. "Poor fellows," Rob lamented, "how they have been slaughtered!" Miraculously, one day later, on the Fourth, the siege at Vicksburg, Mississippi, ended with the surrender of the fortress city to Major General Ulysses S. Grant. The victory divided the Confederacy, separating the western states of Arkansas, Louisiana, and Texas from the rest of the South and allowing U.S. gunboats to sail the length of the Mississippi River.[24]

THE TWIN VICTORIES MADE SHAW ALL THE MORE DETERMINED TO have the Fifty-fourth included in the War Department's plans for the Charleston assault. Shaw had grown friendly with General George Crockett Strong during their few days together on St. Helena, and when Strong's forces were ordered to Folly Island, Shaw wrote to express his distress at "being left behind." He remained convinced that his men were "capable of better service than mere guerilla warfare," and he regretted that his regiment no longer formed "a part of the force under your command." Although Strong was a career soldier, he had been raised in Vermont and was but five years Shaw's elder. Rob did not mention the pay issue in his plea, but he hoped Strong agreed that "the colored soldiers should be associated as much as possible with the white troops," so as to erase the image of them in the white mind as mere laborers and plunderers.[25]

Strong did not reply directly to Shaw's letter of July 6. His response instead arrived at noon on July 8 in the guise of orders instructing the Fifty-fourth to be prepared to move within the hour, bringing only their blankets and rations. By three o'clock, seven companies were loaded into the transport *Chasseur,* with the remaining three aboard the *Cossack,* a steamer they shared, Shaw noted uneasily, with Montgomery and his staff. The skies opened and the long night, one captain groused, "was made miserable by wet clothes" and the "crowded conditions on the small steamers." But shortly after one in the morning on July 9, the transports reached the mouth of the Stono River, and by noon the soldiers had all debarked on the western end of Folly Island.[26]

Already in control of portions of the island, Gillmore proposed to use the flat, northeastern edge of Folly as a staging ground for assaults across a narrow inlet to Morris Island, which he described as an equally smooth "mess of sand about three and three quarters miles long." On the eastern side of Morris, Confederate engineers had constructed Battery Wagner, a beachhead redoubt of fourteen cannons, which together with Fort

Drawn by topographical engineer Robert Knox Sneden for General Quincy Adams Gillmore, this charts the islands and terrain from Charleston Harbor to the Stono River. The Fifty-fourth and Fifty-fifth used Folly Island as a camp; it also served as staging ground for the July 1863 assaults on James and Morris Islands. *Courtesy Virginia Historical Society.*

Moultrie, across Charleston Harbor, guarded the harbor's entrance and protected Fort Sumter. To the north, across Folly River, lay the far larger James Island. On its harbor side, Confederates had strengthened a dilapidated eighteenth-century stronghold, Fort Johnson, to protect against an overland assault on Charleston. Otherwise, General P. G. T. Beauregard, in charge of the city's defenses, relied on the natural barriers of salt marshes, creeks, snakes, and mud to keep U.S. forces at bay. Gillmore's plan was to shell Wagner with shore batteries constructed on Folly Island and, from warships outside the harbor, have General Alfred Terry and 4,000 men—including the Fifty-fourth—launch a feint north onto James Island in hopes of pulling Confederates away from Wagner and Morris Island more generally. To slow the arrival of Confederate reinforcements, Higginson and the First South Carolina were to sail up the South Edisto River and cut rail lines to the south.[27]

The Fifty-fourth had only a few hours' rest before orders arrived for Terry's division to move, but most of the men discovered that anticipation was the enemy of sleep. A monitor, two gunboats, and a mortar schooner began to push up the Stono River, firing on James Island on their right and John's Island to their left. Thirteen transport ships followed close behind. Beauregard was not completely wrong to think his southwest effectively guarded by creeks and swamps. Most of the lower portion of James Island, which faced Folly and Morris Islands, was latticed with twisting rivers and creeks, and even three miles up to the Stono River, on the island's southwestern side, where Terry's forces landed near Holland Island Creek, the island was more marsh than dry land. The soldiers made camp on a spit of higher land roughly three miles long and half a mile wide. Known to locals as Solomon Legare Island, after the largest plantation in the area, the strip was effectively cut off from the rest of James Island by a wide bog; earlier residents had constructed two narrow land bridges of dirt roads just under a mile apart to connect the estate with the northern portion of James. Most of Terry's division made camp on the southern edge of Legare, with the Fifty-fourth guarding its northern shore and the two causeways.[28]

At five o'clock the next morning, the soldiers could hear "heavy cannonading" coming from the direction of Morris Island. Having correctly assumed that Beauregard had shifted troops to the northeastern side of James Island, Gillmore ordered his men to cross the narrow Lighthouse Inlet to Morris Island. The attack began inauspiciously. George Strong was in the lead boat, and misjudging the depth of the inlet, he waded off into what he believed to be shallow waters. The water was well over his head, and all his men saw was his hat drifting on the waves. They fished him out of the water, and pulling off his waterlogged boots, Strong led the charge up the beach, hatless and in his stockings, while gunners in the harbor opened fire on Wagner. Confederate soldiers along the beach scrambled for the safety of Wagner's bombproofs, abandoning their kettles. Although Strong failed to take Wagner itself, the army soon controlled three-quarters of the island. Had Strong pushed on at that moment, his troops quite possibly might have overrun and captured Wagner as well. Union losses stood at fifteen killed and ninety-one wounded, while Confederate casualties were far higher at nearly three hundred, with eleven artillery pieces left behind during the retreat. The news, one officer remembered, was received by the soldiers on James with "rousing cheers."[29]

The following day proved far less successful for U.S. forces on both islands. At dawn on June 11, Strong's brigade advanced on Wagner through heavy fog. But heavy fire from within the battery combined with the narrowness of the beach to keep other units from following. Overly confident, Gillmore ordered no artillery bombardment prior to the attack. Nor were Strong's men provided with covering fire during the assault itself. By the time Strong ordered a retreat, he had lost forty-nine men, with nearly another three hundred either wounded or missing. On James Island, the Fifty-fourth and other U.S. forces were able to advance pickets across the western land bridge, known as Grimball's Causeway, thanks to supporting fire from the gunboat *Pawnee*. But with the grim news from Wagner and their uncertainty about the number of Confederates several miles to their front, they dared advance no further. In the chaos, Private Abraham Brown accidentally shot and killed himself while cleaning his pistol. As it began to pour again, Ned Hallowell rode out to inspect the pickets along the northern edge of Legare and, no doubt, to bolster the flagging morale of his men.[30]

Correctly believing Wagner to be secure, Beauregard reduced his force on Morris Island and concentrated on James. Higginson's expedition up the Edisto River had failed, even before six regiments of Confederate infantry arrived from Georgia and North Carolina to assist in the defense. On June 15, Confederate infantrymen suddenly appeared in front of the Tenth Connecticut pickets, and several pickets from the Fifty-fourth reported seeing scouts close to their lines. At about six that evening, Companies B, K, and H relieved Pennsylvania troops, and the 300 men from the Fifty-fourth spread out in front of the Tenth Connecticut, all of them holding a precarious position, as they had a dense swamp to their rear. It continued to rain, but an officer, climbing atop a house, could see the Confederate signal corps flashing messages. He shouted for the men to remain vigilant and prepare for an attack, his words almost lost in the squall. Undaunted, Private George Brown crawled forward far enough to get a shot off at a Confederate picket.[31]

Around three in the morning on June 16, Confederate sharpshooters began to take aim at the Union pickets, hoping to drive them away from the road and toward the center of Legare Island so that they might advance in greater numbers by daylight. Suddenly, just before dawn, six companies from the Twenty-Fifth South Carolina and two from the Nineteenth Georgia swarmed across River's Causeway, the easternmost land bridge. Despite the warnings of the previous night, the Tenth Connecticut was caught unprepared, and far to their rear the pickets could hear Shaw and Wilkie James bawling for the remaining companies to form lines.[32]

Peter Vogelsang held his position behind a thick palmetto tree, but within moments "one hundred Rebels were swarming about him." Cartridges for Enfield rifles consisted of paper-wrapped powder charges with a lubricated minié ball resting on its top; Vogelsang bit off the end of the cartridge, tasting the bitter gunpowder as he poured the charge down the musket of his gun, frantically inserting the bullet and ramming it down the barrel. He led his men to the left, away from the bridge, firing as they slowly retreated. One Confederate took his bullet and went down, and Vogelsang sliced three more with his bayonet. Swinging his empty musket, Vogelsang caught a fifth soldier in the stomach and "doubled him up" before stabbing down with his bayonet. After the skirmish, Vogelsang remembered that the dying soldier "looked so young," but in the moment he thought only to grab the fallen man's gun. The "rebels came so thick and fast, and on horseback, too." His unit dashed toward a creek and the safety of land beyond. "You know I am pretty good at running," the forty-six-year-old sergeant recalled, "and I did my prettiest." Cut off from the rest of the company, Vogelsang "dropped the old secesh rifle" and waded into the creek. Although not wide, the water was neck deep in the middle, and as he scrambled into the tall grass on the other shore a ball nicked his heel. Just behind him, two slower soldiers, Corporals Harvey Davis and Anthony Schenek, were shot as they tried to swim across; they drowned, their blood oozing into the slowly moving water. Confederates shouted for two others to surrender, and they "very foolishly did so," in Vogelsang's estimation, as they "were afterwards found, tied and shot."[33]

As the Tenth Connecticut scrambled into formation and Shaw's companies fell in on their right, the 300 men of the Fifty-fourth continued to pull back, able only to hinder but not halt the wave of 800 attacking Confederates. "Our picket line retired slowly and reluctantly," George Stephens wrote of Company B, "delivering their fire as if on a skirmish drill." Not far away, Vogelsang heard a cavalryman shout "surrender" and spied a mounted Confederate aiming in his direction. The ball caught him as he spun, hitting him in the upper chest and collapsing his left lung before narrowly missing his spine and exiting through the center of his back. "It made a sort of stinging, numb sensation for a moment," he recalled, finding it odd that the pain was not greater. Vogelsang dropped to his knees and tugged off his cartridge box and haversack and began to crawl away, yet after scuttling but "one hundred feet or so," he passed out.[34]

"Our men fought like tigers," Lewis Douglass assured his parents. "The rebels were held in check by our men long enough to allow the Tenth Connecticut to escape being surrounded and captured." The white soldiers were able to reach the Stono and took shelter under the protection of the *Pawnee*'s guns. Shore batteries succeeded in landing a few shells on the *Pawnee*, but soon the other gunboats, which had steamed north, dropped back downriver and began to rake the Confederate lines. The noise of the ships' guns awoke Vogelsang, but as he had fallen behind the advancing Confederates, he remained where he was, lying "in the blood, mud and water" up to his waist for the next several hours. Unable to see the action, he had no idea "which side would win, or if they would come" and search for him. In the center of the island, the Confederates "yelled and hooted," but the main body of the Fifty-fourth stood their ground. The soldiers poured "volley after volley" into the Confederates, their shoulders bruised from the recoil of their rifles, Stephens reported, "and after a contest of two hours they fled." Sweating and bone-weary, James Henry Gooding lowered his rifle. "It was a warmer reception than they had expected," he said proudly.[35]

Despite the victory, General Terry feared that the U.S. forces could not hold out against a second assault and gave the order to evacuate the island. Search parties located Vogelsang, cut off his clothes, and dressed his wounds as well as they could before carrying him aboard a transport ship bound for Folly Island, and then on to the Union hospital in Beaufort. The Fifty-fourth suffered fourteen killed and twenty wounded, with another thirteen missing. Among the dead was twenty-four-year-old Corporal Charles Holloway, a student from Wilberforce, Ohio, and Sergeant Joseph D. Wilson, an Illinois farmer. Wilson had been surrounded by Confederate soldiers who ordered him to surrender. He bravely "refused to do so," Gooding reported, "and was shot through the head." Because the men who joined the Fifty-fourth had often marched off to Readville with groups of friends or relatives from the same towns and villages, fights such as the one on James Island could have disastrous effects on black communities back home. Although Mercersburg, Pennsylvania, was home to only several thousand residents, four brothers from the Krunkleton family had signed on. All four served in Company K and stood near River's Causeway when the fighting began. James Krunkleton was unharmed, but Wesley and William were among the wounded, and nineteen-year-old Cyrus was killed. The Confederates reported only fifteen casualties, a ludicrous undercount that nobody believed. "They carried cart loads of dead off the field," Stephens remarked.[36]

Worrisome too was the fate of those captured. The thirteen listed as missing were assumed to have been taken prisoner, and rumors circulated within the regiment that Confederate infantrymen had mistreated their black captives. One soldier who had taken cover after being overrun by Confederates reported seeing black prisoners protected by officers, but watched as three others were shot and bayonetted when no officers were nearby. Private George Counsel, a laborer from West Chester, Pennsylvania, was among those unaccounted for, as were William Henry Harrison, a thirty-five-year-old teamster from Chicago, Henry Worthington of Defiance, Ohio, and James Caldwell, the grandson of abolitionist Sojourner Truth. Yet unknown to Shaw and Hallowell was the fact that General Beauregard, unsure of what to do with captured black soldiers who did not fall under the description of men listed in Davis's decree, had written to General Samuel Cooper, the inspector general of the Confederacy, to ask about their status. While he awaited an answer, Beauregard ordered the men imprisoned in Castle Pinckney, a small island fortress previously used as a lockup for prisoners taken during the First Battle of Bull Run. With good reason, Beauregard suspected that a far larger number of black prisoners were about to fall into Confederate hands. It remained "a nice question," commented one Charleston reporter, whether free black troops "are to be regarded as belligerents or outlaws."[37]

At five o'clock that afternoon, the Fifty-fourth prepared to withdraw from James, only hours after the last shots had been fired. As the regiment shouldered their arms and prepared to march, several officers from Connecticut rode in to express their thanks for "the service rendered by the Fifty-fourth." Shaw was even more gratified by a message that arrived from

General Terry: "Tell your Colonel that I am exceedingly pleased with the conduct of your regiment." Brief though the action was, it was the first time in the war that black and white soldiers had fought side by side, and Shaw believed that "what we have done to-day wipes out the remembrance of the Darien affair." Wilkie James, having survived his first taste of battle, was yet more enthusiastic. "For the first time," he wrote his father, "we had met the enemy, and had proven there, fully to our satisfaction at least, that the negro soldier was a fighting soldier." Lewis Douglass, of course, had never had any doubts that men like himself made effective combatants, but even so, he was proud to inform his parents that the battle "earned us our reputation as a fighting regiment."[38]

Sympathetic newspapers concurred. As one correspondent wrote, the "boys of the Tenth Connecticut could not help loving the men who saved them from destruction." The journalist predicted that "probably a thousand homes from Windham to Fairfield have in letters been told the story how the dark-skinned heroes fought the good fight and covered with their brave hearts the retreat of brothers, sons, and fathers of Connecticut." He was not wrong. One white soldier wrote home to his mother, praising the Fifty-fourth for fighting "like heroes." Had it not been "for the bravery of three companies of the Massachusetts Fifty-fourth (colored), our whole regiment would have been captured." Connecticut, of course, was a Republican stronghold. In fact, Lincoln had carried every one of its counties in 1860, and so the state was inherently more sympathetic to Andrew's experiment than were white soldiers from the Midwest. Yet this did not mean that the fight for James Island was not a crucial step in the right direction.[39]

After several hours' preparation, the march back to Folly Island finally began around nine o'clock. The men bundled most of their stores, extra ammunition, and horses aboard the steamer *Boston,* but the transport ship was a small one, and after the wounded were carried on, there was no space for the rest of the regiment. When the pathways through the swamps grew too marshy, the soldiers threw down planks as makeshift bridges. "A driving rain poured down nearly the whole time," one officer remembered. "Blinding flashes of lightening momentarily illuminated the way, then fading but to render the blackness deeper." The boards grew slick from the rain and muck, and it took the regiment from ten o'clock that night until five the next morning, Shaw observed, to travel four miles. "For nearly a mile we had to pass over a bridge of one, and in some places, two planks wide," Shaw remarked, "without a railing, and slippery with rain." Short on both water and rations, the regiment collapsed on the southern shore of Cole's Island, just opposite Folly Island, sleeping until the sun grew too hot. Their trek, Douglass presumed, was surely "one of the hardest marches on record through woods and marsh."[40]

As they lay on the beach awaiting transport ships to ferry them across to Folly, Rob found time to write to Annie, promising her that he "shouldn't like you to see me as I am now." Apart from being washed by the summer rains, none of the men had bathed or shaved in several days. Shaw himself had eaten nothing but "crackers and coffee these two days," and his hunger, combined with his lack of sleep and the incessant bombardment of Fort Wagner in the distance, did little to improve his mood. Leaning over to Hallowell, Shaw asked him if he believed in presentiments, adding that he felt sure he would die in the next battle. Astonished, Hallowell begged him to "shake off the feeling." After a long moment, Shaw replied only: "I will try."[41]

As if Shaw required yet another reason to be disconsolate, word of deadly race riots in New York City began to filter south. Four days before, on July 13, when the new 1863 draft law went into effect, mobs of working-class Democrats and Irish immigrants systematically sacked federal property and buildings associated with the Republican Party before turning on their black neighbors. Rioters burned the West Broadway pharmacy of Dr. James McCune Smith, the attending physician at the Colored Orphan Asylum, before turning on that institution itself. As teachers hurried the 233 children out the rear entrance, rioters brushed aside the two policemen guarding the orphanage and ransacked the building of furniture, bedding, and dishes before soaking the floors with turpentine and setting it afire. The children took refuge at the Thirty-fifth Street police station, where inmates tried to strike at the black orphans "through the bars of the doors." Sarah Shaw and her daughters fled their Staten Island house, while Frank, after arming his gardener and coachman, prepared to defend his home. The mobs left him alone. Overall, at least eleven blacks were murdered during the riots, including one man who was beaten with paving stones, lynched, and then burned. Another of the murdered was the seven-year-old nephew of Sergeant Robert J. Simmons of the Fifty-fourth. Corporal Gooding had survived the fight on James Island only to live long enough to read that his childhood home had been reduced to ashes.[42]

When George Stephens heard the news, he penned a lengthy letter to the *Weekly Anglo-African*. "Are we their enemies? Have we tyrannized over them? Have we maltreated them? Have we robbed them," he wondered of the rioters. Black Americans, he observed, had long been "loyal to the country, in season and out of season," while newcomers to American shores attempted to "subvert the government by popular violence and tumult." Yet the mobs, Stephens believed, were but the tools of influential Democratic politicians who sought to leverage the chaos into "arbitrary power." Despite the fact that for years the federal government, "by its every precept and practice, conserved the interests of slavery, and slaves were hunted down by United States soldiers," blacks remained prepared to "defend it against powerful and determined foes." But having enlisted and been shipped south to fight, black soldiers had to read of "mob-fiends" who "brandished the incendiary torch over the heads of our wives and children and burn their homes." For his part, Peter Vogelsang, despite his worries for his home in Manhattan, tried to remain optimistic about his country's future. Writing from the army hospital in Beaufort, Vogelsang assured his New York friends that he "sympathized with you all in the trials you have had to undergo" during the three days of rioting. "Tis hard, but may be a better day will dawn for us, at least, I hope so."[43]

Not until late that evening did the transport *General Hunter* arrive to ferry the soldiers back to Folly Island, and even then the only way to get the men aboard was by way of a leaky longboat that could hold only thirty per trip. "Rain was pouring down in torrents," Captain Emilio sourly noted, as thunderstorms yet again drenched the regiment. Colonel Shaw himself saw to the embarkation, which took hours, and when the last private was aboard, he chose to remain on deck with his soaked men rather than retire to a dry cabin below. Sailing up Folly River, the transport reached the landing by nine in the morning on July 18. Having not enjoyed a full night's sleep for days, the exhausted men were heartened by the sight of white soldiers cheering their arrival, shouting, "Well done! We heard your guns."

A few soldiers accepted the offered hardtack and coffee, their first meal in many hours. Most of the men wished only to sleep, but the cannonade waged daily against Wagner began around ten-thirty. A few of the soldiers climbed to the top of a sandy hill, from which point they "could see the distant vessels engaging Wagner." Shaw instructed his officers to keep the men "near the shore" while they awaited "further orders." Sergeant Simmons used the opportunity to scratch out a few lines to his mother, although he was unsure as to where he should mail his letter, since not only had his nephew been murdered in the rioting, but his mother's apartment house had been burned down. "God has protected me through this, my first fiery trial," he wrote. "Goodbye! Likely we shall be engaged soon."[44]

CHAPTER FIVE

Battery Wagner

A s most of the Fifty-fourth, exhausted from the long night's march through the swamps, sprawled under pine trees in search of shade and soaked hardtack in their coffee on the morning of July 18, a handful of men climbed atop a sandy rise on Folly Island to watch the distant bombardment of Battery Wagner. "A fresh breeze blew that day," Captain Luis Emilio recalled, "at times the sky was clear; the atmosphere, lightened by recent rains, resounded with the thunders of an almost incessant cannonade." The beachhead fortress was an impressive feat of engineering and a formidable impediment to the capture of Charleston. By definition a battery rather than a fort—the latter having complete walls on all sides—Wagner was a sprawling stronghold. One hundred yards deep and 250 yards wide, the battery stretched north from Vincent's Creek and south to the waves of the Atlantic, so that it completely spanned that section of Morris Island. Initially named Neck Battery, the fortress had been rechristened the previous November in honor of Lieutenant Thomas Wagner, a Charleston slaveholder who had been killed when his cannon exploded during artillery practice at nearby Fort Moultrie. Its rear wall, facing Charleston Harbor, was nothing more than

This bird's-eye view of Charleston's defenses published in *Harper's* on August 15, 1863, reveals the formidable task faced by the U.S. Army. On Morris Island, to the north of Battery Wagner, Battery Gregg and Fort Sumter guarded the southern side of the harbor, and across the narrow opening Fort Moultrie *(right)* and a series of batteries helped keep the U.S. Navy at bay. *Courtesy Harvard University.*

a low rampart, but its sloping front wall rose more than thirty feet from the beach. Built of packed sand and earth and fortified by palmetto logs, Wagner's pitched front was crowned with sharpened stakes, while a canal designed to fill at high tide provided a watery barrier for attackers and their siege works.[1]

The battery boasted fourteen cannon, including a ten-inch Columbiad, which was aimed toward the Atlantic to keep the U.S. squadron at bay. Six guns faced landward, and the beach in front of Wagner lay within range of the cannon at Fort Sumter and Battery Gregg, which sat on the northeastern tip of Morris Island. General William Taliaferro commanded roughly 1,700 infantrymen, artillerymen, and cavalrymen within Wagner, including the Thirty-first and Fifty-first North Carolina, as well as the Charleston Battalion and two companies from the First South Carolina Infantry. During times of heavy bombardment, the soldiers retreated into what one journalist on Folly Island described as "capacious bomb-proof apartments [that] can shelter thousands of men."

Gazing at Wagner's imposing sand walls, Shaw again had a foreboding premonition. For the second time in as many days he remarked to Ned Hallowell that he felt sure he would not survive his next battle.[2]

Despite these shadows, Shaw remained determined that the Fifty-fourth would be included in what everybody suspected was to be an imminent attack on Battery Wagner. Still anxious to prove the value of black troops, he had feared that the assault would take place while his men were relegated to the feint on James Island. He was nearly right. Shortly after the failed attack of July 11, shore and naval batteries began to fire on Wagner each morning like clockwork, with the second assault on the battery initially planned for July 16, at which time the Fifty-fourth was in the thick of battle on James. But the "heavy rain storms materially interfered with the progress of our works," Gillmore later reported. "Nearly all the batteries were submerged and much of its powder spoiled," so that the attack was delayed until July 18. Even then, Gillmore hoped to move "at the break of day," but this goal was pushed back so that his gunners could shift their mortars closer to the battery. Despite these postponements, Gillmore had every confidence that his cannon could pound Wagner into submission, and that the land forces would encounter little opposition once they reached its walls.[3]

The handful of journalists on Morris Island were equally confident. "We seem to have come to the era of triumph," crowed one Amherst newspaper. "Meade's at Gettysburg, Grant's at Vicksburg," and "affairs at Charleston are progressing very favorably." Gillmore's shelling of Wagner gives "every prospect of success," the paper added, and once "Wagner falls, Sumter and Charleston will soon follow." On July 18, the *New York Times* reported that "everything [was] working well" in the siege, with "Charleston and the forts completely besieged." In fact, the *Times* assured its subscribers, "the grand and final attack" had probably already taken place, as it "was assigned for Tuesday," July 14. Common soldiers were less sure. Lorenzo Lyon, a white private with the Forty-eighth New York, wrote home that they needed "more forces in this Regt & hope that Govt will see the necessity thereof & send them *now*." Lyon had gotten hold of a Charleston newspaper that warned that if the Confederate forces "lose Wagner, Charleston is give[n] up." The Confederates well understood the critical role that Wagner played in the defense of their city, Lyon cautioned his father, and "at any time the Rebels may choose to let chime the cast iron dogs of war."[4]

Although General George C. Strong believed that several days of shelling had reduced the interior of Wagner to rubble, the battery's enormous bombproof—capable of sheltering nearly 1,000 of the garrison's 1,700 men and topped by a beam-covered ceiling and sandbags piled twelve feet high—provided ample protection for its defenders just prior to the Fifty-fourth's assault on July 18, 1863. Here, members of the Fifty-fourth stand before the fort after its capture that fall. *Courtesy Massachusetts Historical Society.*

The weaponry at Gillmore's disposal was extraordinary. Starting on the afternoon of July 13, American gunners constructed four batteries of forty-two guns and mortars. Gillmore placed the batteries as close to Wagner as possible, ordering that they be hidden behind dunes "where they will not be seen by the Enemy." Five wooden gunboats and one ironclad joined in the shelling, driving the Confederates into their bombproofed enclosure. Taliaferro's men heaped protective sandbags atop the cannon, and twice his flagstaff was shot away. Watching from their end of Morris Island, U.S. soldiers cheered as the flag fell, believing that the defenders were about to surrender, but a handful of men rushed out of the bombproof to raise their colors again. Deep underground, the Confederates listened to what a defender believed to be one of "the most furious bombardments of the war." The combined shore and naval batteries "poured forth their missiles of death for ten long hours on our little fort," another Confederate remarked, while the huddled Confederates "quietly awaited the time when they would be afforded an opportunity for taking revenge." Watching through field glasses, Northern officers believed the entrances to the bombproofs to be choked with sand, the guns disabled, and the battery itself practically dismantled.[5]

During the shelling, Gillmore discussed the attack with his senior staff. He believed that George Strong should lead the charge, and General Truman Seymour, who remained chief of staff despite the departure of David Hunter, agreed. Journalist Edward Pierce had warned Governor Andrew that Seymour was a racist, and the general confirmed that suspicion by commenting: "Well, I guess we will let Strong lead and put those d——d niggers from Massachusetts in the advance; we may as well get rid of them one time as another." Gillmore, however, was willing to allow the Fifty-fourth to show the nation what they could do. He sent word to Admiral John Dahlgren that he "intended to storm the work about sunset," and that the shelling should continue for the next several hours. By twilight, Gillmore presumed, the stretch of land in front of Wagner "might not be distinctly seen from the James and Sullivan Island batteries and from Fort Sumter." Because of a marshy bog on the northern side of Morris Island, Strong's brigade would have to advance in two columns along a sandy, twenty-five-yard-wide strip of land. The order of attack, Gillmore determined, started with the Fifty-fourth in the lead, supported by the Sixth Connecticut and the Forty-eighth New York, with the Third New Hampshire, the Ninth Maine, and the Seventy-sixth Pennsylvania held in reserve. Owing to a combination of sickness and battlefield casualties, Gillmore added, the "regiments were all small," but the fact that none of them as at full strength little worried the general.[6]

At around two o'clock in the afternoon, Shaw and Wilkie James crossed over from Folly Island and went in search of Strong in hopes of receiving new orders. The general informed them that Gillmore planned to storm the battery that evening. Strong had been impressed by what he had heard of the fighting on James Island, and as he later remarked, perhaps with the benefit of hindsight, he also wished to place the Fifty-fourth in the forefront of the assault so that the honors that would fall to them could be all the greater. "You may lead the column if you say 'yes,'" Strong offered, knowing that Shaw neither could nor wished to disobey the command. "Your men, I know, are worn out, but do as you choose." Shaw's face brightened, and by way of answer he turned to James and instructed him to return to Folly Island, locate Hallowell, and bring up the regiment. When the news arrived, the men struggled to their feet and boarded a steamer to carry them across the inlet to Morris Island. Strong's headquarters sat halfway down the island, and the soldiers arrived at his camp around six. Edward Pierce was present as a guest of the general's, and he thought the men "looked worn and weary." Strong too noticed that the men were fatigued and hungry, not having had rations in two days and nothing to eat since the soggy hardtack that morning. Strong wished there were time for "food and stimulants," but twilight was rapidly approaching.[7]

WHILE SHAW CONFERRED WITH GENERAL STRONG, NED HALLOWELL led the 650 active-duty soldiers of the Fifty-fourth forward. "We were marched up past our batteries," James Henry Gooding remarked, "amid the cheers of the officers and [white] soldiers." When they reached a wide span of low ground, the companies spread into battle formation of two columns. Mindful of what the sudden silence of U.S. artillery meant, Confederate gunners frantically began to unpack their cannon. "About dusk the dark and dense columns were seen moving slowly down the beach," one Confederate observed. At three-quarters of a mile away from the battery, the black soldiers fell within musket range, but those inside Wagner held their fire and instead sent but a few solid balls sailing over the heads of the regiment. Worried that the national colors and the predominantly white Massachusetts state flag were drawing fire, the flag-bearers began to roll them onto staves. Captain William Simpkins drew his sword and pointed at the fort, shouting: "Unfurl those colors," and to cheers, the bearers did so.[8]

Then began the waiting. Behind the lines, Shaw and Strong enjoyed a hasty meal in his tent, where they were served by Harriet Tubman. After thirty minutes, the two officers mounted up and began to ride to the front. Rob turned suddenly and rode back to where Edward Pierce stood. Leaning down, he handed the journalist his yet-unmailed letter to Annie of the previous day, along with a short note to his father, dated that morning. "I enclose this letter for Annie, which I didn't intend to send you," Rob wrote in the latter, "because it is impossible to tell whether I can write again by this mail." As he galloped up toward Hallowell, Luis Emilio could not help noticing that Shaw was as brushed and dressed for the solemn moment as battlefield conditions allowed. His "close-fitting staff-officer's jacket" was set off by the polished eagles on each shoulder, and a "fine narrow silk sash was wound round his waist." An expensive officer's sword of English manufacture hung from his belt, and on one hand shone an antique gem set in a ring. His gold watch, like his sword etched with his initials, was tied in place by a gold chain. Prudently, he retained his pocketbook, in case his body later had to be identified. Emilio observed that Shaw's "bearing was composed," but his cheek had somewhat paled and he was grinding the cigar clenched between his teeth. He dismounted, handed the reins to sixteen-year-old drummer boy Alec Johnson, and walked to where Hallowell waited. "I shall go in advance with the National flag," he told Ned. "You will keep the state flag with you; it will give the men something to rally round."[9]

Most of those in the front, Companies I and C, were also doing their best to remain composed. There "was a lack of their usual light-heartedness," one soldier remarked. Another ball split the air above them, and two of the men shifted nervously, drawing a rebuke from Hallowell. "I guess they kind of 'spec's we're coming," a soldier said aloud. Gazing up the beach toward Wagner, few of the officers were any less anxious. "We have the most magnificent chance to prove the value of the colored race now," Lieutenant James assured a fellow officer, just before spoiling the sentiment by accidently discharging his pistol into the sand, nearly hitting his own foot. Shaw glared in his direction. "I would not have had that happen for anything," an embarrassed Wilkie later admitted.[10]

Strong pulled up in front of Shaw and Hallowell, speaking to the men without dismounting from his gray mare. "Gen. Strong asked us if we would follow him into Fort Wagner," Gooding recalled, with "every man" shouting that they "were ready to follow wherever we were led." Strong too wore his dress blues, with a yellow handkerchief tied around his neck. "Boys, I am a Massachusetts man, and I know you will fight for the honor of the State," he shouted. "I am sorry you must go into the field tired and hungry, but the men in the fort are tired too. There are but three hundred behind those walls, and they have been fighting all day." Confident that they would face little resistance, Strong instructed the men not to fire their muskets "on the way up, but go in and bayonet them at their guns." Then, pointing to Sergeant John Wall, the flag-bearer, Strong asked: "If this man should fall, who will lift the flag and carry it on?" Taking his cigar from his lips, Shaw answered quietly, "I will." As those around Rob hoorayed, Strong rode off and prepared to give the order to advance. Caught up in the moment, Shaw failed to reflect that the Vermont-born Strong had never lived in the Bay State. Also, what no one in the ranks yet knew was that the general's estimate of Confederate strength was off by 1,400.[11]

In the final moments before the advance, Shaw adopted a far less formal approach, walking slowly along the line, speaking soft "words of cheer to his men." Corporal Gooding had always judged his colonel to be a fair but tough taskmaster, yet now he was struck by how Shaw chatted with "the men very familiarly and kindly." His manner was friendlier "than I had ever noticed before," Gooding remarked, yet he observed also how tense Shaw was. His "lips were compressed, and now and then there was visible a slight twitching in the corners of the mouth, like one bent on accomplishing or dying." Shaw reminded one group "how the eyes of thousands would look upon the night's work," gently insisting: "Now, boys, I want you to be men!" As Shaw walked by one private, the soldier impulsively shouted: "Colonel, I will stay by you till I die." Shaw nodded and smiled back.[12]

The signal to advance over the roughly 1,300 yards of sand came at 7:45. Shaw drew his sword, the monogrammed steel scraping against the scabbard's throat. Shaw led the right column, with Hallowell taking the left. The attack coincided with low tide, which afforded the soldiers a wider pathway of firm sand. At low tide the water in Wagner's protective moat would also be lower, between two and three feet. Even so, as the men held formation, the two companies on the right were pushed into the waves, with some of the men wading knee-deep into the ocean. "Move in quick time until within a hundred yards of the fort," Shaw shouted, "then double quick, and charge!" Darkness was coming on fast, but the men could see flashes of light to their front as gunners in Sumter and on Sullivan's Island began to fire. As they reached the widest part of the marsh to their left, soldiers on the edge of both wings were forced to slow and fall back. Only those in the center had a clear path, and they moved smartly behind Shaw and the flag to within 200 yards of the battery's front wall.[13]

Close behind Shaw were Companies I and C and the New Bedford men, including Gooding, William Carney, and brothers John and Charles Harrison. "Fort Wagner is the Sebastopol of the rebels," Gooding later wrote, thinking of the Crimean naval port, "but we went at it." Suddenly, as the gap between the soldiers without and within narrowed, the dark sky exploded. It seemed to Gooding that Wagner's long front wall "became a mound of fire, from which poured a stream of shot and shell." For one too-brief moment, Luis Emilio noted, there was a brief lull as the gunners reloaded, but then came a "deafening explosion" as the cannon fire resumed, "mingled with the crash and rattle of musketry." A sheet of flame, almost "like electric sparks, swept along the parapet" as the Fifty-first North Carolina, lying atop the bulwark, opened fire. The charge up the beach had taken roughly seven minutes. Gooding and those in the lead splashed through the ditch, waded up the sandy wall, and shoved through the wall of spikes at the top of the wall, engaging "the foe [with] the bayonet," but the company was "exposed to a murderous fire from the batteries of the fort." The color-bearer of the regimental flag went down. Shaw seized its staff and forged ahead.[14]

Only then did they realize how wrong Strong had been on the numbers inside Wagner. The earlier bombardment, Hallowell later admitted, which "seemed sure to tear out the very insides of the fort," had "in fact, simply excited a lively commotion in the sand." As hundreds upon hundreds of Wagner's defenders swarmed out of the safety of the bombproofs, Confederate artillery from Battery Gregg and James Island began to rain shells down onto the beach. Racing at the head of Company F were Sergeants Douglass and Swails. "The grape and canister shell and Minnie swept us down like chaff," Douglass swore, but "still our men went on and on." Shells crashed into their ranks, chewing up huge spouts of sand and dust and tearing holes in the columns. "Men fell all around me," Douglass remembered. "A shell would explode and clear a space of twenty feet, [but] our men would close up again." Douglass scrambled up the sloping front wall, waving his sword and screaming: "Come on, boys, and fight for God and Governor Andrew." Grapeshot coming from his left blasted off his sheath and hammered pellets into his pelvis and thighs. "If I die tonight," Lewis thought, as men from his company followed him into the fort, "I will not die a coward."[15]

Dashing toward the fort with the left column, Captain Wilkie James tried to remain only a few paces behind Ned Hallowell and the state flag. Even under what he described as "that mountain of fire," he recalled Governor Andrew's reminder that those "colors had never been surrendered to any foe." As he neared the ditch a shell fragment tore into his side, but in "the frenzy of excitement it seemed a painless visitation." James splashed into the shallow moat, and just when he began to think that reaching the parapet was not "out of the question," he received a second wound, a canister ball in his foot. Stunned, he fell to the ground. His men swept by him and flooded up the walls. Defenders hurled hand grenades down into the lines of the attackers. Somewhere ahead of him in the smoke and din, Hallowell reached the top of the wall. He took a bullet to the groin and rolled back into the ditch, where he received two more wounds. Bleeding profusely, Ned began to crawl away from the fort.[16]

To Hallowell's right, Shaw was one of the first to scale the wall. "With another cheer and a shout," the men from Companies I and C scrambled up beside him and engaged the Confederates in hand-to-hand combat. Shaw was waving his sword and shouting, "Forward, my brave boys!" when a bullet caught him in the breast. He was hit five or six more times before he dropped. Gooding saw him fall, as did Private Thomas Burgess, a young carpenter from Pennsylvania. Although badly wounded himself, Burgess tried to drag Shaw with him as he scuttled down toward the ditch. But Burgess could see that "there appeared to be no life in him," and those trying to retrieve his body, Gooding reported, were themselves "either shot down, or reeling in the ditch below." Twenty soldiers fell close about Shaw, with "two lying on his own body."[17]

Advancing directly behind the Fifty-fourth were the Sixth Connecticut and the Forty-eighth New York. Raised by the Reverend James Perry, the latter regiment had tried to recruit only pious soldiers, and the unit was nicknamed "Perry's Saints." After reaching the ditch, the New Yorkers attempted to swing about and overrun Wagner's seaward wall. "Up the beach we went amidst the iron hail," Private Lorenzo Lyon wrote. "I can't tell you the moans & shrieks of the dying." Confederate canisters hurled spreading cones of bullets into the Forty-eighth. To his left, Lyon could see the Fifty-fourth struggling up the slanting walls, while the "rebels fired everything they could, mowing down a Co. at a time." Facing the Forty-eighth was an iron artillery piece whose eight-inch mouth had been used against the U.S. Navy; filled with grapeshot, the howitzer spewed enough metal to make Lyon feel as though "an entire Blacksmith shop" was flying through the air. The white regiments took heavy casualties, and although Lyon "had made up [his] mind to give all [he] had," the night sky "filled with all the weapons of death that could be invented." Resigning himself to God's "righteous will," he slowly pushed on, even as he thought he "saw hundreds dropping" all about him.[18]

For nearly an hour, soldiers from the Fifty-fourth and the Sixth Connecticut were able to hold the southeastern bastion of the battery. Some of the men lay against the sloping wall, shooting up through the spikes at Confederates; one black soldier, who had lost the use of an arm, piled cartridges atop the parapet for seventeen-year-old Lieutenant Edward B. Emerson to use. Some Confederates shouted, "No quarter," and aware of the fate of those taken prisoner on James Island, no black soldier tried to surrender. Private George Wilson, a laborer from Hudson, New York, was shot in both shoulders but refused to retreat until ordered to do so by his captain. Neither side had time to reload their muskets in the melee, and the attackers, one officer recorded, took "wounds from bayonet thrusts, sword cuts, pike thrusts and hand grenades; and there were heads and arms broken and smashed by the butt-ends of muskets."[19]

Unaware until too late how many Confederates had waited out the shelling deep within the bombproof, Strong and Seymour held back the final three regiments from the assault. Gillmore later suggested that more soldiers would only have congested the chaotic battlefield, and that "the darkness and the [Confederates'] perfect knowledge of the interior" of Wagner "rendered it necessary to relinquish it." Whatever the reason, the assaulting forces were badly outnumbered. Hallowell later complained that a common "characteristic" of Union officers was that they rarely ordered "sufficient numbers to push the advantage gained to complete success." Lewis Douglass also believed that had they "been properly supported we should have held the fort." But "the white troops could not be made to come up," and so "the consequence is we had to fall back." Neither man, however, expressed anything but praise for the white soldiers who fought beside them along Wagner's wall; they claimed only that decisions made by senior officers cost them their prize. With Shaw dead and Hallowell down, and with so many older captains killed or wounded, it fell to Captain Luis Emilio to order the retreat. The son of Spanish immigrants, Emilio had bluffed his way into the army in 1861 by claiming to be eighteen, his actual age on the night of the attack. Both captains from Company K had died on the northern portion of the parapet, one of them in Swails's arms; the black sergeant led the company's survivors in retreat. Still slashing at defenders atop the parapet, Douglass joined the withdrawal down the beach, "dodging shells and other missiles" as he ran.[20]

Nor did the Fifty-fourth willingly abandon the Stars and Stripes. Sergeant John Wall, a twenty-year-old Oberlin College student, initially carried the national flag up the beach but became mired in the ditch. During the chaos, Wall shouted for help, but his company poured by him as they fought their way up the barricade. Sergeant William Carney threw aside his gun, grabbed the flag, and pushed his way to the head of the column. "I found myself alone, struggling upon the ramparts," Carney later recounted, "while all around me were the dead and wounded, lying one upon another." He planted the banner in the sand atop the parapet but was immediately hit in the right arm and leg. Just as the retreat commenced, Carney took a third ball, this one to the chest, with a fourth cracking his left hip. He fell to the ground, still holding the flagstaff. After a struggle, Confederates seized the state flag. But despite the wounds in both legs, Carney crawled down the beach on his knees toward the lower end of Morris Island, keeping one hand pressed to his chest wound while the other carried the flag. He had covered nearly half a mile when he was sprayed in the back of the head by grapeshot, but he nevertheless reached Company D, which had stopped close to where the march began hours before. Seeing the American flag, the soldiers, "both black and white," began to cheer. As Carney presented the flag to a lieutenant, he promised: "Boys, I did my duty; the dear old flag never touched the ground."[21]

Captain Emilio rallied about 100 men along the beach, near to where Carney had crawled. The soldiers remained within firing distance of the Confederates, but they hoped to use the cover of darkness to rescue the wounded, who otherwise might be captured if Wagner's defenders chose to search outside its walls. When General Strong rode forward to "try and rally stragglers," he was struck in the thigh by canister shot. Although a bit of metal passed all the way through Strong's leg, a journalist found him in the hospital tent on Morris and was happy to report that "the wound was less dangerous than was anticipated." As the surgeons worked to stem the flow of blood, Strong lay on a stretcher, worried only about "the poor fellows who lay uncared for on the battlefield."[22]

Among those still on the field was Wilkie James. Wounded in two places, James made it to the water's edge, hoping to find cover behind a ridge of sand. The Confederates within Wagner maintained a "terrific fire," but James reasoned that he would rather die where he lay than be taken prisoner, given Jefferson Davis's "manifesto, ordering the white officers of the 54th Massachusetts hung if captured alive." At length, several soldiers from the Fifty-fourth bearing stretchers found James and began to carry him to the rear. Wagner's guns fired again, and "a round shot blew off the head of the stretcher-bearer to [James's] rear, producing a horrible and instant death." The second soldier dragged James behind a dune, where rescuers found both the next morning. Wilkie was one of the lucky ones. Lorenzo Lyon of the Forty-eighth New York later recalled that even after it was clear that U.S. forces could not renew the attack, "the Rebels kept up with grape & everything, I think on purpose to keep" Union soldiers from "taking off any wounded." As the waves flowed in, George Stephens told the *Weekly Anglo-African*, "dozens of our wounded were drowned." Due to the ongoing fire from Wagner, "before we could secure our dead and wounded the tide came up," Stephens mourned, "and such as could not crawl away were drowned."[23]

Harriet Tubman listened to the distant rumbling from her post by Strong's tent. The deeply religious woman, who began to experience visions and revelations from God after being hit on the head by a heavy metal weight while a young slave, described the faraway battle in elegiac terms: "And then we saw the lightening, and that was the guns; and then we heard the thunder, and that was the big guns; and then we heard the rain falling, and that was the drops of blood falling; and when we came to get in the crops, it was the dead that we reaped."[24]

SUNDAY MORNING BROKE GRAY AS THUNDERSTORMS AGAIN ROLLED in. A correspondent for the Charleston *Courier* reported that hundreds of corpses lay atop Wagner's front wall, sometimes piled two and three

The stormy morning of July 19, as depicted by *Harper's*. In the foreground, Generals Quincy Adams Gillmore and William Taliaferro discuss the care of the dead and wounded as well as possible prisoner exchanges. To the left, the southern wall of Wagner is covered with dead bodies, which can also be seen in the watery ditch. In the distance, lightning strikes above Charleston. *Courtesy Harvard University.*

bodies deep, with others floating in the canal's high tide. The black troops had "received no tender treatment during the skirmish," a reporter for the *Charleston Mercury* added, "and the marsh in one place was thick with their dead bodies." Many of the soldiers had been blown to pieces. "Probably no battlefield in the country has ever presented such an array of mangled bodies in a small compass as was seen on Sunday morning," the *Courier* ventured. General Gillmore wrote to General Taliaferro, requesting "permission to receive and bury the dead of my command left upon the battle field last Evening." Under a flag of truce, Gillmore rode up the island to confer with his counterpart, both as to the bodies of the dead and the care of the wounded, but also to discuss an exchange of prisoners. Gillmore was especially anxious to press the point "that the officers and men of the colored regiment were to be treated like all others." Taliaferro replied that such determinations were made in Richmond, and he promised only to submit the "question for the consideration of his superiors."[25]

Gillmore also hoped to discover whether Shaw was dead or had been wounded and then taken prisoner. That it was even a question was due to the fact that just after the fighting, Confederate private Charles Blake found Shaw's body and, together with several men, carried him into the bombproof, where they stripped him down to his undershirt and trousers. Blake made off with Rob's watch and chain, while others grabbed his sword and sash. One of those who knew his fate was not then in a position to alert Gillmore. The U.S. naval surgeon John Luck had been captured that morning while looking after the wounded, and he saw Shaw's corpse lying within the fort. When he later asked General Johnson Hagood, who arrived just that afternoon to replace Taliaferro, what they had done with Shaw's body, Hagood sneered: "We have buried him in the trench with his niggers." Had the young colonel "been in command of white troops," Hagood admitted, he would have granted "him an honorable burial." Hagood had no idea whether the black soldiers who lay beside Shaw were freemen or runaways, but the planter and future South Carolina governor believed that white men who led black regiments had demeaned themselves, and so Shaw deserved to be buried "in the common trench, with the negroes that fell with him."[26]

After two assaults in quick succession, Confederates had no reason to suspect that the attack of July 18 would be the last. Hagood was understandably wary of allowing sharp-eyed U.S. soldiers into the battery itself to carry away their dead. Given the intense July heat, he ordered the deceased buried as quickly as possible, and as was becoming all too common in the war, that meant that dozens of bodies were piled together in hastily dug pits. There was no time for coffins, and in this case the Union dead—black and white alike—were not even wrapped in blankets. Just in front of the battery, Confederates dug long trenches about six feet wide and four feet deep. Hagood later insisted that they had no leisure to do more than drag bodies to nearby pits, and so "each officer was buried where he fell, with men who surrounded him." In reality, by tradition Confederate soldiers buried white captains with other officers; Rob Shaw, Pen Hallowell later alleged, "was the only officer buried with the colored troops."[27]

On July 24, the Confederates sent out a flag of truce, and Gillmore ordered General Israel Vogdes to ride forward to confer with Hagood. By the time of the parlay, the U.S. surgical corps had already begun moving wounded soldiers from the tent infirmary on Morris to the army hospital in Beaufort. The number of men in hospitals in Hilton Head and Beaufort rose to 144. "A few others died on the boats" as they sailed down the coast, a Worcester journalist noted. Those officers whose bodies could be recovered or who died while under the surgeon's knife were given proper burials after the army shipped their bodies home in "large sized water casks." Vogdes and Hagood discussed an exchange of wounded soldiers, and Vogdes requested, unsuccessfully, the body of Colonel Haldimand Putnam of the Sixth Connecticut. In later years, Hagood insisted that Vogdes did not inquire about Shaw's body, or even his condition, but that was surely untrue; James Henry Gooding wrote later that day that General P. G. T. Beauregard, perhaps at Vogdes's request, sent word to the parlay that Shaw was not being held prisoner in Charleston. Hagood, a graduate of the Citadel, Charleston's military academy, was increasingly embarrassed about his lack of martial courtesy and did not wish to admit to a career officer that he had unceremoniously dumped Shaw's body into a sandy pit.[28]

Word of Shaw's demise spread quickly around the camp. "We have since learned by the flag-of-truce that Colonel Shaw is dead," Gooding reported that afternoon to the *Mercury*. Like Private Burgess, Gooding had seen Shaw fall, and he never had much confidence that his colonel could have survived his wounds. But in the confused aftermath of July 18, faith often proved stronger than dreadful truths. Lewis Douglass initially assured his parents that "Col. Shaw is a prisoner and wounded," although Douglass had not been near Rob in the fort. The grim news reached Charles Russell Lowell on July 26, at his camp just outside of Washington. "I see that General Beauregard believes Rob Shaw was killed in the fight on the 18th," Effie's fiancé wrote his mother. "I hope and trust he is mistaken." As he sought to avoid the truth Lowell rationalized that as Rob had missed serving with "the old Second" at Gettysburg, he would forever escape harm: "I had *always* felt of Rob, too, that he was not going to be killed." An Amherst newspaper flatly reported on July 30 that "Col. Shaw of the 54th Mass. was taken prisoner, but is not dead." Closer to the front in Beaufort, Charlotte Forten prayed "that our colonel, *ours* especially he seemed to me, is not killed." But on the evening of July 24 she received "the news of Col. Shaw's death is confirmed. There can no longer be any doubt." Rob's was surely

THE AMERICAN TELEGRAPH COMPANY,

NORTH, SOUTH, EAST AND WEST.

Connecting with all the Southern, Eastern and Northern Lines of Telegraph.

My letter must not be known to the family until the rumor is verified. Do not let news paper of tomorrow be seen

Ogden

Neither side's military employed a branch to inform families of a loss, so parents and spouses relied on newspaper listings of soldiers killed, wounded, or missing. After the publication of numerous and contradictory reports regarding Shaw's fate, Annie's father cabled his son not to allow Annie or the rest of the family to see any newspapers until he could obtain definitive word on whether Rob was dead or alive. *Courtesy New York Historical Society.*

"a glorious death," Forten reflected. "But oh, it is hard, very hard for the young wife, so late a bride."[29]

The heartbreaking news proved hardest, of course, for those who resided in Massachusetts and New York. Annie's father, Ogden Haggerty, abandoned all hope by July 24, but he counseled his son Charles not to allow Annie or the Shaws to know that "until the rumor is verified." "Do not let news papers of tomorrow be seen," he added in a terse cable. Governor Andrew had yet to receive official confirmation of Shaw's death, but on July 30 he forwarded the Haggerty family a letter he had received from Edward Pierce's wife, together with an account of the attack from the Richmond *Enquirer.* "Candor compels me to say that I have no reason to believe that he survives," Andrew cabled, signing his name with "the deepest sympathy for you and your family." Black editors across the North received word from their soldier-correspondents on Morris Island,

and Manhattan's *Weekly Anglo-African* reported on July 26 that "as we go to press the telegraph brings us the sad news of the death of Robert G. Shaw."[30]

Memorials and testimonials poured in, from the Massachusetts and abolitionist press and also from the officers who had served with Shaw. "If the reports of his death are true," observed the Worcester *Massachusetts Spy,* "his regiment will have lost an able commander and a devoted friend, while the state will mourn the loss of another of her gifted sons." The *Boston Transcript* added that "when record is made up of those who nobly fought and died to save our free nationality, shining high and bright upon it will be the name of Col. Robert G. Shaw." General Gillmore tendered his "heartfelt sympathy & condolence" to the "friends & relations of those brave and gallant men" who perished at Wagner, and Pen Hallowell later insisted "that in the great war with the slave power the figure that stands out in boldest relief is that of Colonel Shaw." Rob, thought his old classmate, "was the fair type of all that was brave, generous, beautiful, and of all that was best worth fighting for in the war of the slaveholders' Rebellion." From Beaufort, General Rufus Saxton sent "a tribute" to the *Liberator,* enjoining William Lloyd Garrison's readers to "cherish in their inmost hearts the memory of one who did not hesitate to sacrifice all the attractions of a high social position, wealth, and home, and his own noble life, for the sake of humanity." Writing only three days after the conference with Hagood confirmed Shaw's death, Saxton thought that the "truths and principles for which he fought and died still live" and would be vindicated "by the ditch into which his mangled and bleeding body was thrown."[31]

Saxton was hardly the only person to be offended by the theft of Shaw's personal possessions and the dishonorable treatment of his corpse. As early as July 24, survivors of the battle began to pool their meager resources— they had still not gotten paid—to locate and send their colonel's body home. The men "all declare that they will dig for his body till they find it," Gooding reported. Evidently embarrassed by their behavior, Confederates in Charleston began to claim that Rob had not been buried with his soldiers, but "was put into a separate grave between two other Union officers." The site might easily be found after the war, one officer maintained.[32]

Frank Shaw was having none of it. On August 24, in what became a widely republished letter, he wrote to Gillmore, observing that any attempt to recover his son's body was undesired by the Shaw family. Transforming a calculated slight into a moral triumph, Frank observed that he believed "that a soldier's most appropriate burial-place is on the field where he has fallen." He hoped that the general "will forbid the desecration of his remains or of those buried with him." The general agreed. "Had it been possible to obtain the body of Col. Shaw immediately after the battle," Gillmore noted, he would have done so. But now that option had passed. "Surely, no resting-place for your son could be found more fitting than the scene where his courage and devotion were so conspicuously displayed." Gillmore assured the Shaws that "on no authority less than your own shall your son's remains be disturbed."[33]

The black press, even as it mourned Shaw, reminded Northern readers that it was not merely white officers who had streamed toward Wagner's guns. Manhattan's *Weekly Anglo-African* listed Shaw's name at the top of its column "Casualties at Fort Wagner," but the paper methodically recorded the name, rank, wounds, and hometown of each dead or injured soldier. The numbers were sobering. Of the 650 men of the Fifty-fourth who marched up the beach, 272, or 42 percent, were listed as casualties. Of the 34 men immediately killed in action, 23 were officers leading the charge; only eight white officers emerged unscathed. The William Henry Harrison who hailed from Michigan lay among the dead. Among the 146 soldiers who were wounded was James Krunkleton, the only one of the four Pennsylvania brothers not to be killed or wounded two days before on James Island. The categories of killed and wounded merged after five later died of their injuries. Private George Washington, for instance, breathed his last on August 3, eight days after his fellow Syracusean Charles Reason died in the hospital of wounds. As Robert Hamilton, the editor of the *Anglo-African,* was quick to point out, since the federal government continued to deduct $3 each month for uniforms, even after the regiment had refused payment, "every man who died in battle, or by disease, died actually in debt to the government." The sad truth was that "the men who gave their lives to the country," Hamilton observed, were "brought in debt on the Quartermaster's accounts for the uniforms which the rebels stripped from their bodies after death."[34]

The white soldiers who supported the Fifty-fourth also paid a heavy price. Of the 540 men in the Sixth Connecticut who engaged in the assault, 15 died, with total casualties of 138. The New Yorkers fared worse still. Their active-duty roster was smaller, at 420, but 54 men from the Forty-eighth died, and their total casualties of 242—or 57 percent of the regiment involved in the July 18 action—was only 30 fewer men than the losses suffered by the Fifty-fourth. In the course of one long night, U.S. forces suffered casualties of 1,515. Within the battery, Confederate losses amounted to 36 killed and 133 wounded.[35]

Northern readers worried not only about the wounded and the families of the dead but also about the 73 soldiers from the Fifty-fourth reported missing or captured. Northern blacks, and especially those parents who had emigrated out of the South early in their lives, had little confidence that Confederate officials would draw a neat distinction between runaways in blue and their sons who had been born free in the North. Lincoln's administration, one Pennsylvania newspaper insisted, "should at once demand from the rebel ringleaders an explicit guarantee of the same treatment that all our soldiers in their hands receive." Among those wounded and carried into Charleston were Nathaniel Hurley, a Douglass family friend from Rochester; Robert Lyons, yet another of the small Mercersburg, Pennsylvania, contingent; and Sergeant Robert Simmons, whose young nephew had been clubbed to death in the Manhattan riots. His arm shattered by a ball, Simmons was moved to a Confederate hospital. Surgeons amputated his arm, but he died in Charleston sometime that August.[36]

IN THE AFTERMATH OF THE ASSAULT ON WAGNER, PEOPLE ACROSS THE North and South took stock of just what the July 18 battle meant against the backdrop of the broader conflict. As the men of the Fifty-fourth had understood as they dashed up the beach, their trial of July 18 was not merely a single battle. It had the potential to shape public opinion. The official Confederate response to the battle, particularly among politicians and senior officers, was a curious mixture of elation that the battery had held and revulsion over the use of black troops. "Praise be to God," Beauregard cabled General Joseph E. Johnston and three other Confederate generals. "Anniversary of Bull Run gloriously celebrated." In a lengthy report on the U.S. assaults of July 11 and 18, General Roswell S. Ripley praised "the brave officers and men" who defended Wagner and condemned Gillmore for putting "the poor negroes, whom they had forced into an unnatural service, in front, to be, as they were, slaughtered indiscriminately." Unable to conceive of a world in which black men actually volunteered to serve their country, Ripley at least took solace in the fact that "the colors under which they were sent to butchery by hypocrisy and inhumanity fell, dragged in blood and sand, in the ditch."[37]

As Southern gentry who defined their sense of self and honor by what they were *not*—which is to say, black or poor or under the authority of another—Confederate officers regarded having to fight against African American soldiers who saw themselves as equals on the battlefield to be especially demeaning. The editor of the Charleston *Courier* was indignant that Confederate troops had to fend off "a mongrel set of trash." A correspondent for the *New-York Tribune,* who had been permitted to attend the officers' conference of July 24 and overheard Hagood's dismissive remark about Shaw's body, chatted briefly with several Confederates. "We are gentlemen," one complained, "and here you are sending us your negroes to pollute our soil." As South Carolina was home to roughly 100,000 more blacks than whites on the day of its secession, the officer's objection had nothing to do with the blackening of his state and everything to do with having to fight black sergeants and corporals. Even army surgeons shared that attitude. When one of the captured U.S. officers grumbled about being housed in the same hospital ward with privates, the doctor sneered "that if they put themselves on a par with negroes as soldiers, the same relation must be maintained under all circumstances while they are in our hands."[38]

The Southern soldiers who actually faced the Fifty-fourth during those July days had a differing opinion, at least of their adversaries' abilities as fighting men. William Ball, a wealthy Carolinian who first encountered the regiment on James Island before being transferred into Wagner on the evening of the assault, was so "despondent" after the battle and sure that his friends within the fort "were all to be destroyed" that his mother begged him not "to give up entirely, before the black servants particularly." William Scott, serving on Morris Island with the Ninth New Hampshire, wrote to tell his parents of a Confederate prisoner he had spoken to on the day after the second assault. The captured soldier "said that he had been in all the

battles in Virginia and had never seen any [of] our troops fight as we did."
Lieutenant Iredell Jones of the First South Carolina told his father a very
similar tale. "The negroes fought gallantly, and were headed by as brave a
Colonel as ever lived." After the battle, Jones spoke to a number of the prisoners, and he admitted that the "negroes were as fine looking set as I ever
saw—large, strong, muscular fellows." Aware that his own clothing was
badly worn and tattered, he could not help noticing that "they were splendidly uniformed." Even the habitually fiery publisher of the Charleston
Courier conceded that the Fifty-fourth performed with enormous courage,
although he grumbled that their "bravery was worthy of a better cause."[39]

In the North, the abolitionist and Republican press was ecstatic in the
face of defeat. Garrison's *Liberator* crowed that while many "had prophe-
sied that the colored man would not stand fire," the bravery of the Fifty-
fourth forced those doubters to "finally yield in his favor." "Fresh honors
crown the colored troops," editorialized the New York *Evening Post*. Their
relentless march up the beach into "a stream of fire," the *Post* maintained,
was a "severe test, which would have tried even veteran troops." The reli-
ably progressive *Boston Transcript* contrasted the "heroic conduct" of the
regiment with the "ruffians and assassins of the New York mob." The editor
hoped that there was no longer "a person in the loyal States" who had read
of the battle "without feeling his prejudices insensibly giving way before
such examples of fortitude and daring." Echoing Lewis Douglass's portrayal
of the skirmish on James Island, the *Cincinnati Daily Gazette,* a Republican
newspaper, reported that the black soldiers at Wagner had "fought with the
desperation of tigers." The *Manchester Daily Mirror* offered grudging praise,
remarking that "the Mass. 54th is composed of good stuff, [even] if they
are colored." The most effusive editorial to appear in a pro-administration
newspaper, however, was published in Horace Greeley's *New-York Tribune*.
The battle, Greeley supposed, "made Fort Wagner such a name to the colored race as Bunker Hill has been for ninety years to white Yankees."[40]

Pennsylvania was less firmly ensconced in the Republican camp than
was New York, yet Pennsylvania's *Washington Reporter* was every bit as
lavish in its praise as Garrison or Greeley. At a time when black men
could not vote in the Quaker State and white "prejudices have hitherto
kept [them] at every conceivable disadvantage," the editor remarked,
black Pennsylvanians had not only marched up to Readville to enlist but

comprised, the editor bragged, the largest state contingent in the regiment. "The experiment has begun," he added, and at Wagner the Fifty-fourth were "magnificent for their steadiness, impetuosity, and dauntless courage." Were all Union troops "as single hearted as these soldiers, our difficulties would disappear."[41]

If a few conservative journalists continued to harbor doubts about black soldiers, they were politic enough to remain silent in the weeks after Wagner. Although no Democratic journal published a formal retraction or apology, one by one they commended Shaw's regiment and called for more black troops. "Not myself a believer in the arming of negroes, free or contraband, as soldiers," one New York correspondent admitted, "I must do this regiment the credit of fighting bravely and well." He reported that some of those who died had the opportunity to become Confederate prisoners, but "they declined in every instance." Far from running from the melee, "several fell pierced by many bullets while fighting singly with half a dozen rebels." The men of the Fifty-fourth were "evidently made of good stuff," the correspondent concluded, "and no better fighting can be asked for than they did on James Island when so furiously attacked." One Democratic paper in Ohio conceded that the men had shown "undaunted bravery" in the fight, while the *New York Times* admitted that such courage under fire proved that black soldiers were "entitled to assert their rights to manhood." In a lengthy editorial, the *Chicago Tribune,* a longtime Lincoln critic, acknowledged that public opinion was evolving rapidly on the question. "Opposition to make a soldier of the negro has nearly ceased everywhere," the editor recognized. The "government and the people have woke up to the importance of negro soldiers in the conduct of the war." Thanks to the events of July 16 and 18, the "thing, therefore, is now settled—the negroes will fight."[42]

With that sentiment, white soldiers agreed. During the first two years of the war, senior officers, particularly those from the Midwest, had routinely insisted that it debased Northern soldiers to have black men anywhere in the Union ranks and that, at the first sign of black enlistments, whites would desert in droves. Junior officers from New England were the first to dissent from that view, but even in that Republican stronghold, Governor Andrew's experiment had hardly been enthusiastically embraced. One lieutenant claimed that while he had never doubted that "Massachusetts and her colored troops" would perform admirably if given the chance, "other regiments declare their surprise, and state that they do not wish better nor braver soldiers" than the Fifty-fourth. Dr. Lincoln Stone, the regiment's head surgeon, had obviously believed in Andrew's cause enough to sign on, but his post-Wagner communications with Boston editors were surely not mere wishful thinking. "I really think they showed themselves very brave, true soldiers, in both of the engagements they have been in," Stone reflected. Two serious fights within the span of two days, he thought, "has gone far to remove whatever prejudice may have existed in this department against colored troops."[43]

Captain Charles Russell Lowell had never hidden the fact that he regarded Shaw's willingness to accept the colonelcy of the regiment a fool's errand. Despite his fondness for Rob and love for Effie, Lowell always doubted that African Americans could make capable soldiers. After Wagner, Lowell converted, and not merely because he mourned the man who was to have been his brother-in-law. "Since Rob's death I have a stronger *personal* desire to help make it clear that the black troops are *the* instrument which alone can end the rebellion," he admitted. "I did what little I could to help the Fifty-fourth for his sake and for its own sake before," a somewhat guilty Lowell pled, "but since July 18th, I think I can do more." Lowell hinted that he would be "very glad to assist in the organization of a black cavalry—if I am wanted," and told another correspondent that since Shaw's death he had developed "a personal feeling in the matter to see black troops made a success," in part as he wished to "justify the use (or sacrifice) made of them at Wagner." Even Charles Francis Adams Jr. dropped his earlier opposition to the use of black troops. "The negro regiment question is our greatest victory of the war so far," he assured his father, adding that "in the army, these are so much of a success that they will soon be the fashion." Writing from Virginia just four days after the battle, Adams had already encountered several senior officers who once held "a conservative's prejudices against their use," but now were "confident that under good officers they will make troops equal to the best."[44]

Remorse was common among white soldiers and officers. Long nights between battles gave even the least reflective soldiers opportunity to examine long-held opinions on black inferiority. Noticing that the camp newspaper was in the habit of routinely "calling all negroes boys," one Ohio soldier realized that it had never occurred to him to question the practice, yet suddenly it "sounds rather strangely." The curious timing between the Manhattan draft riots and the heroism of the Fifty-fourth led another, Private Wilbur Fisk, to understand that his fellow white Northerners had to collectively confront their racism. By mindlessly accepting "wholly wrong, unnatural and unjustifiable" discriminatory practices and laws, he and his neighbors had kept "the souls of the Africans" almost as enchained as did white Southerners. Now, Fisk believed, Northerners had to repent and face up to their "fearful responsibility" in reforming their country. Carlos Lyman, another Ohioan, confided to his sister that many in his regiment had come to believe that the protracted conflict was a compulsory atonement for his state's biased past, and that the only way to justify the carnage was to demand "the equal freedom of all men in this country *regardless of color*."[45]

These anecdotes perhaps reveal a general change of heart, or at least the beginnings of one. But the immediate, dramatic changes brought about by the success of the Fifty-fourth were readily apparent. Writing to Senator Henry Wilson from Beaufort, Colonel Augustus Hamlin, the medical inspector for the U.S. Army, swore that racist "slander will not affect the reputation of that regiment in the two battles in which they have taken part." A Maine Republican and the former surgeon general of that state, the colonel had powerful connections in Washington; his uncle was Vice President Hannibal Hamlin, an early advocate of the use of black troops. Even more influential was the advice of Major General Ulysses S. Grant, fresh from his July triumph at Vicksburg, Mississippi. "I have given the subject of arming the negro my hearty support," Grant assured President Lincoln on August 23. The use of black troops would be the "heavyest blow yet given the Confederacy," Grant believed. By "arming the negro we have added a powerful ally," he added. "They will make good soldiers and taking them from the enemy weakens him in the same proportion [that] they strengthen us." The assault on Wagner, while a military disaster, quickly became a political victory.[46]

LINCOLN REQUIRED NO FURTHER PERSUASION. BY EARLY AUGUST, Lincoln announced plans to enlist "at least a hundred thousand" black soldiers. As Joseph Holt, the judge advocate general of the U.S. Army, put it to Secretary Edwin Stanton that same month, "The tenacious and brilliant valor displayed by troops of this race has sufficiently demonstrated to the President and to the country the character of the service for which they are capable." Now that official Washington was on board, Garrison enthused, both Northern states and the federal government—in the case of Southern units—were in the process of organizing twenty-five new black regiments. A second, Garrison bragged, was already "in the field," an allusion to the Massachusetts Fifty-fifth, which by that date had already debarked on Morris Island to assist in the next campaign against Wagner. Although some of these new regiments hailed from free states such as Pennsylvania, Ohio, and Rhode Island, others were being raised in Baltimore, at Fort Monroe in Virginia, in Tennessee, and in North Carolina, with one regiment from the nation's capital "ready for service" and a second one "nearly half full" at 500 recruits. By year's end, as recruiter Martin Delany reported to the War Department from Chicago, the number of USCT regiments would reach 60, well on the way to the final tally of 175 units, or roughly one-tenth of all the manpower in the American army. One of those recruits would be Delany. His son Toussaint L'Ouverture Delany had survived the fighting on James and Morris Islands; the elder Delany would be commissioned as a major, the first African American to become a field officer in the U.S. Army.[47]

Their numbers did not merely bring fresh muscle to a bloodied army and a war-weary Northern public. Black soldiers fought for more than reunion, and certainly for more than sectional restoration; as Frederick Douglass often remarked, they fought "for nationality and for a place with all other classes of our fellow citizens," as many of the home states of the Fifty-fourth had resolutely refused to recognize them as such. They joined up, as one editor observed, understanding that there must be no further "union with slavery. One or the other must die, *Slavery must perish!*" Rob Shaw, "sleeping in that Southern swamp, beneath twenty-five negroes—all have said it. The negro himself, when he charged on Fort Wagner, said it." And now, because of them, the journalist added, the "Government and the Administration have said it." As black abolitionist and historian William Cooper Nell commented as he introduced John A. Andrew to a conference held in Boston's Twelfth Baptist Church the next summer, when scholars came to write the "history of the Slaveholders' Rebellion," they would have to describe "that memorable and historic scene of daring and gallant service at Fort Wagner." At a time when U.S. forces were preparing to launch major offensives that were likely to bring about both heavy casualties and a renewed working-class opposition to the draft, tens of thousands of young black recruits would help to turn the tide in the coming years.[48]

At the conclusion of the conflict, Horace Greeley gazed back at the events of 1863. "It is not too much to say that if this Massachusetts Fifty-fourth had faltered when its trial came, two hundred thousand colored troops for whom it was a pioneer would never have been put into the field," he wrote in the *Tribune*. The war then might have dragged into 1866. "But it did not falter," and so both the war and the nation changed forever. As a father of two soldiers, Frederick Douglass was more lavish yet in his praise. After Battery Wagner, "we heard no more of sending Negroes to garrison forts and arsenals, to fight miasma, yellow-fever, and smallpox," he later observed. "After the 54th and 55th Massachusetts colored regiments were placed in the field, and one of them had distinguished itself with so much credit in the hour of trial, the desire to send more such troops to the front became pretty general."[49]

Having played a role in the creation of the regiments, Douglass had every reason to be proud. But first he had more pressing concerns. In hopes of putting his parents' minds at ease, Sergeant Lewis Douglass had been less than honest about escaping Wagner without a scratch. In truth, he had been stricken with gangrene and typhoid fever and was deathly ill. As had too many white households across the country, black families from New Bedford to Philadelphia, and from Manhattan to Detroit had received dreadful news from the Southern front in the wake of James Island and Wagner, and they were about to receive far more.

CHAPTER SIX

✦

Hospitals and Home Fronts

A FTER MOST OF THE TOWN'S RESIDENTS FLED IN NOVEMBER 1861 following the arrival of the U.S. Navy, Beaufort had become a village of hospitals. By the time the badly wounded Sergeant Peter Vogelsang was ferried down the coast after the skirmish on James Island, nearly a dozen elegant mansions had been transformed into infirmaries. Slowly on the mend, Vogelsang lay on a cot in what the army numbered "No. 6 General Hospital," an infirmary reserved for black soldiers. So far as hospitals went, it was not a bad one: the mansion on the corner of Craven and New Streets had been one of several owned by the Sams family. Charlotte Forten described it as "a large new brick building—quite close to the water—two-storied, many windowed, and very airy—in every way well adapted for a hospital."[1]

Vogelsang remained pleasantly surprised that he had survived. "I am doing very well," he assured the *Weekly Anglo-African.* "My wounds are healing pretty rapidly." At first, the surgeons believed he had been hit with two balls. After a seemingly endless probing of the wounds, they concluded that one ball had passed completely through him, "but from its very eccentric course they do not see why it did not kill me." His close brush with death, combined with the knowledge of what Confederates on James Island had done to some of the black soldiers who had tried to surrender, elicited from Vogelsang the gallows humor that was common to the Fifty-fourth. "But you know the old saw of the man born to be hung," Vogelsang chuckled, remembering the ancient seamen's saying that a man destined to be hanged would never drown. "May be that is my fate," he mused. "At all events, I am perfectly satisfied as it is."[2]

Vogelsang barely had time to emerge from the ether's fog before the men wounded at Wagner began to arrive. The medical facilities on Morris and Folly Islands amounted to little more than several large tents, which one officer condemned as "poorly supplied with comforts and conveniences for the sick, and also with medicines." Those tended to there were either only lightly wounded or sick from dysentery or fevers. The seriously wounded were evacuated to the hospitals in Beaufort, with the black soldiers destined for No. 6 and the white officers for No. 5 in what had been the home of Robert Barnwell; the injured white soldiers from New York and Connecticut were taken to any of the other ten infirmaries that had sufficient beds. Around nine o'clock in the evening of July 19, the first ships reached Beaufort's docks. A runner came dashing up New Street to No. 6 with the warning: "Prepare immediately to receive 500 wounded men." Of that number, roughly 150 were from the Fifty-fourth. "The brave boys," wrote Dr. Esther Hill Hawks, "were brought to us and laid on blankets on the floor all mangled and ghastly." From his cot, Vogelsang watched as stretcher-bearers carried badly wounded friends from his company into the room. "Such a sight! Blood, mud, sand and water, broken legs and arms, some dying and some dead," he lamented.[3]

The regiment's surgeons were initially overwhelmed by the number of wounded, even though they had the help of Hawks, an 1857 graduate of the New England Female Medical College, and her husband, surgeon John Milton Hawks, who had traveled south together to volunteer in army infirmaries. "We had no beds and no means even of building a fire," Esther fretted. But the newly freed people living in Beaufort "came promptly to our aid and almost before we knew what we needed they brought us buckets full of nice broth and gruels, pitchers of lemonade, fruits, cakes, vegetables indeed everything needed for the immediate wants of the men was furnished." Journalist Edward Pierce also marveled at how the work of the doctors was "being supplemented by those of the colored people here." Harriet Tubman organized the town's black women, and while they cooked and scrubbed, she saw to the soldiers. "I'd go to the hospital," she remarked, "early every morning." Filling a large basin with clean water, she would "take a sponge and begin." The same large windows that let in the sea breeze allowed for flies, and Tubman "thrash[ed] away the flies, and they'd rise, they would, like bees round a hive." After she had cleaned the wounds of four soldiers, the water in her basin "would be as red as clear blood." By the time she returned with fresh water, "the flies would be round de first ones, black and thick as ever."[4]

Despite the serious nature of so many soldiers' wounds, both Hawks and Pierce were stunned by the enthusiasm and bravado of the men in their care. One soldier with a shattered right arm lamented only that he would be unable to "strike another blow for freedom." Some of those who hoped to regain their health quickly and return to the regiment assured Pierce that they were ready "to meet the enemy again, and they kept asking if Wagner is taken yet." Talking with soldiers lying in one room, Pierce was swept along by their good humor and laughed, "Well, boys, this was not part of the programme, was it?" Gazing up from his cot, one soldier replied: "Oh, yes, indeed, we expected to take all that comes." The other men in the room chimed in. "Thank God, we went in to live or die," one swore, while another promised to fight on until "the last brother breaks his chains." Only after "all our people get their freedom," ventured a fourth, "can we afford to die." Frank Myers, a twenty-three-year-old laborer from New Jersey, knew he would not be among those returning to Morris Island. His arm shattered by a shell, Myers was going home, but he assured the journalist that he thanked "God so much for the privilege" to serve. "I went in to live or die as he please."[5]

Charlotte Forten was particularly impressed when she visited the hospital on July 23. Expecting to hear the constant, muted moaning that haunted most battlefield hospitals, she instead found the patients to be "so cheerful" that she first supposed that few of them were badly injured. But as she moved from bed to bed Forten discovered that "among the most uncomplaining" were those "who are severely wounded—some dangerously so."

Among the men she spoke with was Sergeant William Carney, who "suffers great pain, being badly wounded in the leg." Despite taking four balls and having the back of his head raked with grapeshot, Carney was "perfectly patient and uncomplaining." Forten sat with Carney for some time, drawn to his "good, honest face." The story of Carney's return with the flag was already legendary among U.S. soldiers of both races, and Forten heard him described as "one of the best and bravest men in the regiment."[6]

Carney's numerous wounds never improved sufficiently. At first shipped to No. 6 in Beaufort, his leg injuries were too extensive for the surgeons, whose central task was to patch up the soldiers so that they might rejoin their unit. Long-term rehabilitation was hardly their specialty. In late October, the army moved Carney to the large hospital in St. Augustine known as Government House, but the doctors there proved little better. Just before Christmas, Carney received a thirty-day furlough to return home to New Bedford. Still unpaid, Carney borrowed "what money he wanted" from Lieutenant Henry Hooper and asked his doctor to "give his thanks" to Ned Hallowell for the latter's "kindness to him." By January 1864, Carney was able to hobble about with a cane, and the determined sergeant tried to rejoin his company in a noncombat position. But February found him again unwell, this time in one of the hospitals in nearby Hilton Head. Finally, on July 21, a clerk in the Adjutant General's Office stamped his Certificate of Disability. This time Carney sought rehabilitation in Boston, only to discover that even in the capital of Massachusetts army hospitals were understaffed and ill prepared for the rising tide of incapacitated soldiers. As one member of the state assembly complained to Governor Andrew, "sick and wounded soldiers are obliged to take their place in file, in the order of their arrival, and must *stand* for hours, or lose their place in the order of precedence." As a mariner with two blasted legs, Carney's path to restored health and solvency would be a lengthy one.[7]

What worried the patients, Hawks learned, was the fate of their colonel. For the first few days after their arrival, the soldiers peppered the doctors with queries about Shaw. "Do you hear any news from Morris Island," one soldier asked Esther. "Anything of our Colonel?" When definitive word arrived in Beaufort on Friday, July 24, the men were heartbroken. Hawks recorded that they spoke of nothing else. At Readville, Shaw had been a tough disciplinarian, but having ventured his life with theirs, they re-

William H. Carney's heroic protection of the American flag made him an immediate celebrity, and his words upon handing the Stars and Stripes to a waiting soldier—"Boys, I did my duty; the dear old flag never touched the ground"—would be repeated by New England students for generations. He became the most photographed soldier in the Fifty-fourth. *Courtesy National Park Service.*

vered him in death, and their admiration for him, Hawks thought, "has something of the divine in it." Sergeant John Morgan, a Cincinnati barber, anticipated Frank Shaw's views on attempts to recover his son's body. "I suppose his friends will consider it a great disgrace for him to lie buried with a lot of niggers," Morgan assured Esther, "but if they know how all his men loved him, they would never wish to take him to any other resting place." To add to their misery, word arrived that General George Strong, who had been shipped north to an army hospital in Manhattan, died of tetanus on July 30. Only thirty years of age, Strong traveled across one final river and was buried in Brooklyn.[8]

Some of the cases encountered by the medical staff served as depressing reminders that the Fifty-fourth was not a traditional regiment comprising white Yankees. After Private Charles Reason's gangrenous arm was amputated, Dr. Hawks asked if she could contact his parents in his behalf. The twenty-three-year-old Reason had enlisted in Syracuse, but he confided to her that he was a Maryland runaway who had fled his master "only a few years ago." Reason told Hawks his story as she bathed "his head and face." After reaching Syracuse, he had worked on a farm owned by an aged white couple, assuring the family that he was a freeman from Alabama. "As soon as the government would take me I came to fight," Reason insisted, "*not* for my country, I never had any, but to gain one." When Hawks again inquired about his mother, Reason told her that she had died years before. Still pressing, Hawks asked about his father. She blushed at her foolishness when the mixed-race Reason added that his "mother was all I had to love me, and she has gone home." Reason knew that he was dying, but since he would then see his mother "soon," he asked only that the doctor "pray with me." Hawks held his remaining hand as he died, then "kiss[ed] his *white* forehead" and moved on to the next patient. Reason would be one of thirty-eight soldiers from the Fifty-fourth who died at No. 6 over the next two years.[9]

The three Krunkleton brothers were united in the sick ward. Nineteen-year-old James had been wounded at Wagner, and his older brothers Wesley and William were already in No. 6 with the injuries they incurred on James Island. Esther Hawks found the brothers lying "side by side," in some pain but thinking only of their brother Cyrus, James's twin, who had died in the fighting on July 16. "We offered to go when the war broke out," one of the brothers assured Hawks, "but none would have us, and as soon as Gov. Andrew gave us a chance all the boys in our place were ready, [and] hardly one who could carry a musket stayed home." Henry, their eldest brother, had remained on the farm in Mercersburg, but upon hearing of Cyrus's death, he caught a train for Readville and signed on with the Fifty-fifth. Henry would survive the war and return home to marry his fiancée, but William was to die of pneumonia in a battlefield hospital in Georgetown, South Carolina, five days after Robert E. Lee's surrender.[10]

One of the white officers taken to No. 5 was Captain John Whittier Appleton, a thirty-year-old clerk from Boston. Appleton had been wounded at Wagner after crawling into a gun embrasure—an opening cut through the parapet that allowed artillerymen to take aim over a broad piece of ground—to stop the Confederate artillerymen from firing their cannon. Although in need of medical care, Appleton suffered from more than his physical wounds. Black soldiers such as Carney had old friends like Gooding to confide in, while the Krunkleton brothers had one another for moral support or to bolster their courage. White officers, by comparison, felt the need to serve as flawless models for their men, and too often their class and their color isolated them from the men in their command. Appleton's young wife was far away, and at times the stress became unbearable. "His brain has been seriously affected by isolation and exhaustion during the recent field operations on James Island," his doctor observed, "so that an absence from the department is necessary to prevent permanent disability." At length, the captain recovered from his bout of combat stress and returned to the regiment.[11]

When the injuries lingered or worsened, or simply proved to be beyond the capabilities of the surgeons in Beaufort, the soldiers received leaves to return home to seek care in army hospitals in the North, or private care if they were officers of wealth. Wilkie James sailed up the coast, first to Manhattan and then to Newport, but the wound in his foot grew so infected that doctors had to cut away at it during his journey. By the time Wilkie reached his father's house, he was delirious and so near death that the bearers placed his stretcher just inside the front door, judging him too ill even to be carried to an upstairs bedroom. For days, his father Henry James Sr. fretted, the eighteen-year-old remained "excessively weak, unable to do anything but lie passive, even to turn himself on his pillow." His doctors recommended a year's recuperation, and Wilkie resigned from the regiment the next January. Ever the indifferent student, Wilkie had no desire to return to college, and always "vastly attached to the negro-soldier cause," as his father put it, he eventually returned to the Fifty-fourth and served until August 1865.[12]

For a time, Ned Hallowell lay on a cot near Appleton in No. 5, the officers' hospital. On July 24, Charlotte Forten paid him a visit, remarking that the infirmary was housed "in one of the finest residences in Beaufort, and surrounded by beautiful grounds." Only six days after the assault on Wagner, Hallowell was in no mood to revel in his surroundings. The two spoke of Shaw with "deep sadness," and Ned surprised Forten by telling her that Rob, doubting he would survive the battle, had expressed the wish that Charlotte would take charge of his horses until they could be shipped north to his widow. Forten judged Hallowell "to be slowly improving," yet she could not help reflecting on how one tragic week had altered so many lives. "How strong, how well, how vigorous he was then! And now, how thoroughly prostrated." Not unlike the enlisted men in his regiment, Ned remained "brave, patient" with his wounds, despite the fact that the army, with its customary inefficiency, remained unsure as to whether the lieutenant colonel was "absent, wounded or a prisoner." After the battle, an officer with another regiment stumbled across Hallowell's cloak and "a bag filled with horse equipment," which he wished to return. But as late as August 6, few outside of No. 5 appeared to know the details of Ned's whereabouts.[13]

In fact, by that date, Ned was back in his parents' Philadelphia home at 912 Walnut Street, being cared for by his father, surgeon Morris Hallowell, his mother Hannah, and a series of doting sisters. On August 1, Dr. William Hunt and Massachusetts state medical director Joseph Swift visited the Hallowells to report on Ned's recovery. The two "carefully examined his wounds of scrotum, left thigh, & hip," and concurred that "he will not be able to resume his duties in a less period than twenty days." The familiar surroundings and the plentiful fare helped restore Ned's body and soul, and on August 6 he assured John Murray Forbes, the governor's adviser, that his "wounds are improving rapidly, & I hope in a few weeks to rejoin my command." Even so, four weeks later Hunt recommended an additional furlough of another twenty days.[14]

Family friends who themselves had loved ones in harm's way took great interest in Ned's welfare. Amelia Holmes, the mother of Pen's friend Oliver Wendell Holmes Jr., assured Emily Hallowell from Boston that she wished she could take a turn "in nursing him or rather in sitting by his bedside and fanning away the flies." Amelia knew the torment that came with having a family member in the army, and she encouraged Emily not to work herself too hard while caring for her brother. "The *shaving*, Emily, how could you have the courage to do it!" Holmes marveled as she remembered Ned's elaborate mustache. "I suppose you are now the family barber." Charlotte Forten, visiting her own relatives in Philadelphia, stopped in to see Ned on August 13 and "found him much improved; sitting up and looking quite cheerful and happy." She noted that Ned tired easily, but thought his "stately mother and sisters were very gracious." Meanwhile Ned himself worried about the welfare of his men and talked of returning south.[15]

As he improved his thoughts turned to who should lead the Fifty-fourth in his absence. Seeking "to straighten out our shattered ranks," he recommended that temporary command of the Fifty-fourth be given to Lieutenant Colonel Alfred Hartwell. Briefly a captain in the unit before being transferred with Pen Hallowell into the then-forming Fifty-fifth the previous May, the twenty-six-year-old attorney had known Pen and Shaw at Harvard, and Ned regarded him as one of the few officers who possessed both ability and racial sensitivity enough. Hallowell also considered recommending Captain William Simpkins for the position, but presumed, based on the limited information he had, that Simpkins was "missing and probably dead." Sadly, as it turned out, Hallowell was correct, and so Hartwell's was the name he advanced to General Gillmore. On September 26, the War Department approved Hallowell's promotion "to be Colonel" in place of "Shaw killed in action." Soon after, Ned, although not completely mended, donned his uniform and caught the train for Manhattan in preparation for sailing back to Morris Island.[16]

At about the same time that Hallowell readied to again sail south, army surgeons grew concerned about the health of Sergeant Major Lewis Douglass. Although raked hard enough by grapeshot at Wagner to have his scabbard blasted away, Douglass judged himself lucky by comparison to those ferried to Beaufort's No. 6, as did the doctors at Morris Island's hospital tents who plucked the tiny shot out of his thighs. By mid-August, however, Douglass admitted to Amelia that he was "suffering slightly from a pain in the head caused by the climate." Although a number of men, including Massachusetts farmer George Pell, contracted typhoid fever while stationed on Morris Island, Lewis's self-diagnosis was incorrect. Two weeks later, Douglass assured his fiancée that he felt good enough "to be able to attend to [his] duties again," even though honesty forced him to add that he was "in no wise enjoying perfect health." Lewis hoped to remain in South Carolina long enough "to see rebellion crushed," even if "some of us will die crushing it."[17]

Just as Douglass was falling ill, John Andrew was considering promoting the sergeant major to the rank of lieutenant, or at least trying to, as the promotion of a black soldier into commissioned ranks would require the intervention of the War Department. Having been too sick to ship south with the Fifty-fourth, Charles Douglass had remained in Readville as an army clerk, and on September 18 he notified his father of rumors at Camp Meigs "that Lewis is going to have a commission as Lieut. as soon as Gov. Andrew returns from Washington." But just days after Charles posted the letter, his desperately ill brother arrived in Manhattan aboard the steamer

Fulton on a thirty-day furlough. Because the city as yet had no segregated hospital for black soldiers, the army lodged Lewis at the Brooks House at 513 Broome Street. As a hotel for well-to-do African Americans, the Brooks House was doubtless far more sanitary than any of the army hospitals for white soldiers in the city. Attending on Douglass was Dr. James McCune Smith, the Glasgow-trained doctor who had become the head physician at Manhattan's Colored Orphan Asylum in the year of Gooding's arrival at the institution. Douglass "was then very ill with Diarrhea, Cachexy [a marked state of constitutional and pituitary disorder] and spontaneous gangrene of the left half of the scrotum," Smith reported on October 6. "He continues seriously ill at the present date, the slough having separated, leaving the part entirely denuded." Douglass was "now too feeble to be safely removed from this city, and, in our judgment, several months must elapse before he will be able to do even the lightest military duty," Smith believed. Sergeant Major Douglass, then just three days away from his twenty-third birthday, might live, but he could never father children.[18]

Frederick Douglass, and presumably Anna as well, hastened to Manhattan and took a room at the Brooks House, fearing that their eldest son was near death. For three weeks, Frederick later told Gerrit Smith, he spent every waking moment "bending over the sick bed of my Dear Son Lewis who has been until now quite too ill to be removed home" to Rochester. Despite the fact that Lewis's condition was so dire that the army made no attempt to treat him at either Morris Island or in Beaufort, Frederick and Anna hoped that Dr. Smith might perform miracles that could return Lewis "to his post as soon as his health is restored."[19]

Within a month, it became clear that Lewis could never do so. Mid-November found him at home in Rochester, one newspaper reported, "slowly recovering from a severe attack of typhoid fever," which was either an error on the part of the reporter or the story Lewis wished disseminated to the public. Mustered out for "disability" on February 25, he would not be the soldier to break the color barrier and earn his commission as a lieutenant. That grim realization was not merely a calamity for Lewis, but, Frederick Douglass evidently believed, a setback for the cause of black militancy, as the most celebrated black abolitionist now had only one son in the army. As a company clerk, Charles was hardly earning the accolades heaped upon Lewis. In November, and then again in early December, Manhattan's

Weekly Anglo-African reported that Frederick Douglass Jr., the middle son, had "enlisted in the 54th Massachusetts" in his brother's place, "and will proceed immediately to the camp at Readville."[20]

When Frederick Jr. arrived in Massachusetts, however, Governor Andrew decided to employ him "in the recruiting service" rather than in one of the state regiments. The Douglass family consented, in part because they found a better candidate for the army in Nathan Sprague, a twenty-four-year-old Maryland runaway and the fiancé of Rosetta Douglass, their eldest child. The tall, handsome Sprague had been working as a gardener in a nursery near the Douglasses' home, and while he had won Rosetta's heart, the semiliterate laborer seems to have had less luck impressing her eloquent father. At length, an understanding appears to have been reached: the family would approve of their marriage, after which Sprague had to prove his worth by joining the Fifty-fourth. The wedding date was set for Christmas Eve. Lewis was still convalescing, and Charles applied for a furlough to attend the nuptials. Nathan, however, found excuses not to join the regiment until the following September, at which time Rosetta was eight months pregnant. He was signed into the army under his father-in-law's signature.[21]

ROSETTA SPRAGUE WAS NOT THE ONLY WARRIOR'S WIFE TO FACE tough challenges on the home front. As was the case for tens of thousands of young women in both sections of the nation, the sort of debilitating injuries sustained by Lewis Douglass at Wagner posed profound dilemmas for wives and sweethearts. Amelia Loguen had known Lewis for years; they were bound together not only by their affection for one another but by their fathers' joint antislavery labors. Their engagement had been public knowledge in both Syracuse and Rochester before Lewis first caught the train for Readville. But now Amelia began to reconsider. She wrote him to say that she was thinking of leaving Syracuse and accepting a position as a teacher, perhaps for several years. For his part, witnessing the marriage of his sister led Lewis to think of his immediate future. "I have just had my attention attracted to those whom God has put together," he wrote to Amelia in an anguished letter just after the ceremony. Lewis "was attracted by their whispering" and suspected that he "was the subject of their conversation."

Nathan and Rosetta, no doubt, wondered if he was to one day share their happiness. "You are thinking of teaching school for two or three years," Douglass asked, "what will become of your promise to me?" Barely nineteen years of age, Amelia needed time to evaluate her desire to be a mother against her love for Lewis, and also to ponder her duty and proper role in a conflict that demanded almost as much sacrifice from young women as it did from young men.[22]

After Amelia left to teach in Binghamton, Douglass was disconsolate. He traveled to Syracuse to visit her parents and wrote her long missives about sitting alone in his room, "that dear box full of your own dear letters to me, close at hand." He still one day hoped "to call you my own and to be your own and then to live on happily together." When the first anniversary of his return to Rochester arrived, he wrote to say that he "should have pressed you to marry me two years ago." While Charles and Nathan continued to serve, Douglass felt "so unsettled" and "very gloomy and discouraged." By the spring of 1865, as the end of the war neared, Lewis was eager to be married. But after a business trip to the South, he returned home to Rochester, and five weeks passed before a single letter from Amelia arrived. "Why has thou forsaken me?" Douglass lamented. Amelia was to keep Lewis waiting for another four years.[23]

Sadder still were the residents of the Shaw home in New York. Rob's mother and four sisters dealt with their sorrow by throwing themselves into charity work, most of which was done with the U.S. Sanitary Commission. The five spent hours rolling bandages for Union hospitals and knitting socks and mittens for the survivors of Wagner. "We five knit 10 pairs a week," bragged Anna, the eldest, although she admitted she found the endless production of mittens "tiresome." Sarah Shaw devoted three days each week to cutting out shirt patterns for local women to sew into uniforms. Each Thursday, Anna reported, she and her mother went "to the Society at New Brighton & cut for three or four hours, tiresome work." Fridays were spent handing out the cut cloth to the "sixty to seventy women" who came to the house "to receive the work & be paid for what they bring home." (Most of the seamstresses were working-class Irish, and Anna complained that the house smelled for hours "after they leave.") By sewing for wounded soldiers, whom Rob might have fought beside in South Carolina, the Shaws performed the sort of work that Rob would have valued. "And this is the reason why, though I feel for you the tenderest sympathy," Henry James Sr. promised Frank, "I cannot help rejoicing for him even now with unspeakable joy, that the night is past, and the everlasting morning fairly begun."[24]

There were not enough socks and mittens in the world to assuage Sarah's pain. "Since Robert's death, Sarah Shaw writes very seldom, and her letters are intensely sad," commented Lydia Maria Child. "A cold indifference to everything seems to have taken complete possession of her." Like so many American mothers, Sarah had encouraged her son to march off to war, knowing that he might perish for a cause in which she passionately believed. But just as the conflict had at last become the holy crusade that abolitionists had demanded since April 1861—thanks in large part to the heroism of the Fifty-fourth—her only son had been martyred. "I have great faith that our land is to be rid of slavery," Sarah wrote shortly before the fight at Wagner. "Would God have inspired now again thousands of mothers and young wives to look upon it with resignation, but for some great end?" But now that Rob was gone, Sarah was no longer sure that her family contribution to the crusade was worth it. "The cup of life for me is poisoned," she confessed to a friend.[25]

As did the Douglass family, the Shaws found some small solace in the ongoing lives of their other children. Yet fate, tragically, had not yet finished with the Shaws. On October 31, just three months after Rob's death, Josephine married Charles Russell Lowell in a simple ceremony at the Shaw home on Staten Island. The following year Effie was seven months pregnant when Russell and the Second Cavalry were ordered south into Virginia's Shenandoah Valley to serve in General Philip Sheridan's army. Impending fatherhood made the young soldier cautious for the first time in his career. "I don't want to be shot till I have a chance to come home," he admitted. But Russell caught two bullets on October 19 at the Battle of Cedar Creek; the first broke his arm and collapsed his lung, while the second severed his spinal cord. He died the next day, having assured the surgeon that Effie, then on the eve of her twenty-first birthday, "will bear it, Doctor, better than you & I think." Their daughter, Carlotta Russell Lowell, was born five weeks later on November 30, 1864.[26]

Effie's sister-in-law Annie Haggerty Shaw was not present at the birth of her niece. Following Rob's funeral, Annie sent a note of thanks to Alec

Only twenty-six days after marrying Robert Gould Shaw, Annie Haggerty Shaw watched from a second-floor balcony at 44 Beacon Street with Rob's mother and sisters as the Fifty-fourth marched through Boston before sailing for South Carolina. She saw her husband for the last time when he paused on his horse, gazed up, and touched his sword to his lips. *Courtesy Boston Athenaeum.*

Johnson, the drummer boy who had held Shaw's horse during the battle; she then fled to Switzerland. Having no desire to be the famous widow of a celebrated martyr, the twenty-eight-year-old Annie would not return to Massachusetts until forty-one years had passed.[27]

AT LEAST ANNIE AND MANY OTHER WOMEN ATTACHED TO THE FIFTY-fourth knew, without any doubt, what had happened to their relatives under arms. In the aftermath of the fighting on James Island and at Wagner, many women did not. For the loved ones of men who were taken on June 16 or those who did not join the retreat out of the fort on July 18, their grief was compounded by uncertainty. Northern families had been aware of Jefferson Davis's edict of December 1862, but only in the weeks before the two July battles had they learned that, on May 1, 1863, the Confederate Congress had amended the president's decree. Instead of turning captured black soldiers over "to the respective States to which they belong," the Congress adopted a resolution calling for black recruits and their white officers to be prosecuted by military courts as war criminals, subject to a potential death penalty.[28]

As the Confederate Congress debated this escalation in retribution, Senator Charles Sumner drafted a public letter to Lincoln on May 20. "I have been horror-struck by the menace of Slavery to our colored troops & of death to the gentlemen who command them, should they fall into the hands of the rebel enemy," he wrote. Sumner urged the president to issue a formal proclamation promising American soldiers that they would "be protected by the Govt. according to the laws of war, & that not one of them shall suffer without a retaliation." By mid-June, the Confederate Congress's resolution had been picked up by newspapers in both sections of the nation, and thirty-four "friends, kinsmen and neighbors of Massachusetts Officers" had seconded Sumner in a petition to Andrew (which the governor forwarded to Lincoln). The petitioners, many of them conservative businessmen, wished it understood that they "express no opinion as to the original policy of enrolling Blacks in our National Army." But since their state had taken that step, they wished "to deter that enemy from outrages wholly unjustified by the usages of modern warfare." Governor Andrew submitted a separate plea that Lincoln issue a "clear avowal" of his determination to "punish, promptly, unhesitatingly," every infringement of the rights of black soldiers. Secretary of War Edwin Stanton assured Andrew that the administration would protect black volunteers "as well as their white officers," but William Lloyd Garrison worried that absent an unambiguous statement from Lincoln that "he will retaliate," Stanton's pledge hardly proved "that it will be done."[29]

Unsure as to whether the thirteen men captured on James Island were to be treated as conventional prisoners of war, as criminals, as runaway slaves, or as some combination thereof, General Johnson Hagood contacted Assistant Adjutant General William Nance, then in Charleston, on July 16. "Thirteen prisoners Fifty-fourth Massachusetts, black," Hagood wrote. "What shall I do with them?" The Confederate general had obviously questioned his prisoners, as he informed Nance that only two of the thirteen were "refugee slaves, the balance free." Curiously, the details of the May 1 edict appear to have been better known in Boston than along the Carolina coast. While he awaited a reply, Nance ordered the captives moved into the city "under a strong guard, without their uniforms," and after that imprisoned within Castle Pinckney. The following evening, General P. G. T. Beauregard, commander of the Department of South Carolina, drafted a similar request to General Samuel Cooper, the inspector general of the Confederacy. Beauregard reported that they had fourteen, not thirteen, prisoners, and that "several of the latter claim to be free, from Massachusetts." Unaware of the Confederate Congress's resolution, Beauregard assumed that Davis's edict of the previous December remained in force. "Shall they be turned over to State authorities?" When four days passed without a response, Beauregard again cabled Richmond. "What shall be done with the negro prisoners who say they are free," he wondered. "Please answer."[30]

While Beauregard impatiently waited for a reply, Isaac W. Hayne, the South Carolina attorney general, submitted his opinion on the matter to Governor Milledge Luke Bonham. Writing on July 18, Hayne referred the governor to the 1740 Negro Act, a comprehensive slave code passed in the wake of the previous year's slave rebellion along the Stono River. As its title suggested, the ancient law drew no distinction between slaves and free blacks, a notion that was easily maintained in a state in which only 2.4 percent of African Americans were free in 1860. "By the laws of South Carolina a negro is presumed to be a slave until the contrary appears," Hayne reminded the governor. Unless captured or wounded soldiers could prove otherwise, their "color is prima facie evidence that the party bearing the color of a negro, mulatto or mestizo is a slave." Since the soldiers in question were within South Carolina's boundaries, Hayne argued, the army was required to turn the captives over to state authorities.[31]

That night and the next morning, following the assault on Wagner, the number of captured soldiers rose precipitously. To the fourteen men held in Castle Pinckney the Confederates added another seventy-three, twenty-nine of whom were wounded. On the morning of July 19, all of the prisoners were taken under heavy guard into Charleston, where, one soldier later remembered, "they were greeted by the jeers and taunts of the populace." Handed over to the provost marshal, the forty-four healthy soldiers were first ferried out to Pinckney, while the wounded were carried to a hospital for captured soldiers on Queen Street. One of the wounded, Daniel States of Philadelphia, later told Captain Luis Emilio that "the colored prisoners were somewhat separated from the whites" of the Connecticut and New York regiments "and received treatment last." A large crowd assembled outside the hospital's windows to witness the curious scene, including a journalist from the Charleston *Courier*. "Yankee blood leaks out by the bucketful," he reported. "Probably not less than seventy legs or arms were taken off yesterday, and more are apt to follow today."[32]

Armed with Hayne's opinion, Governor Bonham fired off letters to both Beauregard and Secretary of War James Seddon. The governor was also evidently unaware of the congressional resolution, as he referred only to Davis's edict of Christmas Eve in his letter to Seddon. Eager to punish the men of the Fifty-fourth, Bonham—an attorney previously elected to both the U.S. and Confederate Congresses—sought to enlarge upon his president's proclamation. Where Davis had ordered that captured blacks be turned "over to the executive authorities of the respective States to which they belong," Bonham chose to interpret that phrase to mean "the executive authorities of those States in which the offense might be committed." On July 22, Seddon cabled Beauregard to inform him, incorrectly, that the "joint resolution of the last Congress" had endorsed the governor's understanding of the situation, and that the soldiers were "to be handed over" to the state. A perplexed Beauregard telegraphed Richmond that he knew "of no joint resolution about the disposition of captured negroes," having heard rumors that "it failed to pass." Meanwhile Beauregard dragged his feet in replying to Bonham, who wrote again the following day.[33]

The precise meaning of this flurry of communications was unknown to officials in Washington and Boston, but as early as the July 24 conference between U.S. general Israel Vogdes and Hagood, it was clear that the Confederates intended to treat their black prisoners differently from white soldiers. When Vogdes pressed the issue, Colonel Edward Anderson, a Confederate commissioner present at the parlay, replied only that "in compliance with instructions, all information or conversation upon these troops was declined." Three days later, when word of this impasse reached Boston, John Andrew fired off a short letter to Lincoln. Having "never received any reply to my letter" of June 18, the governor pointedly observed, "I am unable to assure the friends and relatives of these prisoners as to the treatment they will receive from their captors." Three days later, on July 31, Frank Shaw weighed in as well. His only son, Shaw reminded the president, "was killed on the parapet of Fort Wagner, in South Carolina, & now lies buried in its ditch, among his brave & devoted followers." In

the battle of July 18, Shaw believed, the regiment "proved their valor &
devotion," and now it was time for the administration to clearly "proclaim
to the world" that it would "extend the protection of the United States
over his surviving officers & men." In closing, the grieving father wrote
that if "our son's services & death shall contribute in any degree towards
securing to our colored troops that equal justice which is the holy right of
every loyal defender of our beloved Country, we shall esteem our great loss
a blessing."[34]

On that same late July day, a second parent posted an extraordinary
letter to the president. Hannah Johnson, then living in Buffalo, was the
daughter of a slave who had fled Louisiana. "I have but poor edication but
I never went to schol," Johnson admitted, "but I know just as well as any
what is right." Hannah's son served in the Fifty-fourth and "fought at Fort
Wagoner but thank God he was not taken prisoner, as many were." Like
so many mothers, Johnson had not wanted her son to enlist, but he had
assured her that "Mr. Lincoln will never let them sell our colored soldiers
for slaves." Should the Confederate government refuse to exchange black
prisoners as it did whites, or worse still, force them to labor, the president
"must put the [captured] rebels to work in State prisons to make shoes and
thing." If that seemed harsh, she added, "a just man must do hard things
sometimes, that shew him to be a great man." Her son counted on his commander-in-chief to ensure fair and equal treatment. "You ought to do this,
and do it at once," Johnson lectured. "Meet it quickly and manfully, and
stop this, mean cowardly cruelty." Even after a thousand years had passed,
"that action of yours will make the Angels sing your praises."[35]

Unbeknownst to both Johnson and Shaw, on the day that they signed
their letters Lincoln issued General Order 252. The families of the soldiers
in the Fifty-fourth desired a firm, unambiguous statement, and Lincoln's
order was just that. The laws of nations, Lincoln warned, "permit no distinction as to color in the treatment of prisoners of war." To "sell or enslave any captured person" was not merely a violation of standard rules of
warfare but "a relapse into barbarism and a crime against the civilization
of the age." The president wished it known by friend and foe alike that
his government would afford "the same protection to all its soldiers," and
that if either the Confederate government or any of its states attempted to
enslave black soldiers, "the offense shall be punished by retaliation upon

the enemy's prisoners in our possession." The public directive was as extraordinary as Johnson's private plea. Only months before, only the most progressive Northern whites approved of the use of black troops. Now, however, Lincoln counted on the general outrage over the Manhattan draft riots, together with the praise heaped upon the Fifty-fourth after Wagner, to result in support for his threat that "for every soldier of the United States killed in violation of the laws of war a rebel soldier shall be executed, and for every one enslaved by the enemy or sold into slavery a rebel soldier shall be placed at hard labor on the public works."[36]

Despite, or possibly because of, Lincoln's statement, a bellicose Governor Bonham chose to escalate his demands. On August 8, he again wrote to Secretary Seddon, insisting that any white officers captured leading black soldiers be turned over to him as well. Referring to Davis's December 24 edict, Bonham claimed that "commissioned officers" were also insurrectionists under the state's 1805 law. The Secretary of War cabled back that while none of the captured men from the Fifty-fourth were either from South Carolina or "slaves at the commencement of the war," he had instructed Beauregard to surrender the "negroes captured in arms" to the "authorities of the States in which they are taken." Seddon said nothing, however, about their officers. While he awaited Bonham's anticipated complaint, Seddon approached Davis in hopes that he might resolve the issue. Although he believed that black captives should not "be regarded as regular prisoners of war," but rather "dealt with in some exceptional way to mark our stern reprobation of the barbarous employment" of African Americans, he wanted Davis to endorse his view that they should be put "to hard labor" instead of being "promptly executed." In response, Davis—a man normally criticized for being overly attentive to the business of his cabinet members—drafted a vague nonreply. While it was true that the congressional resolution granted him the power to commute the sentences of white officers, Davis conceded, he did "not see how a definite answer can be given." A frustrated Seddon finally informed Bonham that the May 1 resolution "annulled" the president's earlier order and required that white officers be tried in military courts. In "consequence the officers demanded by you cannot be delivered."[37]

Southern editors, who were as likely as Bonham to suspect that all black soldiers were, or at least should be, slaves, endorsed the governor's tough position. Although J. J. Pennington, publisher of the Raleigh *Daily Progress,* initially admitted that the soldiers captured on Morris Island carried the Massachusetts flag, he concluded his story by observing that "if our own slaves, taken in arms against us, are to be treated as prisoners of war by the Confederate government, we had better give up the contest at once." A similar conflation of freemen with Southern runaways appeared in the *Richmond Dispatch.* While "the Yankee Government" had a right to enlist "free negroes," just as they did "to make war upon us with elephants," the editor huffed, they had "no right to steal a man's negro, and arm him against his master." Emboldened, Bonham persevered in his plans. On August 10, he instructed Attorney General Hayne to convene a court for the trial of those captives who might have once been slaves or who were freemen born in Confederate states. By then, only twenty-four of the captured soldiers were well enough to stand trial, which suggests that twenty initially judged to be fit had fallen ill. Bonham appointed a three-member commission comprising two men from his personal staff and one "prominent" citizen to question the soldiers. Held within the bowels of the cavernous city jail, all but one of the prisoners, though they were intimidated and scared, answered the questions put to them. Four days later, the commission reported back to Bonham. Of the twenty-four, they concluded, only four had been born slaves. Two of the men—Privates George Counsel and Henry Worthington—had once been enslaved in Virginia, while two others—Henry Kirk and William Henry Harrison—were Missouri natives. Kirk had been captured during the retreat from Wagner, while the other three had been taken during the fighting on James Island.[38]

The four perhaps told their inquisitors the truth about their childhoods, or possibly the commissioners coerced the captives into supporting a narrative they had made up to appease the governor. Kirk listed his home as Galesburg, Illinois, at the time of his enlistment, and Harrison was living in Chicago. Henry Worthington may in fact have been born in Virginia, the state that his father, Archibald Worthington, told census takers was his birthplace. But Henry appeared in the 1850 census as a three-year-old child living in Union, Ohio, so if he had been a slave, he was freed at an early age. Counsel had signed up in West Chester, Pennsylvania. Based on the commission's findings, Bonham urged that they be put to trial on two charges. The first held that being slaves, they were in rebellion against the state, while the second alleged that the four had been "concerned and connected with slaves" in insurrection, as the Fifty-Fourth's camp at the time was not far from Higginson's First South Carolina regiment.[39]

Under the 1740 Negro Act, African Americans were not afforded a jury trial, since that would imply that they were the peers of white jurors. Instead, they faced a board of magistrates. The trial of the four men was set to begin on September 8 in the provost marshal's court for the Charleston District. Attorney General Hayne and Alfred Proctor Aldrich presented the state's case, while two Charleston-based attorneys spoke for the defense. In typical cases, court-appointed attorneys wasted little effort on behalf of their clients, but one of the Charleston attorneys, Nelson Mitchell, was a Unionist who had spoken out against secession in December 1860. According to captured private Daniel States, Mitchell "came to the jail and offered to defend" the black prisoners. Although States, a teamster from Philadelphia, was not accused of being born a slave, he noted uneasily that authorities had begun to erect a gallows "in the jail-yard," and that his captors taunted them that it was "to be used for hanging all our colored boys." Mitchell took the case without compensation, "and he was very kind to us at all times," States later recalled. Perhaps unknown to Mitchell was that General Thomas Jordan, Beauregard's chief of staff, was quietly telling anybody who would listen that "retaliation would fall alone upon the military forces of the Confederacy" should the four men be executed.[40]

The editor of the incendiary *Charleston Mercury* demanded that the court ignore Lincoln's order despite the risks, as did one of the magistrates, who assured diarist Henry William Ravenel that the "conviction & execution of these negroes" could not "be avoided by us, though it inaugurates bloody acts of retaliation." The *Savannah Republican,* however, argued "against a rigid execution of the law" and suggested that the soldiers might strike "a plea in defence that they were acting not of their own free will." In the event, Mitchell provided a majority of magistrates with the pretext they sought. The four were subject to neither Davis's edict nor the congressional resolution, he skillfully claimed. The soldiers in question might have been born into slavery, but they had been legally freed years before by their masters, who in any case could not be located. Since the Confederate Congress had overruled Davis and handed jurisdiction to the army, the men could also not be tried in a civilian court. Although it was hardly the intent of that Congress, Mitchell argued that by placing black soldiers and their white officers under military law, the Confederacy had implicitly recognized them as legitimate soldiers protected by the rules of war. Convinced more by General Jordan's admonitions than by Mitchell's logic, a majority of the magistrates directed Charleston authorities to return the four to the city jail and ordered that "the governor be informed of the action of the court."[41]

Despite Mitchell's small victory, the Confederate Congress approved another resolution backing "the actions of the Executive" when it came to the treatment of black soldiers. Speaking before that Congress in Richmond, Alabama's Jabez Curry insisted that arming blacks was "not among the acts of legitimate warfare" but rather akin to "the right to use poisoned weapons or to assassinate." By mid-September, Edwin Stanton ordered General Gillmore to investigate the treatment of the men of the Fifty-fourth. "If no satisfactory reply could be got from Beauregard," Stanton assured a subordinate, "we should assume the worst, and should retaliate."[42]

As ever, black activists did not wait for events to unfold but lobbied the government to act. During the trials, Frederick Douglass was speaking in Philadelphia, and Major George Luther Stearns, the chief recruiter for the Fifty-fourth, encouraged Douglass to go to Washington and press Stanton. Upon reaching the capital on August 10, Douglass was accompanied to the War Department by Kansas senator Samuel Pomeroy. As did most visitors, Douglass thought the humorless, asthmatic Stanton "cold and business like throughout but earnest." The abolitionists promptly brought up the issues of discriminatory salaries and a guarantee of treatment at the hands of the Confederates. As to the first, Stanton bluntly replied, he had publicly endorsed Thaddeus Stevens's bill of the previous January, which had died in the Senate. Yet he pledged himself committed to providing "the same pay to black as to white soldiers," just as he was open to the possibility of promotion for meritorious black soldiers.[43]

As to the problems posed by Jefferson Davis and the Confederate Congress, Stanton observed, that question lay with the commander-in-chief, and the secretary proposed that Douglass and Pomeroy pay a call on Lincoln. Douglass had recently published an angry essay in his *Monthly* on the question, charging that until "Mr. Lincoln shall interpose his power to prevent these atrocious assassinations of Negro soldiers, the civilized world will hold him equally with Jefferson Davis responsible for them." Yet Douglass later recalled that Lincoln "quickly [and] completely" made his guests feel welcome, saying: "I know who you are, Mr. Douglass; Mr. Seward has told me all about you. Sit down. I am glad to see you." The president encouraged the editor to consider his policies regarding black soldiers as parts of "the whole slavery question." Lincoln admitted that the unequal pay offered black combatants was unfortunate, but he insisted that Northern Democrats "despised" the enlistment of black men, and that their lower salaries helped "smooth the way." The time would come, Lincoln promised, when that would change. Though he stood behind his July 31 order, Lincoln said, he worried about using the "terrible remedy" of retribution. "Once begun, I do not know where such a measure would stop." Although Douglass left the meeting without any firm assurances, he took heart in the president's denial that he was guilty of "vacillation" on these questions. As Lincoln had put it, "I think it cannot be shown that when I have taken a position, I have ever retreated from it."[44]

When the Confederates remained inflexible, Lincoln made good on his promise and announced the suspension of prisoner exchanges on November 22. According to a statement released by the War Department, the "rebel authorities, so soon as we placed colored soldiers in the field, proclaimed the purpose of handing over their officers when captured to their several states' authorities to be punished under their states' laws as criminals engaged in slave insurrections." Though the four soldiers of the Fifty-Fourth had escaped this fate, the policy had not been rescinded. With his term drawing to an end, and having been rebuked by his own court, Bonham chose to wash his hands of the matter. On December 8, he notified Secretary Seddon that he was turning the men back over to the Confederate military. "A few of them, it is supposed, may be slaves," he groused, "but the State has no means of identifying them or their masters." The Confederate War Department opted to keep most of the prisoners in the Charleston jail but moved some to its prison camp in Florence, South Carolina. Not until the final moments of the war did Davis relent and agree to exchanges on a color-blind basis. Henry Kirk and George Counsel survived long enough to be exchanged, but both Harrison and Worthington died of typhus in Florence in early 1865. Another nineteen men of the

Fifty-fourth died while in Confederate custody, either of wounds received at James Island or Wagner or from poor prison conditions. Among the dead was nineteen-year-old Nathaniel Hurley, the Douglass family's friend from Rochester.[45]

THE DEATH OF A SON OR HUSBAND WAS TRAGEDY ENOUGH FOR AMERican women in the years after 1861, but for those who had loved ones in the Fifty-fourth, the death often also signaled a descent into poverty. Many of the soldiers in the regiment were but one generation removed from bondage; "laborer" was the occupation scrawled on countless induction records. Even in peacetime, their families had struggled to get by. Now, in many cases, the youngest, strongest male, and the future of the family, was gone. Amelia Nelson of Montrose, Pennsylvania, lost her son Daniel to smallpox late in the conflict. Daniel's father had died in 1847, and Private Nelson, a single mechanic in civilian life, had been her sole support, "providing her with food and Clothing, and . . . sending her money while in the service." Also destitute was Sarah Vorhies of Philadelphia, whose son Isaac had died of "chronic dysentery" on Morris Island just after the attack on Wagner. Isaac had worked as a teamster, earning "$10 to $15 per month & contributed thereof to his mother's support." Having no property of her own, Sarah hired "out as a servant at $5.00 per month."[46]

Complicating matters for both grieving loved ones and army bureaucrats was the lack of documentation for those soldiers newly arrived in freedom. Sarah Dorsey was the mother of Isaac Dorsey Jr., who died on Morris Island during the fall of 1863, and the widow of Isaac Sr., whom she had married in Washington, D.C., in 1837. But "her husband being at that time a slave, no records [of the marriage were] made or kept." Private Wesley Ryal died on Folly Island during the fall of 1863, leaving two young children behind in Sandusky, Ohio. Ryal had married Julia Rice in 1856, but after he enlisted she vanished, leaving the children in the care of neighbor John Mackey. Acting as their guardian, Mackey applied for a pension for Ryal's children, although he conceded that he possessed no evidence of a legal marriage for the deceased private, and he did not know "the exact day" of either child's birth.[47]

The instability of slave marriages was brought home to Harry Jarvis, the oysterman who had stolen a boat and sailed to Fort Monroe during the summer of 1861. Not wishing to endanger his wife, Jarvis had left her behind but promised not to forget her. After taking a job with a ship sailing to Liberia, Jarvis then booked passage for Massachusetts. On arriving in Boston, he somehow got word to her that he was back, and that he planned to join the Fifty-fifth. But "she sent word she thought she'd marry anoder man." After the war, Jarvis returned to his native Virginia, by which time his ex-wife's husband had died. Hurt by what he regarded as her betrayal, and unmindful of her need to survive during his prolonged absence, Jarvis replied that she should "a kep' me when she had me, 'n I could get one I liked better." Jarvis, never having been legally wed, married Mary Jane White, a far younger schoolteacher.[48]

Jarvis might have been a bit more forgiving had he known of the plight of Patsey Leach, a Kentucky slave whose free husband, Julius, journeyed to Massachusetts to enlist. After word arrived that Julius had died in late 1864, Patsey's owner, Warren Wiley, whipped her severely, "saying my husband had gone into the army to fight against white folks." Fearing that one day Wiley would whip her to death, she took her baby and fled to Lexington, leaving Julius's four other children behind. "I dare not go near my master," Patsey agonized, "knowing he would whip me again."[49]

Sarah Thompson, the mother of Stephen Swails's children, struggled in her own ways. On September 22, Sergeant Swails was granted a two-month furlough to return home to New York State. Since Swails had seen Sarah nine months before, it is possible he was given leave to see his new daughter, Minnie Swails. At the time, Sarah was living with Stephen's brother Jesse, who worked as a porter at the Frasier House in Corning. As the abolitionist press continued to hammer away on the issue of unfair wages, the family of the soldier now being considered by Governor Andrew as the test case for black promotion—as Lewis Douglass was in the process of being mustered out—made for good copy. "Think of their starving families!" editorialized William Lloyd Garrison. "There is Sergeant Swails, a man who has fairly won promotion on the field of battle." Yet while Swails was atop Fort Wagner, "his wife and children were placed in the poor-house at home." The publisher of the *Weekly Anglo-African* quickly corrected Garrison, noting that "some friends were kind enough to loan Mrs. S. sufficient [funds] to take her to her mother's house in Elmira." The fact that she was not in a public institution, editor Robert Hamilton added, was "no thanks either to the General Government of the authorities of Cooperstown." But however often the press referred to Sarah as "Mrs. Lieut. Swails," they never married, and their relationship evidently remained a troubled one.[50]

Most of the marriages of the soldiers in the Fifty-fourth survived the war, but not without considerable adjustment. Private David Demus, a young farmer from Mechanicsburg who was wounded at Wagner, chided his wife, Mary Jane, for working the fields of a white neighbor. But since Demus was among those who refused to accept segregated pay and had declined the $90 yet owed him, she had no other option. Other soldiers were engaged, and most of those promises too survived. William Carney, only twenty-two on the day of his enlistment, was engaged to Susanna Williams. Peter Vogelsang had begun to court his sister-in-law, Maria Margaret DeGrasse, shortly before enlisting; she made do thanks to the help of Vogelsang's eldest son, George Peter, who was now twenty-two, worked as a clerk in Manhattan, and helped care for his two younger siblings. Virginia Isaacs of Chillicothe, who was engaged to James Monroe Trotter, one of the first recruits of the Fifty-fifth, had the financial and emotional support of Sally, Trotter's sister, and her own married sister, Mary Elizabeth Dupree. Charles Francis Adams was not engaged at the start of the war, but while on sick leave in Newport in 1863 he met Mary Elizabeth Ogden, eight years his junior. Although the Adams men prided themselves on their lack of emotionalism, Charles gushed that he had "never met so charming and attractive a person." The Ogdens were in mourning, having lost their only son in battle in Virginia, a tragedy that reminded the young pair that romance during wartime could be all too fleeting. Within the week, they were engaged.[51]

As difficult as it could be when soldiers spent time on the home front, once these men returned to the war, their families had to again face a gloomy existence of infrequent letters and intermittent and inaccurate news reports. The question of how captured black soldiers and the whites who led them would be treated by the Confederacy remained an open one, but that was not the only source of the constant uncertainty most families experienced. When the war began, both the American and Confederate governments established agencies to compile records for wounded or deceased soldiers, and copies of the resulting reports were submitted to bureaus in Washington or Richmond. But no copy was sent to the families of the soldiers, and no officers were tasked with traveling the countryside to notify parents or wives of casualties. Newspaper editors attempted to fill the breach, and chaplains routinely mailed lists of their regiment's dead and wounded to sympathetic journalists. As a result, most wives first heard of their husband's death or injury by reading the Manhattan newspapers. In the months before Wagner, Lydia Maria Child confided to Sarah Shaw that each day, as her husband walked out to collect the newspaper, she was "all of a tremble, [and] urged him to take a quick look for the killed and wounded." Although each afternoon, at least until July 1863, revealed that "your darling" was alive, Child had to steel herself for the following day, wondering "what tidings the next paper might bring." Since letters from old friends often brought unhappy news, Child was always anxious when receiving missives covered with familiar handwriting. Before she opened the envelopes, she invariably hoped her correspondents had "not sent anything about the war." Aware that initial reports were often inaccurate, Lewis Douglass had once cautioned Amelia to "never give [him] up for dead until you are certain of it." Douglass feared that he might "be reported dead when I am not, [as] it is often the case in battle."[52]

Yet the soldiers on Morris Island were most worried about the ability of their wives and parents to provide for themselves, and not only in cases where a soldier was killed or permanently debilitated. Months had gone by since the Fifty-fourth first refused to accept the government's racially biased salary structure. "How do the authorities expect our families to live without the means to buy bread, pay house rent, and meet the other incidental expenses of living in these terrible times, we know not," one soldier complained to the *Weekly Anglo-African*. Another soldier broke into tears after he received a letter from his wife, who related that she had been sick for several months and begged him to send her fifty cents. But as this was "not a question of pay but of equality," another soldier reminded Garrison, the regiment refused to give way, and so it fell to their "parents, wives, children and sisters to suffer," while they remained down the coast from Wagner, "fighting the battles of the nation." The pleas from Northern families so demoralized the men, one admitted, that he begged editor Robert Hamilton to spread the word that the "good wives at home" should avoid sending "such down-hearted letters" to their husbands. "Every heart-burning letter makes us less contented and gives us a very bad disposition."[53]

As early as May 1861, as Lincoln issued the call for volunteers in the wake of the attack on Sumter, Massachusetts had passed "An Act in Aid of the Families of Volunteers," which was designed to supplement household income by providing $1 per dependent. Not only was that a paltry amount, but having been designed originally for white soldiers who enlisted in their town of residence, it was not available to the majority of the families of the Fifty-fourth or Fifty-fifth who lived outside Massachusetts. Since governors in New York and Ohio were uninterested in raising black regiments, wives and parents in those states, complained one soldier, were "often refused [help] at the almshouse for their color." Richard Hallowell, Ned and Pen's brother, began a fund for those families who lived beyond the borders of Massachusetts, but to the dismay of the soldiers stationed in South Carolina, Philadelphia philanthropists disliked ceding control of the organization to Boston donors. "The best people here refuse to having anything to do with it," Morris Hallowell confessed to Governor Andrew, "and some are exceeding disgusted with it." This bickering among white reformers did little to put food into the stomachs of soldiers' children, and Congress, having dragged its collective feet when it came to enlisting blacks, failed to provide for even the widows of black soldiers until July 1864.[54]

As a result, those black women who could afford to help stepped forward, aided in some cases by the mothers and sisters of white officers in the regiment. In the fall of 1863, former slave Harriet Jacobs organized the New Bedford Relief Society to provide for the children of black soldiers. Martha Gray, the wife of Sergeant William Gray, who had been wounded at Wagner, and the cousin of two other men in the regiment, collected medical supplies for the soldiers and their families. Yet she continued to think her labors inadequate and so contacted her congressman for permission to "go south as a nurse for the sick and wounded." The Colored Ladies Sanitary Commission of Boston sought to alleviate the "suffering among the families of these noble men," and the Colored Ladies of Stockbridge held "a festival for the benefit of the 54th Massachusetts Regiment" and their dependents. By the war's end, the New Bedford Ladies' Soldiers' Relief Society, a private committee, was able to donate $25 to the family of every black soldier who had enlisted from the seaport.[55]

The regiment's supporters were also mindful of the "sick and wounded" soldiers of the regiment, both those who were slowly healing at Beaufort's No. 6 and those, such as William Carney, who had been mustered out because of their injuries. Emily Hallowell donated $100 to a fund "for the benefit of the sick." On March 18, 1864, the women of New Bedford held a fund-raiser featuring "essays, recitation and music." A trio of young women "sang several patriotic pieces," while a "committee of ladies" set out several tables "laden with the substantials and dainties of the season." The evening raised "more than exceeded their expectations," and the *Weekly Anglo-African* urged the women to continue in their efforts "until this country shall be set free from the curse of slavery and every soldier be permitted to see the sun rise and set on a glorious and free republic."[56]

By mid-October, Ned Hallowell had recovered from his wounds sufficiently to say his farewells and again ship south. This time Pen Hallowell and the soldiers of the Fifty-fifth were there to greet him. Both now colonels, each in charge of one of the two sister regiments, they joined the hundreds of black recruits in leaving behind worried wives, sweethearts, and families who would have to cope with their absence as best they might. New to coastal Carolina were Lieutenant George T. Garrison, former schoolteachers Nicholas Said and James Monroe Trotter, and Henry Jarvis. Private John M. Smith, a troubled young man from Maine, arrived several weeks after his regiment, having briefly deserted the Fifty-fifth at Readville before being arrested in Boston. As the Fifty-fourth again began to fill with new recruits to replace those men killed or captured at James Island and Wagner, the Hallowells and their men returned to the unfinished task of capturing the battery and fighting their way into Charleston.

CHAPTER SEVEN

The Siege

I N THE LATE SPRING OF 1863, ANY BLACK MAN WHO ASKED THE
Boston stationmaster for a transfer ticket to Readville could be assured
that every other African American aboard the car was heading toward
Camp Meigs to join either the Fifty-fourth or, if all of its companies had
been filled, its sister regiment, the Fifty-fifth. Even as Rob Shaw and his
regiment broke camp on May 28, dozens of recruits continued to arrive
at Readville's gates. By May 31, the first five companies of the Fifty-fifth
had been mustered in, and the new soldiers were settling into the barracks vacated only a few days before. Two more companies, F and G, were
mustered on June 15. Joshua Dunbar, a forty-year-old plasterer, arrived
on June 5 and assured the regiment's clerk that he hailed from Ohio. (In
truth, Dunbar, the father of the yet-unborn poet Paul Laurence Dunbar,
was a former Kentucky slave.) Three days later, Nicholas Said stepped off
the train. The harried clerk scribbled "servant" into his regimental Descriptive Book and, not noticing Said's ritual scars, listed the African as being
a native of Detroit. Twenty-one-year-old James Monroe Trotter also hiked
the short distance from the station to the camp. He went into the book as
a "school teacher" and as being of "light" complexion; before the day's end,

an officer—perhaps Pen Hallowell—promoted him to first sergeant. John Smith was mustered in on June 22. Twenty-seven-year-old Henry Jarvis was not far behind, looking, as one admiring white abolitionist gushed, like a "young Hercules in bronze, or a gladiator ready for the imperial review."[1]

Because of the groundwork laid by the Fifty-fourth's Black Committee, recruitment for the overflow unit was easier. John Mercer Langston and George Luther Stearns continued in their efforts, mostly in Ohio. The Ohio legislature, having little interest in black soldiers, refused to provide a bounty for black enlistees. Since Massachusetts governor John A. Andrew continued to promise to assist his state's black soldiers "on equal terms" with white combatants, Langston and Stearns had little trouble in convincing "the colored men of Ohio [to] leave their own State, and go to Massachusetts." Cadiz, Ohio, home to only about 1,000 residents, contributed 21 men, who left their families on June 2 "amid many tears and good wishes." In the East, Manhattan's enlistment office at 55 West Broadway remained open, advertising for "able bodied colored men desirous of going South [to] join the Massachusetts Regiments." Even so, money remained an issue. A second Black Committee, co-chaired by entrepreneur John Murray Forbes and Richard Hallowell, was organized in late July with the goal of raising at least $50,000 to assist in the "prompt enlistment of colored men." The usual roster of Boston Brahmins opened their checkbooks, with the initial membership list boasting Cabots, Lowells, Lawrences, and even an Oliver Elsworth, a descendant of the Supreme Court justice of the same name. As ever, black residents of Massachusetts responded as well, contributing anywhere from a few dollars to one hundred.[2]

Pen Hallowell, who had been stationed at Meigs since February, had already helped organize and train one black regiment. "Promoted from Lieut. Colonel 54th Regt. Mass. Vols. Infantry," the clerk dutifully recorded, Colonel Hallowell now took command of the next regiment, effective May 30. Transferring alongside Hallowell was twenty-seven-year old Alfred Hartwell, whose Harvard career had overlapped with Pen's and whose temporary command of the Fifty-Fourth would come to an end after Ned Hallowell returned to the Carolina coast in October 1863. Now he rose to lieutenant colonel, a rank shared by Charles Fox, a civil engineer who had served with the Second Massachusetts Cavalry. William

Penrose Hallowell, six years Ned's senior and the eldest of the four brothers, signed on as first lieutenant and adjutant; he was a married merchant
in Philadelphia at the time of his enlistment, and the position marked
William's first association with the army. Among the second lieutenants
were George Garrison and Robertson James, Wilkie's younger brother.
Though he continued to object to his son's military service, William Lloyd
Garrison could not resist proudly printing George's name and rank in the
pages of his *Liberator*.[3]

None of the new black recruits expressed anything but praise for their
colonel, tested as he had been at Antietam. They had similar confidence in
Hartwell, who had risen to the rank of first lieutenant in the Third Missouri. Robertson James—Bob to friends and family—was an altogether
different matter. All of sixteen, James was perhaps the youngest soldier
at Readville, and certainly the youngest officer. Like William Hallowell,
James had never held a musket, let alone faced one from across a smoky
field. Undeniably, James's principles were sound, and he later complained
of "the contempt which was shown to these humble" black soldiers. But
James, Garrison, and William Hallowell owed their rank to race and family connections. Although at this point the Fifty-fourth had yet to see
action on James or Morris Islands, by late June there were noncommissioned officers from that regiment who were far more qualified to serve as
lieutenant. Older black recruits in the Fifty-fifth complained about being
led by unqualified teenagers "whose antecedents or sentiments we know
nothing of." One officer advised Trotter that it was "too soon" to discuss
black promotions, insisting that "time should be granted white officers to
get rid of their prejudices, so that a white Lieutenant would not refuse to
sleep in a tent with a colored one." When another assured Trotter that no
federal law explicitly allowed a black soldier to receive a commission, his
reply echoed the thoughts of many in the regiment: "Do you know of any
law that *prohibits* it?"[4]

Still, more recruits arrived daily. Stearns and Langston had done their
job well. Although Ohio had provided the third-largest contingent for the
Fifty-fourth, the Buckeye State furnished the new regiment with an additional 222 men. Pennsylvania was second, with 139 recruits, while New
York, which had supplied the Fifty-fourth with its second-largest group,
this time sent only 23 men to Readville. Indicating how rapidly the war

was shifting south was that soldiers claiming a Virginia birthplace numbered 106 and Kentucky supplied 68, Missouri 66, and North Carolina 30. Despite the fact that the new regiment would march under the Massachusetts flag, the Bay State contributed to the regiment only 22 men, fully 75 fewer recruits than hailed from Indiana. More than half of the unit—596 soldiers—listed their occupation as farmers, with "laborers" a distant second at 76, followed by barbers, waiters, and cooks. Said and Trotter were two of the six teachers. Lieutenant Colonel Fox dutifully recorded that the regiment's average age was just over twenty-three, while their average height was five feet, seven inches. Though the men were relatively young, 219 were married; only 52 professed to be members of any congregation. As a white New Englander, Fox was also fascinated by the men's racial background. More than half, or 550, were "pure blacks," while the other 430, Fox guessed, were of "mixed blood." But the one demographic that truly set the Fifty-fifth apart from the Fifty-fourth was that roughly one-quarter of them, or 247 men, had been born into slavery.[5]

Since the last of the Southern recruits had signed on prior to Lincoln's July 31 order of retaliation, runaways such as Henry Jarvis enlisted with the grim knowledge not only that they would be paid less than white soldiers and take orders from unprepared white officers, but that they would risk reenslavement if captured. Although they possibly knew nothing of the Confederate Congress's May 1 resolution, all Northern men were aware of Davis's Christmas Eve threat, and unlike the vast majority of freemen in the Fifty-fourth, many of these new soldiers had living masters; their enlistment dovetailed perfectly with Davis's promise to reenslave runaways in blue. Samuel Flora enlisted at Fort Monroe, in Virginia, shortly after escaping to freedom, while twenty-one-year-old Theodore Clark, who had fled up the coast from Savannah, was one of six soldiers who listed Georgia as their birthplace. A few others may have been born free but probably lacked the documentation to prove it if captured. The man calling himself Private John Brown listed his home as "Zanzibar, Africa." Mariner Donald Cardoron, who enlisted as a paid substitute for white draftee Daniel Campbell, was a native of Valparaiso, Chile, which was also the home of seaman Joseph Crooks, age thirty-four. Earlier recruits such as Lewis and Charles Douglass had fathers who had been slaves, but they themselves, though intimately familiar with Northern racism, had never known Southern bondage. For so many freedmen in the second regiment, slavery had defined their lives and their view of the war—as it did, of course, for the loved ones they had left behind in the Confederacy.[6]

Because so many privates in the Fifty-fifth were Ohio farmers or former bondmen from the South, the level of literacy was far lower in the new regiment than in the Fifty-fourth. Fox placed the number of men who could read at 477, while another 319 could both read and write. That meant that roughly one-third of the unit was illiterate, and for the half who could read but not write, that skill surely did not come easily. The Reverend William Jackson, who ministered at the camp, discovered that a "large number" of the recruits "did not know the alphabet or could not read nor write one word." The soldiers requested that one of the buildings at Meigs be converted into a school, and both the white commissioned officers and the noncommissioned blacks who had "enjoyed the advantages of a liberal & professional education" devoted their afternoons to teaching privates who may have been weary from the day's long drills but were anxious to "improve themselves." George Garrison threw himself into teaching, an activity that helped to dissolve barriers between him and the men in his company. By July 18, Jackson reported, most of the recruits were "making a laudable progress in the Elementary studies," and the Ohioans especially "distinguished [themselves] for sound practical sense & steady habits."[7]

Although only fifty-two of the recruits identified themselves as formal members of any congregation, that hardly implied that they lacked religion. One evening, just after the conclusion of the tattoo and roll call, a soldier solemnly stepped forward and delivered "a simple and appropriate prayer." The entire regiment joined in, singing what one mystified white officer described as "one of their peculiar hymns." The simple act inspired a camp tradition: each night a different company continued the prayers and hymns. The singing was "really fine," the officer conceded, and soon the men formed several glee clubs. One, from Company F, was considered the best, and they were invited to give a concert at Dedham that also served to raise money for the soldiers' families. For these Christian soldiers, the Bible and the Enfield went hand in hand in triumph's song against slavery.[8]

Nicholas Said, owing to his unique background and fluency with languages, was a favorite of the press, particularly the abolitionist journals that wished to play up the regiment's capacity for achievement. In a profile published by the *Boston Evening Transcript* and picked up by a number of other newspapers, a journalist chronicled Said's "curious and romantic history," praising his ability to speak five languages. The Fifty-fifth's officers thought his "French is quite Parisian and his Italian correct," the paper reported. In the days just prior to the assault on Wagner, at a time when many Northern whites continued to doubt that black men were either intelligent or brave enough to serve, progressive publishers wished to emphasize Said's "deportment and intelligence," observing that his "acquisitions and behavior go far to dispel ignorant and vulgar prejudices against the colored race." The *Weekly Anglo-African* proudly listed him as a subscriber. Said assured the reporter that he had enlisted "because all his folks seemed to be doing so." Yet after a long lifetime of serving others, the former slave quickly realized that he lacked the capacity to lead. Promoted to sergeant on July 30, Said was soon "reduced to the rank [of private] at his own request."[9]

Rather less enamored of military life was Private John Smith, the twenty-one-year-old stove-maker and sometime peddler from Maine. Having survived a rugged childhood and a stint in the Brunswick poorhouse, he evidently thought that the army might provide him with a new and better life. He enlisted at Readville on June 9. Smith's papers described him as single, five feet, four inches tall, with "light" skin and dark hair and eyes. On July 20, shortly before the Fifty-fifth prepared to ship south, Smith failed to report, and the company clerk listed him as a deserter. Instead of returning to Maine, Smith ventured only as far as Boston. He then had a change of heart and returned to Camp Meigs, but not before contracting syphilis. Smith assured the guard that he always intended "to rejoin his Company before the Regiment left the State." Unconvinced by the confession, the camp commander ordered Smith "apprehended" and instructed Fox to try Smith on charges of "absence without leave." While Smith awaited trial, he was held in various military jails in Massachusetts, New York City, and Washington.[10]

Possibly because the regiment's white officers wished to avoid the bad press that would follow a trial and hanging, Alfred Hartwell lobbied for "mercy" and pretended to believe Smith's promises that he had planned to rejoin his company after a few final days of pleasure along the Boston waterfront. Another officer also embraced the excuse that Smith "deserted before the Regiment was fairly organized and in the field." By October 15, the army ruled that "it will be no injury in the service, if he is thus returned to duty," on the condition that Smith "make good the time lost and forfeit all pay due up to the time of pardon." Within the year, Hartwell and Fox would come to regret their leniency.[11]

Army incompetence being what it was, an overly officious clerk also reported Lance Corporal Charles Douglass as absent without leave. While training at Readville, Douglass had fallen ill and so was not with his company when they shipped out on May 29. Douglass was granted "sick leave" until June 29, but instead of returning to Rochester, he remained in the camp hospital. Unaware that Douglass was within the walls of the camp, the clerk then listed Charles as being "a deserter from this regiment in the month of July." In fact, long before that, Douglass was well enough to return to his duties. Somebody finally noticed his presence and scribbled "Corp. Douglass remains in Massachusetts" into his regimental account. "Reported as deserter by error," the clerk confessed.[12]

Having located him, how best to use Douglass's talents became the army's next question. Although hardly the natural leader that his older brother was, Charles was the perfect corporal—organized and systematic and far from the type of inept administrator who might report a famous corporal missing. In a day when military forms had to be copied in triplicate, the neat script he had learned in Rochester's schools was much in demand. General Edward Pierce, the commandant at Meigs, praised Douglass "for keeping things neat and orderly about the camp when all were sick." Douglass cheerfully adopted the responsibility of tending to the sick; he "wrote to their friends and in fact [did] most all that was to do except doctor them." Still in Readville in mid-September, Douglass feared that Pen Hallowell might place him in charge of "a batch of conscripts" for the Fifty-fourth and have him escort them to Morris Island. But as he told his father, Lieutenant Erik Wulff sought to keep him as a clerk in Massachusetts, "as I suit him first rate." That suited Douglass just fine too; as an administrator, he spent a good number of days in Boston. Nevertheless, the army continued to ponder Charles's role, and Frederick Douglass assured Gerrit Smith that his youngest would soon be transferred to the Fifty-fifth.[13]

One of Douglass's trips into Boston served as a grim reminder that even in the North many remained furious at the sight of a black man with a corporal's winged chevron on his sleeve. Douglass was chatting about General George Gordon Meade, the victor of Gettysburg, with some white soldiers and remarked that he was pleased that the Army of the Potomac finally "had some sort of Gen. now." An Irish tough overheard the conversation and "stepped in front" of Douglass, shaking his fists and shouting: "[A]in't McClellan a good Gen. you black nigger. I don't care if you have got the uniform on." Mindful that his father regarded his youthful fight with a Maryland slave-breaker as his passage into manhood—not to mention his older brother's courage under fire—Charles, still only nineteen, threw off his coat "and went at him." A policeman broke up the fight and marched the ruffian off, which only made "all the other Irishmen mad." Charles promised his father that he felt sure he "could whip a dozen irish," especially as he had his "pistol and it was loaded." He might allow Boston whites to swear at him, Douglass admitted, but he was determined "to shoot the first Irishman that strikes me."[14]

While Corporal Douglass filed and copied paperwork, the Fifty-fifth reached its complement of 1,000 men and the Fifty-fourth began to replenish its depleted ranks. Although few Massachusetts residents joined the new unit, many flocked to the pioneering Fifty-fourth. Of the 286 men who joined after the original regiment had sailed south, 161, or 56 percent, listed the Bay State as their current home. Among the new recruits were brothers Warren and William Freeman, ages eighteen and twenty-two. Both were farmers, as was Private Charles Bateman from Northampton. William Henry Morris, yet another mariner from New Bedford, signed on, as did Evan Carrington, a troubled youth who would die the following year in an insane asylum near Washington. The influx of New Englanders— another 24 percent of the new arrivals came from Vermont—helped to preserve the original regiment's somewhat refined culture. Roughly 90 of these recent recruits eventually transferred to the Fifty-fifth, including Private Charles Cassell, a stove-maker from Baltimore, and Jerome Cross, an upholsterer from Richmond. Joseph Crooks, one of the two recruits from Valparaiso, Chile, also transferred, as did Luke Foutz, a laborer from far-off Denver, and James Hamilton, a farmer from Jackson, Mississippi. At a time when most white soldiers fought beside friends and kinfolk from the same small town, the two black regiments claimed half a dozen nations and nearly every state in the Union as home.[15]

On Tuesday, July 21, the new regiment, together with some of the fresh recruits for the Fifty-fourth, prepared to break camp and sail for South Carolina. The Fifty-fourth had trained over a period of nearly four months, but after just slightly more than two months of drilling, the Fifty-fifth was deemed prepared for duty. Eager to emphasize their state's contribution to the Fifty-fifth—and also to remind Easterners of their state's discriminatory "black laws" and stubborn refusal to raise a black regiment—the "colored women of Ohio" sent four flags for the unit to carry South. One featured a silver shield, with the words God and Liberty emblazoned upon it. A second, sewn from "heavy blue silk," featured the motto Liberty or Death, an appropriation of slaveholder Patrick Henry's Revolutionary slogan for black soldiers. Recruiter John Mercer Langston, who had signed so many of the Ohio men, arrived at Camp Meigs to present the banners.[16]

Initially, Governor Andrew had planned to ship the Fifty-fifth by rail to Manhattan, stage a parade down Broadway, and then embark for New Bern, North Carolina. After the draft riots earlier in the month and the lynching of black men, the soldiers, Fox reported, "had been carefully drilled in street-firing." But Horatio Seymour, the state's conservative governor, begged Washington to cancel the parade, and at length the War Department agreed. The men were keenly disappointed. While "taking counsel of fear was wise," Fox conceded, the entire regiment regarded the prospect of "marching firmly and boldly, as they had a right to do, through New-York streets" as the best way to win "new friends of freedom" while intimidating their foes. Just days after the courageous assault on Wagner, one officer groused, "what a re-action in public feeling might have been produced by a thoroughly drilled and disciplined colored regiment" marching through streets that had recently seen black men hanging from streetlamps.[17]

The regiment's departure from Boston was disappointing in its own way. Governor Andrew had planned a send-off to rival that of the Fifty-fourth, but Wednesday, July 22, was unseasonably chilly, and torrents of rain forced the cancellation of speeches on Boston Common. Despite the raw weather, a good-sized crowd turned out to cheer. "Many bouquets were thrown to the officers by their lady friends," Fox remarked, Colonel Hallowell "being particularly favored." George Garrison thought it "cruel and cowardly" of the state to cancel their parade on the Common, which he attributed, incorrectly, to the governor's fear of mob violence. "We feared no attack," Garrison assured his mother, "and if there had been one we were abundantly able to take care of ourselves, as our muskets and revolvers were loaded." William Lloyd and Helen Garrison had braved the storm to wish their son farewell, but the soldiers moved too quickly and the "rain poured heavily down," and so they were forced to "beat a retreat—keenly regretting that we could not, even from a distance, shout farewell." By two o'clock that afternoon, all of the men were loaded aboard the steamer *Cahawba*.[18]

The voyage south took four days, and the soldiers endured seas as stormy as what those aboard the *DeMolay* had faced the previous month. "Rough is a mild expression for the state of the water," Fox complained, "and very few of us have escaped the fate of novices upon the sea." Hallowell too suffered from "the usual intervals of sickness," but he refused to retreat to his cabin, instead joining the men on deck, who huddled beneath makeshift tents constructed of blankets. By Friday morning, one soldier wrote the *Weekly Anglo-African*, "every person was well, and our sea-sick men were as hungry as wolves." The *Cahawba* reached Morehead City, North Carolina, on Saturday afternoon. There they found New York papers that chronicled the assault on Wagner. The men were disconsolate. "If the fort is not taken before we get there, we shall have our turn at it, and I hope with little better success," Garrison assured his mother, grimly adding that the "chances of our being badly cut up are, I suppose, as good as that of the 54th." Such grim bravado was hardly what Helen Garrison wished to hear, although the entire family concurred in George's vengeful promise that if the Fifty-fifth successfully fought its way into Charleston, "the intention is, I think, not to leave one stone upon another, but to level it to the ground."[19]

Lieutenant Colonel Fox appraised their temporary base of New Bern, which they reached by train from Morehead City, with the eye of a trained civil engineer. "Situated between two rivers in a comparatively healthy location, with many fine residences often reminding one greatly of the New England origin of its builders," he explained to his wife, the town suffered from the "two spirits of evil, [which] have made it not a garden, not a desert but to a great extent a wilderness—The blight of the demon of slavery" and "the demon War." While his men bivouacked below Fort Spinola, just across the Trent River, Pen Hallowell rode over to the office of General

Edward Wild, a Harvard-trained Massachusetts doctor who had briefly served as a medical officer in the Ottoman army during the Crimean War. Rumor had it that Wild planned to employ the Fifty-fifth on raids into the state's interior. But on the evening of July 29, orders arrived from General Gillmore at Morris Island, instructing the regiment to join his command and together with the restored Fifty-fourth take part in further assaults on Wagner. The embarkation began early the next morning, and the soldiers quit New Bern as they had Boston, "in the midst of a pouring rain."[20]

Once again, high winds and relentless torrents tossed the three transport ships. "A nice sick time we shall have of it," Fox groaned. "Our little Schooner pitched nicely." Officers plied the wet, miserable men with ham, sugar, and coffee during the three-day voyage. The ships finally docked on Folly Island on the morning of August 2 and set up camp in a palmetto and evergreen grove on the north end of the island, roughly one-quarter mile from Lighthouse Inlet, just across from Morris Island. One soldier in the Fifty-fifth worried that they "were but poorly drilled, and had not been in the service long enough to become acquainted with military discipline." Corporal Gooding, who wandered over a few days later in search of old friends from New Bedford, at least judged the new arrivals physically "superior in material to the 54th." But after a few months on the Carolina coast, he supposed, "the hardships incident to a soldier's life" would take a toll on their health.[21]

Gooding's judgment was prescient. By the end of the month, Dr. Bernard Beust, the medical director on the island, reported "an alarming increase in the number of sick" men. Of the 1,000 soldiers in the regiment, 105 men were in a battlefield hospital on Folly Island, with another 70 so ill that they had been transported to Beaufort. As the men grew acclimated to the Lowcountry, however, they began to recover. "The health of our regiment is somewhat better than it was at our old camp," George Garrison assured his brother. "Most all our officers are now enjoying pretty good health." At least, one correspondent informed the *Boston Daily Advertiser,* the regiment had suffered no deaths.[22]

The weather was foul for several weeks. When the winds blew, the few trees on Folly and Morris Islands provided poor shelter. On August 19, the gales were so fierce that even after the soldiers tied their tents closed, sand continued to blow in. The men used boards to shovel out the floors of their tents, which one soldier reported to be "several inches deep" with sand, and he refused to try to sleep for fear "of being buried alive." Those born in the North complained about the hot, muggy temperatures and fretted about the impact of the dampness on their gear. "Every piece of brass and button about me is tarnished beyond repair almost," one officer worried. "The scabbard of my sword is as rusty as though it were a trophy of the Revolution." No matter how carefully cleaned or polished, anything metal was after "three hours exposure to the air as bad as ever." At least the evenings were "cool and bracing," another soldier wrote to the *Weekly Anglo-African,* "so much so, that woolen blankets are not uncomfortable."[23]

The Fifty-fourth was encamped roughly ten miles away on Morris Island, and the men of the two units saw one another too little to suit either regiment. Those officers who had enlisted just after Sumter were accustomed to army regulations, but newer captains, such as George Garrison, found the military's rules infuriating. "It requires almost as much red tape to go from one [island] to the other as it would to get North on a furlough," he complained. "It is only, therefore, by accident that we occasionally meet each other." Garrison was able to visit Harriet Tubman, however; the forty-one-year-old abolitionist had remained on the South Carolina coast, helping settle black refugees onto abandoned estates and leading the occasional raid into the interior. When Garrison found her in her cabin, she was ironing, but she "instantly threw her arms around" the young captain and gave him "quite an affectionate embrace," somewhat to his discomfort and "much to the amusement" of the soldiers accompanying him. Tubman confided in Garrison, telling him that she wished to return north but General Gillmore had begged her to remain. Tubman interviewed all the "contrabands escaping from the rebels," Garrison observed, and the former slave was "able to get more intelligence from them than anybody else."[24]

For the time, Ned Hallowell remained in Philadelphia convalescing; he would not return to the Fifty-fourth until mid-October. When he at last arrived, Gooding was cheered to find him "looking quite hale and hearty," and his "familiar voice acted like electricity on the men." Hallowell promptly wrote to John A. Andrew on the issue of black men under his command being promoted into the ranks of commissioned officers, as he knew that the governor had long considered Stephen Swails a potential test case with the War Department. While he awaited an answer, the colonel set out to reward the noncommissioned officers who had helped to run the regiment in his absence. Corporal Gooding, one of the most literate soldiers on Morris Island, was "detailed on Daily Duty at these Head Quarters as Clerk," and Peter Vogelsang was promoted to quartermaster sergeant. Swails advanced from sergeant to acting sergeant major.[25]

The Hallowell brothers could do little, however, to combat the lingering racism in the all-white First and Second Brigades. "Notwithstanding the bravery of the 54th Mass. which has earned a certain position for them," Fox confided to his wife, "the colored troops" remained unpopular with white soldiers recently arrived for the siege. "There is a strong feeling against them," he added, a sentiment not found among the white Connecticut soldiers who had fought beside the Fifty-fourth on James Island. General Gillmore, at least, praised the regiment for its "cleanliness of dress, good conduct, and proficiency," and so, Gooding hoped, the Fifty-fourth might "live down all prejudice against its color, by a determination to do well." Despite this, one week later, after being dismissed while on dress parade, one of the regiment's black sergeants marched his company to the front, as had white sergeants leading white companies. Three days after, the soldiers "were informed by an order (without any signature) that they need not march to the front" of the columns, as that appeared to place black men at the head of white soldiers. So "the prejudice against negro troops still exists," William Lloyd Garrison editorialized. Despite their July heroism, their efforts to redeem America were not the work of a day.[26]

Black men wearing officers' straps on their arms especially infuriated commissioned officers in white regiments. While Ned Hallowell was still absent, Captain J. A. Burns of the 140th Pennsylvania made it his business to check on the soldiers of the Fifty-fourth, and he complained to his superiors that he noticed "the guard is sometimes turned out and sometimes not." In early September, Burns took it upon himself to reprimand Sergeant Newton Williams for "neglect of duty in this particular." Burns ordered Williams arrested and confined to his tent, and he demanded that Colonel M. S. Littlefield "see that a proper rebuke be administered." When the punishment failed to suit him, Burns again ordered Williams held, this time in the guardhouse. Weary of these escalating demands and requiring his sergeant back with his company, Major Henry Hooper, recently transferred to the Fifty-fourth, wrote Burns a curt note, insisting "that Sergeant Williams be returned to his command."[27]

When a soldier from the two black regiments needed to be chastised, the men preferred to do it themselves, or with the assistance of one of their own officers. After one unnamed private in the Fifty-fifth committed the unpardonable sin of stealing from a fellow soldier, Fox sentenced him to be "marched down the line of the regiment, with the word 'thief' printed on a board around his neck." Being humiliated in front of his own company was too much for the young private, and when it came time for the unhappy ceremony he "absolutely refused to march down the line." Ned Hallowell "was not in sight," so Fox thought he had no choice but to order "two of the guard to load and cap their rifles, fix bayonets, and take their places behind him." The prisoner obeyed, but Fox regretted the incident. "War is an institution of the Devil," he admitted, "only justifiable to prevent greater evil." Lieutenant Garrison took away a different lesson from the affair, and one that served as a sad reminder of the cultural gulf between the enlistees and even the most well-intentioned white officers. "Most of the colored men with us are rather inclined to be dishonest, I think, than otherwise," he wrote to his brother, before admitting that his suspicion "may be a slander upon them to a certain extent."[28]

As the soldiers of both regiments settled into their new lives on the islands, the U.S. Army of the South returned its attention to the problem of Wagner and the siege of Charleston. After two failed frontal assaults on the battery, General Gillmore had finally learned the virtue of patience. "I don't think there will be any more storming parties here," one soldier assured his mother. The "fighting will be with artillery mostly with infantry as reserve." Gillmore and his senior advisers decided on a two-pronged attack in which the blockading fleet would first shell Sumter and Wagner day and night, and then Gregg and Moultrie, while the Massachusetts soldiers advanced a series of trenches toward the battery's front wall. With Sumter reduced, one soldier believed, "we can starve the garrisons of forts Greg & Wagner to surrender." Major George Brooks, an engineer, was put in charge of the trenches—formally known as parallels—and because the digging was to take place under Confederate guns, Brooks wished to employ the Fifty-fourth, "it being desirable to have older troops for the important and hazardous duty required in the advance." All of the soldiers understood, according to one, that they faced a "long siege of it here." Gooding warned the readers of the *Mercury* that they should "not expect Charleston to be taken in two minutes." Even after the capture of Wagner and Sumter, "there is still a few miles between Sumter and the city, backed by heavy batteries on each shore."[29]

In the weeks after the fighting on July 18, General P. G. T. Beauregard ordered Wagner's defenders to hold the battery "at all costs." Five hundred Confederates remained within its walls, most of them living within the comparative safety of the bombproofs. Beauregard hoped that the number was sufficient to hold Wagner until reinforcements could arrive. The U.S. guns began the bombardment on the afternoon of August 17. Lieutenant Colonel Fox and five soldiers of the Fifty-fifth climbed a tree to get a bird's-eye view as "the Ironsides, all the Monitors and wooden gunboats crossed the bar and ranged themselves along the harbor from below Fort Wagner to nearly under the walls of Sumter." As black smoke clogged the harbor's mouth, the soldiers could see only "the continuous flashes of the guns." Gooding watched in fascination from the Fifty-fourth's camp on Morris Island. "Such a roar of heavy cannon I greatly doubt has been heard since the art of war has been known," he marveled. "Shot after shot tears up the bricks and mortar of Sumter's walls," and while Sumter's flag "floats defiantly from the battlement," Gooding was confident that his readers could "anticipate the fall of secession's mother before the genial days of September are gone." Fox agreed: "The scene was grand and terrible."[30]

By August 20, the incessant shelling had eroded Sumter's parapets; twice its flagpole was shot away. Using spyglasses, gunners counted at least nine large holes in Sumter's walls, while the northwest wall was a ruin of rubble, fallen arches, and shattered guns. On Saturday, August 22, alone, the U.S. Navy aimed 604 shots at Sumter and claimed that 419 of the shells hit their target. Fox guessed that Sumter could "not withstand the bombardment if continued for forty-eight hours longer, some portions look like a perfect honeycomb." On Morris and Folly Islands, when the soldiers were not watching the shelling they tried to sleep, and after the "thunder at greater or less intervals during day and night," the men "gradually became acquainted to their sound." "The next time we attack the rebels, it is the intention of Gen. Gillmore to pretty effectually use them up with artillery before the troops attack them," George Garrison guaranteed his worried mother. "There is a very large fleet here."[31]

Even before the defenders within Sumter abandoned the wreckage, the fort ceased to provide artillery protection for Wagner. One U.S. officer aboard the steamer *Quaker City* reported the fort's surrender as early as August 29, having mistaken its shattered flagpole as a signal of capitulation. That was premature, but as a soldier in the Fifty-fifth notified the *Liberator* on September 1, Sumter had "not fired a gun for a long while." A second black private also wrote to Garrison, adding that the fort had "not sent a shot from its shattered walls since last August, with the exception of a few grape and canister thrown at the picket boats." But its guns could no longer reach the ironclads, nor stretch across Wagner onto the beaches of Morris Island. The fact that the forts would soon be captured by black regiments, the private remarked, was something the *Liberator*'s readers "might be pleased to know."[32]

While the navy continued to hammer away at Sumter and Wagner, Gillmore ordered the Fifty-fifth to construct a battery in the marsh between Morris and James Islands and to drag an eight-inch Parrot gun—a rifled artillery piece invented by Robert Parker Parrot—to the site. Although formally known as a "siege rifle," the eight-inch gun was 162 inches long, weighed 16,500 pounds, and was capable of launching a 150-pound projectile 8,000 yards. By August 21, the massive piece, dubbed the "Swamp Angel," was in place, and gunners from the Eleventh Maine informed Gillmore they were ready to fire. That afternoon, Gillmore sent an ultimatum to Beauregard, threatening to "open fire on the city of Charleston" if Wagner and Sumter were not immediately evacuated. The Confederate general was away inspecting the city's defenses. Upon finally receiving the message, he scribbled an angry response, complaining about the lack of a "timely notice." When no move was made to evacuate the forts, Gillmore ordered the first round fired at 1:30 A.M. the next morning. By dawn, gunners had rained sixteen shells down into Charleston. "It is a sad day for poor old Charleston," Henry William Ravenel wrote in his diary, "so long defiant, & the first to strike the blow in this revolution—now about to feel the foot of the foul invader on her neck." An American naval officer saw it differently: "Charleston is being ground to powder thanks to Treason."[33]

With ironclads just outside of Charleston Harbor bombarding Sumter and Wagner, fatigue parties began to construct the trenches toward the battery's front wall. Initially the Fifty-fourth was assigned the task, but after it became clear how slow and arduous the chore would be, the Fifty-fifth joined in. No white soldiers from the regiments stationed on the islands were assigned this task. Major George Brooks typically placed three companies in each fatigue unit, and they would dig in eight-hour shifts. Brooks hoped to work nonstop, with one unit starting at 4:00 A.M., the second relieving them at noon, and the third picking up their shovels at 8:00 P.M. But "the enemy's sharpshooters were quite annoying during the day," one officer reported, "and it seemed impossible to drive them from the shelter." Instead, Luis Emilio grumbled, "most of the work had to be done at night." During the day, some soldiers remained in the unfinished trenches, standing guard to repel any potential attacks. Each morning at sunup, the weary black soldiers stumbled back into camp and fell onto their blankets, their grim expressions showing "plainly at what cost this labor was done." Within days, their uniforms "were in rags, [with] shoes worn out, and haversacks full of holes."[34]

While the fatigue crews dug, other companies were assigned the task of cutting and dragging timber for the trenches' sides and floors. As the parallels advanced soldiers from both regiments hauled forward the heavy siege guns, which were only slightly smaller than the famous Swamp Angel, their labors made more difficult as the "sling carts" that carried the guns sank into the sand. Those soldiers in the Fifty-fifth who were not digging stood picket on Folly Island. "All details for fatigue were made from the colored troops," Charles Fox noted sourly. "If there were any exceptions to this rule, they did not come to [his] notice." George Garrison was pleased that the men of the two regiments at least got to see one another as the fatigue companies came on and off duty, and a sort of friendly regimental competition emerged over which company had moved the most sand. One soldier in the Fifty-fifth bragged that most of the digging was "done under fire of the enemy, and the men, more or less all of the time, are obliged to dodge the shot of the enemy." But the pressure was "good experience for them," he thought, for they learn to "keep cool" under fire.[35]

By early September, a pleased Pen Hallowell reported, a series of five trenches ran across the island from just above the shore to the marshes facing James Island. Sitting within the front lines were three 200-pound siege guns. The zigzagging troughs allowed the soldiers to advance more than 600 yards from their initial lines; most of the parallels came within 250 yards of Wagner's face, with a winding branch of the fifth parallel approaching 100 yards from the wall. The diggers encountered a number of buried land mines, "which were removed," Pen remarked, but "not without some distressing casualties." The soldiers were so close that late one night a number of men from the Fifty-fifth crept up the battery's sandy wall and removed "a sort of palisade made up of projecting spikes and sharp-pointed stakes." Warned of the crown of spears that sat atop Wagner's front wall by the survivors of July 18, the new arrivals hoped to remove the impediment in preparation for a potential third assault.[36]

Transporting the heavy mortars through the trenches, one private informed the *Liberator,* "was the hardest night's work I have yet had." Just as they were getting the gun into place, a Confederate shell "burst not a great way" above their heads. A shell fragment pierced the ground where he had just been standing. "The whole time we were there, we were under tremendous fire from our own and the rebel guns," and the fifth parallel ran so close to Wagner "that the men in it were more afraid of our own shells than they were of the enemy's." But the soldiers got the mortar into place and returned fire, "almost every shot coming down plump into Wagner." The men earned the praise of their colonel, as Ned "thanked them for their coolness." Even the habitually critical *New York Times* admitted—but without dropping its patronizing language—that "the darkies stand fire well amidst the bursting of shell." But some of the Fifty-fourth were less lucky. Private John Green of Brooklyn died in the trenches, as did Alexander Hunter, a laborer from Cleveland. Shells from Wagner also took the lives of Lennox farmer Charles Van Allen and eighteen-year-old George Vanderpool of Coxsackie, New York. "A man dies none the less gloriously standing at his post on picket, or digging in the trench," Gooding reflected, as "his country needs him there, as he is as true a soldier as though he were in the thickest fray." Even if they thought their work important, the hard labor served to further infuriate the men about the ongoing pay dispute. As one soldier of the Fifty-fifth observed, the "men need money badly." Yet if "Charleston is taken," he added, *"it will be owing to the hard labor and exertions of the colored troops here."*[37]

After the two failed assaults on Wagner, General Gillmore chose to reduce the battery with shelling from the water and from trenches on Morris Island. Most of the hard, dangerous work of moving sand and placing guns was given to the Fifty-fourth and Fifty-fifth, who were only rarely assisted by white soldiers or prisoners taken after the draft riots. *Courtesy Massachusetts Historical Society.*

If the black soldiers lacked the assistance of white troops in the trenches, they greatly enjoyed the company of more than 200 prisoners who had been arrested in the wake of Manhattan's July draft riots. Gooding had lost his boyhood home when the rioters torched the Colored Orphan Asylum, and the soldiers relished the sight of the convicts being put to work "at the very front" of the parallels where they were all "the time under fire from the enemy." The army pitched their camp close to the tents of the Fifty-fourth's, and the prisoners "have behaved themselves quite respectfully," Garrison remarked, with the exception of a dozen toughs, who then found themselves in the island's guardhouse, where they were watched by armed black men. That, Garrison laughed, "had the effect of curing their prejudices at once." The prisoners also turned out to watch the Fifty-fourth on dress parade, and Garrison suspected that "from their looks that they were getting some new ideas into their heads in regard to the negro."[38]

By the end of the first week in September, Gillmore estimated that his shore-based guns alone had landed 1,247 shells within Wagner's walls and that, of those, 1,173 had smacked into the roof of the bombproof. Despite the vast sacks of sand protecting the soldiers inside the bunker, at least 100 of Wagner's defenders were killed or wounded, with another 50 casualties suffered at nearby Battery Gregg. Beauregard and Colonel Lawrence Keitt, in command of Sumter, finally determined that both batteries had to be evacuated. Late on September 6, Keitt ordered all of his cannon but the remaining Columbiad to be disabled. As his men quietly boarded forty skiffs and barges that would ferry them into Charleston, Keitt packed the Columbiad with a double charge, but when the order was given to fire, the gun refused to go off. The few defenders tried again, and when the Columbiad still sat silent, they attempted, unsuccessfully, to remove the spike they had just hammered into the touch-hole of a nearby cannon. At around 1:00 A.M. on Monday, September 7, after a siege of fifty-eight days, the two batteries stood empty.[39]

Noticing less activity to the front of the trenches, Gillmore sent word to Pen Hallowell that "black troops shall again have the honor" of entering Wagner. Hallowell in turn instructed Bob James—who, despite his young age, had recently been promoted to first lieutenant—to take several companies of the Fifty-fifth and advance through the trenches. When they reached the end of the fifth parallel, two soldiers "crawled belly-wise" through the watery ditch and up Wagner's front wall. Both disappeared over the parapet, and for several minutes, James admitted, the hearts of those still in the trenches seemed "as if in concert to stop beating." Then one of the men reappeared atop the wall, and by the gray light of morning they could see him waving his cap. As a "great cry" went up, detachments from the Fifty-fourth and the Tenth Connecticut dashed along the James Island side of the battery and captured the last three Confederate barges as they shoved off. A few Confederates dove over the side and drowned. About 100 were taken prisoner, "and to a man," Private George Stephens commented, they denied "having been in the fort" on July 18. The black soldiers discovered the bodies of two Confederate officers and eight privates within the bombproof, together with "two wounded men who had eaten nothing for three days." The deceased, a soldier reported, "were decently interred by our own men," and although they tried to care for the two survivors, both died while being removed to the camp hospital.[40]

That night, Admiral John Dahlgren, commander of the South Atlantic Blockading Squadron, decided the time had arrived for an amphibious landing at Sumter, whose south-facing wall had been breached by Gillmore's guns. September 8 was a moonless night, and Dahlgren estimated that they would find "nothing but a corporal's guard" within the fort. Four hundred sailors and marines paddled out from Morris Island aboard thirty skiffs, quietly rowing across the narrow channel. Despite the darkness, the defenders either heard or guessed that they were coming. As the marines landed Confederates inside responded with muskets and hand grenades, while gunners across the harbor at Fort Moultrie poured metal into the storming party. Shells smashed three boats. The "barges in the rear, terror stricken by the concentrated fire," gloated the *Charleston Mercury,* "abandoned the attack, leaving the Yankees who had landed" to be killed or taken prisoner.[41]

Even so, as James Henry Gooding informed his readers, "Sumter is a mass of shapeless ruins," and Battery Gregg "is occupied by our forces, a small detachment of men, to repair and hold it." Although yet in Confederate hands, "the deserted castle," as Gooding described it, "fires no guns now," and soldiers from the Fifty-fourth rarely spied "any men on the ruined walls." Sumter's flag had been shot away fourteen times, and while its defenders continued to restore the flagpole, they now raised it "but a very few feet above the ruined walls," and soldiers could see it only by standing on the distant hills of Folly Island. Naval gunners returned to their daily bombardments, Fox wrote his wife, so that "Sumter is being rapidly reduced to a pile of bricks." The daily shelling began at dawn, so "there is no danger of our losing our habit of early rising at present," he observed.[42]

Meanwhile, for the soldiers of the two black regiments, and particularly for the men who had survived the assault of July 18, the fact that Wagner was "now in our possession" was a grand victory. The men yanked the pikes out of the ditch and the parapet and carried them back to their camps as souvenirs. Ned Hallowell sent Jesse Benton Frémont, the wife of abolitionist general and politician John C. Frémont, a "piece of a rebel gun taken at

Fort Wagner," and she in turn praised the young colonel as "a quaker of the war kind." Garrison's *Liberator* reminded its subscribers "that Fort Wagner was one of the strongest works ever constructed by the rebels." For Gooding, who had lost so many comrades in the battle, Sumter's temporary survival mattered little by comparison to the fact that "at last Wagner and Gregg have the old flag waving over them." One soldier wrote the *Boston Traveler* to insist that the "fort was taken by the spades and shovels of the 54th,—deny this who dare." Given the friendly rivalry between the sister regiments, it was hardly surprising that the only writer who accepted the dare was a soldier in the Fifty-fifth. The soldier wanted it understood that although the newer arrivals did not "lay claim for our brigade to *all* the fame earned by colored soldiers at that well known siege," he believed that "we of the 55th [performed] as much hard service as any other regiment in the field."[43]

With the entirety of Morris Island under U.S. control, relatives of some of the white soldiers who perished at Wagner begged the army to retrieve their loved ones' bodies. The family of Augustine Webb, a lieutenant in the Forty-eighth New York, requested "permission to disinter [his] remains and send them to Mass." Ignoring Frank Shaw's public letter of August 24, the army began to search for Rob's body. Writing again to General Gillmore, Shaw insisted that "such efforts are not authorized by me, or any of my family, and they are not approved by us." Gillmore deferred to the family and ordered that Rob's grave not be disturbed. The army could not control the waves, however, and for months afterward the tide disclosed the soldiers' final resting places. Susie King Taylor, a former slave turned nurse who assisted the First South Carolina, routinely noticed "many skulls lying about" as she walked along Morris Island. "They were a gruesome sight," she remembered, "those fleshless heads and grinning jaws."[44]

The failed incursion against Sumter served as a grim reminder that Charleston's fall was hardly imminent. As the correspondent for the New York *Herald* reported, the Confederates still controlled shore batteries on James Island, as well as Battery Bee and Fort Moultrie on Sullivan's Island. Moultrie's cannon were no longer effective against Wagner, but the sands near Gregg remained unsafe. "Around Castle Pinckney they have built up huge barricades of sand extending to the very parapet," the journalist noted, "and have thus rendered that work capable of a strong defense." While rid-

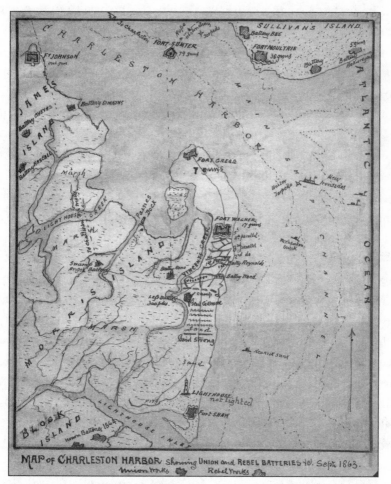

This September 1863 map shows the trenches immediately below Wagner, as well as the U.S. batteries that were relentlessly shelling Wagner and Fort Sumter. On the southern tip of Morris Island, the newly created Fort Shaw guarded the entrance to the inlet above Folly Island. *Courtesy Virginia Historical Society.*

ing along the beach, Ned Hallowell had his horse shot from beneath him; the shell fragments miraculously missed him. Gooding supposed that the forts on Sullivan's Island held very few men, but "they *must* be got out." The weary corporal proposed that a "steam force engine" shoot "petroleum, or kerosene, or any other combustible fluid or oil," into Sumter and Moultrie, and then ignite the liquids "by the bursting of a few shells." Although cruel, Gooding admitted, such tactics would ultimately save lives that might be sacrificed in conventional campaigns. "War is nothing but

barbarism at the best, and those who can excel in that, to put an end to a
longer train of barbarisms, are in the end the most humane of the two."
The former sea cook, who had turned twenty-five the previous August, was
among those who had seen Shaw fall, but his opinions were likely shared
by those soldiers who could remember being slaves.[45]

While shore gunners and monitors continued their daily barrages
against the remaining harbor fortifications, the black regiments were far
from idle. "Our regiment has been working very hard at what is called
'fatigue duty,'" one soldier in the Fifty-fifth complained, "and I can assure
you it is rightly named." Each morning, between 50 and 200 soldiers received orders to perform various labors, "mostly in unloading vessels of
freight and ammunition of all kinds." Sixty soldiers were detached to the
First New York Engineers, where they "were set to work leveling ground
for the Regimental Camp, digging wells &c pitching tents and the like,"
even though white soldiers had long performed such labors themselves.
The regiments' sick lists increased daily. "We perform the same duties of
other Massachusetts troops," snapped Private Stephens, "and even now we
have to perform fatigue duty night and day." Yet they were "offered $10 per
month or nothing until next December or January! Why, in the name of
William H. Seward, are we treated thus?" Stephens had enlisted to fight,
not to dig wells, and the battleground, he argued, was "the proper field for
colored men." But because they were black, even in the aftermath of Wagner, the army thought them fit only for "menial work."[46]

A handful of white progressives also began to speak out. Colonel Thomas
Wentworth Higginson published a public letter, widely reprinted in the
abolitionist press, denouncing "the cruel fatigue-duty" imposed on black
recruits only. It was as if the army had "calculated to destroy all self-respect
in the soldiers," Higginson observed, "because no *esprit de corps* can be
created in a regiment" that existed only to unload vessels. Yet in the same
way that the valor shown by the Fifty-fourth at Wagner had softened the
hearts of some white critics, watching fellow soldiers perform backbreak-
ing labor forced others to reexamine their long-held assumptions about
race. Although he wanted it known that he was no "nigger worshiper,"
Private John Westervelt of the First New York Engineers concluded that
it was simply wrong for black troops to be "ill used by those whose duty

it is to look after their interest and see them get what Uncle Sam intends to provide for all alike both white and black." After the battles on July 16 and 18, Westervelt admitted, "there is no longer any question about their being good fighters," yet they are "put at the hardest as well as the meanest kinds of work."[47]

As the morale of the black soldiers continued to plummet, their commanders found it necessary to make a stand. Colonel James C. Beecher, the half-brother of antislavery novelist Harriet Beecher Stowe, filed a complaint against Gillmore on September 13. Beecher commanded runaways in the First North Carolina, and his soldiers, he reminded the general, "have been slaves and are just learning to be men." It was bad enough that they were daily "called d——d Niggers by so-called 'gentlemen' in uniform of U.S. Officers." But now that sin was compounded by having them "policing camps of white soldiers." Beecher threatened to "forward" his objections to the highest levels of military authority. Ned Hallowell began to refuse to allow soldiers from the Fifty-fifth to perform manual labor, prompting Gillmore to inform General Wild "that the excuse offered by Col. Hallowell for not Complying with the order detailing 200 men from his Regiment is insufficient and cannot be accepted." Wild was unhappy at being caught up in the growing dispute, and unhappier still when Ned was openly rude to the unfortunate captain who was tasked with delivering Gillmore's commands. Wild commanded Hallowell to be "severely reprimanded for disobedience" and warned him that "hereafter any disrespect shown to any one of my Staff Officers, when representing me, shall be regarded as disrespect shown to myself." Quakers, even fighting ones, answered to a higher authority than generals, and Ned stubbornly continued to back his troops.[48]

James Henry Gooding concluded that complaining to senior officers was not enough. On September 28, the young corporal decided to submit his grievance to his ultimate superior: Abraham Lincoln. Gooding hoped that the president "will pardon the presumption of an humble individual like myself, in addressing you," but he wished Lincoln to know what the men thought about the interconnected problems of unequal pay and unfair treatment. "Now the main question is, Are we *Soldiers,* or are we *Labourers?*" Gooding declined to mention that he had stood atop Wagner's parapet two months before, but he did observe that the Fifty-fourth had "shared the perils and Labour of Reducing the first stronghold that flaunted a Traitor Flag." Since Lincoln had warned "the Rebel Chieftain, that the United States knows no distinction in her Soldiers," would it not then be "consistent to set the example herself by paying all her *Soldiers* alike?" Although he was certain that the service of former slaves was "undoubtedly worth much to the Nation," the recruits in his regiment had not "enlisted under any 'contraband' act." He and those who had signed up with him were "American *Soldiers,* not menial hirelings." Gooding promised to fight on, but he prayed that the president might fight for him as well. "We feel as though our Country spurned us," he concluded, "now that we are sworn to serve her. Please give this a moment's attention." Although Lincoln declined to reply, he clearly read the letter and forwarded it to the War Department.[49]

The scandal threatened to become even more embarrassing when Southern newspapers picked up the story and argued that if black men could perform manual labor for the American military, "the Confederate Government should place in [its] army as many negroes as may be needed to do all fatigue duty." Pressured by influential journalists, and perhaps also by the War Department, Gillmore assured correspondents for a number of Northern newspapers in early October that it had only recently "come to his knowledge that detachments of colored troops" were being employed to "prepare camps and perform menial duties for white troops." Having given an explicit order to use only "colored troops" on August 2, the discomfited general now condemned "these details as unauthorized and improper." On November 25, Gillmore elaborated in his General Order No. 104, in which he promised that "colored troops will not be required to perform any labor which is not shared by the white troops." A vindicated Ned Hallowell retained a copy of Gillmore's order, and a soldier from the Fifty-fourth assured the *Weekly Anglo-African* that the general's "second order against the unequal distribution of labor" had resulted in "the greatest improvement imaginable." Neither the officers nor the men trusted Gillmore, but as both regiments returned to regular training with "the most rigorous drill and discipline," they hoped the time had arrived "for the bravest troops" to again see combat.[50]

THE PAY DISPUTE WOULD PERSIST, HOWEVER. UNFORTUNATELY, THE fatigue and pay issues coincided, so that each problem served to exacerbate the other; the soldiers returned from arduous days on fatigue detail to discover pleading letters from home describing hungry children and unpaid rent. On August 5, Colonel Milton Littlefield, the acting paymaster, arrived on Morris Island. Calling the regiment together, Littlefield promised them that they "need not be afraid . . . that you won't get your thirteen dollars per month, for you surely will" when Congress again met. He then encouraged them to temporarily accept the lower pay of $10, asking those who would do so to "raise your right hand." The men glanced up and down the lines, seeing who might break ranks. "I am glad to say not one man in the whole regiment lifted a hand," Gooding proudly observed. Littlefield warned the unit that by refusing their wages, they might not receive any money until Congress convened in December. His company "had been over five months waiting," Gooding replied. "Too many of our comrades' bones lie bleaching near the walls of Fort Wagner to subtract even one cent from our hard earned pay." Not a soldier among them would "sell our manhood for ten dollars per month."[51]

In hopes of ending the crisis, Governor Andrew traveled to Washington in September to meet with Lincoln and members of the cabinet. The president offered vague promises of reforms but hinted that the fault lay with Congress and the wording of the Militia Act. Frustrated, Andrew remarked that, as the navy paid black and white sailors the same wage, "therefore the Navy is daily breaking the law." But the terrible news from the late September debacle at the Battle of Chickamauga, which ended the U.S. offensive in southeastern Tennessee and resulted in the greatest casualties since Gettysburg, occupied the attentions of policymakers in Washington. The pay scale for black soldiers, Andrew understood, would not soon be resolved. Instead, acting upon the recommendation of longtime adviser John Murray Forbes, Andrew decided to call the state assembly into a special session and ask them to pay the difference between what the two regiments were promised and what the federal government offered. Forbes urged the assembly to act quickly "in view of the suffering of the families of these soldiers." At least initially, Robert Hamilton, the editor of the *Weekly Anglo-African,* supported the idea. "This will be cheering news to our brethren in arms, and will show them how wisely they have acted in relying upon the Commonwealth of Massachusetts."[52]

After the legislature agreed to Andrew's proposal, the governor appointed Major James Sturgis and Republican businessman Edward Kinsley as his special envoys to carry the payments south and explain the compromise to the two regiments. The emissaries docked on Morris Island on December 12 and stood ready to disburse the wages. Sturgis and Kinsley were stunned, therefore, to find the Massachusetts regiments hostile to the offer. One soldier announced his "surprise and disappointment" that the state, "in effect, advertises us to the world as holding out for *money* and not from *principle*." The newer recruits of the Fifty-fifth also held firm. The men should die rather than accept unequal pay or agree to serve only as "menials in the Union army," Sergeant James Monroe Trotter insisted. Ned Hallowell was proud of his men. By accepting the cash, he agreed, they "would be acknowledging to the world that the money is what they fight for." Hallowell called in all of the sergeants under his command to read them Andrew's message to the legislature, but "every one has reported that his Company would refuse now and always to take any part of their just dues, until the US was ready to give them the same as other soldiers." The sergeants were concerned about their relatives, they admitted, yet "nothing but the starvation of their families will make them back down."[53]

Sturgis and Kinsley "pleaded with the men by every argument, by every persuasion they could command," Hallowell observed, but "[i]n vain." A handful of contraband soldiers from the Third USCT, who had never drawn a day's wages in their lives, expressed a willingness to take the proffered $10, but the Massachusetts regiments "did not falter." They were "soldiers of the Union, not of a State," Hallowell added. George Garrison proudly assured his family that "there was hardly a baker's dozen of men in the regiment that would consent to take" the money. Aware of the hardships this protest imposed on their families back home, the white officers "advised them to take it," Garrison noted, "but it had not the slightest effect upon them." One soldier promised Garrison that if they had "to work their whole three years for nothing," they were prepared to do so.[54]

The soldiers in both regiments were grateful to Andrew and the legislature for their "kindness in offering to make up to us the amount which we enlisted for," one man informed the *Liberator*. But they signed up "with the same patriotic motives as actuated any white soldiers," another told the *Weekly Anglo-African*. Both regiments had tasted Confederate fire, so "we consider ourselves as manly and as soldierly as any other troops *of our experience, and therefore their equals.*" The units took pride in the fact that Massachusetts "was first to send two colored regiments in the field," but in reality every state was represented in the units, and they had signed on as soldiers of "the U.S. Government on the same terms as her other Regiments." Those recruits from outside New England had long faced discriminatory laws, segregated or nonexistent schools, and ballot boxes reserved for white voters. Racially based unequal pay was the final insult, and so the soldiers collectively decided they "must respectfully and yet firmly reject [Andrew's] generous offer."[55]

As had become his custom, James Henry Gooding was no longer content to submit his opinions only to the *New Bedford Mercury*. Having already filed a complaint with the president, he now drafted a response to the governor—and sent a copy to the press. The young corporal worried that if Massachusetts paid the difference, there would be no motivation for Congress to address pay inequality. "As men who have families to feed, and clothe, and keep warm, we must say, that the *ten* dollars by the greatest government in the world is an unjust distinction to men who have only a black skin to merit it," Gooding argued. All Congress had to do, he believed, was to acknowledge that black men were soldiers and not hewers of wood; no special legislation was necessary. As it now stood, no matter "how brave they had been" at Wagner, their contribution "was spurned, and made mock of."[56]

Governor Andrew, who had called his state assembly into a special session to address the problem, was unamused at being lectured by a black corporal. "While I fully appreciate his intelligence and good will," Andrew huffed, "I can only say that *I* have no time for the effort to explain to those who do not understand what is so clear." Since the governor completely agreed that the two regiments had "the clear right to be treated, in all respects, by national and State governments as *soldiers,*" he did not appreciate the men turning down the legislature's compromise. Anticipating that Gooding's missive would strike a nerve, Ned Hallowell wrote to Andrew in hopes of explaining why the offer was "received unfavorably by the enlisted men of this Regiment." Hallowell hastened to assure Andrew of the unit's gratitude in his "efforts to establish their just rights," but he pointed out that to accept lower federal pay "would be acknowledging a right on the part of the United States to draw a distinction between them and other Soldiers from Massachusetts." Since the War Department paid white privates $13, to agree to less, regardless of who made up the difference, was to concede "that because they have African blood in their veins they are less men than those who have Saxon."[57]

Although they led black regiments, the segregated pay did not extend to white officers. As did most of the officers of the Fifty-fourth and the Fifty-fifth, Lieutenant Colonel Fox offered to serve without pay, but the men "requested them" to accept their salaries. The black soldiers regarded their collective position as a matter of racial solidarity, and while they respected most of their white officers, they regarded the pay dispute as their own cause. Certainly the gap between what Congress paid officers and privates was substantial. George Garrison informed his brother that his "salary I believe is over $1,000 a year," which allowed him to "be of some service to Father and Mother if they are in need of it." Even as they accepted their pay, however, most of the officers felt guilty in doing so, and their letters home spoke of their anguish and resentment. "I would be overjoyed if the men could only get that which belongs to them," Bob James told his parents. "It is disgraceful, the way in which the Govt. is treating them." Fox agreed, telling his wife that he wanted "to see justice done to the men."[58]

According to one of his advisers, Governor Andrew "was at first considerably put out by the complete overthrow of his plan." But as it became clear that the white officers (and their influential families) supported the "uncompromising spirit shown by the men," he returned his attention to Washington. On December 14, Congressman Thaddeus Stevens introduced a bill to equalize the pay of all U.S. soldiers. Since Massachusetts senator Henry Wilson had taken a hand in creating the confusion in the first place by demanding the withdrawal of Stevens's bill of the previous winter, it was fitting that he now joined with the Pennsylvania radical to advance a bill through both houses. As Gooding had feared, Maryland's Reverdy Johnson insisted that if Andrew had promised his recruits $13 in violation of the 1862 Militia Act, "let Massachusetts redeem it." But even alleged supporters, such as William Pitt Fessenden, a Maine Republican, wondered as to the wisdom "in our going back and paying them this increase for services already rendered." The Senate, he maintained, "must not consider that the Treasury can meet everything."[59]

This view prevailed, and when word of this latest setback arrived on Morris Island, Sergeant Major Stephen Swails decided he was done with the army. He had "performed the duty of a soldier" at Wagner, Swails reminded Adjutant General E. D. Townsend. "But the Government having failed to fulfill its part of the agreement, in as much as it refuses me the pay, and allowances of a Sergeant of the regular Army," Swails "respectfully demand[ed] to be mustered out of the service of the United States." Instead of responding to the request, Gillmore scribbled, "The tone of this communication is disapproved" across the bottom of the letter.[60]

As if the ill will created by fatigue duty and unequal pay was not enough to dispirit the regiments, by the late fall of 1863 Pen Hallowell's health again worsened. His Antietam wounds continued to plague him, and under the heat and dampness of the Carolina coast, the pain in his arm grew unbearable. In September the War Department granted him another thirty days' leave to recover in his parents' Philadelphia home. There, he tallied up the number of months he had missed while convalescing. Over the past thirteen months, he had been "off duty" for seven, on special assignment at Readville raising the two regiments for another four, "and in the field [only] two months." Less concerned about his own health than what he owed to his regiment, he fretted that he "shall be partially disabled for a long time to come." And so, on October 5, he wrote to the adjutant general and tendered his resignation as colonel of the Fifty-fifth. Norwood Penrose Hallowell was not yet twenty-five.[61]

Andrew responded in a gracious letter, commenting that he was aware that Hallowell had agreed to organize black troops "at a time, when the undertaking was not a popular one, or its success guaranteed." He hoped that Pen's "health, when no longer taxed by exertions, perhaps too great, will be fully restored." The governor also accepted Hallowell's recommendation that Alfred Hartwell take command of the Fifty-fifth. The loss of Hallowell "was a source of great regret" to all the men in his regiment. "Universally beloved and respected as an officer and a man," Fox observed, "all felt that his place could not be easily filled." Garrison agreed. Apart from the fact that the Fifty-fifth was "now very short of officers," he judged Hartwell "to be a man unable to hold out against any one," as he "lacks firmness." Fearing just the opposite, curiously, Pen's last words of advice to Hartwell, according to surgeon Burt Wilder, were "to refrain from the 'gruffness' (something like hauteur, too) to which he is prone." Pen divided the contents of his trunk between his junior officers, said his final farewells, and sailed for Philadelphia.[62]

Christmas Day 1863 was "cold and windy," but the soldiers welcomed the festivities, even as they thought about distant loved ones. For both regiments, cooks prepared special dinners, with apple dumplings, minced pies, beefsteak, mutton, and ham added to their usual fare. "It was the best time I ever had," one soldier marveled, and although it was "about as cold a morning as we have here," it was nothing like "the weather at home." Pen Hallowell shipped a case of wine south for the officers of the Fifty-fifth. The soldiers received the day off, and most celebrated the holiday with "various games and amusements." To remind the Confederates that wars take no holiday, U.S. gunners, Captain Emilio remarked, "sounded their fearful Christmas chimes by throwing shells into the city after one o'clock." For the next three hours, shells slammed into Charleston as fast as the artillerymen could reload. That evening the soldiers on Morris Island could see fires in the city that "illuminated the whole sky and destroyed twelve buildings."[63]

Far grander still were the celebrations of liberty that greeted January 1 along the coast south of the harbor. To commemorate the first anniversary of the Emancipation Proclamation, Colonel Benjamin Tilghman marched a company of enlisted men from the Third South Carolina down to Beaufort to assist in a "Freedmen's Celebration." On Morris Island, Sergeant William Gray organized a "Solemn Convention" for the Massachusetts regiment. At thirty-eight, Gray was one of the older soldiers in the Fifty-fourth; a New Bedford mariner, he had enlisted with Gooding and, like his friend, had survived the assault on Wagner. Dressed in their cleanest uniforms and "fully armed and equipped," the Fifty-fifth marched to the parade ground. Some of the recruits had formed a "Musical and Vocal Club," and after a prayer offered by Chaplain Samuel Harrison, the club sang "Year of Jubilee." Gray ascended the dais to speak. As did all of the men, Gray resented the lack of pay and the long hours spent on fatigue drudgery and was saddened by the loss of the younger of the Hallowell brothers. But instead of dwelling on that unhappy past, Gray ventured that the year 1864 was for looking ahead. He thanked his comrades for the "accumulated testimony of negro patriotism and courage" they had demonstrated the previous summer and fall. He asked his "fellow soldiers" to reflect that it would someday "deck the page of history, that on South Carolina soil the race that her laws have been studiously framed to oppress" now stood ready "to make their liberty permanent." Their government and some of the white men they served beside scorned their contribution, but "our children will refer with pride to their fathers, who, for the sake of the liberty of the human race, suffered the baptism of fire."[64]

Corporal Gooding reported on the day's events to his loyal readers back in New Bedford, adding that "all is quiet and evidently settled for the winter." He knew of nothing "very exciting in the military line" and assumed that the regiments would remain on Folly and Morris Islands until the fall of Charleston. For once, the young corporal was wrong. Lincoln hoped to return Florida—the least populous of all of the Confederate states—to the Union, while General Gillmore wished to secure a source of cotton, turpentine, and lumber, sever Confederate supply routes for beef and salt, and liberate more contraband troops to hurl against Charleston. By the month's end, the Fifty-fourth and Fifty-fifth would receive orders to ship south. For the newer recruits, who had not taken part in the battles of the previous July, tests of their courage and mettle awaited them on fields that carried strange names, including the one the Creek called "black water"—Olustee.[65]

CHAPTER EIGHT

Florida

N ED HALLOWELL WAS RESTLESS. LIKE SOME OF THE ENLISTED
men, the colonel worried that the regiment was doomed to months
of tedium and fatigue work while the navy lobbed shells into Charleston.
Hoping to prod his superiors into action, he steamed down to Hilton
Head on February 3 to remind them "that his 10 companies are full &
that he has 52 unassigned recruits from Vermont." Doubting that the
Fifty-fourth was as battle-ready as Hallowell claimed, General Gillmore
accompanied Ned back up the coast, where he ordered a grand review
of all troops. Although rarely inclined to give black soldiers their due,
Gillmore was impressed by what he saw, and after the drill he told Hallowell to prepare to break camp. On February 5, orders arrived just as
the men were eating dinner. Gillmore directed General Truman Seymour
to sail for Jacksonville, Florida—which had already changed hands several times—"effect a landing there," and push forward to Baldwin, a rail
junction twenty miles to its west. The Fifty-fourth was to be part of a
force of 7,000 men. The soldiers shipped out that night under the cover
of darkness, although a movement that large was visible even in Charleston, where General P. G. T. Beauregard guessed that they were headed

for Savannah. Twenty-eight ships sailed south, with Hallowell aboard the *General Hunter,* a transport named for the relieved commander.[1]

By comparison to the regiment's earlier voyages, the short trip down the coast was smooth. The first two steamers entered the mouth of the St. Johns River and began the twenty-five-mile trek upriver to Jacksonville. Just as the vessels rounded the point above the town late in the afternoon on February 7, about fifty Confederate cavalrymen rode into sight and fired a volley at the *General Hunter,* wounding its mate. "Every man began to load without orders and rushed for the gangway to get on shore," Gooding reported. Soon "the men were rushing pell-mell up through the streets" in pursuit. Most of the Confederate riders escaped, but the Fifty-fourth captured thirteen prisoners. Hallowell posted seven companies around the town as advanced pickets, with the black soldiers supported by mounted riflemen from the Fortieth Massachusetts Infantry.[2]

None of the men was impressed with Jacksonville. After being abandoned by Southern forces, occupied by U.S. soldiers, and then evacuated once more, much of the town was in ruins. "Poverty, ignorance, filth, fleas, alligators and rebellion encompass the State from the bar on the St. Johns to Apalachee Bay," groused a journalist traveling with Seymour's troops. Nor were the locals welcoming. "The faces of the ladies in Jacksonville indicated a sort of Parisian disgust as the well-appointed Union army, composed in part of Lincoln's 'niggers,' filed through the streets," Gooding observed. But the men maintained a "respectful silence" and refused to respond in kind. If they acted the part of professional soldiers, Gooding hoped, the Floridians might respond with "respect and courtesy." Whatever the behavior of the women who watched the Fifty-fourth march by, their reaction to seeing black men in blue was no worse, Gooding mused, than what they faced while on leave "in some parts of the free North."[3]

Having secured Jacksonville, the Fortieth Massachusetts and five companies from the Fifty-fourth followed the railway west toward Baldwin. Hallowell ordered a dozen men to secure the telegraph lines, while others found themselves back in the familiar role of fatigue duty, chopping and hauling the wood "kept constantly on hand" for arriving locomotives. On February 8, about ten miles into their march, the vanguard stumbled into an equally surprised Confederate encampment. The "sable sons of Africa charged with a yell that sent utter terror and confusion into the hearts of the enemy," one soldier later boasted. The two regiments captured a rebel battery of five guns, more than 100 horses, and a large number of small arms. The Fortieth pursued the fleeing Confederates, and roughly 100 threw down their arms and promised to take an oath of allegiance to the United States.[4]

Finally, on February 13, the soldiers, all "well tired out," arrived at Baldwin, an unimpressive hamlet but a junction of four railroads and so, one captain remarked, "quite an important place to hold." While the companies awaited further orders, the men constructed tents from rail timbers and rubber blankets. Then the skies opened, and the makeshift shelters proved inadequate. "Here's two inches of water in my boots," a soldier complained. "No tea or coffee, no meat, no bread." Worse yet, Gooding's hope that their polite efficiency might bring out the latent Unionism in the local population proved misplaced. While patrolling the streets, one white officer happened upon a hostile woman who warned him that he was "in a terrible position." When he paused to ask why, she snapped that "if you are taken prisoner, you will surely be hung because you command nigger troops."[5]

With the siege of Charleston continuing to require no infantry support, Gillmore decided to reinforce the troops already in Florida by ordering the Fifty-fifth and Colonel James C. Beecher's contraband regiment, the First North Carolina, to sail for Jacksonville. Orders arrived to break camp on February 10; in a lament common to soldiers everywhere, George Garrison was surprised by both the abrupt departure and Gillmore's disinclination to inform them whether they were "to remain in that place or go on some expedition after getting there."[6]

The steamers docked at Jacksonville on the afternoon of February 15. Colonel Alfred Hartwell marched the regiment through town and reported to Seymour, who, unsurprisingly, thought the best use of the men was in fatigue duty. The regiment bivouacked seven miles outside Jacksonville at Fort Finnegan, an abandoned Confederate camp the soldiers promptly renamed Camp Shaw. "Our officers and men place but little confidence" in Seymour, one soldier admitted, as the general was known to be a close associate of conservative former general George McClellan, who was running for the Democratic presidential nomination. But the newer recruits of the Fifty-fifth were pleased to be near the seasoned men of the Fifty-fourth. The former "are soldiers, and only care to be treated as such," Fox confessed, "while our men are fearful all the time," having not yet tasted battle. Fox suspected his company yet required "a little stricter discipline." Private John M. Smith and three others were about to show just how tragically prescient he was.[7]

After deserting from Camp Meigs on July 20, 1863, Private Smith had been recommended for mercy upon his arrest in Boston. The hard-luck soldier, who had either lost his father or been abandoned by him as a child before being raised in a predominantly white poorhouse in Brunswick, rejoined his company on Folly Island in early October. But he spent most of the winter suffering from syphilis in the regimental hospital, where he was dosed with potassium iodide and small amounts of mercury. The twenty-one-year-old was finally ready for duty on January 15, but the other men in Company B thought him one of the worst soldiers in the unit. Charles Fox regarded Smith and his only two friends, Privates Spencer Lloyd and John Wesley Cork, as "known rascals."[8]

Cork and Lloyd, ages twenty-three and twenty-one, respectively, were evidently old friends. Both hailed from Wilmington, Delaware, and had been mustered in on the same day in May. Lloyd listed his profession as a porter, while a company clerk identified Cork as simply a laborer. As the company marched down the road to Camp Shaw, they passed an isolated house and noticed that the only inhabitants appeared to be a young wife, her infant, and an old man. Cork and Lloyd had been in Florida only two days before they approached Smith and a fourth, unnamed, soldier with their plan.[9]

Aware of the hardships facing Floridians, and especially single women whose husbands were away with the Confederate army, the four approached the house on February 17. They assured the woman, Sarah Hammond—a widow, as it turned out—that the army had "lots of provisions" to spare, which they were disbursing to the local population. With her baby on her hip, Hammond set out for the camp, but she had gone only 200 yards when the four caught up to her. Lloyd asked her "for a hug." Hammond tried to walk around them and headed back toward her house, yelling as she went, but Lloyd threatened to shoot her if she "hallooed so as to alarm the people at the house." Lloyd threw Hammond to the ground, and as she told it later, he "then violated my person first—then Private Cork violated me while [Smith] held [her] down." Hammond's child was crying, and Smith promised to kill her "and the child too" if both were not quiet. "I cried and screamed and begged them to let me loose," she later insisted, but Cork and Lloyd held her "down by the arms" while Smith raped her. The fourth assailant, never named, "then violated my person—He then got up and broke and ran ways towards Jacksonville." The other three shouldered their packs and strolled off toward the camp, leaving Hammond to stumble back toward her home.[10]

Just as Hammond was heading for a neighbor's farm in search of help, Captain J. D. Hodges, a white officer with the First North Carolina, happened by. Sarah rushed to the fence, shouting that "those four men with packs on their backs that has just gone down the road did what they pleased to me [and] threatened me with their guns." Hodges galloped after the men and followed the three soldiers—the fourth assailant having vanished—back to the camp. As they entered the gate Hodges instructed Lieutenant George Mussey of the Fifty-fifth to watch them while he reported the incident and rounded up a guard of eight soldiers. The posse arrested the men, and with the permission of the camp's commander, Hodges escorted them back to Jacksonville and delivered them to the provost marshal. Military justice being swift, trial was set for the following evening.[11]

Around sunset, General Seymour ordered a panel convened "for the trial of four Soldiers of the 55th Mass. Vols., charged with committing Rape upon the person of a white woman." The four-person tribunal included Charles Fox, who just months before had advocated lenience for Smith as a deserter. Captain William Anthorp of the Thirty-fourth USCT was assigned the unenviable task of defending the accused. Unaware that the army considered abusing local "secesh" women a serious offense, the three regarded the brief proceedings as a mere formality to appease local sensibilities. After Hammond and Hodges provided testimony, Cork rose to ask Sarah if he "threaten[ed] to take your life, if you did not let [him]." Lloyd also implied that Hammond had initiated the encounter, asking: "Did you not pick your own place to lie down?" Hammond responded that Smith had in fact "threatened to shoot me while [Cork] was struggling with me," and in reply to Lloyd, she insisted that when she refused to lie down, "he then took hold of me and pushed me backwards." The hearing lasted seven hours, ending at four in the morning of Thursday, February 18. "The evidence here closed and the prisoners having no defense to make," the clerk scribbled, "the Court was then closed." The three prisoners were instructed to await the verdict outside.[12]

The court sent a chaplain to find the three, who were sitting under guard by a campfire, "engaged in light and easy conversation." The soldiers glanced up, reading their fate in the chaplain's somber expression. "Are we convicted?" one asked. When the minister remained silent, they again argued that Hammond "was *particeps criminis*"—a willing accomplice—and that the incident hardly "amounted to rape." As their courtroom demeanor had indicated, "they were astonished that so much importance should be attached to so unimportant an affair." When the chaplain informed them that they would be executed that evening, Smith was stunned. "Why were we not taught that such consequences would result from such an act?" Smith wondered. Fox then called the regiment together to announce the men's sentences and to emphasize the importance of keeping "their good name." Aware that many white Americans regarded black men as barbarous savages, Fox "could not help showing [his emotions] a little in [his] voice." The ranks were silent, but Fox guessed the regiment "to be on the right side" of the matter.[13]

As the sun began to set, the provost marshal marched the condemned men to an awaiting wagon. "Calmly, and with a firm step, they took their seats in the cart," the chaplain observed, before he stepped forward to deliver a prayer. General Seymour lived down to his reputation by barking: "Served them right, now let any other man try it if he dares," as if the three were somehow representative of the nearly 1,000 soldiers in the regiment. A driver carried Lloyd and Cork to a hastily constructed gallows at Camp Shaw, where their deaths were witnessed by the Second and Third South Carolina. Private John Smith, age twenty-one, was hanged before the Fifty-fifth in the town square of Jacksonville, illuminated, Fox recorded, only by "the dim moon-light." The regiment "could but see the justice of the sentence," he added. The army left the bodies hanging for twenty-four hours.[14]

The executions were widely reported in the Northern press, including in Smith's Maine, and reaction broke along predictable lines of race and political affiliation. One conservative Manhattan paper ran the headline

"Wholesome Hanging at Jacksonville," maintaining that the three soldiers "shared a righteous fate." Most Republican papers covered the story without editorial flourish, other than to note that Smith had previously "been pardoned for desertion" and that the three "were among the hardest men in the regiment." Writing to the *Weekly Anglo-African*, Private George Stephens conceded that "the base crime of rape [was] second in its heinousness to willful murder," yet he thought it wrong that "a black man should be hung for a crime if a white man is not treated with the same punishment." That sentiment was shared by Dr. Esther Hill Hawks, who took offense at General Seymour's words. "If the same measure had been meted out to white officers and men who had been guilty of the same offense toward black women," she confided to her diary, Seymour "might have grown hoarse repeating his remarks."[15]

Hawks was more right than she knew. Twenty-one percent of all U.S. soldiers executed by the military were black, although by the war's end they constituted only 8 percent of the army. In every case where a black soldier was hanged for rape, the accuser was white. Southern whites, of course, had long employed rape as a weapon of terror against black women, and during the war years reactionary whites used the threat of assault to intimidate black women and their families. But the men of the Fifty-fourth and Fifty-fifth understood that John Smith's behavior endangered their hopes of exchanging military service for citizenship. As one white New York feminist argued, were Congress to give the vote to black men but not to women, the result would be "fearful outrages on womanhood, especially in the southern states."[16]

As the men sorted out their emotions the morning after Smith's execution, they all assumed that they were in for a quiet, lengthy stay in northern Florida. Literally without loss of life, the regiments had successfully carried out Gillmore's plan, capturing Jacksonville and the rail junction of Baldwin and driving Confederate cavalrymen into the backcountry. Despite being instructed to entrench and await further orders, Seymour wrote to Gillmore on February 17, informing his commander that he intended to take portions of six regiments and destroy the railroad near the Suwannee River, roughly 100 miles from Jacksonville.

The thirty-nine-year-old Seymour, a veteran of the Seminole War, thought himself familiar with Florida's terrain, and he also suspected that he faced only tattered remnants of cavalry and militia units. "Greatly surprised" to hear of the incursion, Gillmore dispatched his chief of staff to Jacksonville "to stop the movement." Choppy seas prevented the order from arriving at Camp Shaw until midday on February 20, by which time Seymour and the troops would be in the thick of the largest battle waged in Florida.[17]

General Beauregard had initially guessed that Gillmore's intended target was Savannah, but as it became clear that the objective was the Jacksonville area, he moved to bolster Florida's defenses. General Joseph Finnegan was already posted at Olustee Station with several regiments, and Beauregard ordered General Alfred Colquitt to hurry south and guard the rail lines west of Baldwin. By February 18, Finnegan commanded 4,600 veteran infantrymen, 600 cavalrymen, and three batteries of twelve guns. Serving with the Confederates was Colonel Abner McCormick, who in a reference to the Smith hanging assured his men that the invading force was "made up largely of negroes from Georgia and South Carolina, who have come to steal, pillage, run over the state, and murder, kill, and rape our wives, daughters and sweethearts." McCormick exhorted his troops to "teach them a lesson," vowing that he would "not take any negro prisoners in this fight."[18]

The order to move reached Hallowell's hand on the morning of February 19, and by 8:30 A.M. five companies of the Fifty-fourth were marching behind their colonel as part of the 5,500-man-strong force, a larger number of Union soldiers than were engaged at Wagner. Three New York regiments took the lead, advancing along the bed of the Atlantic and Gulf Central Railroad. Companies from two New England regiments trailed, with Pennsylvania recruits in the Eighth USCT next. Inexplicably, almost all of the regiments in the front were untested raw recruits. As part of Colonel James Montgomery's brigade, the First North Carolina and the Fifty-fourth brought up the rear in what quickly became a very long column. After marching twenty miles, some members of the Fifty-fourth wondered if "there was any danger of the rebels getting into our rear." Seymour, unworried, pushed forward and declined to send scouts or skirmishers in advance of his main force. That night the soldiers unrolled their blankets along the track, the full moon, one soldier remembered, "brightening the white, sandy earth" and the "moss-laden limbs of the huge pines which stood sentry-like on the roadside."[19]

Hard marching began again the next morning at eight-thirty. At the top of each hour, the soldiers paused to catch their breath, "but we cannot say the troops fairly rested," an accompanying journalist reported. The road they followed was "of loose sand, or boggy turf," and in low areas the soldiers were "covered knee-deep with muddy water." Noon passed, but Seymour refused to break long enough for the men to gnaw at their hardtack. Having covered sixteen miles, the procession ground to a halt at two o'clock on Saturday, and the Fifty-fourth, "weary, exhausted, faint, [and] hungry," yanked off their knapsacks and fell to the ground in the shade of some fallen trees. Suddenly, from far to their front, they heard an explosive volley, followed by the roar of cannon. "That's home-made thunder," one soldier said aloud. Ned Hallowell was already on his feet, yelling at the men to grab their rifles, when an orderly galloped up, asking to see their colonel.[20]

The Fifty-fourth was two miles behind the fighting, and Hallowell ordered his men to abandon all gear but their firearms and cartridge boxes and "move forward at the double-quick." As they closed in on the mayhem, they encountered "hundreds of wounded and stragglers," many of them from the untested Eighth USCT, who begged them to retreat, shouting, "We're badly whipped!" and "You'll all get killed." Seymour's advance forces, Hallowell quickly grasped, had blundered into entrenched Confederates concealed behind a thick wood. Although the Confederates, it was later discovered, had five fewer companies than did Seymour, their 5,000 soldiers—3,000 more than had defended Wagner—had begun to dig defensive lines, while other companies started shifting to the side to flank the panicked American troops. While Hallowell brought his men into formation, Seymour galloped up. "The day is lost," the dumbfounded general shouted, "you must go in and save the corps." Hallowell pulled out his saber, the familiar metallic hiss lost in the din, and led the Fifty-fourth to the left, while the First North Carolina charged to the right of the Seventh Connecticut. The Fifty-fourth dashed into the melee "with a cheer," remembered a white soldier, with Company D bawling out their battle cry: "Three cheers for Massachusetts and seven dollars a month."[21]

Having led his invasion force into a trap, Seymour compounded his errors by maneuvering his advance regiments onto a small patch of high ground between two swamps, one to the front, which hindered their advance, and the other to their rear. Finnegan's men, who knew the area well, continued to flank Seymour, so that the Confederates fired from both an entrenched front and from the side, with sharpshooters hidden in the trees. Hallowell and his men splashed through 200 yards of swamp, he later reported, "driving the enemy from some guns, and checking the advance of a column of the enemy's infantry." As the shattered companies of the Eighth USCT and Seventh Connecticut—most of whom had enlisted only two months before—fell back in disarray, the Fifty-fourth and the black soldiers in the First North Carolina continued to advance, protecting both flanks. Colonel Charles Fibley, commander of the Eighth, took a bullet to his heart, and five Confederate balls killed as many color-bearers. Each time, soldiers from the Fifty-fourth recaptured the Eighth's flag. To the rear, the Fifty-fourth's band struck up "The Star Spangled Banner," and one veteran swore that even above the unceasing musket fire, the "soul-stirring strains" could be heard, inspiring "new life and renewed energy into the panting, routed troops."[22]

To better make sense of the chaos swirling about him, Hallowell mounted a stump about fifty feet behind the front. Despite the danger posed by Confederate sharpshooters, he could not resist being proud of his regiment. One soldier glanced up and "observed Col. E. N. Hallowell standing with a smile upon his countenance, as though the boys were playing a small game of ball." The determination of the Fifty-fourth encouraged the battered New York regiment; although nearly out of ammunition, they fixed bayonets and raced forward to join the black troops. Some of the newer black recruits, who had joined after the fight at Wagner, were so nervous that they forgot to pull the ramrods out of their muskets and sprayed the Confederates with both balls and short spears. A sergeant bawled for those who had lost their ramrods to drop the balls down the barrels and then hammer the stocks hard against the ground. Not only was the tactic successful, but some of the veterans realized that they could load and fire faster using that method than with a ramrod.[23]

The firefight continued for more than two hours, the Fifty-fourth standing their ground and pouring withering fire into the gray line. "The

In this 1894 lithograph of Olustee produced by the Chicago firm of Alexander Allison and Louis Kurtz, black troops march across a cleared field toward entrenched Confederates, while smoke rises into gently rolling hills. In reality, the battle was waged in a pine forest, neither side had the opportunity to fortify the flat, swampy ground, and the rail line was not as close to the fighting as depicted. *Courtesy of National Park Service; photograph by author.*

musketry firing had now increased to one loud, continuous peal, amid which was heard the rapid crackling of guns," one officer recalled. But after firing nearly 20,000 cartridges, they began to run short. Hoping to drive back the Confederate left flank, Lieutenant Colonel William Reed of the First North Carolina led his regiment in a charge. The outnumbered black soldiers got within twenty yards of the Confederate line before a murderous volley took Reed's life and forced them to retreat. From his position on the left, Private Joseph Wilson of the Fifty-fourth squinted across the field toward the North Carolinians. "Men fell like snowflakes," he later wrote. Grasping their banner in his left hand—his right hand all but shot off—the First's color sergeant led the survivors back toward American lines. Colonel James Montgomery turned to the officers nearest him, urging them to save themselves. "Now men, you have done well," he sighed. "I love you all. Each man must take care of himself." The Fifty-fourth had never cared much for Montgomery or his instructions, and nobody, one soldier sneered, planned "to retire in his bushwhacking way." Sergeant James Wilkins, a twenty-one-year-old housepainter from New Haven, instead shouted "Rally!" and his company shifted behind him, forming a neat line along the dirt road. We would "not retreat when ordered," a member of the Fifty-fourth later bragged.[24]

But they would listen to Ned Hallowell, however reluctantly. By dusk, he understood that if they remained on the field, his men would be either killed or taken prisoner. The First North Carolina continued to fire, but their methodical retreat exposed his right to Confederate horsemen. "Both flanks were being folded up," a soldier observed, "and slaughter or capture would have been the inevitable result." Seymour decided to pull out and limp back toward Baldwin. The conservative general who had never had any use for black soldiers admitted that the Fifty-fourth "was the only colored regiment that was worth a d[am]n," and he ordered Hallowell's men, together with what remained of the First North Carolina and the Seventh Connecticut, to form a rearguard to protect his retreating forces. Even then, one soldier insisted, their blood was up, and "the men had no idea of obeying the firm order." Hallowell had to tell them three times to leave the field. "It was a sorrowing spectacle to see our little army, so hopeful and so gallant," wrote Private George Stephens, "in such a precipitate retreat."[25]

Their retreat back down the tracks "was steady and cool," one soldier maintained, but the danger was far from over. The Fifty-fourth paused to fire every 200 yards, the black smoke briefly enveloping the kneeling men. The Confederate infantrymen chose not to follow, but cavalrymen on their right continued to shoot, and sporadic cannon shot fell into their ranks. A stray ball creased Sergeant Swails's right temple, gouging a furrow "two inches long and fracturing the skull." More concerned for his company than his own well-being, Swails herded his men toward Baldwin until he grew insensible and "fell exhausted beside the road." Captain Lewis Reed, age twenty-one, bundled the bleeding sergeant into a nearby cart. Swails "deserves special praise for his coolness, bravery, and efficiency during the action," Hallowell later reported.[26]

So ended the fight at Olustee, the bloodiest battle fought in Florida during the Civil War, as well as Lincoln's hopes of having a restored government for the state in place in time for the November elections. It was another defeat for the Fifty-fourth, but another grim test of their mettle, and so another victory for their growing reputation. Captain Luis Emilio recorded total American losses at 193 killed, 1,175 wounded, and 460 missing, for a total casualty list of 1,828, or 34 percent. Ten more later died of their wounds, making total U.S. losses at Olustee approximately the same as at Wagner. The Fifty-fourth suffered three officers wounded, 13 soldiers killed, 63 wounded, and eight missing. The First North Carolina paid a higher price, with 230 casualties, as did the undertrained recruits in the Eighth USCT. Confederate losses were far lighter. Ninety-three men died, 847 were injured, and six went missing, a casualty rate of 19 percent. "The losses of the 54th Mass. were not severe," Fox assured his wife. Yet the clash proved devastating for one family in New Bedford. Our "hearts are saddened by mournful events and our eyes moistened with tears of grief," a soldier wrote to the *Mercury* and the *Weekly Anglo-African*. "Corp. James Henry Gooding lost his life in that battle." Gooding was in the thick of the melee, "carrying the flag on to victory," when he was shot, the soldier reported. "He enlisted from the highest motives, believing the destiny of the black man of his country was in this rebellion," as he believed "that now was the day of salvation."[27]

The Fifty-fourth reached the encampment near Baldwin around one o'clock on Sunday morning, just as companies from the Fifty-fifth, led by Sergeant Major James Monroe Trotter and including Private Nicholas Said, began to arrive from the east after marching more than twenty-four hours. "Here a scene that beggars description was presented," one soldier wrote. "Wounded men lined the railroad station, and the roads were filled with artillery, caissons, ammunition and baggage wagons, infantry, cavalry, and ambulances." Still leery of a Confederate counterassault, the Fifty-fourth secured the disordered withdrawal by securing the road that ran beside the rails. "Exhausted as was our black regiment," Captain Wilkie James bragged, "it was still necessary to cover the retreat of our men as best they might." After marching 110 miles and taking part in a bloody battle, the soldiers reached Camp Shaw near Jacksonville on Monday afternoon, but not before having to lash their horses to a disabled train filled with the wounded, which they dragged for the last ten miles of the retreat.[28]

Although all present praised the Fifty-fourth for the unhurried, orderly fashion in which they protected the rear of the retreating forces, there had been no time to collect the bodies of the slain or assist those who were badly wounded and assumed to be dying. The "greater part of the wounded and all the killed were left on the field," one soldier lamented, and a reporter for the Savannah *Republican* agreed that both the "dead and wounded" of the retreating army "lay thick on the field." Before the battle, Colonel McCormick had threatened to give no quarter, and his men hastened to make good on that warning. One young Georgia cavalryman reported hearing shots coming "from every direction" after the battle was over. When he inquired of a Confederate officer what the cause of the firing was, the man coolly replied: "Shooting niggers, Sir." The officer explained that he had tried "to make the boys desist but I can't control them." Yet another officer conceded that after the Fifty-fourth were gone, "our men slayed the Negrows & if it had not been for the officers their would not one of them be spaired." After several junior officers sought to put an end to the executions, Confederate infantrymen simply switched to quieter methods. The "boys went over the battlefield and knoct the most of the wounded negros in the head with lightwood knots," Private Joab Roach explained. The brutal retaliation was both revenge against black soldiers who fought them as equals and a lesson for those slaves yet at home. One soldier urged his wife to tell their slaves, "if they could have seen how the negroes are treated" at Olustee, "I think that would cure them of all desire to go."[29]

In the aftermath of the battle, Seymour was skewered by the Northern press for leading his troops into a trap, and Gillmore, having no desire to take the fall for the disaster, publicly announced that Seymour had defied his orders by leaving Baldwin. Gillmore also leaked the rumor that he intended to have Seymour arrested, and while he did not follow through, he did make sure that Seymour understood that his career was over. Gillmore ordered General Israel Vogdes, who was then taking part in the Charleston siege, south to Jacksonville to take over Seymour's division. Not surprisingly, conservative editors contended that the fault lay not with the invasion's commander but with his black troops. A lieutenant from Rhode Island reported that it "was our misfortune to have for support a negro regiment, who, by running, caused us to lose our [five abandoned artillery] pieces." The comment was picked up by the Democratic press, which railed against "the cowardice of negro regiments" and used the debacle as "conclusive proof that the blacks are unfit for soldiers."[30]

The Republican press fired back, with the Hartford *Connecticut Courant* writing, for instance, that "[o]n the battle-field [the black soldier] is fast vindicating his claim to the respect of the world." But now, for the first time, a large number of whites—many of them self-identified as previous skeptics—were willing to say the same. "Had it not been for the glorious Fifty-forth Massachusetts," one soldier ventured, "the whole brigade would have been captured or annihilated." While other companies panicked, he added, the Fifty-fourth "was the only regiment that rallied, broke the rebel ranks, and saved us." Even Seymour admitted that the "colored troops behaved creditably—the Fifty-fourth Massachusetts and First North Carolina like veterans." (Anxious to parcel out blame, the general instead pointed to the Seventh New Hampshire, "a white regiment from which there was every reason to expect noble service.") Yet another white soldier marveled at the Fifty-fourth's refusal to "retreat when ordered." If the Fifty-fourth "has not won glory enough to have shoulder straps," he wondered, "where is there one that ever did?" The Amherst *Farmer's Cabinet* agreed: "They fought gallantly and lost heavily, sustained the reputation they had gained at Wagner."[31]

Perhaps the strangest praise came from three Confederate deserters who wandered into the Fifty-fourth's camp a month after the battle. Deciding their war was over, they arrived at the garrison in search of food, raising their hands in surrender. The "three rebs" hardly cared for their black captors, but neither did they wish to fight on against them. "You black soldiers fight like the devil," one admitted. "It is twice we met you. Once at James Island, and the other day at Olustee. We know all the Massachusetts flags. You peppered us like hell." Coming from battle-hardened Carolinians, such compliments meant a good deal to men far from their homes and families. The exchange, which the soldiers were anxious to share with the *Weekly Anglo-African,* might help erode "prejudice, the curse of the North as slavery is the curse of the South." If so, one wrote, "then we will suffer more, work faster, fight harder, and stand firmer than before."[32]

ONCE THEY COULD BE SHIPPED UP THE COAST, THE WOUNDED FROM the Battle of Olustee kept the doctors busy at No. 6. Dr. Esther Hill Hawks was stitching a wound in a soldier's arm when he looked up. "Is you Mrs.

Hawks," he asked. "There is only one woman in dis world who could do that." The soldier identified himself as Henry Krunkleton, the eldest of the five Pennsylvania brothers to enlist. Hawks had cared for his three brothers the previous July, when two were wounded on James Island and one at Wagner. "My brudder told what you did for the 54th soldiers in the hospital." Upon inquiring, Hawks discovered that Henry had remained in Mercersburg to look after the family farm. But after his brother Cyrus was killed on James Island, Henry "had come out with the 55th." He lived to return home and marry his fiancée.[33]

Also resting in No. 6 was Acting Sergeant Major Stephen Swails, although not for long. The bullet had cracked his skull along his left temple, and the only remedy then available was time and patience. The doctors judged his wound to be "severe but not mortal," and Gillmore granted Swails a two-month furlough to convalesce. Mid-April found him boarding the Elmira train for Manhattan and then transferring on to Boston for shipment back down the coast. (The army deducted $9 for transportation costs from the salary he still refused to accept.) While in Elmira, Swails presumably visited Sarah Thompson and their children in nearby Corning, but as always, he evidently had no interest in legalizing their relationship.[34]

On the battlefield, however, he displayed no ambivalence. Now thirty-two years of age, the former wastrel had discovered that he was a skillful leader of men, a gifted practitioner of the dark trade—as did his colonel. Shortly after Olustee, Hallowell wrote to Governor Andrew, insisting that Swails had "fought so splendidly" that he deserved promotion to second lieutenant "whenever he recovers from his wounds and rejoins the regiment." Weary of battling with Washington over pay and doubting that the Lincoln administration would soon consent to promote a black man, the governor decided his title gave him power enough over state regiments, and on March 11 he agreed. Swails was informed of his promotion when he reached Jacksonville on May 12. His men were overjoyed. "Swails, colored, has received his commission as a 2d lieutenant," one informed the *Weekly Anglo-African*. "That is a starter." The men in the Fifty-fourth saluted him as a commissioned officer, but as Andrew had feared, General John Foster, the latest commander of the Department of the South, refused Swails's "muster into service in that grade" unless explicitly granted authority to do

so by Washington, "he being partially of African blood." The army continued to pay Swails as a sergeant major, a moot point so long as the entire
regiment declined wages.[35]

Foster was undoubtedly being honest about awaiting orders from Lincoln or Stanton, as his post had evolved into an unstable, rotating position; over its three-year existence, six men had held command of the
Department of the South, with David Hunter and Gillmore each serving
twice. Yet Foster's response also masked his genteel racism. "Sergt Swails is
so nearly white that it would be difficult to discover any trace of African
blood," he remarked. Maybe, Foster reasoned, that explained why Swails
was "so Intelligent." Charles Duren, himself a second lieutenant in the
Fifty-fourth, agreed, finding it unfortunate that Swails had decided not to
pass for white at the war's start. "About Sergeant Swails there is some doubt
about his being a black man," Duren wrote to his father in Maine. "I know
he is not black, but I mean a negro," he continued, trying to puzzle his
way through his confusion. "White or black he is brave" and "qualified for
the position of an officer." Still, Duren could not bring himself to support
the "*mixing* [of] colored officers with white." Perhaps the answer was the
complete segregation of America's armed forces, at which time Duren was
"ready to step out" of the Fifty-fourth and turn the regiment over to black
officers.[36]

Just as Swails was in transport down the coast from Boston, a curious note appeared in the New Bedford *Republican Standard.* "'James
Goodrich,' Co. C., 54th regiment, reported a prisoner in the hands of
Florida rebels, is supposed to be James H. Gooding, of this city, who
was said to have been killed at Olustee." For Ellen Gooding and her
parents, this glimmer of hope, coming two months after the battle, was
almost too unlikely to credit. But corroboration came within the week,
as the *Weekly Anglo-African* included Gooding in their list of wounded,
placing his injury in the hip. Normally the last to know about battlefield
losses, the War Department listed Gooding as being "wounded in thigh,"
although they mistakenly bucked the young corporal back down to the
rank of private.[37]

The reports were not wrong. Gooding was alive, if wounded, and
was among the eight men missing from the Fifty-fourth, as were George
Brown, a twenty-year-old farmer from West Chester, Private Isaac Hawkins

of Medina, New York, and one of the regiment's three George Washingtons, this one a Philadelphia-based mariner. The prisoners also included soldiers from the Eighth USCT, the First North Carolina, and the Seventh Connecticut. For several weeks, Confederates held the Olustee wounded in Tallahassee, but as they improved, survivors were packed into boxcars for shipment to Camp Sumter, a prisoner-of-war camp adjacent to Andersonville, Georgia. Eleven black soldiers arrived on Sunday, March 27, Gooding apparently among them. Given Davis's edict and the Confederate Congress's resolution, a colonel responsible for their induction questioned General John Winder, the officer in charge of prison camps, as to whether the captured blacks should be treated as soldiers or fugitive slaves. Winder replied, as had so many before him, that they should be treated as ordinary prisoners of war until he heard from his superiors. In the meantime, the black soldiers were segregated into a small encampment near the fort's south gate.[38]

Built only several months before, in February 1864, the prison camp originally covered roughly sixteen acres, although during Gooding's time there its fifteen-foot-high walls would grow to encompass another ten. The first contingent of 860 U.S. soldiers had arrived on February 15, but by the summer's end the total number reached 31,693. Winder appointed Henry Wirz, a Swiss-born captain, as the camp's commander. The Confederates initially planned to construct wooden barracks, but wartime shortages forced the prisoners to instead put up ramshackle huts made out of sticks, clay, and tattered tents. The wounded were treated in thirty-five large tents judged too worn for army use. Medicine was nonexistent. By early March, of the 13,218 soldiers who had arrived at the Andersonville depot, 1,026 had died. The conditions appalled even Confederate surgeons, who complained that the beef rations were crawling with maggots and that soldiers suffering from gangrene lacked clean water to wash their sores. Rations were invariably in short supply, and when prisoners reached the final stages of emaciation from chronic diarrhea, the camp's officers simply cut off their food and allowed them to die. Some corpses lay in the sun for days before burial.[39]

Much of the manual labor within the camp was delegated to what was known as "the Negro Squad," comprising the approximately seventy black prisoners. The group was put to work burying the dead in ditches seven feet wide by three feet deep, but only after stripping the deceased of their

Over the course of the war, Andersonville Prison housed 45,000 U.S. prisoners, nearly 13,000 of whom died, most from scurvy and dysentery. This August 1864 image shows tents and shanties built up to the "dead line," a light fence twenty feet inside the stockade's main wall. Any prisoner who even touched the "dead line" was shot without warning by guards. *Courtesy Library of Congress.*

uniforms and washing their clothing. On one occasion, Wirz fired a warning shot at George Brown, whom he had sent to collect shovels but who did "not run as fast" as the captain wanted. Wirz originally ordered George Washington to be whipped, and for the crime of "carrying [stolen] onions to the sick men of the hospital," Isaac Hawkins received 250 lashes. Wirz had sentenced Hawkins to 500, but after it became clear that the New York mariner would die before the whipping was finished, the captain ended the torture.[40]

The prison authorities reserved their greatest animosity for black men who wore stripes on their shoulders and believed themselves to be the equal of Southern officers. Wirz especially disliked those he dubbed "white negroes—mulattoes—in the prison." That meant that light-skinned Corporal Gooding faced hardships unique even by the violent, heartless standards of Andersonville. Either because of his wounded thigh or owing to his pride, or both, the young sea cook—who had braved arctic winds and drafted letters of complaint to presidents and governors—refused to labor with the "Negro Squad." For this offense, he was beaten so badly that his body was broken and limp when his tormentors finally dragged him away. James Henry Gooding died on July 19, 1864—a year and a day after Wagner— five weeks shy of his twenty-sixth birthday. This time the army would not hear of his fate until May 22, 1865. Wirz, for his part, would be executed for war crimes the following November.[41]

"WITH A RETURN TO THE MONOTONY OF CAMP THE QUESTION OF PAY again became a source of discontent," Luis Emilio observed. Friendly Northern editors reported that just before Olustee, Hallowell had promised that he would refuse to allow his regiment "to fight as they had received no pay." But when the orders to march arrived, William Lloyd Garrison wrote, "there stood the old 54th with levelled bayonets." Even so, the fighting at Olustee aggravated their grievances. They had fought bravely, more so than some white regiments, yet those white units continued to receive higher pay. Emilio was right in thinking that growing discontent over the seemingly endless pay issue was eroding morale in both regiments. The Fifty-fifth had now been in the field for six months, and Charles Fox guessed that "much suffering must exist among" their families back home. George Garrison also noticed that men in his company were "beginning to show signs of insubordination," warning his mother that "if they are not soon paid you need not be at all surprised if you hear of some serious outbreak." Just prior to the battle, Stephen Swails had sparked talk among the regiments by demanding to either be paid as a white soldier or be released from duty, as Garrison agreed that "we ought at once to be mustered out of the service by the Government." Unless Congress resolved the matter quickly, "our efficiency as a Reg't will be at an end."[42]

The inevitable explosion came in late May. A detachment from Company A refused to turn out for guard duty. "Great turmoil" shook the Fifty-fourth, one officer wrote. Hallowell ordered his captains to load their pistols, and then he shouted for the regiment to fall in. Instead, the men continued to loiter about, and the commotion drew spectators from other units. A frustrated Hallowell adopted a balanced policy of coercion and conciliation. Drawing his revolver, he marched down the line of resisting soldiers, pointing the barrel at each of their heads while barking: "Do you refuse to go on guard?" One by one, the cowed men shouted: "No, sir!" The crisis momentarily averted, Hallowell then promised the men that if they would continue to perform their duty, he would leave for Washington to plead their case.[43]

Aware that the army had little interest in fending off angry colonels, Hallowell bypassed General Foster and sought out one of his subordinates for permission to travel, hinting that he had already received "authority from the War Department" to travel to Washington "on important military business." Even with a pass in hand, Ned was risking severe reprimand, but he was desperate, and in any case, fighting Quakers like the Hallowell brothers had long ignored secular authorities in pursuit of a moral good. Worried junior officers wished him luck. Hallowell "left here yesterday for the North to hurry up the payment of our two Reg'ts," George Garrison told his mother.[44]

Compounding Hallowell's anger was the fact that he and the white officers in the Fifty-fourth had not been paid since November 1, 1863, the paymaster apparently thinking that nobody in the regiment would accept their wages. Hallowell demanded that Washington "send some one with funds to pay them," adding that it might "save useless trouble to state that the enlisted men will refuse to take pay unless you are prepared to pay them according to the terms of their enlistment." The soldiers knew of their colonel's efforts on their behalf, but Hallowell's labors did little to dampen their anger, especially as the government's decision to charge black soldiers for uniforms resulted in a growing debt. One private in the Fifty-fifth calculated that the "average amount of clothing charged to each man is $53," which the War Department continued to deduct from their accounts. Even worse, when the Fifty-fourth was ordered to Olustee, they took only "what they had on their backs." Upon returning to Jacksonville, they discovered that much of their clothing and equipment had been accidently destroyed by a fire—yet the government planned to charge them for new uniforms. "In many cases the men's clothing account amounts to so much, that when pay comes but little will be due them," Ned complained. "It seems that the 54th is bound to fight its way through everything." Most of the soldiers, as one groused, came to doubt they would live to see "the day when the government will do justice to the 54th and 55th Regiments, and pay us what is justly our due."[45]

Each mailbag brought plaintive letters from home, reminding the troops that the problem extended far beyond their perceived rights as soldiers of the republic. "Is it not perfectly delightful," one private derisively asked, "to hear your wife and darling babies crying to you for the necessities of life." A desperate wife wrote to beg her husband to accept any pay, however modest, as she "had been driven by want and the cries of her children for bread, to yield to the tempter," that is, to sell her body. How "our families are to live and pay house-rent, I know not," lamented another soldier. James Monroe Trotter was not yet married, but the sergeant major knew what was being said around the Fifty-fifth's campfires. "That the American Congress should regard us so indifferently makes us sometimes sad," Trotter reported to a friend of the governor's. But that was nothing by comparison to the sorrow of "thinking of the necessities of a dear wife and little ones and other beloved ones at home." If the men in his company remained patient, he decided, it was only thanks to "Jehovah, who will not suffer this war to end until every trace of Slavery is gone."[46]

As the temperatures rose, so too did the men's anger. It helped little that both regiments were ordered to return to the Carolina coast. Lincoln had promoted Ulysses S. Grant to lieutenant general, handing him command of all Union armies. After Grant assigned General William T. Sherman the Division of the Mississippi, Washington believed that their combined efforts would place pressure on the Confederate interior and weaken the defense of Charleston. The War Department ordered Gillmore to take 16,000 men and leave the coast to participate in the march against Richmond, while the two Massachusetts regiments, joined by the newly formed Eighth USCT, would return to Folly and Morris Islands. Of this larger, grand strategy, the men knew nothing, only that their unpaid sojourn in the heat and sand was to continue.[47]

In early June, Lieutenant Thomas Ellsworth of the Fifty-fifth ordered his company turned out for inspection. Among those caught unprepared was Private Wallace Baker, a Kentucky-born farmer. Although he had seen action at Gettysburg with the Second Massachusetts, the youthful Ellsworth was regarded by his men as "one of the new batch of Lieutenants promoted from some white regiment." Ellsworth ordered Baker back to his quarters, but the private refused. "I shan't do it," he snapped, "I'll go to the guard house first." Had wiser heads been present, the spat might have been defused. But Ellsworth, all of twenty-three, feared his authority was in danger, while Baker, equally young and aggressive at nineteen, was weary of taking orders from sons of privilege. Ellsworth was drawing his sword when Baker landed "two violent blows" to his face, shouting: "You damned white officer, do you think that you can strike me, and I not strike you back again?" Baker lunged for Ellsworth's sword, unsuccessfully, and as two black sergeants ignored the lieutenant's pleas for assistance, Ellsworth finally subdued the smaller man and dragged him off to the guardhouse.[48]

Unlike John Smith, who was surprised by his sentence of death, Baker knew exactly what was coming. By the war's end, black men constituted one in thirteen U.S. soldiers, but nearly 80 percent of those executed for mutiny. Even Boston newspapers denounced Baker as "a hard character." When Chaplain John Bowles went to tell Baker of his fate, he found him "sitting on the side of his bunk in his shirt sleeves with quiet indifference." Bowles tried to convince Baker to kneel and pray together, but the condemned man instead suggested that the chaplain might simply pray for him. "I came out here to fight the rebels and I would not mind being killed in battle," he told Bowles. But he had "done nothing worthy of death, and they might shoot and be d[amne]d! God would make it all right." Baker did ask that somebody write his mother in Kentucky "and let her know what had become of him." Should they ever get paid, he added, his salary should be sent to her.[49]

The morning of June 18 found Baker calm and prepared, one witness observed, to meet "his death with stoical indifference." A detail of white soldiers from the Fifty-fourth New York marched him down the beach on Folly Island "into an open space of ground, where the grave was already dug." The entire regiment had been ordered to observe the execution, and to several of his friends, Baker shouted, "They have me in a pretty tight place today, boys." Baker took a seat on his coffin, with his hands tied behind his back and a blindfold covering his eyes. The Reverend Bowles dutifully reported that Baker "fell pierced with five balls," including two to the head. "The Government which found no law to pay him except as a nondescript and a contraband," Governor Andrew noted mordantly, "nevertheless found law enough to shoot him as a soldier." A private in the Fifty-fifth agreed. "As the Government has refused to pay us," he insisted, one might "argue from these premises that the court had no jurisdiction in the case."[50]

At long last, embarrassed by the press attention devoted to Baker's execution, Washington began to act. Though the Massachusetts soldiers did not know it, Governor Andrew had kept up a steady flow of complaints to Lincoln, Stanton, and Attorney General Edward Bates. "I will never give up the rights of these men while I live, whether in this world, or the next," Andrew assured Senators Charles Sumner and Henry Wilson. The sly politician also used a recent act of Congress against the administration. As a new law allowed Northern states to meet their military quotas by recruiting runaways from Confederate states, Andrew informed Lincoln that Massachusetts was prepared to entice black Virginians north with a generous state bonus, which would dash the president's hopes of enlisting Southern blacks in the USCT. The governor wrote Lincoln again on May 27, immediately making a copy of his missive available to the *Liberator*. Black soldiers "have fallen in battle on James Island, in the assault upon Fort Wagner, or in the affair of Olustee," he reminded the president, so these men, "bearing honorable wounds," were hardly mere laborers. At the same time, both Ned Hallowell and Alfred Hartwell—despite being instructed not to by General Foster—posted letters to Andrew and Stanton, demanding that their regiments either be paid in full or "be sent back to Massachusetts and mustered out of the service."[51]

As Andrew suspected, Bates desired a quick end to the debate. Despite his Virginia birth and reputation as a conservative legalist, the attorney general submitted a short, almost brusque opinion to the president on April 23. Ignoring the Militia Act, Bates instead pointed to the Second Confiscation Act of 1862, which authorized the president to employ African Americans in any way he saw fit. Bates chose to focus on the case of Reverend Samuel Harrison, the Fifty-fourth's unpaid chaplain. Harrison was neither a soldier nor a laborer, he reasoned, and so under the terms of the July 1861 Volunteer Service Act the chaplain was entitled to the same monthly salary of $100 paid to white ministers. Although Bates avoided any mention of black combatants, the logic of his opinion pointed to equal pay for all servicemen. As William Lloyd Garrison crowed, the attorney general essentially ruled not only that black men deserved the same pay as whites, but that if "persons of African descent could be lawfully accepted as private soldiers, so also might they be lawfully accepted as commissioned officers." Bates even encouraged the president to consider it his "duty to direct the Secretary of War to inform the officers of the Pay Department of the Army that such is your view of the law." If Lincoln desired legal cover, he now had it.[52]

Yet Congress continued to muddy the waters. After Senator Wilson introduced a resolution to eliminate racially based salaries the previous February, Sumner was able to advance legislation to equalize pay for all soldiers as of January 1, 1864, with the law retroactive to the final months of 1862. Sumner was unable to defeat an amendment, however, favored by moderate Republicans who continued to fret about the costs involved, a complaint they never once advanced regarding white soldiers. The amendment sought to underpay the first contraband regiments. Under the law, finally passed in mid-June, only African Americans who were free as of April 19, 1861—just days after Lincoln called for troops following the attack on Fort Sumter—would be eligible for back pay. "The argument which prevails in the Senate," William Lloyd Garrison fumed, "is simply that it costs too much to be honest." And even then, 49 of 184 House members cast a no vote, all of them Democrats and most from the Midwest and the new state of West Virginia.[53]

Lincoln signed the bill into law on July 4, even though he professed to find the Congress's distinction regarding back pay and enlistment dates confusing. So too did the attorney general, who confessed to Edwin Stanton that he thought the law "very peculiar in its phraseology," and he urged the War Department to pay all soldiers according to the promises made at the moment of their enlistments, "and not under the act of June 15, 1864." Although the vast majority of original enlistments in the Fifty-fourth had been born free—or, like James Henry Gooding and William Carney, pretended that they had been—that was not the case with newer recruits in the Fifty-fifth. When the paymaster issued a circular directing commanders to question each soldier, "under oath," as to their status, Hallowell supplied the obvious solution. In what came to be known as the "Quaker Oath," he suggested that his men swear only that they "owed no man unrequited labor on or before the 19th day of April, 1861." Since neither former bondmen nor white abolitionists believed that slaves owed anything to their previous owners—just the reverse, in fact—the vast majority of black soldiers raised their right hands and swore the oath. By summer's end, most white officers of black regiments had adopted the strategy. A handful of soldiers, still offended by Washington's cheapness, refused to take the pledge. "But we have no harsh words for the many who were equal to the occasion by swearing to their freedom," remarked an approving Pen Hallowell. Those bondmen, such as Henry Jarvis, who had risked their lives to race for Union lines, Pen reasoned, "had overcome too many difficulties in their escape from the South, to be seriously annoyed by this grotesque proposition to swear away their back pay by denying their freedom."[54]

WITH THAT, NED HALLOWELL CALLED BOTH REGIMENTS TOGETHER to "announce that the question is justly settled," and that the paymaster would arrive soon. "I pray that soon all will be all right," James Monroe Trotter sighed. While the troops awaited his appearance, the soldiers idled away the hot afternoons, reading and rereading shared copies of the *Weekly Anglo-African*. Trotter and Nicholas Said had been teachers during their civilian days, and the Fifty-fifth pitched two large tents, salvaged some "suitable desks and benches" for furniture, and turned the shelters into evening classrooms. Other soldiers poked into holes in the sand to extract the egg sacs of spiders, which one private found surprisingly good. "Wash them down with brackish black coffee." The Fifty-fifth, another soldier wrote the *Liberator*, "in all probability, will see no more active service for the remainder of the season, stationed as it is, in its old position on Folly Island." As ever, soldiers made that assumption at their own peril.[55]

Although the Confederates had abandoned the southern coast of James Island during the siege, the northwestern edges remained vital to Charleston's defense. Fort Pemberton, a hastily constructed battery of some twenty guns, sat far up the Stono River, guarding the waters west of the harbor. Confederate skirmishers used Pemberton, as well as the smaller Fort Lamar, as bases from which they occasionally harassed U.S. gunners on the lower portions of the island. Most of the time, soldiers from the two Massachusetts regiments exchanged only a few random shots with Confederate pickets. George Garrison and three companies from the Fifty-fifth clashed with a small number of pickets on May 21, driving them three miles north toward Pemberton. The companies suffered no serious casualties, although the "Rebels, so far as could be made out, lost quite heavily in killed and wounded," Garrison reported. "Three of their officers were shot by our men, and even seen to fall from their horses." Just days later, Garrison's company ran into another patrol, but running short of ammunition, the "Rebels occasionally shake their guns at our men, but don't venture to fire them," Garrison observed. Reporting back to Colonel Hartwell, Garrison noted that "the rebel pickets have their horses with them, which is a pretty good sign that they have but a small force to oppose us." Hartwell, in turn, sent word along to General Foster that south of the fort, James Island was lightly defended, at best.[56]

With Fort Pemberton removed, shore guns could be advanced closer still to Charleston, and so, in late June, Foster began to plan for what became the largest military maneuvers of the summer in coastal Carolina. Deciding upon a three-point assault, Foster ordered two divisions to shift west before striking north up the Edisto River and across John's Island to disrupt the Charleston and Savannah Railroad. At the same time, Hartwell was to march the Fifty-fifth into the central portion of James Island, quite near to where the Fifty-fourth saw their first action one year before, and take Fort Lamar before advancing on Pemberton. Because so many of the officers in the Fifty-fourth were ill or temporarily assigned to other units, Foster instructed the 103rd New York and the Thirty-third USCT (formerly the First South Carolina Infantry) to accompany them, while the navy outside the harbor kept up its fire on the city. For the Fifty-fifth, who had missed most of the fighting at Olustee, the incursion was an opportunity to at last prove their mettle.[57]

On the night of June 30, four companies from the Fifty-fifth boarded boats on the north shore of Folly Island that would ferry them across the inlet to Long Island. Initially, Sergeant Trotter wrote, their landing "was disputed only by the mud and some of them sunk nearly up to their necks in the mire." The trek toward Fort Lamar involved "plunging, wading and part of the time almost swimming" across a series of swamps, but just as dawn broke they reached dry land. Suddenly, they could hear rifle fire to their front. As they had been at Olustee, the Confederates were fewer in number but well entrenched, and soldiers from both the New York and USCT regiments panicked and began to race by the Fifty-fifth in retreat. Hartwell tried to slow their flight, but when that failed, he shouted to "bring forward the 55th!" Trotter's company had already fixed bayonets and were charging ahead, cheering and shouting, "Remember Fort Pillow," invoking the name of the Tennessee fort where victorious Confederates had massacred defeated black soldiers the previous April. The ground to their front was littered with trees felled by the defenders, who added grapeshot to their musket volleys, raking the field before them. "But onward we plunged," Trotter remembered, "getting nearer and nearer the battery and very soon the enemy seemed to get confused." When the Fifty-fifth got within 200 yards of the Confederates, they made a final, desperate rush, "yelling unearthly" cries. Having first believed they had won the day, the Confederates realized they were about to be overrun. The skirmishers broke, racing for their horses and abandoning two cannon. Company F reached the cannon first; they spun it around and fired a farewell blast at the retreating Confederates. "O how they did fly!" Trotter would recall. But the Fifty-fifth was weary following two days and nights of "wading through the mud and water." And with the 103rd and Thirty-third in full flight, Trotter sourly observed, they "had no support, the other Reg'ts having failed us."[58]

Wounded soldiers were carried back to a battlefield hospital on Long Island, where harried surgeons did their best, one remembered, "in the open air, without tents." The colonel of the New York regiment reported that the opening Confederate volley "killed seven of my men and wounded many others"; the Thirty-third USCT suffered six killed and thirteen wounded. Hartwell recorded twenty-nine casualties in the Fifty-fifth, including eleven dead and another eighteen wounded. Among the dead was Sergeant Alonzo Boon, an illiterate laborer who had been befriended by Trotter. At Readville, Trotter had impressed upon Boon "the importance of learning, telling him that I would gladly help him, and that when he could read I would recommend him for sergeant." Boon had taken grapeshot to his leg, and he died while surgeons attempted an amputation. His company buried him near where he fell, hammering a crude board into the ground that read: As HE DIED TO MAKE MEN HOLY, LET US DIE TO MAKE MEN FREE. Despite Hallowell's failure to successfully promote Swails in rank, Alfred Hartwell forwarded Trotter's name to the War Department for promotion to second lieutenant. That did little to ease Trotter's pain. "No one's death has made me feel so sad as his," he admitted. "In truth I loved him."[59]

The two westward thrusts were also slowed by boggy terrain, and while the three-pronged assault succeeded in driving the Confederates back into

James Monroe Trotter was born to an enslaved mother and a white father who evidently cared enough for James and his mother to liberate them. When Trotter enlisted, he was teaching in Chillicothe, Ohio, a haven for freed slaves where he met Virginia Isaacs, his future wife. He would be the second man of color in the U.S. Army promoted to second lieutenant. *Courtesy Cornell University.*

the northern edge of James Island, the effort to coordinate the incursions failed. Unable to march north, the weakened Fifty-fifth dug in where they were, and several companies of the Fifty-fourth were moved up from Morris Island to support their lines. Although the skirmish of July 2 was thus of less consequence than the fighting on James Island the previous year, and although it received far less press attention than did the battles at Wagner or Olustee, the hitherto untested troops were justifiably proud. "I say, could you have seen the old 55th rush in," one soldier wrote the *Liberator,* "you would have thought nothing human could have withstood their impetuosity. We know no defeat." Garrison agreed, reporting that "this was the first time this regiment was ever under a hot fire," and that their task was especially difficult, as "they had to charge through retreating white and black troops in the face of murderous fire." This time no editor confused the Massachusetts regiment with the faltering troops of the USCT. That criticism, in fact, was made by a soldier in the Fifty-fifth, who complained that "conscript regiments here will not fight." Had there been more companies from the Fifty-fifth and Fifty-fourth in the skirmish, he believed, "Charleston to-day would either be ours or else we would be at her gates instead of occupying an old post."[60]

The Fifty-fifth was still basking in the glow of their well-deserved laurels when late in the day on September 28 word spread that the paymaster had arrived and would begin disbursements the next morning. Some of the earliest volunteers in the Fifty-fourth had enlisted eighteen months before. Soldiers reached for their fiddles, one officer chuckled, and "songs burst out everywhere." Veterans of Wagner and Olustee danced about the camp, and "boisterous shouts [were] heard." It took $170,000 just to pay the men of the Fifty-fourth, each soldier receiving on average $200. Not having been paid for months, Hallowell stepped forward to collect $562.64. Although a few soldiers indulged in what a disapproving Luis Emilio described as "lavish and foolish expenditures," the vast majority made plans to ship their earnings home, either through Adams Express Company, a freight and cargo business, or one of the chaplains. The Fifty-fourth shipped $100,000 home, while the newer recruits of the Fifty-fifth hurried an equally impressive $60,000 to their families. Some were in debt to sutlers, the civilian merchants who sold provisions to soldiers in the field, and they paid those men off too. Among those on Morris Island working as a sutler was disabled veteran Lewis Douglass. Still awaiting a response to his proposal from Amelia Loguen, he had returned to the regiment he missed and treasured. "I feel more self reliant, more independent than I should had I forever hung around home," he confided to his fiancée. After collecting the money owed him, both by the army and by his employer, Lewis shipped home $50.[61]

Enlisted men and officers alike decided that an official day of celebration was in order. As overjoyed as the soldiers were, their victory was about far more than money in their pockets. "No, it was because a great principle of equal rights as men and soldiers had been decided in their favor," Trotter reflected, "that all this glorious excitement was made." The Fifty-fifth's band led the regiments "toward a piece of rising ground" on Folly Island, where the men adopted a series of resolutions. The soldiers vowed to "stand now, as ever, ready to do our duty" in "crushing this wicked rebellion, and preserving the national unity." They promised also to forgive those who failed to "appreciate our motives, in connection with the pay question," being convinced that their critics would one day "see the error of their way." Most of all, they swore to prove themselves "worthy of the responsible position assigned us by Providence in this, the grandest struggle of the world's history between Freedom and Slavery." White Northerners, in the main, had enlisted to stitch their torn nation back together. But from the day they stepped down from the train in Readville, the black recruits had sought to bring on a revolutionary conflict and to "prove our fitness for liberty and citizenship in the new order of things now arising in our native land."[62]

As October began, the Fifty-fourth was given the task of guarding Confederate deserters and prisoners of war, not so much as an intentional insult to Southern whites but rather because General Rufus Saxton could imagine "no better officer than Colonel Hallowell" to perform the task. Problems at home in Elmira, on the other hand, continued to bedevil Stephen Swails, who was given yet another thirty-day furlough on November 6. As the War Department was not yet prepared to recognize his commission, Hallowell reluctantly ordered Swails not to wear his lieutenant straps home, but rather "in future wear the uniform of a 1st Sergeant." Two days after Swails's departure came Election Day. Most of the men cheered the news of Lincoln's victory, some because they regarded the Great Emancipator as God's chosen instrument of freedom and others, still irritated with his administration over the protracted pay fight, because they loathed George McClellan and the Democrats' conciliatory platform. Hallowell was thrilled. He thanked "God that 'long Abraham was [president] four years longer' and that he was an honest man." Ned confided to his father that he was "very tired of the war" and longed for home, yet he was "determined to see it through." In northern Virginia, "Grant has the rebel power by the throat," and to the Fifty-fourth's west, "Sherman is tearing their vitals out."[63]

Hallowell was more right than he knew. Three days after Lincoln's reelection, Sherman, then in Kingston, Georgia, telegraphed Washington, requesting that General Foster sever the Charleston and Savannah

Railroad. That crucial lifeline had been the target of the unsuccessful July incursion by the Fifty-fifth, and Sherman wanted the task accomplished by December 1. Foster handed the assignment to General John Hatch, who began to select the 5,000 men believed necessary. Hatch intended to steam upriver past Beaufort, land at Boyd's Neck, and then march overland to capture the junction at Grahamville. As part of his Second Brigade, Hatch decided to take companies from both the Fifty-fourth and Fifty-fifth, with Lieutenant Colonels Charles Fox and Henry Hooper—who had been promoted from major after Olustee—under the joint command of Colonel Alfred Hartwell. Although this would be the first time the two units might see combat together, Foster thought it unnecessary for Hallowell, who knew the regiments better than any other officer, to participate, opting to leave him behind with two companies to guard the islands.[64]

Foster hoped that Charleston would not notice the departure of so many men, so he ordered the tents left standing on Morris and Folly Islands. The troops slipped away to Hilton Head late on the night of Sunday, November 27, leaving behind a disconsolate Hallowell. He rode down the beach, "the empty tents looking like ghosts." With eight companies of his "beloved regiment" gone, he found the camp too quiet; "everything is so lonely," he complained to his mother. After Hatch and the men vacated the island, Hallowell contacted Foster, begging him "to send some one to relieve me in time for me to catch the regiment before it went into action." The young colonel had stood with his men at Wagner and Olustee, and the thought that they might see combat without him left him nearly frantic with worry.[65]

His brother Pen, reading about the affair in Philadelphia, later concluded that the two regiments were doomed to be ordered into indescribable folly by senior officers who had been promoted far above their level of competence. And nature was of no help. As the troops sailed up the winding tributaries that poured into Broad River, heavy fog and hidden undergrowth slowed their advance and snagged their boats. Some of the companies were forced to disembark about half a mile below their designated target of Boyd's Neck; others reached the dilapidated wharf, but "not an army transport was to be seen," according to one officer, the vessels having either gotten lost in the fog or sailed up the wrong estuary and

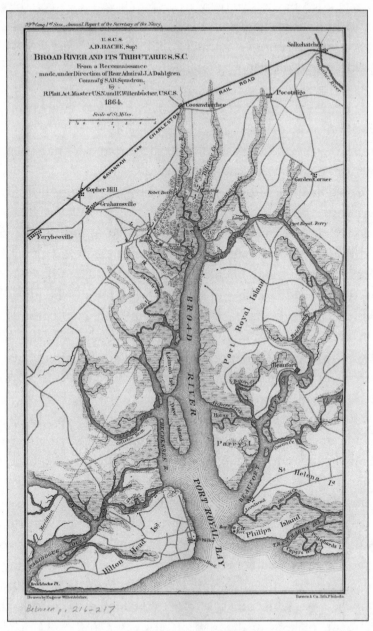

In an effort to sever the Charleston and Savannah Railroad line in support of General Sherman's arrival from Atlanta, Colonel Alfred Hartwell and sixteen companies from the Massachusetts regiments ran into entrenched Confederates at a rise called Honey Hill two miles east of Grahamville (here spelled Grahamsville). For advancing the colors into heavy fire, Corporal Andrew J. Smith became a posthumous recipient of the Medal of Honor in 2001. *Courtesy Library of Congress.*

become grounded in the shallow waters. Yet all was not lost. The railroad was guarded by Confederates stretched thin along its line, and a picket force of roughly seventy-five Southern soldiers was all that stood between the U.S. forces and the depot at Grahamville. Hatch instructed Hartwell's regiments to bivouac at the Neck, while he scouted ahead with several regiments of USCT and a small contingent of sailors. But his maps were worthless, and twice they got lost, losing valuable time.[66]

Not until daybreak on November 30 did the troops finally begin moving down the main plantation road toward Grahamville. Portions of two New York regiments led the way, followed by the Twenty-fifth Ohio and the Third Rhode Island Artillery. The second brigade followed, led by Hartwell and sixteen companies from the Massachusetts units. But downed and damaged bridges slowed their progress, and by 11:00 A.M., they had advanced only three miles. By then, Confederates in the interior had grasped the objective of the invasion and shifted troops toward the junction. Led by Colonel Charles Colcock, between 1,400 and 2,000 troops dug in along the crest of Honey Hill, two miles east of Grahamville. Although the hill was little more than a rise in the road and the semicircular line of earthworks was crudely constructed, Colcock placed seven cannon atop his lines. The road turned just before reaching Honey Hill, so attacking troops would not spy his earthworks until the last moment. To one side of the road sat an empty field of tall grasses, and beyond that a cotton field. On the other side stood a small, whitewashed church backed by a swampy forest that followed the highway for nearly forty yards, transforming the path almost into a narrow bridge, and one easy to defend.[67]

The advance portions of Hatch's force walked directly into the teeth of the Confederate defenders. "The enemy came by the former road, and turned the angle apparently before they were aware of an opposing force," reported a journalist traveling with Colcock's men. Infantry inside the church opened fire, while others set fire to the high grass, forcing the New York regiments to keep to the road or seek cover in the swamp. Colonel James Beecher, now leading the Thirty-fifth USCT, led his men forward, but "our batteries," the Southern journalist recorded, "opened upon them down the road with a terrible volley of spherical case." The regiment fell back in disarray. As at Olustee, the Massachusetts men were far in the rear when they heard the first sounds of gunfire. Hartwell was immediately in the saddle, his sword in one hand, his hat waving like a flag in the other. "Follow your colors," he bellowed as he galloped to the front, directing companies of the Fifty-fifth up the side of the road toward the guns, while shouting for those in the rear to divide up, with some wading into the swamps and others racing through the still-burning fields. Sergeant Trotter led one of the companies toward the guns. At one point, the path grew so narrow that the men raced only four abreast, making the Confederate use of grapeshot murderously effective. "It was like rushing into the very mouth of death going up this road facing 7 pieces of death dealing cannon," Trotter remembered. "But when commanded to charge 'twas not [ours] to refuse," and "in we rushed cheering and yelling."[68]

As Hartwell galloped toward the hill's crest, a charge of canister caught him, blasting his sword from his hand and killing his horse. The dying animal rolled, pinning the young colonel beneath it in the mud. A lieutenant ran forward, cut the saddle from the beast, and helped Hartwell to stagger toward the safety of the woods. Two more balls caught him, and Hartwell shouted to be left behind, but two other men turned to help. One was himself then wounded, but the four eventually made it to the trees. The men bound Hartwell's wounds before returning to the fray. Sergeant Robert King, the eighteen-year-old color-bearer of the Fifty-fifth, Charles Fox later wrote, "was blown to pieces by the explosion of a shell," but Corporal Andrew J. Smith picked up the banner and advanced toward the hill. As they approached the earthworks, a strange moment of silence was followed by a renewed explosion of "grape, canister, and bullets at short range," and the survivors fell back in retreat, tripping over the bodies of the fallen.[69]

At the same time, Hooper arrived with two companies of the Fifty-fourth. He had posted the remainder of the regiment along the road all the way back to Boyd's Neck to secure the column's rear. Just then, General Hatch's chief of staff appeared on the scene, looking, Hooper thought, much "excited." The general demanded that the Massachusetts men again "charge." Hooper was stunned. "Where?" he asked. "Charge! Charge!" was all the aide could say. Wisely, Hooper avoided the main road, instead leading his men into the trees, warning them to seek cover as they advanced and to use their ammunition as sparingly as possible. Beecher and what was left of the Thirty-fifth followed. "It was a perfect jungle all laced with grape vines," he remembered. One of those in the second assault later told Trotter that the forest was so "dense and marshy [that] it was almost impossible on this account to maneuver more than half our troops." As that side of the Confederate earthworks was "very much exposed," the journalist from the *Savannah Republican* worried, the black soldiers might have flanked their lines had enough made it "through the swamp and up the hill," but the bog made for a good barrier.[70]

A few made it across the marsh. Two of those who did were Virginia runaways Peter Drummond and Henry Jarvis, whose company briefly captured one of the Confederate guns. "O God, I've got you," Jarvis shouted in triumph. To his side, Confederate infantrymen spun about and fired. Jarvis took a ball in the arm. "I kep' on fightin' till a ball struck my leg an' I fell," he said later. He was struck "once more in de same leg," the second ball shattering the bone. Drummond and Jarvis had been friends since age six; they had run away together, sailed to Liberia together, and enlisted together, and Peter was not about to leave Henry behind. Together with Augustus Brooks, Drummond dragged Jarvis back into the trees. "I should have bled to death ef all our men hadn't been drilled in usin' a tourniquet, an' supplied wid bandages." The two barely had time to tie up Henry's leg, stick a knife into the knot, "an' twist it tight 'fore I fainted." As a second retreat began in earnest, Sergeant Trotter was also hit, although the wound was not severe enough to keep him from leading his company back down the road toward Boyd's Neck.[71]

After what had transpired at Olustee, the black soldiers refused to leave any wounded behind. Even so, the next morning the Confederates were stunned by the carnage that lay in front of their lines. The bodies "lay five deep as dead as a mackerel," sighed a Confederate gunner. The reporter for the *Savannah Republican* concurred, writing that he "counted some sixty or seventy bodies in a space of about an acre, many of which were horribly mutilated by shells, some with half their heads blown off." At No. 6 General Hospital in Beaufort, Jarvis "stood it all for to keep my leg," and the surgeons tried to save it, but "pieces of de bone [kept] a comin' out," and at length they sawed it off four inches below his pelvis. American casualties were severe, with 89 killed, 629 wounded, and, despite the best efforts of the troops to leave no man behind, 28 captured. Confederates reported only 47 total casualties, with 8 killed and 39 wounded. Trotter guessed that the Confederate casualties were not that much less than U.S. casualties, "although they try and make it so." But while that was invariably true, they had, as Trotter conceded, "such natural positions as more than made up for such deficiencies" of numbers.[72]

The Northern press largely blamed the tragedy on fog, shallow inlets, and poor maps rather than Hatch's inept leadership. In truth, all played a role in the defeat. But in later years, one soldier concluded "that the Rebels had a trap set for us and we were marched right into it." Reading of the battle, Pen Hallowell agreed that if Hatch could not be blamed for the miscalculations that took place on November 29, the next day's order to storm the hill was "not free from the charge of down-right recklessness." The narrow roadway and the swamps to one side made the assault, Pen decided, sadly reminiscent of Wagner. A veteran of the Fifty-fourth who survived both battles drew a similar comparison. "Wagner always seemed to me the most terrible of our battles," thought Sergeant Charles Lenox, "but the musketry at Honey Hill was something fearful." As the sad news filtered back to Morris Island, Ned Hallowell thought the only positive aspect to his missing the action was that he was "alive to comfort those who lived through it." He understood that had he been there, it might have been him, rather than Hartwell, who lay in a bed in Beaufort, or even in the ground. "It's very hard Mother to make up your mind that you are willing [to] die," he wrote home, "but it's ever so much harder to content yourself at [camp] while others are suffering. Oh Mother I wish I was a boy, so that I might cry out."[73]

Hallowell sent that letter in December, by which time the Fifty-fourth and the Fifty-fifth were preparing to celebrate their second Christmas on the islands. Despite their losses, the men rightly took heart in the Northern praise for the way they fought in the face of impossible odds. William Lloyd Garrison anointed the Fifty-fifth as "heroes of all the hard fights that have occurred in the department since their arrival" on the coast. (Privately, Garrison was happier yet to hear from George, who miraculously "escaped without a scratch.") The festering issue of pay had at long last been resolved, if not before the tragic execution of Private Wallace Baker, a man, unlike John Smith, mourned by his fellows. Though the matter of black

promotion and advancement remained a source of discontent, the bombardment of Charleston continued, and from the number of Confederate
deserters who wandered into the camps, it was clear that the city would
soon fall, and if so, that was in no small part thanks to their sacrifices.[74]

On December 18, however, word arrived that General Sherman was
displeased that the rail lines were not yet severed. Both regiments understood that their battles, both political and military, were far from over.

CHAPTER NINE

Liberation

"**P**URSUANT TO AUTHORITY RECEIVED FROM THE U.S. DEPART-
ment of War," the *Weekly Anglo-African* reported in early January
1864, "a regiment of Cavalry Volunteers, to be composed of men of color,
is now in process of recruitment." The essay carried a lengthy description of
promised state compensation: a $325 bounty to enlist, another $50 upon
successful completion of training at Camp Meigs, and then a monthly
salary of $20, "in addition to the pay now or hereafter received by him
from the United States." As John Andrew took "great satisfaction [in] the
progress made" by the Fifty-fourth, the newspaper remarked, the governor was equally confident in a regiment of black riders designed to "illustrate their capacity for that dashing and brilliant arm of the military
service." The men of the Fifty-fourth and Fifty-fifth contested with the
black soldiers in the First Kansas Colored Volunteers and the First South
Carolina Volunteers, which had been reorganized as the Seventy-ninth
and Thirty-third USCT, respectively, over pride of place as the army's
first black regiment—although those units were fairly unknown to white
Americans—so Andrew wished it known that his would be the first black
cavalry regiment anywhere in the country. The "destiny of their race is in

their own grasp," the governor insisted. It "is in the hands of those now invited to unite in the final blow which will annihilate the rebel power, [so] let no brave and strong man hesitate."[1]

For Andrew and the black soldiers already in the field, the right to serve as cavalrymen was every bit as critical as equal pay or promotion in the ranks. Cavalrymen were elite troops, as evidenced by their higher pay as well as their reputation for dash and courage—and by the dangers they risked, as men on horseback made inviting targets. Midway through the war, however, advances in the technology of the rifled musket—now able to reach 300 yards—had effectively put an end to the cavalry charges that had been pioneered in Europe during the Napoleonic era. Although trained as a cavalryman, for instance, U.S. General John Buford had come to regard the old saber charges as anachronistic, in part because of the disastrous assault made by his friend Elon Farnsworth and the First Vermont Cavalry at Gettysburg. Buford instead advocated transforming cavalry regiments into mounted infantry units armed with carbines, which could be fired at twice the speed of the muskets carried by infantrymen, so that they might move quickly during battle but also dismount and fight on foot. Some more traditional Confederates, such as General Jeb Stuart, remained wedded to the old concept, but Andrew saw the logic in the new tactics (while Stuart was destined to be shot by a dismounted Union private). As with the two black infantry regiments, Andrew's newest experiment would not be created under the auspices of the USCT. There already being four Massachusetts cavalry regiments, this was to be the Fifth Massachusetts Cavalry.[2]

If anything, Andrew faced even more formidable obstacles than he had the previous January when creating the Fifty-fourth. For one, most Northern whites had an even harder time visualizing African Americans as elite cavalrymen than as common infantrymen. The cost of arming and mounting 1,000 men, moreover, far exceeded the price of outfitting as many infantrymen, and the expense of maintaining ten companies in the field did not decline once the men left camp. The War Department's Cavalry Bureau also struggled to maintain a "supply of public animals to our gallant armies in the field"; the high combat losses incurred by 1864 had increasingly forced the army to purchase inferior mounts at ever-rising prices. And even for those recruits who were accustomed to working with farm horses, learning to conduct complicated maneuvers as part of a mounted group required months of training.[3]

To command the unit, Andrew tapped Henry S. Russell, then a lieutenant colonel in the Second Massachusetts Cavalry. Just shy of twenty-six, the Harvard graduate had seen considerable action in Virginia, fighting beside the late Charles Russell Lowell. But what most recommended him for the post—as the antislavery press enthusiastically emphasized—was that he was a cousin to Rob Shaw. As had his kinsman, Russell initially preferred to stay with his old regiment, but after reflection, he concluded that "Bob would have liked to have me do it." Several white officers from the Fifty-fifth shipped back north to join the new regiment, but no black private from either of the two Massachusetts regiments joined them, though they were given the option. Black newspapers understood that the recruits would come from the South, especially from among the refugees in Washington who had once been grooms or had cared for their masters' finest steeds. "Let us astonish Gen. Lee and the pride of the old cavalry brigade," the *Weekly Anglo-African* proclaimed, "by the novel spectacle of their own servants sabreing their old masters to the tune of Yankee Doodle!"[4]

Andrew wanted to have a sound Massachusetts man as the regiment's second-in-command. Several advisers advanced the candidacy of Charles Francis Adams Jr., who had by then advanced to the rank of captain in the First Massachusetts Cavalry. The Adams name meant more to the public than did Russell's, and Charles Sr.'s long-standing support for free-soil politics had led Andrew to believe that the son was more devoted to the cause than he actually was. But if Adams continued to harbor racist assumptions about the character of African Americans, the Fifty-fourth had erased any doubts he had about the ability of black men to fight. White soldiers might eventually capture Richmond, Adams thought, but America's fight to overcome racism would never "take a step backward" if it was a "success to which 200,000 armed blacks have contributed." When contacted by the governor, Adams hesitated, but not for long. Russell was an old friend from college days, and Adams, who was typical of the cold, dour men in his family, knew that there were few in his regiment "who know or care for me." He later insisted that he cared little "for the increased rank, still less for the pay," but while the latter was surely true, Adams men always strove for excellence, and upon achieving success they invariably wished the world to acknowledge it. A "colored regiment would prove an interesting study," he mused. And so, provided that the army granted him seventy days' leave for a voyage to Britain to visit his father and brother, as well as a few days in Boston to see his fiancée, Mary Elizabeth Ogden, Adams accepted the commission and promised to be at Readville by March.[5]

Of the noncommissioned officers, the final one to sign on was Charles Douglass. Content to remain in Readville and process paperwork for both the Fifty-fourth and Fifty-fifth, the young corporal had little interest in equestrian pursuits or in shipping south. Organized and possessed of a clear script, Douglass enjoyed the clerical life at Meigs, which often allowed him to venture into Boston on army business. On several occasions, Douglass had been instructed to prepare to escort new recruits for the two regiments to Folly or Morris Islands, but each time those orders fell through. Of all the black soldiers in the Fifty-fourth and Fifty-fifth, in fact, only Douglass transferred to the cavalry, and perhaps not of his own volition. But the Fifth required his skills, and so, on March 26, he signed on for another three years—provided the war lasted that long—and was promoted to sergeant. At the same time, his older brother, Frederick Douglass Jr., received a commission from Andrew to journey south down the Mississippi in search of former bondmen who could ride.[6]

ON MAY 13, THE *LIBERATOR* REPORTED THAT 1,000 CAVALRYMEN were "mounted, armed, equipped, and ready for service." Frederick Douglass Jr. and the other recruiters had found enough men with experience in the saddle, and in less than four months the companies had mastered "the cavalry drills," although the task of training "the horses to the motion of different exercises" remained unfinished. The men grumbled a bit when the paymaster arrived, since the salary issue had not yet been resolved in Washington; even Sergeant Charles Douglass was paid a private's wages. Unlike the Northern freemen in their sister regiments, however, the unit's black Southerners did not refuse to accept the proffered payments. Also unlike the Fifty-fourth and Fifty-fifth, the Fifth was roughly two-thirds former bondmen, and possibly because of that, the men were quick to take offense at slights to their manhood. When a white officer slapped a recruit with the flat of his sword, the private spun about, bayonet at the ready. "God damn you!" he shouted. "You will not strike *me* that way." The unnamed officer wisely let the incident drop, but the point had been made. Former slaves—some of whom carried the scars of their previous lives on their bodies—were done being battered about by white sons of privilege.[7]

The largely different background of the soldiers in the Fifth set them apart from the black infantrymen in other ways as well. All black soldiers sought to eradicate slavery, but many of the soldiers from New England boasted of ancestors who had been free for generations. Many of the refugees who joined the Fifth Cavalry, by comparison, left wives and children behind when they ran for Union lines, and so for them the war against slavery took on a personal dimension. Peter Vogelsang had enlisted in the Fifty-fourth in the hopes of forcing his nation and state to recognize his claims of citizenship, but for most of the black cavalrymen such a dream stood far behind a desire to free yet-enslaved families. For them the North was not a refuge, merely a place to train before returning as liberators to their native South. Although most of them became politicized during the last years of the war, their backgrounds made them almost as culturally distant from Sergeant Douglass as they were from Colonel Russell.

Readville could be damp and muddy, but the spring of 1864 was warmer and dryer than usual. The men's health was "pretty good," one private informed editor Robert Hamilton, and the "officers are much respected." That was surely due in part to the fact that upon joining the regiment Adams confined his opinions of black capabilities to his letters home. Like many white Republicans, Adams, as he explained it to his father, based his "opposition to slavery" on the notion that the peculiar institution was nearly as harmful to national progress as it was to the slaves themselves. The former bondmen in his new regiment would certainly have disagreed with his assumption that the vast majority of slaves "were not, as a whole, unhappy, cruelly treated, or overworked." Nor did they refer to their unit, as did Adams, as "nigger all over."[8]

Not even Adams, however, could miss the readiness of the men to defend their honor. In early May, as the Fifth departed Readville for Point Lookout, Maryland, and traveled through Philadelphia, a man on crutches hobbled into the street and broke one over the head of a soldier. The assailant was saved only when an onlooker knocked the man to the ground.

Even then, a white officer had to protect the attacker from the sabers of half a dozen soldiers of the Fifth. Upon reaching Baltimore, one of the soldiers involved "shot at a rough for insults." At length, the regiment reached their camp, which Adams derided as "a low, sandy, malarious, fever-smitten, wind-blown, God-forsaken tongue of land dividing Chesapeake Bay from the Potomac River."[9]

Having arrived without most of their horses, the Fifth was put to work guarding roughly 1,400 Confederate prisoners. The enormous depot at Point Lookout was under the command of General Edward Hinks, who was appalled, despite his Maine origins, by the idea of black cavalrymen. As had Rob Shaw and Ned Hallowell before him, Colonel Russell feared that his men were doomed to endless guard duty and fatigue work. "Hurrah for the day that we shall throw aside our muskets for sabres," one officer confided to his brother. Each man stood guard on alternate days, a schedule that gave the soldiers leisure time, Sergeant George Booth informed the *Weekly Anglo-African,* to fish "for oysters, crabs, rock or tailor fish, of which there are not a few." Douglass's company raided a nearby farmhouse and confiscated seven chickens. The soldiers performed "their duty cheerfully," Booth insisted, but they longed to see action and prove their mettle. Russell continually lobbied the War Department to assign the regiment to the campaigns in Virginia, and in June he was able to announce that horses would soon arrive. "Then we shall show ourselves one of the best cavalry regiments in the service," Booth boasted.[10]

THE FIFTH DID NOT HAVE LONG TO WAIT. AFTER ASSAULTING ENtrenched Confederate lines at Cold Harbor, Virginia, with disastrous results, General Ulysses S. Grant had refocused his armies on Petersburg. The town, roughly thirty miles south of Richmond, was held by a force of only 2,500 men under General P. G. T. Beauregard, who had been transferred from Charleston. Petersburg was crucial to the Confederate supply lines into Richmond, and General Robert E. Lee hurried reinforcements to bolster Beauregard's thin line. The attack called for General Quincy Adams Gillmore—now stationed in Virginia—to lead two columns of USCT across the Appomattox River, while cavalrymen swept around the city and attacked from the southeast. This third column was led by General August

Kautz, the German-born commander of the Second Ohio Cavalry. The Fifth was in his rear when Kautz unexpectedly encountered Confederate pickets. "We had gone but a short distance before we came upon the ambulance train," Douglass noticed uneasily, "then I knew some of us were not coming back again."[11]

Just days before, Charles had confided to his father that he was "not over anxious" to see battle, but "our boys are very anxious for a fight," and if it came to that, he promised to "meet the devils at any moment and take no prisoners." In fact, however, Douglass had done just that the previous week when he encountered a Confederate deserter while standing picket. The deserter got within a dozen yards of Douglass before the two spied one another. The Confederate ducked behind a tree, but Douglass shouted for him to step out "or I would knock a hole through him." The white soldier, half-starved, did so, and Douglass could see that he was unarmed. Douglass ordered the man to start marching, cocking his rifle as he did so. As terrified of black soldiers as Douglass was nervous, the prisoner asked if Douglass intended "to murder him." Upon reaching the camp, Douglass and his captain searched the man and discovered papers indicating that he "owned the land where we picketed." If Douglass felt a bit foolish in arresting a deserter on his own farm, he did not indicate as much to his famous father or war hero brother. Rather more satisfactory was that Douglass, while riding his gray mare, discovered six runaways hiding in a nearby farmhouse, whom he shepherded to safety.[12]

By sunup on June 15, the Fifth was within five miles of Petersburg. Moving toward the American forces was a dense swarm of refugees, both white and black, trying to escape the coming battle. "Buggies, hacks, and vehicles of every description were in use, carrying off the women and children," one soldier reported. "Hundreds, nay thousands of colored people [and] women, poor harmless looking creatures, with rags for clothing" clogged the roads. To one side of the Fifth marched six USCT regiments, while more than 20,000 white soldiers under the command of General Lysander Cutler advanced to their left. Facing them were Confederates sheltered in rifle pits and protected by a system of trenches and breastworks twenty feet thick and backed by four cannon. The Fifth dismounted and "moved forward down the hill into a wheat-field, forming two lines of battle," Douglass wrote. "Sending out skirmishers, we soon met the enemy's advance pickets and drove them back through two pieces of woods. Our regiment was in the second line of battle." As the Confederate pickets retreated, one shouted: "Lincoln's Massachusetts niggers are on us. They are coming, the damned black bastards, but we'll give 'em hell."[13]

"As we came through the second piece of woods, the enemy opened on us with solid shot and shell," Douglass remembered. The Fifth plowed ahead, taking brief shelter in some woods to their front. "Then we were only about a quarter of a mile from the enemy, they being drawn up in line of battle behind their breastworks," he added. "All this time we were under a withering fire from the rebel batteries." The underbrush was thick, slowing down the charge and hindering their ability to remain formed in battle lines. The Confederates opened with "shell, grape and canisters" that raked their lines "cruelly," Private Charles Beman recalled, but "we rallied" and continued the charge "amidst pieces of barbarous iron, solid shot and shell." The first line of attackers faltered, and Colonel Russell bawled to fix bayonets. Charles Douglass was immediately to Russell's right. "Come on, brave boys of the Fifth!" Russell screamed, just as a ball snapped off his shoulder-strap. "In an instant our men began to fall around us pretty fast," Beman later wrote, but those still on their feet poured over the breastworks, driving "the desperate greybacks from their fortifications," and captured two of the cannons. "Young, middle-aged and old men, fearful of their doom, were flying before the negro legions of Massachusetts," a third cavalryman reported. Two hundred Confederates threw up their hands in surrender, and standing atop the captured fortifications, the Fifth "gave three cheers for our victory." Douglass then noticed that it was not merely Russell's strap that had been hit: a second ball had found his upper arm. Bleeding profusely, Russell refused to leave the field until a surgeon insisted he do so; Douglass then helped him stagger toward the rear.[14]

There Douglass fell to the ground, exhausted. "I am yet unhurt, but am much worn out; my shoulders are raw, from the straps of my cartridge-box, as I had forty rounds in my box, two days' rations, canteen, blankets and musket," he wrote home. But the Fifth felt vindicated. "It was rather interesting to see the old veterans of the A[rmy of the] P[otomac] stare when they saw the works we had captured," one soldier marveled. In the attack, another wrote to the *Weekly Anglo-African*, the Fifth "not only proved themselves valorous men, but added fresh laurels to the already imperishable laurels of the glorious Bay State." In what became known as the Battle of Baylor's Farm, the Fifth suffered three men killed, with nineteen more wounded.[15]

Fearful of Confederate reinforcements and sharing Hinks's distrust of black cavalrymen, General William Smith had refused to allow either the Fifth or the USCT units to pursue the retreating Confederates. Grant was furious at Smith's decision, believing that a perfect opportunity to capture Petersburg had been lost. "There was nothing—not even a military force," he groused, "to prevent our walking in and taking possession." The result would be a lengthy siege of the city.[16]

ALTHOUGH HE WOULD LIVE, THE POPULAR RUSSELL WAS TOO INJURED to carry on as the Fifth's commander. The colonelcy was temporarily handed to Henry Bowditch, but only until Governor Andrew and the War Department could permanently assign the position to Lieutenant Colonel Adams. Once again, Adams assured his father, the offers of promotion arrived "unsought by me and undesired." By the mid-nineteenth century, politicians had abandoned the quaint early American custom of pursuing office while loudly announcing their indifference, but the tradition remained strong in the Adams family. Now twenty-nine, Adams awaited only the arrival of his orders before briefly heading to Washington, "and immediately afterwards," he told his mother, "I shall join my colored brethren." Thanks to hearty exercise and heavy doses of quinine, he was free of earlier touches of malaria and jaundice and ready to command. "You will agree with me that '64 came to me full handed and has been to me a pleasant and a prosperous year," he bragged to his still-unconvinced father.[17]

If ready to lead the regiment, Adams's brief tenure as the Fifth's second-in-command had not altered his opinions of blacks. Of their "courage in action," he conceded, "there can no doubts exist," particularly after the fight below Petersburg. But of "their physical and mental and moral energy and stamina I entertain grave doubts," he wrote. Although sound enough as infantrymen, blacks, Adams maintained, were "wholly unfit for cavalry service, lacking absolutely the essential qualities of alertness, individuality, reliability, and self-reliance." Few of the wealthy white officers in any of the three black regiments had been close to black men before the war, and both Shaw and Hallowell had preferred to promote light-skinned soldiers in rank. But only Adams, surrounded by dark-skinned freedmen, never grew to appreciate the men he led, no matter how well they performed. Even when he praised them, it was in a patronizing, racially tinged fashion. "You never saw such fellows to eat and sleep!" he wrote to his brother Henry. "Then they're built so much better than white men. Their feet—you never saw such feet." At least, Adams considered, the army was "the proper school for the race," for in the army "they learn to take care of themselves." It never occurred to Adams, evidently, that while enslaved, his recruits had cared for themselves, their families, and their masters' horses, all without the supervision of Massachusetts Brahmins.[18]

Much to the dismay of Adams's men, following their June action near Petersburg they were ordered back to Point Lookout to continue guarding Confederate prisoners and construct floating bridges. "After escaping rebel bullets, railroad iron, and harrow teeth," one soldier complained, they were "sent to the front with inexperienced officers to make pontoon bridges." Others were set to labor at "removing the rubbish which had accumulated" at the camp of a departing USCT regiment. The soldiers had joined up to fight, but "drilled in Cavalry tactics," they instead found themselves, as had the Fifty-fifth before them, routinely abused as common laborers. "The regiment has been worked harder than any regiment that ever left the state," one officer believed. Ever ready to strike back at white tormentors, one soldier warned that should such "outrages" continue, they "shall be under the painful necessity of turning our arms against these demagogues, who, daringly, insult and trample on our manhood without just cause."[19]

As colonel, Adams performed no labor, but he was as bored by the inactivity as were his men. The Fifth were perhaps fortunate to miss out on the July 30 Battle of the Crater, in which Confederates slaughtered a USCT force after U.S. miners blew a hole in Southern fortifications by packing 8,000 pounds of gunpowder into an underground shaft. "I did not see the mine exploded," Adams lamented. After the detonation, orders to ride in support arrived too late. "The cavalry did not reach [Petersburg] until the assault had failed," he told his father. "The march was difficult, but it was possible," he wrote, but "it was not accomplished" owing to a badly coordinated effort. The disheartened men returned to camp, where Adams announced his desire "to see the war over, so that I may see my way out of the army" and get home. "I am tired of the Carnival of Death," he told Henry, melodramatically. In the meantime, he occupied his time by drafting "a somewhat stately paper" for Governor Andrew on how best to organize a cavalry regiment. The essay, he assured his father—himself a celebrated author and editor before turning to politics and diplomacy—was "distinguished by unusual ability even for me." Otherwise, "I wait here and kill time."[20]

As much as Adams might doubt his men's abilities, as their colonel he wished them properly outfitted. Too many rode old, tired mounts, and some cavalrymen had no horses at all. Determined to obtain an adequate supply of first-rate animals, Adams caught the train for Washington, a town he thought he knew how to navigate. From the first moment of his arrival, however, he found himself in a bureaucratic quagmire. After being told by two War Department staffers that all available horses were needed for the Petersburg siege, Adams knocked on the door of Colonel James Hardie, who referred him to Charles Dana, assistant secretary of war. "Dana suggested Colonel This or General That," Adams sighed, and when that failed he tried Henry Halleck, general-in-chief of all U.S. armies. "In about one minute he signaled an emphatic disapproval of me and of my plan," before slamming his door in Adams's face. The frustrated colonel tried Secretary of State William Henry Seward, an old family friend, and he even encountered Governor Andrew and adviser John Murray Forbes, as both were then in Washington. The two were encouraging but lacked authority with Secretary of War Edwin Stanton. Adams next tried General George Gordon Meade, the hero of Gettysburg, who promised nothing more than a letter of introduction to Grant. Adams had heard little good of the hard-drinking general, and he expected even less. But quitting Washington for the Virginia countryside, Adams thought it worth a try.[21]

Adams found Grant sitting in front of his tent, chatting with several staff members. The young colonel explained why he was there, and Grant asked him to be seated. Grant sat, "puffing at his eternal cigar and stroking his beard as he listened to what I had to say," Adams told his mother. Staring hard at Adams, Grant surprised him by replying only: "I will approve your plan and request the Secretary [of War] to issue you the horses and have an order made out to you to go to Washington to attend to it yourself." Adams was stunned, admitting that this "was three times what I had expected to get from him." While Grant dashed out the order on the back of Meade's letter, he chatted with Adams "as he would had he been [just] another Captain of Cavalry." The young officer promptly announced himself to be "a violent Grant man," and Adams returned to his regiment with 700 of the best horses, "without exception," that he had "ever seen in Virginia." Being an Adams, however, meant never being content with success, and he complained to his brother Henry that while they now had excellent mounts, he "didn't have one tolerable blacksmith."[22]

Though fortified by his exercise regime and doses of quinine, Adams fell ill as fall turned into winter. October 1864 was an unusually wet and cold one, even in Virginia, and on November 17 he was granted one month's sick leave. Although he spent the time in wintery Quincy, Adams could at least enjoy hot food and a warm hearth's fire rather than remain ill in a damp tent. Suffering too was Sergeant Douglass, whose lung ailments contracted at Readville nineteen months before had never completely mended. As a result, "I am Honorably discharged [from] the service of the United States," Charles informed his parents. Douglass first had to travel to Washington to have his "papers made out for pay," after which he planned to sail north to Boston before catching a train for Rochester. "Love to you all," he finished his brief note, before signing off with: "Your Aff. Son, Charles R. Douglass, civilian."[23]

ALTHOUGH HE PERHAPS WAS UNAWARE OF IT, DOUGLASS PASSED through the War Department in the same month that another black soldier arrived to make his case for promotion. The previous spring, in the days after his heroics at Olustee, Stephen Swails had been promoted to second lieutenant by Governor Andrew on the recommendation of Ned Hallowell. The unprecedented action made news across the North, with the *Liberator* praising Andrew for having "dealt a sturdy blow to colorphobia." But General John Foster, the latest commander of the Department of the South, had refused to muster him out as a sergeant major without authorization from Washington. Word shortly arrived at Hilton Head that Secretary Stanton approved of Foster's delay, pending action by Congress. Hallowell was furious. He ordered Swails "to discard his officer's uniform," but also procured him a furlough to travel to Hilton Head to see Foster himself. Foster in turn extended Swails's furlough so that he might go to Washington and present his case. The general was at least willing to arm Swails with a letter remarking on the "several occasions" in which he "distinguished himself in battle." Foster also assured an annoyed Andrew that "in refusing to discharge him as an enlisted man," he had "acted under particular orders from the War Department."[24]

Hallowell had no interest in letting the matter drift. On June 1, he informed Captain William Burger, Adjutant General for the Department of the South, that he was again asking that Swails "be discharged in order to accept promotion," insisting that as a "vacancy exists in the grade" of second lieutenant, his regiment was short on senior officers. At about the same time, Alfred Hartwell added to the pressure by recommending James Monroe Trotter for the same rank. Once again, the promotion was denied on the grounds that "no law existed for their muster as commissioned officers." Trotter was particularly incensed, as some white officers made little effort to hide the fact that they took a "most lively satisfaction at the result." One pulled Trotter aside to counsel patience, advice that white conservatives had dispensed for decades—and would do so for years to come. "An officer told me that it was 'too soon,' that time should be granted white officers to *get rid of their prejudices*," Trotter fumed. The "U.S. government has refused so far to muster them because *God did not make them White*," Trotter wrote to the *Weekly Anglo-African*. "No other objection can be offered. *Three cheers for 'our country.'"*[25]

With the pay issue at last resolved, the question of promotions became the new flash point for the soldiers of the three Massachusetts regiments and the abolitionists who held the top positions in each. As a good abolitionist, Hallowell saw only the injustice of denying promotion to a deserving sergeant who had "distinguished himself for coolness and bravery." Swails's crime in the eyes of the War Department, Hallowell supposed, was that his "skin is rather darker than most officers." The dark-skinned soldiers in the regiments, however, could hardly fail to notice that the men most quickly promoted at Readville were of light complexion. Almost all of those promoted to sergeant or corporal by Shaw or the Hallowell brothers had other attributes to recommend them—literacy, age, family connections—yet invariably they were also mixed-race. Swails, Vogelsang, Trotter, Gooding, and even Charles and Lewis Douglass had white fathers or white ancestors. Swails was "as brave as any of the commissioned officers," one soldier admitted. Yet "we cannot call the promotion of Swails a triumph, as he is too near white." In most states, if not told that Swails was a man of color, "he would be a white man, [and] therefore the victory is barren."[26]

In the spring, though, there did appear some cause for hope, at least with regard to the basic question at hand. Attorney General Edward Bates's public letter to Lincoln of April 23, 1864, on the salary dispute already hinted that the commander-in-chief could do as he wished under the Second Confiscation Act. "I have already said that I know of no provision or law," Bates had concluded, "which prohibited the acceptance of persons of African descent into the military," and consequently there was also no law that forbade them from being "lawfully accepted as commissioned officers, if otherwise qualified." Garrison's *Liberator* continued to publicize Bates's ruling, which mirrored the argument that Trotter had been making almost from the day of his enlistment: "Do you know any law that *prohibits*" black promotion? In the meantime, one soldier grumbled, African Americans awaited the advancement of "men from their own ranks" while continuing to serve "under command of [white] vagabonds and upstarts" who were approved by the board merely because of their race.[27]

WHILE WASHINGTON DITHERED, THE FIFTY-FOURTH AND FIFTY-FIFTH were ordered to again try to sever the Charleston and Savannah Railroad, this time by capturing the junction at Pocotaligo, a hamlet far above Hilton Head on the river of the same name. Sherman's forces continued to advance from the southwest, and the general also sought intelligence on the size of Confederate forces below Charleston. As acting assistant adjutant general, Lieutenant Leonard Perry, an officer in the Fifty-fifth, placed the Second Brigade—which included the Thirty-fourth USCT—under Hallowell's command. Perry then ordered Hallowell to take portions of the Fifty-fourth, together with Alfred Hartwell and the Fifty-fifth, and move inland. The march began on the afternoon of December 20, 1864. After riding ahead in reconnaissance, Lieutenant Colonel Charles Trowbridge of the Thirty-third USCT reported back that the main road toward the junction was littered with felled trees, while impassible swamps to the lane's left would require the black troops to thin out into a long, vulnerable line.[28]

The advance forces were within a mile of Pocotaligo when they encountered roughly 300 Confederate cavalrymen, spread from the river on Trowbridge's right into the swamp on his left. The Thirty-third attempted to fight their way into a small gap near the marsh, but the Confederates retreated into nearby woods, "opening a brisk fire" on the advancing soldiers. The soldiers charged into the woods "and routed the enemy, who broke and fled in the direction of the railroad," Trowbridge later reported. But Hallowell, upon moving to the front, ordered his brigade to pull back down the road. The narrow causeway prevented him from utilizing most of his troops, and he suspected that the Confederates would dig in outside the town, turning any attack into a second Honey Hill. He reported that his men had "captured some of their blankets, overcoats, haversacks, canteens, &c.," and guessed at twenty to thirty Confederate casualties. Hallowell's brigade suffered seven casualties, two of them mortally wounded. Among the wounded was Colonel Alfred Hartwell, with three more wounds to add to the two balls he took at Honey Hill, although this time none were serious. As ever, the Confederates minimized their losses and exaggerated their victory. General Beauregard informed Richmond that they had captured much of Hallowell's "transportation, baggage, and supplies" and that the retreating American forces had abandoned "many dead negro troops on the road." The black soldiers burned "Government and railroad buildings" as they "retreated in the direction they came," he added, and that was probably true enough. Hallowell's temporary setback, however, did little to slow the overall Union strategy, and Sherman expected to capture Savannah within days.[29]

Five days later Christmas arrived, and almost magically at noon so too did a basket for Hallowell from Philadelphia. "I jumped with joy," he assured his mother, adding: "I love thee and some day I'll try to be worthy of thee." The package was bursting with "Turkey, Cranberries, Mince pies, Cake, sugar, plums, tooth powder, Cigars, tobacco, Whiskey, poetry & Butter." It was hard to be so far from home during the holidays, and Hallowell wished "it was not my duty to fight, then I'd come home & be thy darling." Hallowell also informed his sister that "a party of ten contrabands came into our lines," having hidden "all night in the swamp, the little children nearly dead with cold." The soldiers ate well, including a slaughtered cow taken during the Pocotaligo skirmish, and that made up for "the life we lead in the field," which was at once "cruel, inhuman, awful, but exciting and jolly." Wilkie James could hear the distant guns shelling Charleston, which gave his men "the merriest Christmas wish we possibly could."[30]

New Year's Day of 1865 found the Fifty-fourth back in their old quarters on Morris Island, and the Fifty-fifth, temporarily under the command of Lieutenant Colonel Charles Fox until Hartwell mended, returned to their camp on Folly, hard beside Trowbridge and the Thirty-third USCT. Most of the soldiers were allowed to journey down the coast to Beaufort to help celebrate the second anniversary of the Emancipation Proclamation. "The many bleeding and bruised of the 55th, who had poured out their life's blood free as water, at the fight of Honey Hill," deserved the day off, remarked the Reverend John Bowles, the regiment's chaplain. As their transport steamer neared the landing, the soldiers spied a procession of freed men and women "moving down to the dock to receive" them. Behind the crowd marched a band, and behind the musicians came a wagon bearing the "Goddess of Liberty," drawn by six white horses and "filled with a score or more of boys and girls, bearing Union flags in their hands." The goddess, Bowles noticed, was "a good looking colored woman dressed in white," with an American flag tied as a sash over one shoulder. As the soldiers tumbled off the boat, the woman "sang a national song, assisted by the children." The children, Bowles later discovered, were being taught to read by a black-run school in Beaufort. "What a sight in South Carolina!" the reverend marveled.[31]

By the month's end, Hallowell had received orders to sail again upriver toward Pocotaligo. "The men will carry in their knapsacks and haversacks five days' rations" only, his orders detailed, with the rest of their gear stored in Hilton Head. Confederate forces had evacuated Savannah on December 20, and Sherman's army arrived around noon on the following day. Sherman had placed the city under martial law, a new experience to white Georgians, who found themselves prisoners in their own town. Savannah's blacks had crowded into the Second African Baptist Church to celebrate their liberation. One bondwoman "screeched and screamed" when she saw the general; her voice finally gave out, and so she took off her apron and waved it in salute as he passed by. Sherman next planned to move north, and he wanted either Pocotaligo captured or the rail lines cut. This time Hallowell was to be given both cavalry and artillery support.[32]

At about the same time, five companies of the Fifth-fifth sailed for Savannah, with the remaining forces remaining on Folly Island to assist with the Charleston siege. Hartwell had recovered enough to rejoin the departing companies, and when the noncommissioned officers heard of his return, Sergeant Trotter recalled, "we made the old tent ring with cheers." After an uneventful journey, the soldiers established their encampment at Fort Camp Barton, a large fortress about four miles from Savannah, "named after a prominent slave holding Rebel," Trotter noted sourly. There was no other black regiment in the region, and the white residents of the city "did not fancy being guarded by colored soldiers," one Northern journalist remarked. Or, as Trotter put it, invoking the biblical story of God's judgment on Babylon: white Georgians "are trembling because of our proximity" to Savannah, "and the expectation of our coming to town to them was [as] Belshazzar reads the handwriting on the wall."[33]

The end was in sight, and the men knew it. Better yet for morale, on Saturday, January 21, Edwin Stanton notified Governor Andrew that he was "authorizing Swails being mustered" as a second lieutenant, making him the first man of color in the entire army to become a commissioned officer. New England newspapers uniformly praised the promotion, noting Swails's "conspicuous gallantry in action, and his merits as a man of character." William Lloyd Garrison, of course, applauded Stanton's decision but correctly observed that somebody in Washington "might have done this piece of justice long ago." Reformers recognized that Swails's promotion would establish a precedent for others, but Stanton's silence on Hartwell's recommendation of a lieutenancy for Trotter led one soldier to write to the *Liberator* to wonder "about other colored men who have already given, or who may hereafter give, good cause to be recommended for promotion." Would Trotter's and Vogelsang's names be submitted to the board of examiners as if they were white men, "or is each such instant to be made the subject of a protracted correspondence, a series of postponements, and finally a special order from the War Department?" If Stanton had hoped that a single promotion would silence the black community and their allies, he had missed that the debate was over principle. Black soldiers wished to be treated precisely as were whites, as if color were simply not a consideration.[34]

The Fifty-fourth found little time to celebrate. With Sherman slicing a path toward the South Carolina state capital of Columbia, Confederates abandoned Pocotaligo on January 14 and retreated into the interior. Hallowell and his Second Brigade—which had grown with the addition of two companies of white Ohio soldiers—marched into an abandoned junction. Word then arrived for him to move north along the rail line toward Charleston, while conducting "a reconnaissance of the enemy's position" on the southern side of Charleston Harbor. Hallowell's superiors expected him to move fast, and his orders were to take only "two days' rations and sixty rounds of ammunition per man." The companies of the Fifty-fifth who remained on Folly received orders to sail down the coast and then up the Edisto River and to connect there with the Fifty-fourth. With Confederates racing west to support Columbia, General Foster hoped to encircle Charleston's rear from the southwest. Small bands of retreating Confederates "halted on every bit of rising ground, or on the farther side of swamps, to throw up barricades of fence-rails," reported one soldier in the Fifty-fourth, "and delayed our advance by shelling us with their field-pieces." But Hallowell's "skirmishers moved on steadily through water, swamp, and heavy under-growth, until their flanks were threatened, when, after exchanging shots, they would retire to new positions."[35]

Confederate guerrillas succeeded in killing a white lieutenant under Hallowell's command on February 8, but their march was hampered more by rains "drenching us to the skin," remembered Captain Luis Emilio, "and making the road a quagmire." Hallowell's brigade continued to inch north. "My life is now very active and exciting," he reported to one of his sisters. "We are following the Rebs very close and hope to be in Charleston when Sherman compels them to evacuate it." Runaway slaves arrived daily at his camp, providing intelligence on Confederate movements. Hard marching meant that some days his regiment had "to go hungry," but mostly, he chuckled, "we 'live high,' [as] the country is well stocked with cattle, poultry, rice, etc." His men applied "torch & axe" to the mansion houses they passed, always taking care to "leave the Negro shanties" undamaged. "It makes me sick to see such elegant furniture destroyed, but it's South Carolina and it must be." Although yet a devout Quaker, Hallowell shared

Sherman's view that his country had not started the war, and that Jefferson Davis could end the "havoc" at any moment by surrendering. The Fifty-fourth had learned to dig about in the basements of the mansions they marched by, and they routinely uncovered large quantities "of china, silver ware etc" buried beneath floors. "There's wine & cider in the cellar," so Ned's men drank well too. "I never was better in my life," he concluded, "& I shall never be happier if we only march into Charleston."[36]

HALLOWELL AND HIS MEN WOULD SOON GET THEIR WISH. ALL BUT surrounded within Charleston, the demoralized defenders, one officer reported, deserted "at every opportunity." Shells continued to rain down on the city, reaching as far north as Calhoun Street, a boulevard on Charleston's northern border named for the deceased senator and states' rights advocate. On the night of February 17, most of the remaining soldiers abandoned the city, hoping to avoid Sherman's advancing forces by retreating north across the Santee River. A Union prisoner witnessed some of the Confederates mourning their defeat by getting "drunk and crazy [on] turpentine whiskey." Other defenders blew up the remaining ironclads in the harbor, set fire to the Ashley River Bridge and the shipyard, and burned vast stores of cotton and rice. A handful of boys decided to join the mayhem after stumbling across a cache of gunpowder stored in the Northeastern Railroad Depot. They threw handfuls of the powder onto the already blazing cotton fire, which eventually set off the entire stock, killing several hundred poor white and black refugees who had sought shelter in the depot. By sunup on February 18, nearly all of the homes and buildings along Chapel, Alexander, Washington, and Charlotte Streets were ablaze.[37]

That morning, Hallowell and the Fifty-fourth were some forty miles west, on the upper Ashepoo River. They had to repeatedly stop and backtrack after encountering burned bridges and abandoned ferries; they also marched by an abandoned wagon filled with 300 pairs of shoes, which the tired soldiers were happy to confiscate. They bivouacked at the estate of Dr. Theodore Dehon, the men feasting on his previously hidden supplies of "corn, poultry, sweet potatoes, and honey." Happy to see a white face, Dehon complained to Hallowell that his former slaves had been "helping themselves and carrying furniture off by whole boat-loads."

Hallowell was unsympathetic to his host, who also begged Ned to urge his self-emancipated workers to return to his fields. Ned called them all together and told them they were free to stay or to leave, and as a result, Emilio laughed, Dehon lost "all his slaves, young and old." Just then, a rider brought news of Charleston's evacuation. "Cheer after cheer rang out; bonfires were lighted; and the soldiers yelled long and frantically," Emilio wrote. "Far into the night, nothing else was talked about around the campfires."[38]

The first soldiers to enter the charred city on February 18 were the Twenty-first USCT, joined by a handful of soldiers from the Fifty-second Pennsylvania. They were met by Mayor Charles Macbeth, who handed them a note: "The military authorities of the Confederate States have evacuated the City. I have remained to enforce law and preserve order until you take such steps you think best." The Twenty-first's commander ordered the regiment to assist the local freedmen in extinguishing the numerous fires that still burned around the city. The next day the Fifty-fifth quit Folly Island and pitched camp at Mount Pleasant, directly across the river from Charleston; a few companies settled nearby on the coast of Sullivan's Island. Because the slave pens that once marred the island were long gone, it is likely that few of the soldiers knew that at least 40 percent of the Africans imported into North America came ashore on that island, including, undoubtedly, many of their ancestors.[39]

Two days later, on February 21, the Fifty-fifth entered Charleston, parading through the city on their way to their new camp on the Neck, at the city's northern edge. "Many of Charleston's wealthier citizens had fled with the Confederate army," and those whites who remained behind, Fox observed, stayed indoors. But the black residents "turned out *en masse,*" pouring into the streets to cheer. One soldier rode at the head of the column, carrying a large banner emblazoned with the word LIBERTY. "Bless de Lord," shouted an old woman, her arms raised toward heaven. "Bless de Lord, I's waited for ye, and prayed for ye, long time, and I knowed you'd come, and ye has done come at last." The soldiers returned the favor, singing "John Brown," "Babylon Is Falling," and the "Battle Cry of Freedom" and "cheering for Abraham Lincoln and Governor Andrew" as they marched through what they regarded as "the chief seat of that slave power." One soldier pulled down the bell from the city's slave mart, which

The soldiers of the two Massachusetts regiments had long dreamed of capturing Charleston, which they regarded as the heart and soul of proslavery secession. This *Harper's* image depicts the tumultuous reception for Colonel Alfred Hartwell and the Fifty-fifth as they marched into Charleston on February 21, 1865. *Courtesy Library of Congress.*

he promised to ship to Wendell Phillips. "The glory and triumph of this hour may be imagined," Fox wrote in later years, "but can never be described. It was one of those occasions which happen but once in a lifetime, to be lived over in memory for ever."[40]

On the morning of February 27, the Fifty-fourth's turn came. The regiment crossed the Cooper River aboard the *Croton* and then marched up King and Meeting Streets, Charleston's two major thoroughfares. "We could not but be exultant," Luis Emilio admitted, "for by day and night, sunshine and storm, through close combat and far-reaching cannonade, the city and its defenses were the special objects of our endeavor for many months." Emilio guessed that the city's population had dwindled to about 10,000, down from its prewar peak of roughly four times that. Once again, whites were nowhere to be seen, but black Charlestonians filled the streets to cheer their liberators. "I saw an old colored woman with a crutch," Sergeant John Collins reported to the Philadelphia *Christian Recorder,* "who, on seeing us, got so happy that she threw down her crutch, and shouted that the year of Jubilee had come." Collins, a Chicago printer who had been wounded at Wagner, waved back, perhaps recalling one of the final statements of Corporal James Henry Gooding: "For the sake of the national honor let Charleston be taken before the war is over." Glancing up, Emilio spied the towers of the jail and the Workhouse; like Hallowell, he was anxious to rescue any soldiers who remained behind its walls.[41]

The presence of U.S. troops in what was once the soul of the Confederacy transformed the city overnight. "During the last three weeks, more and more radical, anti-slavery speeches have been delivered in the city of Hayne and Calhoun than in the home of Phillips and Garrison," remarked a correspondent for the *New-York Tribune*. Northern journalists crowded the liberated city, interviewing black residents and describing the physical devastation and human optimism they saw all about them. A Boston reporter was thrilled to hear several men from the Fifty-fifth cheer the American flag, the state of Massachusetts, and Governor Andrew. Yet another noticed a young officer barking out the command to "shoulder arms," and taking a closer look, he recognized him as "the son of William Lloyd Garrison!"[42]

Amid the celebrations, a company marched to the Workhouse and discovered that four prisoners from the Fifty-fourth were still being held there, nineteen months after capture: Sergeant Walter Jeffries, a thirty-eight-year-old Ohioan, and Privates John Dickinson and John Williams, all of whom were captured during the fighting on James Island on July 16, 1863. The fourth was George Prosser of Pennsylvania, age twenty-one, who had been taken two days later during the assault on Wagner. Much to everybody's surprise, the four were in reasonably good health and able to rejoin their companies.[43]

The regiments' liberation tour was not yet at an end. On February 28, General Hatch instructed Hallowell to take his brigade—now 1,800 strong—toward Savannah and to encourage "the lately freed people" he encountered to "come into the city." Hoping to pacify the countryside, and aware of the Fifty-fourth's reputation for enjoying captured bounty, Acting Assistant Adjutant General Perry directed Hallowell's black soldiers not to confiscate any foodstuffs, warning that "not even a chicken can be taken." Hallowell was in no mood to comply. Planter Henry William Ravenel awoke on March 2 to discover that black troops were banging on his door and entering his "negro yard" to speak with his slaves. "They soon entered the house, (four or five colored men) armed & demanded to see the owner of the house," he scribbled into his diary. They "demanded his horses & wagons, his guns, wine &c" before marching into the quarters "to tell the negroes they were free & should no longer work for him." When Ravenel objected, they responded with "very threatening language [and] with oaths & curses." Some of the soldiers handed out confiscated guns to the now-liberated freedmen before marching to a neighbor's estate, where they dug up seventy-five bottles of wine and "10 to 12 gal. French Brandy." Most dismaying of all for Ravenel, two of his favorite domestics opted to leave "with the black troops wild with excitement." Masters like Ravenel had always assured themselves that they were beloved by their human chattel, but thanks to the presence of black troops, he fretted, "some of the very peculiar traits of negro character are now exhibited."[44]

About three weeks later, George Garrison's company of the Fifty-fifth found itself on reconnaissance far up the Cooper River, liberating slaves and searching for Confederate cavalry. One planter fled as they approached, "leaving to our tender mercies everything he possessed," a soldier reported. The planter's slaves, however, poured out of the quarters "and gave us a warm and hearty greeting." Despite orders to spare civilian property, Garrison confided to his diary that they came across a second estate, with its "furniture and goods packed and ready to be carried off." Garrison's men "completely sacked it of everything to be of value, and ruined what they could not bring away." The Fifty-fifth proved far kinder to the common folk. A good number "of rebel deserters and stragglers came or were brought in," Charles Fox recorded. "They were mostly from the poor whites, and almost all expressed themselves as tired of the war." The deserters undoubtedly told Fox and Garrison what they wanted to hear, yet it was also true that middle-class disaffection with the planters' war had emerged early on, leading to the Confederate Conscription Act of April 1862, and by war's end President Davis was a deeply unpopular figure. Confederate yeomen were surprised "at the good treatment they received from the colored troops," Fox noted, as their officers had warned them that black soldiers would shoot them "at once if officers were not present." The actual treatment they received, Fox hoped, might "greatly enlarge their knowledge of national affairs and of Yankee character."[45]

FIVE HUNDRED MILES TO THEIR NORTH, COLONEL CHARLES FRANCIS Adams was well enough to return to the Fifth Cavalry's camp at Point Lookout, Maryland. While the siege of Petersburg dragged on, Adams spent his days studying cavalry tactics in the mornings, "and in the afternoon drill[ing] the regiment." Adams rarely left his tent in the evenings to join his men—even the white officers—around the campfire, "and people rarely drop in on me," he proudly assured his brother. The men continued to guard Confederate prisoners, a task that required 276 soldiers, while another 58 were tasked with guarding the camp itself. As was their colonel, the men of the Fifth were bored and hoped to either soon see action or return to their families. "The love of liberty alone induced me to leave the comforts of home and take up arms," one sergeant wrote, "but I still hope that some good may come out of Nazareth [as the] Lord is in the work."[46]

The Fifth was not destined to be bored for long. Just before dawn on April 2, U.S. forces punched through Confederate lines along the Boydton Plank Road. Although Confederate defenders slowed their advance, Lee was forced to pull his remaining troops out of Petersburg and Richmond that evening and flee west. He hoped to unite his armies in Danville, Virginia, which would also serve as the new home of Jefferson Davis's government. General Richard Ewell, in charge of Richmond's defenses, was ordered to destroy all bridges, military stores, and warehouses that might be of use to American soldiers. As civilians looted the city, fires spread, burning roughly 800 buildings and reaching the edge of Capitol Square. Southeast of Richmond on the Darbytown Road, U.S. soldiers heard what sounded like "the exploding of shells in the city," and a reporter from the Philadelphia *Press* described "immense flames curling up" into the sky, indicating "that they were destroying all that could not be taken away." The Fifth were anxious to move, but prudence demanded that they wait until dawn. Adams curled up in a blanket by the side of the road, oblivious to the inferno over Richmond.[47]

By six o'clock the next morning, the Fifth was mounted and riding up Darbytown to the Charles City Road, on the outskirts of the city. The Union command was nearly as confused by the chaos as were Confederate generals, and orders soon reached the Fifth to dismount and be "prepared to fight on foot." They marched for the better part of an hour before yet another order arrived for the Fifth to halt. Still in the saddle, Adams was "fretting, fuming and chafing" at the delay. When no further instructions arrived, and with it clear that the road before them was vacant of Confederates, Adams "concluded something was up and it was best to push ahead." The cavalrymen could still hear explosions to their front and see the flames from boats, bridges, wharfs, and even one blasted ironclad. "We entered the city about 9 o'clock a.m. Monday, April 3d," Private Charles Beman wrote to the *Weekly Anglo-African*. The Fifth passed several forts and breastworks, some of them topped with heavy guns, while others were "Quaker guns," thick logs painted black, the soldier noted, "to frighten Uncle Sam's boys with." The Fifth were the "first mounted men in the city," Beman bragged, not without cause. Davis, they were told, had fled, "but no matter where he has gone," Beman added, "the Confederate States of America have fallen."[48]

As in Charleston two months before, the black residents cheered the conquering army. The cavalrymen, already tall upon their mounts, stood up in their stirrups and waved their swords above their heads, sparking "the wildest demonstrations of joy on the part of the colored people." Seeing their burned city liberated by proud, mounted, well-dressed men of their own race was a spectacle most could never have imagined. "They danced and shouted and prayed and blessed the Lord and thanked him that the Yankees had come," one officer wrote. "It will be an event in history that colored troops were the first into the city," marveled another.[49]

From second-floor windows, a few war-weary residents of both races unfurled American flags. Richard Forrester, a seventeen-year-old freeman and errand boy for the legislature, scrambled to the top of the capitol building to raise the same, enormous American flag that he had been instructed to pull down in 1861, and that he had hidden for the past four years. The past several days had been gray and wet, but the morning, as if in promise of a new day, was bright and sunny. Leading his men through the streets, Adams wondered at "the good fortune which brought me there." To have "led my regiment into Richmond at the moment of its capture is the one event which I should most have desired as the culmination of my life in the Army," he told his father. Upon hearing the news, even the disapproving Charles Francis Adams Sr. was impressed. "It was a singular circumstance that you, in the fourth generation of our family, under the Union and the constitution," the diplomat wrote from London, "should have been the first to put your foot in the capital of the Ancient Dominion, and that, too, at the head of a corps which prefigured the downfall" of slavery. Choosing to forget that he had been furious at his son's enlistment, the elder Adams forwarded Charles Francis's description of the day to his mother, who was then touring Rome.[50]

Alongside soldiers from the Thirty-sixth USCT, the Fifth set to work putting out the still-burning fires, throwing buckets of water on roofs and pulling down smoldering buildings that threatened to spread the conflagration. By midafternoon most of the fires were extinguished, and the tired soldiers set up camp at Capitol Square, breaking out their rations and sharing their meals, and especially their sugar-sweetened coffee, with the city's hungry residents. In exchange, grateful whites broke into a nearby warehouse and "dashed in the heads of several hundred barrels of whiskey," a commodity, unlike coffee, never in short supply in the South. Adams, different in this way from Hallowell, did not permit his soldiers to drink, at least while on duty, and he quietly cursed civilians for sharing liquor with his men. But he refused to allow the day to be spoiled and admitted that he witnessed no misbehavior on the part of his regiment.[51]

Among those observing firsthand the Fifth's victorious entrance into Richmond were the roughly thirty-five black Confederates who represented Jefferson Davis's last-minute effort to purchase, free, and arm bondmen—he had planned on putting 40,000 into the field. Ironically, the sterling service of the Fifty-fourth helped to prod Davis into action. "Some people say negroes will not fight," one adviser to the Confederate president remarked. "I say they will fight. They fought at Ocean Pond [Olustee], Honey Hill, and other places." Following an acrimonious debate, the Confederate Congress finally voted to arm selected slaves, but not to free them. Understanding the absurdity of that position, on March 23—just ten days before the Fifth entered his capital—Davis overruled his legislature with General Orders No. 14, granting any recruit "the rights of a freedman." Instructed to raise a company of black troops, Major J. W. Pegram placed a notice in the Richmond newspapers, begging those masters who had "freely given their sons and brothers, their money and property," to the Confederacy to now donate their slaves as well. Editor Robert Barnwell Rhett was apoplectic. "It was on account of encroachments upon the institution of *slavery*," he editorialized, that his South Carolina had seceded. "*We want no Confed-*

erate Government without our institutions." About half a dozen free blacks enlisted, and Virginia governor William Smith donated two slaves who had been sentenced to hang for burglary. "Dey was mostly poor Souf Carolina darkies—poor heathen fellers, who didn't know no better," reported one black Virginian, when asked by a journalist about the short-lived unit. With the arrival of black troops in the city on April 3, the thirty-five melted into the cheering crowd—and into history as the basis for the modern myth of black Confederates.[52]

On April 10, rumors reached Adams and the men of the Fifth that Lee had surrendered his Army of Northern Virginia to Grant the day before at Appomattox Court House. "So much for my experiences," Adams lamented, "so far in the most interesting bit of campaigning it has yet been my fate to take part in." Other Southern armies remained in the field, but Lewis Douglass, back in Rochester, guessed that "by the 1st of July this 'cruel war' will so far as any more pitched battles are concerned be over." If so, the abolitionist press wished it known, many of the final victories were due to the soldiers in the three black Massachusetts regiments. "The whole number of colored troops which have been credited to Massachusetts, during the war," William Lloyd Garrison reported, "including the Fifty-Fourth Infantry, Fifty-Fifth Infantry, [and] Fifth Cavalry, and their recruits, is 4731." Governor Andrew "believed in colored men," Garrison added, while "others did not. We assumed the hazards of the enterprize, but the country reaps the reward of its brilliant and assured success." J. C. Malone, a cavalryman with the Fifth, agreed: "The colored soldiers in this four years struggle have proven themselves in every respect to be men." Denied basic civil and political rights throughout the United States, black men nonetheless "fought for the freedom of a country whose liberties were threatened by traitorous slaveholders and their infamous allies, the Copperheads [Democrats] of the North." As did most white soldiers, Adams supposed the "war is really over," and he was ready to ship home. Malone, however, understood that the struggle for liberty was far from over, and that his war was merely entering a new phase.[53]

CHAPTER TEN

Occupation

"THE SOUL AND SPIRIT OF [CHARLESTON,] THAT HEROIC CITY lives on," insisted a Confederate journalist on April 11, two days after General Robert E. Lee surrendered his forces at Appomattox Court House. "When the sons of South Carolina, now in the army, read of the desolating passage of a hated foe over the fields and cities of their native State, they will swear a deep oath [to fight on] until they have met those blue rascals of Sherman's face to face, and settled accounts with them once and for all." Although the Confederacy was rapidly collapsing, that was not mere bravado. Richmond and Charleston had fallen, but General Joseph Johnston's Army of Tennessee, roughly 28,000 strong, remained in the field in North Carolina, and Jefferson Davis planned to shift the war to the trans-Mississippi. Davis cabled Johnston, ordering him to disband his infantry, then re-form them at a designated rendezvous point to fight on as guerrillas. Much of South Carolina either remained under Confederate control or had lapsed into chaos. Few whites in Charleston and Richmond had resigned themselves to defeat, so some U.S. Army companies needed elsewhere had to remain as occupying forces. The soldiers of the three black Massachusetts regiments were far from finished with their labors.[1]

Early April found Ned Hallowell and most of the Fifty-fourth still stationed in Georgetown, some sixty miles up the coast from Charleston. Nestled behind Pawleys Island on Winyah Bay, the "sleepy little town," as Hallowell described it, provided his men with quick access to the plantation districts to Georgetown's north and west. On April 3, Ned wrote to Pen that while his orders were to "drive in Contrabands and distribute proclamations" of freedom, the "real object is to fight guerrillas and destroy the country generally." Daily raids into the hinterland led to the liberation of both slaves and foodstuffs, and Ned assured his mother that he would never starve "in a country as well stocked with chickens & rice as this seems to be." The Fifty-fourth continued to drink well too, digging up the cellar floors in each plantation they overran. "There are hundreds of bottles of splendid wine in these old mansions," Hallowell marveled. "What lords these people must have been, with their thousands of acres & hundreds of slaves!" Although he admitted enjoying "some of the most refined juice of the grape Europe ever exported," particularly savoring an 1839 Madeira, the industrious Quaker in him detested wealth accumulated from the sweat of others. "It was high time a revolution had smashed their luxury," he reasoned, and he was content to lead his men in the smashing.[2]

Also on April 3, Alfred Hartwell received orders to take a detachment from the Fifty-fifth, along with white soldiers from the New York Fifty-fourth, and march north toward Lake Moultrie. Soon enough, Hartwell found that they had no further need to inform black Carolinians of their emancipation. As the Fifty-fifth marched through the countryside, black refugees ran out to greet them. "At one house we passed," Garrison wrote, "three or four colored women came out to see us go by, who were barefooted." More black women than men remained in the Lowcountry, Garrison noted, as masters had often tried to drag their most valuable bondmen with them when they fled upcountry. "They were so delighted and astonished" at seeing black soldiers "that they fairly danced with joy, turning round and round, and jumping up and down." Most asked if the regiment was heading to Charleston, before rushing "back to their shanties [to] grab a bundle, and fall in the rear of us." A few elderly blacks told Garrison that "they would come with us if they were not so old, or had not children to care for." By the time the Fifty-fifth returned to Charleston in mid-April, an awaiting William Lloyd Garrison proudly assured his wife, the regiment brought with them "1200 slaves, now freemen."[3]

The editor of the *Liberator* had traveled to Charleston to witness the April 14 rededication ceremony at Fort Sumter, set to take place four years to the day from its 1861 capitulation. George reached the city in time to join his father, who had arrived with Senator Henry Wilson and with the Reverend Henry Ward Beecher, whose son James was a colonel with the Thirty-fifth USCT. At eleven that morning, a small flotilla of ships sailed out toward the ruined fort. Among them was the *Planter,* a stolen Confederate transport, once again piloted by former slave Robert Smalls and carrying Dr. Esther Hill Hawks and the recently liberated Robert Vesey, an aged carpenter who was the son of the black abolitionist hanged by city authorities in 1822. The various guests and dignitaries scrambled onto a wharf recently constructed on the fort's western side, and a flight of steps led them down to the parade ground. An honor guard of soldiers drawn from the Fifty-fourth and Fifty-fifth, "the survivors of the assault on Sumter," formed neat lines on either side of the flagstaff. Those atop Sumter's south wall could gaze below at what remained of Fort Wagner, where so many in the honor guard had lost comrades nearly two years before.[4]

That evening, General Quincy Adams Gillmore hosted a celebratory dinner. Fireworks lit the sky. Just around ten-fifteen on that Good Friday, actor and Confederate sympathizer John Wilkes Booth entered the president's box at Ford's Theater in Washington and, with a single bullet from his derringer, assassinated Abraham Lincoln. Word reached Charleston of the president's death on the morning of April 19. Black Americans "sobbed and cried in the streets," one journalist reported, shouting, "My God! My God! Our friend is gone." Lieutenant Colonel Charles Fox remembered that "scarcely a colored person could be met in the streets, who had not assumed, in some form or other, the badge of mourning." Fearing retribution, most white Charlestonians condemned the assassination or wisely avoided gloating in public. One exception was the rector of St. John's Episcopal Church, who refused Unionist demands to conduct a special service for the murdered president.[5]

HALLOWELL AND MOST OF THE FIFTY-FOURTH, WHO REMAINED IN the field above Georgetown, would not hear of Lincoln's assassination for another four days. Instead, on April 5, the young colonel took his brigade—now consisting of a majority of the Fifty-fourth and thirteen companies from two USCT regiments—and left the port, setting off on a march nineteen miles north. As they moved along the Sumterville Road, Hallowell dispatched companies to burn bridges across the Black River. Small groups of Confederates appeared from time to time, firing a few shots before disappearing back into the woods, but Hallowell's men suffered no casualties. On April 9, just below Sumterville, they encountered approximately 500 entrenched Confederates, backed by three artillery pieces. But the Southerners were hungry and tired militiamen, and Hallowell's far larger force had little difficulty in pushing up the road. The Confederates fled, leaving behind their wounded and dead, as well as their artillery.[6]

Two days later, Hallowell ordered Lieutenant Stephen Swails to march several companies to Wateree Junction, where rumors placed eight locomotives and as many as fifty boxcars. By the time the small group reached the rail lines, night was setting in. One of the engines had its steam up, and sharpshooters fanned out in hopes of picking off any engineers who might try to escape with at least one train. Swails led nineteen men forward, leaping over a trestle and vaulting into the engine cab. Waving his hat in triumph, Swails took a ball in his right arm, fired by one of his own sharpshooters, who in the darkness mistook the light-skinned New Yorker for a Confederate engineer. As had many soldiers by the final year of the conflict, Swails had grown accustomed to being shot, or shot at, and he merely tied his arm into a sling while continuing to bark orders. Swails packed the wounded aboard the steaming train, while his men worked to connect the captured cars. As they backed the train away from the junction the soldiers set fire to the trestle and bridges, and after it became clear that they had attached too many cars, they uncoupled most of them, setting fire to them one at a time. The group returned to Hallowell's camp the next morning, the fit marching down the tracks and the wounded riding on what Captain Luis Emilio cheerfully dubbed "Lieutenant Swails's locomotive."[7]

The bandaged Swails was still with the Fifty-fourth on April 18 when Hallowell led them out of Camden, northeast of Columbia, along the Statesburg Road. "From some contrabands," Emilio wrote, the regiment learned that roughly two miles up the road, a large number of Confederates had thrown up a breastwork of cotton bales at a place called Boykin's Mill, alongside an impassible swamp. As the Fifty-fourth had discovered far too many times in past years, such a Carolina bog diminished their numerical advantage by requiring them to attack in nearly single file. Hallowell sent a small force of scouts ahead, and one of them, Private Stephen Morehouse, returned with the sobering news that "there's a lot of Rebs through there in a barn." The soldiers slowly crept ahead until a bend in the road revealed several mills, each fed by a stream too deep to ford, "forming a sort of island," Emilio thought. Behind the bales, they discovered, was the so-called Orphan Brigade, a unit of Kentucky infantrymen who had opted to march south when their state remained loyal to the Union.[8]

With their way forward blocked, Company F attempted to flank the Confederates by inching across a ruined bridge, but anticipating that, the Kentuckians fired a volley that killed Corporal James Johnson, a young barber from Oswego, New York, and mortally wounded Corporal Andrew Miller, a blacksmith from Elmira. The company retreated, but only to regroup and join the 102nd USCT, who were advised by "an old white-headed negro" of a place to ford the stream about a quarter of a mile behind the Confederate barrier. The Kentuckians were prepared for that too. As Company A rose from the brush to wade across the stream, a Confederate ball struck Lieutenant Edward Stevens in the head, killing him instantly. Stevens pitched forward into the water, his body seemingly too close to the Kentucky sharpshooters to be safely recovered. But Stevens, who had left Harvard during his senior year to serve in the Fifty-fourth after hearing of Shaw's death, was popular with his men, who "promptly presented themselves for that duty." They recovered his body and buried Stevens just behind their lines. At the age of twenty-one, Stevens would be the last U.S. officer to die in the war.[9]

While black soldiers continued to search for weak spots in the Confederate flanks, Lieutenant Lewis Reed led a single-file rush toward the Kentuckians' front. "The charge was a plucky affair," Emilio remembered, "under exceptionally adverse conditions." With their front line collapsed, the Confederates turned and ran. Hallowell ordered the mill burned, and as his men watched the flames those companies he had sent to the flanks rejoined the brigade. The final advance cost the regiment six casualties, but no deaths. Especially lucky was Private Clayton Johnson of West Chester, Pennsylvania. Johnson had been briefly hospitalized after Wagner with a shell fragment, and at Olustee, a tree branch shattered by Confederate guns had fallen on his head. During the fight at the mill, a minié ball snipped the little finger from his left hand. Although they could not know it, Boykin's Mill was to be the final battle on South Carolina soil.[10]

Not that Hallowell thought his task finished. The Fifty-fourth advanced farther into the interior the next day. They encountered a small force near Rafting Creek, but the Confederates were easily flanked, he reported, and "driven in confusion through Statesburg." On April 20, his brigade "destroyed fifteen steam-engines and a large number of box-cars" at Middleton Depot. After that, the march encountered no further resistance. One of Hallowell's captains reported 60 Confederates taken prisoner—most of them probably deserters—5,000 bales of cotton burned, 100 cotton gins demolished, and 5,000 bushels of corn destroyed. The destruction of corn was hard to justify, given the growing number of white and black refugees, but upon hearing of Lincoln's assassination on April 23, Hallowell was in no mood to be magnanimous. The march paused after word reached them "of an armistice between General Sherman and the rebel General Johnston," but when those negotiations briefly broke down, the Fifty-fourth returned to their crusade with a vengeance. "Tonight we have heard of the resuming of hostilities, & we rejoice," the twenty-eight-year-old Quaker informed his mother. "In a few days thy devoted son will be off again killing & destroying, avenging the murder of our leader." Hallowell prayed the war would soon end so that he might return home, "but my soul is in it," he confessed, "it is my duty, the race must be exterminated, unless they quickly get down upon their knees, we can trifle no more, we must hunt them down till there is not a vestige of a Rebel left in the land." Shortly after Hallowell wrote those words, on April 29, Johnston formally surrendered all active Confederate forces in the Carolinas, Florida, and Georgia, an act of capitulation that the still-fleeing Jefferson Davis denounced as treasonous.[11]

As word spread that the war was all but over, Hallowell marched his brigade back toward Georgetown, "rais[ing] merry Hell with the Rebs" as they returned to the coast. His men had run out of rations, so they helped themselves to "the best of sherry wine, and at the best of rebel swine."

But on Hallowell's order, the destruction of private property stopped. "I didn't steal anything on the march but a silver soup ladle to dip out punch with," he laughed. In his report on the twenty-one-day expedition, General Edward Potter wrote that he could "not too highly praise the conduct of officers and men" who had endured long marches and almost daily skirmishes with "great dash and courage." Potter singled Ned Hallowell out for special commendation, telling his superiors in Washington that Hallowell was "at all times prompt and efficient in the discharge of his duties." On May 5, new orders reached Hallowell's tent, instructing him to return to Charleston and rejoin the detachments of the Fifty-fourth and Fifty-fifth still in the city. Hallowell was given the responsibility of coordinating the "defenses of Charleston Neck, Saint Andrew's Parish, and James Island." Formal combat had ended, but the duties of occupation had only begun.[12]

WITH NOBODY SHIPPING HOME ANYTIME SOON, HALLOWELL AND John Andrew began to press the War Department for further promotions. They were assisted by a petition that had been circulated in Washington during the previous January and signed by ten former noncommissioned officers from black regiments, including "Lewis H. Douglass, late Sergeant Major 54th Massachusetts Volunteers [and] Charles R. Douglass, late Sergeant 5th Massachusetts Cavalry Volunteers." The petitioners observed that while "many of the noblest of our race have sprung to arms with alacrity in defense of the Government," other black men held back, rightly worried that "the hope of promotion [would be] denied them." By this point, the majority of black men in the armed forces were former slaves, but the sergeants and surgeons who signed the petition were men of learning and relative prosperity, and they took pains to assure Secretary Edwin Stanton "that others of our educated men, anticipating the granting of commissions to colored men, have applied themselves to the study of military tactics." The petition was signed or endorsed by a number of antislavery activists, including Frederick Douglass, James McCune Smith, Senators Charles Sumner and Henry Wilson, and editor Horace Greeley.[13]

In the past, Governor Andrew had taken advantage of black heroism to push the issue, and when word arrived in Boston of Boykin's Mill and the second wounding of Stephen Swails, he wasted no time in issuing a new round of promotions. In early May, just days after the Fifty-fourth returned to Charleston, Andrew informed Stanton that as "Governor and Commander-in-Chief" of Massachusetts forces, he intended to elevate "Second Lieut. Stephen A. Swails of Elmira, to be First Lieut.," in place of the fallen Edward Stevens, and to promote "Quartermaster-Sergeant Peter Vogelsang of Brooklyn to be Second Lieut." This time there was no delay in Washington, and the two New Yorkers promptly received their new commissions. Although Robert Hamilton, editor of the *Weekly Anglo-African,* shared the concerns of many dark-skinned soldiers that Swails was "far from being a distinctly marked colored man," he conceded that Swails could have chosen to pass for white, yet opted not to. "To Lieut. Swails himself we offer our hearty congratulations for his promotion," Hamilton wrote, "the more so that his truthful adhesion to his descent has enabled him to gain a triumph for our people."[14]

As the campaigns of the previous months gave way to the onerous duty of occupation, those black men who wore stripes had ample opportunity to prove their mettle. From the Fifty-fourth, Peter Vogelsang was promoted again, to first lieutenant, as was Frank Welch, a Connecticut barber who had been wounded at Wagner. James Monroe Trotter of the Fifty-fifth, who had been recommended for promotion the previous June, finally became a second lieutenant, as did John Freeman Shorter, a Washington-born mechanic who was nearly crippled from wounds received at Honey Hill. Shorter had just returned to the regiment, and his men "cheered the officer's advent and at Headquarters we gave him a hearty welcome," noted surgeon Burt Wilder. The black officers "have at last been permitted to wear straps on their shoulders and cords down the seam of their pants," wrote a former chaplain from the Fifty-fifth. "The ball does move."[15]

NED HALLOWELL WOULD DEMAND MUCH FROM HIS BLACK OFFICERS during the coming months, as his formal task of defending, policing, and maintaining order in Charleston ultimately amounted to using the two black regiments as armies of occupation to reconstruct the most troublesome city in the South. Within weeks of Lee's surrender, Northern women began to clamor for the return of their husbands and sons, a demand that politicians who worried about the cost of maintaining an army of one million men were happy to oblige. Although which regiments would be mustered out, and when, was the prerogative of the War Department, the majority of black soldiers had no farms or businesses to return to. Even those Northern freemen, such as Stephen Swails, who held jobs before the war often preferred an officer's pay in Charleston to a waiter's apron back home. Hallowell settled into an abandoned mansion at 8 Meeting Street, "down near the Battery, hot & cold water with the most refined modern conveniences," as he assured a worried sister, who urged him to resign his commission. "I would give my left hand to think it right, but I can't," he told his family. "I must stay with the men till they are mustered out." Although major combat was over, "still there is much work for such as I to do & would feel very mean to leave the men in the lurch."[16]

The men of the Fifty-fourth and Fifty-fifth took shelter in accommodations less grand than that of their colonel. Some bunked in the Citadel, an arsenal turned military academy that fronted Citadel Square, where the black troops conducted a changing of the guard each morning, accompanied by "martial music," a ceremony, one officer wrote, that "always attracted numbers of colored people, young and old." The editor of the Augusta *Daily Constitutionalist* groused that the military academy was being used as "barracks for the nigger soldiers." Other companies camped on the grounds behind the Workhouse and the adjacent city jail. The former had been reserved for runaways and recalcitrant slaves—Denmark Vesey had been tried behind its walls in 1822—and until the city fell to American troops, the latter held prisoners taken on James and Morris Islands. The walls of both castlelike structures were thick, however, and provided refuge from the heat and sun as the spring grew increasingly warm. Vogelsang, who was among those lodged in the Citadel, spent his off hours helping to organize a black masonic lodge that met just across the square.[17]

The two regiments' mission was complicated by the fact that Charleston lay in ruins. "Nearly all the mansions in this once proud part of the guilty city are windowless; many of them roofless," the *Liberator* reported. "Except a few negroes who have nestled in the deserted chambers, they are tenantless." The so-called Secession Hall on Meeting Street, where disunion had been declared in December 1860, was a charred shell, which one journalist judged to be an apt metaphor for the Confederacy's fortunes. A soldier in the Fifty-fourth thought the destruction "a terrible retribution of

Almighty God upon these candidates for Satan's mansions," but as black refugees from the countryside crowded into the city, it was not merely "the slaveholding aristocracy" who suffered. Reduced to army rations, the Fifty-fourth no longer ate well on purloined foods from rural estates. White grocers had fled the shelling, and the enslaved market women who had sold vegetables and eggs in the antebellum city each Sunday no longer resided on plantations just across the Ashley and Cooper Rivers, as they too had flocked into Charleston at the war's end. Colonel William Gurney of the 127th New York Volunteers hurried a desperate missive to Manhattan's Produce Exchange, begging for food. Hallowell confessed that he and his troops were "mighty glad to rest awhile" after their weeks of hard marching, yet he was "very sorry to be in Charleston, it's an awful place!"[18]

As soon as the city had fallen, the army declared martial law and suspended the remaining civil authorities. In hopes of keeping the peace, the Fifty-fourth was ordered to patrol predominantly black neighborhoods, while Gurney's white New Yorkers acted as military policemen in white areas. But unlike Northern cities, prewar Charleston had been segregated more by class than by race, and even near the Battery, where Hallowell slept in his elegant mansion, narrow alleyways housed black servants and artisans. Confederate veterans returned to the city to find their world turned upside down. Black residents strolled along the Battery's seawall—a promenade banned to them before the war—while white veterans, a Northern journalist noticed, found "their streets patrolled by colored soldiers, and Massachusetts ones at that." One white lady mourned that she rarely left her home, as "the streets are so niggery and Yankees so numerous." Veterans who ran afoul of the law were marched off to jail by black officers, a reversal of old power relationships, another journalist remarked, that was "a little too much for Southern chivalry." What Southern whites regarded as intolerable, black soldiers simply saw as "God's inevitable law of righteous compensation." By merely following orders and performing simple duties, one soldier explained to a reporter, they were "making reprisals on the South for years of wrongdoing to their race."[19]

Even when not out on patrol, the very existence of literate black men on Charleston's streets was an outrage to Southern sensibilities. A Rhode Island journalist thought the Fifty-fourth "well behaved gentlemen" and asked a local resident why she complained "of them as insolent." The soldiers performing provost-marshal duty, the woman replied, routinely stopped whites to examine their passes. That too was a stunning reversal of antebellum norms, in which African Americans had to carry documentation when they left their owners' homes. "Oh, they won't turn out of the sidewalk for you," she added, "and they will go up to a white man and ask him for a light for their cigars." The black soldiers no doubt knew they were flouting long-held social customs; their habit of politely stressing that they were the social equals of the former master class surely provided an extra measure of satisfaction. Angry whites were powerless to halt this social reformation and were reduced to threatening, one black soldier wrote, that if Union occupiers continued "to ask a white man for the countersign after [the] 10 o'clock p.m. [curfew], they will be compelled to leave the city. It is getting too hot for them."[20]

Any evidence of black social advancement, no matter how innocuous, attracted the ire of white Charlestonians. When English-born reformer and journalist James Redpath, acting under his new authority as the first superintendent of public schools, seized two abandoned, half-destroyed buildings for an orphanage and school for black children, whites denounced the appropriation. Undeterred, Redpath named the institution the "Col. Shaw Orphan House" and asked congregants in a nearby black church to help repair the buildings and sew clothes for the children. On occasion, the soldiers had to battle the racism of Northern whites. After "a Copperhead [Democratic] clergyman of the 127th N.Y. Volunteers" attempted to placate local convention by announcing that black Charlestonians who attended the Citadel Square Baptist Church had to worship from the balcony, "and if they did not a guard would be there to compel them to go," an unnamed black officer from the Fifty-fourth "led a party of four to five hundred colored persons" into the church and took seats in the front pews. Should any minister dare to complain, the soldier announced, his company "will see that he is enrolled for a chaplaincy in one of Jeff's [Davis] broken party which may be *en route* for Mexico."[21]

As the first black man to rise into the commissioned ranks, Lieutenant Stephen Swails found his days long and his roster of duties longer still. On July 1, he was detailed "as Acting Adjutant" for his entire regiment, and Major George Pope, the young former Brookline clerk who scribbled out his orders, thought to add that Swails "will be obeyed and respected accordingly." That curious addendum indicated that even some white Union officers objected to taking orders from a man of color. At some point in his duties, Swails met Susan Aspinall. Born and raised in Charleston, the light-skinned, twenty-one-year-old Susan was the daughter of Albert and Mary Aspinall. Census takers in 1860 had characterized Albert as a "mulatto" sailor, and his prewar property was valued at an impressive $1,500. Although mixed-race, the Aspinalls evidently did not associate with the city's "brown" elites. Swails had turned thirty-three the previous February, and faced with the prospect of returning to a troubled relationship with Sarah Thompson and a life as a Cooperstown waiter, the ambitious officer had found yet another reason to remain in the South.[22]

With the arrival of summer, the muggy, unhealthy weather added to the burdens of the occupying forces. Word reached Charleston on May 22 that James Henry Gooding had died at Andersonville the previous July, putting an end to any false hopes that he had endured captivity. Hallowell had more immediate concerns too. "This is our third Summer in this warm climate and it bids fair to be very sickly," he wrote to the surgeon general of Massachusetts on May 1 in hopes of obtaining more doctors and medicine. "Even now our Surgeon finds it almost impossible to [do his] duty thoroughly," he added, in part because the "large number of 'Contrabands' recently brought into the Department has created an unusual demand for Medical Officers." Yellow fever struck that summer, and Charlestonians who had means to do so fled into the upcountry. James Williams, a young farmer from the Cincinnati area, lived through war only to die of pneumonia, the same fate to befall James Halpin, a Baltimore boatman.[23]

When not interring fallen occupiers, a company from the Fifty-fifth also ventured out to James Island in search of bodies from the skirmish of the previous July. The detail uncovered a number of decomposed corpses, one soldier noted sourly, "whose bodies were left lying where they fell by the barbarous rebels." The soldiers heaped the bones into coffins and carried the remains to a bluff overlooking the city. "The escort was commanded by Captain Goodwin, who was wounded in the fight," the *Liberator* reported, "and the pall-bearers were mostly men wounded at the same time." Most of the missing had hailed from Ohio, and the state assembly shipped an Ohio flag to be draped over the coffins, a curious tribute from a Midwestern state that continued to deny its black residents voting rights. Members of the Fifty-fourth attended the ceremony, and as they walked down the hill toward the harbor, Corporal Charles J. Howard glanced out at Wagner and reflected on those friends who had not made it back up the beach when retreat was called. "It makes us sad to think of the many bereavements that have been experienced during this war," he recalled. Howard reminded himself to "dry our tears," for those who fell at Morris Island "have gone to reap their rewards in a better world."[24]

THE RELENTLESS HOSTILITY OF WHITE CHARLESTONIANS TO THE black army of occupation began to erode the two regiments' morale, with the incessant glares and angry words proving almost as hard to endure as the heat and the mosquitoes. One furious resident complained that Northern blacks were far more "ignorant & degraded" than former slaves, as they had never "had opportunities of spiritual instruction, or of forming attachments to their masters." Due to the "defiant and discourteous spirit manifested in the city," Lieutenant Charles Joy of the Fifty-fourth moved the curfew from ten to eight o'clock on July 12 and banned whites from "any discussions or assembling in groups on the streets or other public places, day or night." Even so, two weeks later, Private Alfred Lee, a young Pennsylvania farmer who had been wounded at Wagner, finally reached his limit after a hot day of guard duty. Lee drank until "in a state of beastly intoxication," and wandering into "the Public streets," he "did aim a loaded musket at a number of Citizens." The army briefly brought Lee up on charges, but as the white officers were equally weary of the local populace, he was eventually ordered back to his quarters to resume his regular duties.[25]

In one instance, a troubled soldier even led to friction between the two black regiments. Alfred Pelette of the Fifty-fifth deserted, but having no place to go, he remained in Charleston for several months. Hartwell finally ordered black sergeant Andrew Smith to "bring him in dead or alive." Smith located the deserter and locked him in the guardhouse, only to hear that Pelette had escaped, evidently with the help of friends. When Smith again found the soldier, he was "with a crowd of men belonging to the 54th Massachusetts, thinking himself well protected." Smith fired a shot just above Pelette's head and, when the group of soldiers moved toward him, waved "his pistol in their faces." At length, Hartwell had to intervene. Pelette was tried and sentenced to three years at hard labor, although he finally received a pardon from General Gillmore, but not before causing hard feelings between the two units.[26]

Tempers rose with the temperature. In the Fifty-fourth, Private Samuel Benton, a Manhattan waiter, murdered Corporal William Wilson, a thirty-one-year-old Indiana soldier. Ned Hallowell sat on the court-martial, which sentenced Benton to hang, a punishment that was later commuted to ten years' imprisonment. The Fifty-fifth fared no better. A black sergeant shot Private William Matthews for attempting to avoid arrest, and a long-standing feud between Privates Lewis Dickinson and John Shaw ended only when Shaw struck the Ohio farmer "on the temple with a thick sapling, fracturing his skull so that he died in a few moments." Shaw too was to be executed, but in his case a flaw in the legal proceedings led to a reduced sentence. If black soldiers initially expressed little desire to quit the army, the pressures of serving as an occupying force prompted a change of heart, and the men of the two regiments began to look forward to following their white brethren back into civilian life at the first opportunity.[27]

That was not to be, owing in large part, ironically, to the racism of white Northern troops. Equally anxious to return home, soldiers in the 127th New York took their frustration out on local freedpeople. As the tragic draft riots of 1863 had demonstrated, a good many Manhattanites wished to retain prewar racial prerogatives. When newly freed blacks sought to challenge antebellum etiquette by not giving way on the sidewalks, New Yorkers shoved them into the streets with a "boot or perhaps the point of a bayonet," a journalist for the *Boston Commonwealth* charged. Working-class soldiers were especially incensed by the relative prosperity of the city's light-skinned elites, and they routinely kicked African Americans "out of their homes, knocked [them] down in the streets," attacked them "with brickbats and bayonets, cut [them] with knives," and smashed their stalls in the marketplace. The situation grew so dire that James Redpath finally wrote to General Oliver O. Howard, the commissioner of the newly created Bureau of Refugees, Freedmen, and Abandoned Lands, and recommended that Colonel William Gurney be court-martialed unless he began to discipline his troops. The entire New York regiment should be withdrawn, Redpath added, as "unfriendly to the only loyalists whom S.C. has produced."[28]

The War Department shipped the 127th home in late June, only to replace them with another New York regiment, the 165th. According to one captain in the Fifty-fourth, the new squad promptly fell into their predecessor's habit of "robbing, clubbing, [and] stabbing colored citizens." The long-simmering tensions erupted into violence on Saturday, July 8, after a company of New Yorkers were dispatched to patrol the market. The white soldiers later insisted that they were attacked by a knife-wielding James Bing, who sold eggs in his stall, while blacks swore that "the white soldiers were the aggressors." Beyond dispute was that fifteen of the soldiers, "with loaded muskets and fixed bayonets," began to chase Bing through the crowded marketplace. The soldiers killed Bing and soon found themselves surrounded by soldiers from the Fifty-fourth and the Twenty-first USCT. At least one New Yorker opened fire, wounding one of the black soldiers. "All that night confusion reigned in Charleston, and, at intervals, shots were exchanged," General William Bennett reported of the event, which constituted the city's first race riot. As the violence spread, with white and black soldiers involved in countless "street-broils," the army gave up trying to count the wounded. "The disturbances were not confined to any particular locality," Bennett observed, "but they prevailed throughout the city."[29]

Although Bennett's formal report claimed that it was "impossible to definitely ascertain the origins of this particular disturbance," his subsequent actions indicated that he blamed the white soldiers. He ordered the New York regiment relocated to Morris Island, although they were not disarmed, as one black newspaper optimistically reported. As replacements, Bennett brought in the Forty-seventh Pennsylvania Infantry. Until the ostensibly more pacific Pennsylvanians could restore order, General Gillmore instructed the Fifty-fourth to remain in their quarters at the Citadel. Bennett ordered the newly arrived white soldiers to enforce the curfew and warned "the enlisted men in this city that they behave insolently to no person, of whatever color." He also required Charleston's citizens to turn all firearms over to the army, so that they could be "stored away until more peaceful times." On the face of it, the order was color-blind, but since many Confederates had drifted home with their weapons, the threat to arrest anyone "found carrying firearms" or even a sword clearly pertained more to whites than to black residents.[30]

When word of the riot reached Washington, General Grant, who remained the army's highest-ranking officer, directed Gillmore to resolve the racial tensions in Charleston by discharging all of the white regiments of occupation in South Carolina. Grant's recommendation was consistent with congressional hopes of saving money by mustering out white troops as quickly as possible, and in any case, since some of the white soldiers had served longer than the men of the Fifty-fourth, Grant reasoned, they deserved to return home first. By that date, there were 11,200 black soldiers and 2,800 white soldiers in the state. Gillmore urged Grant to amend the order so that only the 300 white New Yorkers would be relieved, leaving him with just over two regiments of white soldiers stationed in major South Carolina cities. Having not been allowed to enlist until January 1863 due to discriminatory policies in Washington, the men of the Fifty-fourth were penalized again, this time for the racism of their white comrades, by being among the last to be mustered out.[31]

WHILE HALLOWELL AND THE FIFTY-FOURTH STRUGGLED TO IMPOSE order and a measure of justice on Charleston, Hartwell and portions of the Fifty-fifth were tasked with the same responsibilities in the countryside around Orangeburg, a town roughly halfway between Charleston and Columbia. The move upcountry proved slower than expected, as the rail lines had either been destroyed by Sherman's corps or not been cared for in months. The tracks were so overgrown with weeds and grass, one officer complained, that the wheels on the engine car slipped "as if they were greased." The black companies, together with the 102nd USCT, finally reached Orangeburg on Sunday, May 21. As the men pitched camp, Charles Fox wrote, nearly 1,000 freedpeople crowded into the site, "to see the 'Black Yankees,' witness the parade, and attend the religious services of the day." The former slaves were so captivated by Chaplain John Bowles's sermon, and comforted by the presence of black troops, that as the sun began to set many began to settle in for the night, and Hartwell had to instruct his sergeants to "clear the camp of all strangers at retreat."[32]

The Fifty-fifth had orders to administer the oath of allegiance to Southern whites, so that the state could prepare for its reentrance into the Union, and to set up a Commission of Labor, which was designed to instruct both landlords and laborers as to the new order of things in the postwar South. Captain Charles Soule, the acting chairman of the commission, guessed that within two weeks of his speaking tour around the county he had addressed 2,000 whites and 10,000 freedpeople. When speaking to former masters, Soule emphasized "the necessity of making equitable contracts with their workmen" and counseled them to stop using "corporal punishment" on their former slaves. When talking to blacks, Soule sought to explain "in plain and simple terms their new position as freedmen, their prospects, [and] their duties." A white Harvard graduate, he cautioned former slaves "that all your working time belongs to the man who hires you." Lieutenant Trotter, by comparison, was far more concerned about the behavior of ex-Confederates, and his plantation visits were designed "to see that they were treating properly the colored people." Rather to his surprise, Trotter discovered that the planter class was "perfectly cowed down" and "completely satisfied that they are whipped."[33]

Southern whites "protested in terror against colored troops being sent out for this purpose," Fox observed. But increasingly aware that many of the white officers came from money and harbored grave doubts about laboring people of any color, landlords appealed to men of their own race to intercede with their former slaves. "Throngs of planters" poured into Orangeburg each day, one journalist wrote, "begging Col. Hartwell to send officers to their various localities to make contracts between them and the freedmen, and to induce the latter to remain." Those planters who hoped that racial solidarity might trump sectional loyalty had their prayers answered on May 22, when Hartwell issued a widely distributed circular. Although the young colonel did promise freedpeople that "no one will be allowed to abuse you like slaves," he encouraged them not to leave for Charleston, as there they "could find nothing to do to get a living." Many former slaves had taken to appropriating their former masters' property as a form of back wages, but Hartwell wished them to understand that they "will not be allowed to take what does not belong to you," and he urged black Carolinians to "make a bargain for work as soon as you can."[34]

A journalist with the *New-York Tribune* denounced Hartwell's circular as leaving the freedpeople "at the mercy of any proslavery military commander." Certainly, the black officers and enlisted men under Hartwell's command took a very different approach. Like Trotter, they devoted their energies to protecting the rights of black laborers. They demanded that contracts "be simply worded," and one officer objected to a planter who wrote "freed by the acts of the military forces of the United States" into a labor agreement on the grounds that it gave "the appearance of an intention at some future day to contest the question of emancipation." When freedpeople saw black soldiers riding toward them, they hastened to complain "of the brutality of their former owners." Indeed, some landlords treated their workers like slaves, prohibiting them from leaving their estates without a pass, whipping their children for quitting the fields for Bureau schools, and threatening to shoot them for demanding wages or a share of the crops. When word reached the Fifty-fifth that a white planter had murdered a freedman in a labor dispute, a squad galloped off "to arrest the murderer." Despite Hartwell's circular, one white Carolinian complained of "the great difficulty in making contracts in this District on account of the refusal of the negroes to sign [them] except in the presence of a U.S. officer."[35]

Defeated Confederates dreaded the interference of black soldiers, knowing they were powerless to intimidate armed and battle-hardened veterans. One planter complained of "two of the coloured soldiers" who arrived on his porch, asking permission to pick a few peaches from his trees. As they did so they questioned his laborers as to conditions on the estate and "expressed some disapproval (to the women) of their working in the hot sun." The planter guessed, probably correctly, that "their visit was rather to spy out domestic arrangements, than to get peaches." Other whites had returned from the war only to discover that their former slaves had moved into their mansions, which in some cases they had helped build. "Some have made the effort to remove them to their former homes," one white officer reported, "but without success," as the freedpeople grew stubborn "when they see a soldier approaching." For the enlisted men of the Fifty-fifth, liberation and reform, not saving the Union, were the causes that had prompted them to sign up, and although formal combat had ended, they regarded their new battles with ex-Confederates as an extension of the war itself. While the "strictly military duties of the troops [were] of necessity very few," a soldier admitted, they were "engrossed in their Efforts to obtain for the Freedmen their just due." When Corporal Charles J. Howard encountered an aged former slave who swore he was 108 years old, the old man insisted that he "had been praying 75 years for this war to come, and God had answered his prayers at last." A waiter in civilian life, Howard was far from his home in Carlisle, Pennsylvania, but he wrote that it "made me feel joyful to see one of his age so happy."[36]

Much like the soldiers stationed in Charleston, the Fifty-fifth understood that the responsibility of occupation also meant assisting recently freed slaves with their transformation into freemen. "Arrangements are also to be made for the education of the children," Trotter reported. "Soldiers are to be teachers." The men took some glee in converting an abandoned building "formerly belonging to the Confederate Government at White Bridge" into a schoolhouse. During the previous year's shelling of Charleston, the city's orphan asylum had been relocated to Orangeburg. A number of white Northern women had arrived to assist with the asylum and the new schools, most of them funded by the American Missionary Association, but arriving also were white women from Charleston who hoped to find work as teachers with the Freedmen's Bureau. A "goodly number" of them, Charles Fox observed, were "willing to consort with the Yankees, and even with officers of negro troops." With black refugees crowding into Orangeburg as well as Charleston, Stephen Swails was not the only soldier to find romance in South Carolina. About a dozen enlisted men married local women that summer, Fox counted, and their brides were anxious to return "with the regiment to Boston" when their tour of duty finally ended.[37]

Also as in Charleston, the very presence of armed black men emboldened people who had long practiced obsequiousness as a survival tactic. Black troops on one occasion marched up to a predominantly white Baptist church and demanded access to the front pews. When refused, they returned to their camp for arms and then marched back with their muskets. The minister responded by locking his doors and refusing to hold services. "Was there ever such an outrage committed on any people by its own govt.?" fumed Henry William Ravenel. The soldiers "knew full well the peculiar & intense sensitiveness of the whites as to social distinctions."

He added that "it is not confined to the South, but equally felt at the North," a fact that the Ohio farmers knew to be too true, but one that they intended to rectify after being mustered out.[38]

Mindful that they would not remain forever in South Carolina, the Fifty-fifth prepared local blacks to protect themselves. One soldier, known only to hostile whites as Johnson, urged freedmen to form "military companies" to defend their rights, their schools and churches, and their growing demands for land reform. Blacks in the district sought to arm themselves "as best they could," an effort made easier by the actions of impoverished Confederate veterans who had returned home with their muskets. "Large numbers of arms and some ammunition have been sold [to] the negroes by whites," planter James Bucher complained. "A low class of whom are in league with them." In the months after Appomattox, upper-class whites continued to regard any act of self-preservation as tantamount to servile insurrection, just as they had during the antebellum era. Another terrified landlord worried that the armed blacks "intended to kill every white man they could find, and take what they wanted." No such rebellions shook the countryside, but the presence of the Fifty-fifth would not soon be forgotten by many Carolinians.[39]

THE FIFTH CAVALRY EXPERIENCED MANY OF THE SAME TRIALS AS AN occupying force in Richmond. Even more than in South Carolina, white Virginians insisted that the end of the war meant nothing more than a formal end to slavery, and that former masters should be able to reassert other kinds of controls. Joseph Mayo, who had served as Richmond's mayor during the 1850s, was reelected to his old post, and according to the abolitionist press, Mayo "re-appointed his rebel policemen, who were notorious and famous negro hunters." He also reinstituted the old pass system, in which freedpeople had to obtain a pass from a white employer just to be able to "attend to their daily occupation." Although the city's black leaders promptly appealed to Republicans in Washington, most African Americans instinctively turned to the Fifth, especially since a majority of the cavalrymen had been born into slavery. The soldiers were happy to oblige. In yet another reversal of antebellum norms, one cavalryman demanded to see a white traveler's pass. When the furious matron huffed that he was as "ill-bred as old Lincoln himself," the soldier "cursed" at her, shouting: "You haven't got things here no long as you did. Don't you know that?"[40]

The mayor found allies in a few Union officers from white regiments, who also fretted about the social interaction between freedpeople and black soldiers. One reported that the Fifth held "very bitter feelings toward the rebels." But when complaints to white officers proved largely ineffective, Richmond whites instead began to protest that far from being a "force for the preservation of order," the cavalrymen were stealing and robbing the local populace. Though he still generally disdained his own men, Colonel Charles Francis Adams Jr. thought the allegations without merit, but to appease the mayor he clapped a "heavy guard" around his camp so that nobody came or left without authorization. Still, senior officers believed that there was evidence enough to place Adams under "arrest for neglect of duty in allowing [his] command to straggle and maraud" on April 16. He was ordered to report to Fort Monroe to answer charges.[41]

Later that afternoon, Adams arrived at the fort, where, as he complained to his father and Governor Andrew, he remained "apparently utterly forgotten and unnoticed" for eleven days. After mailing out a number of missives, all without response, Adams finally obtained an interview with General Edward Ord. Adams wisely chose "not to defend [his] regiment," but rather "simply to demand facts on which to punish officers and men." As he suspected, they had none, and the sympathetic Ord quickly defended Adams as "an ill-used, injured man to whom redress was due." On April 27—one month shy of Adams's thirtieth birthday—Adjutant General Edward Smith ordered him "relieved from arrest and [to] resume command of the 5th Mass. Cavy." By then, the young patrician was sick of the army and weary of his men, complaining to his father that they "are as hard a pack to manage as any I ever had to handle." Although Adams would return home having forged no lasting friendships with men of any race, he was particularly out of sorts with the black cavalrymen. "I no longer wonder slave-drivers were cruel," he remarked. "I no longer have any bowels of mercy."[42]

He would soon find himself free of his men. Sporadic resistance to federal authority continued in faraway Texas, and for the War Department, shipping the Fifth to the West could reduce racial tensions in Richmond while at the same time probably spelling the end of Confederate general

Edmund Kirby Smith's cavalry forces. As did Ned Hallowell, Adams thought it "would not do for a Colonel to set the example of resignation in the face of a distant and dangerous expedition," and he prepared for Texas. But his two weeks' residence near swampy Fort Monroe had made him sick, and on May 29 he received twenty days' leave to return to New England. Adams "dragged [himself] to [his] horse," reaching Quincy five days later, "much reduced in weight, wretchedly weak, mentally depressed and quite broken in spirit." Adams's doctors dosed him with liberal amounts of opium, which eased his intestinal cramps but acted on his "nerves [and] drove [him] almost to insanity." He would never return to his regiment.[43]

On June 28, Doctor Ebenezer Woodward examined Adams and found him "suffering from chronic diarrhea, and general disability" due to "attacks of dysentery and malarial fever, the gradual results of long military service." Another doctor seconded that diagnosis in late July, declaring Adams an "invalid in Quincy." Several days later, on July 21, Adams formally tendered his resignation to the secretary of war, providing documentation that his condition "utterly precluded [his] doing any further service for an indefinite period." Stanton agreed and signed his discharge papers on August 1. And so, Adams concluded, "after an active service of three years, seven months and twelve days, [he] turned to civilian occupations." Or, as his diplomat father, at long last finally satisfied with his son, put it: "This act of the drama is over."[44]

THE FIFTY-FOURTH BEGAN TO FEAR THAT THEY TOO WOULD SEE FURther service in the West. In early June, word reached Charleston that Governor Andrew and Adjutant General William Schouler intended to start discharging soldiers in state regiments who had signed on in the months just after Bull Run, starting with those whose terms of service were to expire in the early fall. That meant that the Fifty-fourth, Schouler explained, "mustered May 13, 1863," and the Fifty-fifth, "mustered June 22, 1863," both colored, have a year longer to serve." Faced with further service, perhaps in Texas or in the upper Midwest, where a series of Sioux uprisings had recently led to the largest mass execution in army history, Hallowell began to favor General Rufus Saxton's suggestion that he remain in the South "for the purposes of assisting the Freedmans Bureau." Ned longed for home, but Saxton, a reformer and abolitionist, played on Hallowell's crusader sensibilities by emphasizing the ongoing need to settle freedpeople on abandoned lands along the coast. If the choice was between that and the Indian wars, Hallowell told his father, he would most likely "consent to it."[45]

Inexplicably, on the morning of Thursday, August 10, orders arrived from General Gillmore stating that both black regiments were about to be mustered out. "I will keep you posted as to our movements," an overjoyed Hallowell wrote his parents; "we are ordered to get ready to GO HOME" and would probably sail by early August. "Hip Hip sing out wild belles, I am wild with delight." Robert Hamilton, editor of the *Weekly Anglo-African,* was ecstatic too, informing his readers that "there will be a time when these boys come home." But as the army was still in need of soldiers to occupy parts of what had been the Confederacy, Gillmore also requested that his senior staff "nominate such officers of their commands as are in their opinion deserving [of] appointment in other colored regiments." Gillmore could not provide assurances that such nominees would receive appointments higher than second lieutenant, which eliminated the two men most interested in remaining with the army: First Lieutenants Swails and Vogelsang.[46]

While the men packed and prepared for departure, they were relieved of garrison duty and relocated across the river to Mount Pleasant. "Make thy arrangements to be in or about Boston some time in August so as to welcome the 54th back to the State of their adoption," Hallowell notified his family. In recompense for his meritorious service, the War Department promoted Ned to Brevet Brigadier General—a rank that conferred honor, but without real authority or a raise in salary—so he was now, he chuckled, "thy affectionate Genl. Hallowell." Late in the evening of August 21, Hallowell bundled his men aboard the steamers *C. F. Thomas* and *Ashland,* which set sail the next morning at five o'clock. Left behind were fifty-nine men too sick to travel and Lieutenant Stephen Swails, who chose not to return home to Elmira, opting instead for a new life with Susan Aspinall. He collected his final pay and was "honorably discharged" in Charleston three days later on August 24.[47]

At nine o'clock on the morning of September 2, the steamers docked at Boston's Commercial Wharf. Andrew thought it proper for the Fifty-fourth to retrace their steps of sixteen months before, after they had quit Read-ville. The streets were "thronged with people," Captain Luis Emilio mar-veled, "who greeted the veterans with repeated cheers." Back in May 1863, a handful of whites had turned out to jeer or had watched quietly. This time Emilio witnessed nothing but "great enthusiasm." At last the regiment snaked onto the Common, where they were met by Andrew, Mayor Fred-eric Lincoln, and former sergeant William Carney. The soldiers formed into a neat square around Hallowell, who first, in the sentimental fashion typical of the time, thanked his officers "for the efficient and manly way they had performed their service." He then addressed the enlisted men, praising them for their courage and remarking, with considerable understatement, that "whenever a 'forlorn hope' had been called for, the Fifty-fourth had been ready and prompt to respond." When they had sailed for the Sea Islands, Massachusetts had been the only state "to recognize them as citizens," but "now the whole country recognized their soldierly qualities." Perhaps soon, Hallowell hoped, the nation might also reward them with citizenship. Their blood had "enriched the soil" of South Carolina, Georgia, and Florida, and they had shown "themselves to be men, without respect to color or former condition."[48]

Never one for public speaking, the twenty-eight-year-old Hallowell paused, drinking in the glorious day. Now, Hallowell shouted, it was time for farewells. He was "glad to disband them," he promised, but equally "sorry to part from them." From the early spring of 1863, he had been at Camp Meigs, together with his brother and Rob Shaw, "and he knew they looked upon him as their friend." For his part, he "felt sure that wher-ever he might go, he would find friends among colored soldiers and col-ored men." His men responded with "repeated cheers," and then, Captain Emilio scribbled into his journal, "the regiment was disbanded." Company C, most of them from New Bedford, departed in a group, but without the young sea cook who had rallied them nearly two years before. Upon reach-ing the port, they were welcomed by black veterans known as "the Carney Guards" and the city's band. Altogether, 1,442 black and white men had served in the Fifty-fourth. Ninety-three, including Shaw, had been killed or died shortly after being wounded; 43 had been declared missing. An-other 107 had died from disease or accident, and 34, including Gooding, had died while prisoners of war.[49]

Several weeks later, on August 24, the Fifty-fifth broke camp and boarded "a long train of rickety baggage cars" in Orangeburg. White soldiers from the Fifty-fourth New York drew up in line to wish them off. The two regiments, one black soldier later remembered, "had long been brigaded together." They had "marched, drilled, fought and encamped side by side, and loud and hearty were the parting cheers they gave each other." Most of the regiment sailed out of Charleston aboard the *Karnak* and the *Ben Deford*—the same steamer that had ferried the Fifty-fourth down the coast two summers earlier—while a few companies awaited transportation at Mount Pleasant. After a rough passage, in which the *Ben Deford* was twice struck by lightning, the steamer reached Gallops Island in Boston Harbor, where the men awaited final payment and discharge.[50]

On Monday, September 25, the Fifty-fifth, as a thrilled William Lloyd Garrison wrote, were warmly "received by the people of Boston." Andrew was in Manhattan, as was Pen Hallowell, the regiment's "first accomplished commander," so their places were filled by Senator Charles Sumner and Alfred Hartwell. Some veterans of the Fifty-fourth had remained in the city for the ceremony, and Garrison was elated to "be permitted to see [his] son in the flesh." As with the welcome for the Fifty-fourth, the city's sidewalks and windows were "occupied by many ladies," Garrison reported in his *Liberator*, "who joined with the other sex in commending the Union soldiers passing in solid column through the avenue." The regiment then "quietly disbanded," Charles Fox remembered, with the Ohio farmers "taking the afternoon trains for their homes at the West." Of the 1,226 who had joined the regiment, 62 men had died in battle, and another 120 had perished of disease. Only one man died while in Confederate hands.[51]

Most of the Fifth Cavalry, absent Adams and Charles Douglass, shipped out to Texas, only to find that Edmund Kirby Smith had surrendered on June 2 before fleeing into Mexico and then on to Cuba to avoid what he assumed would be prosecution for treason. By October, they had boarded transport ships in New Orleans for Boston. They too enjoyed a final ceremony, if a far smaller and frostier one, occurring as it did just days before Christmas. A healed Charles Francis Adams Jr. donned his old uniform and led the regiment through Boston's streets. Those few soldiers from the Fifty-fourth and Fifty-fifth who lived in Boston or the vicinity turned out to march just behind them. In all, 1,386 cavalrymen had served in the

Fifth; only 5 had died in battle. Another 121 died from accidents and disease, and 2 more perished while in Confederate custody.[52]

Not surprisingly, the abolitionist and black-run press devoted a fair amount of ink to the three regiments' mustering-out ceremonies. Louis Charles Roudanez, the publisher of Louisiana's first black-owned newspaper, the *New Orleans Tribune,* ran a lengthy story on Peter Vogelsang's rise through the ranks of "the regiment, until it was disbanded with satisfaction to his superiors." Ominously, however, the White House did not offer its own encomium. In an October speech, President Andrew Johnson praised white soldiers as his "countrymen" and "his fellow citizens," but in what amounted to an afterthought, he referred to black soldiers only as "his friends." Without the two Massachusetts infantry regiments, Roudanez observed, "the war would not have ended yet," for without their courage at Wagner, the United States might not have raised an additional "two hundred thousand [black] men." However reluctant Johnson might have been to characterize black veterans as full citizens, Roudanez added, "they are the countrymen of the gallant Colonel Shaw, who fell at their head before the walls of Wagner." Where was the American, he wondered, who in the presence of these regiments, and in "the sight of the shattered flags, hesitated to call these gallant sons and saviors of his country, by the name of countrymen or fellow-citizens?"[53]

For the Douglass brothers, and for James Monroe Trotter and Peter Vogelsang, who regarded their military service as merely one stage—albeit a defining and bloody one—in their longer, ongoing struggle for justice and democracy, and for Stephen Swails, who planned to exchange his lieutenant's stripes for a politician's suit, the so-called accidental president's tepid praise revealed how the postwar era was to be defined as much by the antebellum decades as by the final years of the war, which had appeared so full of promise to the veterans of the three black regiments.

CHAPTER ELEVEN

The Veterans

T HOSE WHO RETURNED HOME DID SO AS CHANGED MEN. THEY
had spent almost two years in the company of one another, forging
bonds in the crucible of war. Even those who had wives or fiancées before
their enlistment faced the daunting task of reestablishing family relations
with those on the home front, who were now nearly strangers, who could
not understand what they had endured—even if these women and children had faced challenges of their own. Once the cheering stopped on
Boston Common, the black veterans had to find employment or go back
to what for the most part had been low-paying jobs. A majority of soldiers
from the three Massachusetts regiments traveled home to states that denied them the right to vote. But they had proven their worth as soldiers to
their nation—the federal government, after all, was happy to have them
fight on against Native Americans—and proven their manhood, both to
themselves and to their communities. Because they had been paid only
at the end of the war, most black veterans had considerable cash in their
pockets, so they were relatively better able than other black Northerners
to improve their economic position, obtain federal or state patronage jobs,
and advance the cause of political reform. They had stood their ground

when faced by formidable odds at James Island, at Wagner, at Honey Hill, and at Olustee, and they were not about to be intimidated by white conservatives who wished to restore the antebellum social and political order.[1]

ON THE DAY HE WAS MUSTERED OUT, NED HALLOWELL FOUND HIM-self in the arms of a large, loving, and supportive family, including a brother who understood what he had been through. But although he was still young, Ned's health, damaged by Confederate bullets and weakened by two exhausting years in the Carolina Lowcountry, never fully recovered. Because he did not wish to be treated as an invalid by his sisters, he chose to remain in Massachusetts rather than return to Philadelphia to work again as a stockbroker. He may also have wished to trade on his own name and reputation, rather than his father's. So life in Medford in a partnership with brothers Pen and Richard as a wool merchant—always a respected occupation for a Quaker—it was to be.[2]

Shortly thereafter, Hallowell met Charlotte Bartlett Wilhelma Swett, a dedicated activist seven years his junior. Ned married Wilmina, as she preferred to be called, on February 2, 1869, in a simple Quaker service. They settled into Pierpont House at 51 Mystic Street in West Medford, just around the corner from Pen and Richard. While her husband labored in his new profession, Wilmina became a patron of the arts, serving as a trustee of the Boston Museum of Fine Arts, where she became friendly with painter Winslow Homer. Hallowell remained a Quaker, if a not very conventional one, but Wilmina joined the Free Religious Association, a movement that sought to "emancipate religion from dogmatic traditions" while affirming "the supremacy of individual conscience and reason." In later years, together with her brothers-in-law Pen and Richard, she became a financial backer of the Calhoun Colored School in Alabama. Even before the war, Ned had broken with his faith on the question of voting, and on February 17, 1880, the year after the state assembly granted women suffrage in school board elections only, Wilmina and her sister-in-law Anna Hallowell registered to vote.[3]

Tragically, Ned did not live to see his wife cast her first ballot. Nor did he get much time with his daughters Charlotte Bartlett, born on January 22, 1870, and Emily, born on June 5, 1871. A little less than two months after Emily's birth, the ailing veteran passed away. "Gen. Edward N. Hallowell died at his residence in West Medford Wednesday afternoon at the age of 34," the *Boston Journal* announced the next day, July 28, 1871. Obituaries published from Philadelphia to Maine, and as far south as Virginia, spoke of his service in the Twentieth Massachusetts and especially the Fifty-fourth. "He was a brave man and a good citizen," the *Lowell Daily Citizen and News* observed. In honor of "the late Brevet Brigadier-General," ordered Governor William Claflin, Hallowell's death was "officially communicated to the militia throughout the Commonwealth."[4]

Ned predeceased his parents by a number of years, a common if tragic reminder that the war's death toll did not cease in the spring of 1865. Morris Hallowell, his father, lived until 1880, and Ned's mother, Hannah Penrose, outlived her son by twenty-eight years, dying at the age of eighty-seven in 1899. The decade between 1900 and 1910 found Wilmina still living in Pierpont House with her unmarried daughters, both of whom became typists and teachers. Wilmina died on December 18, 1919, and was buried beside her husband at Mount Auburn Cemetery in Cambridge. Charlotte died at home on Mystic Street in 1943, and Emily lived on until the age of ninety-six, dying in 1967. The two sisters, who never knew their father, were buried under a common tombstone next to their parents.[5]

As for the Shaws, they too mourned the early death of their son Rob and their son-in-law Charles Russell Lowell. "I have passed *through* the state where you now are," abolitionist Lydia Maria Child counseled Frank seven years after the events at Wagner, "that of looking for *peculiar* spiritual significance in the Bible." Frank was still searching for the next great reform crusade that might fill the void left in his life by Rob's absence when he contracted pneumonia in the fall of 1882. He died only a few days later. After Frank's death, Effie and Sarah purchased adjoining brownstones in Manhattan on East Thirtieth Street. In 1892, Effie founded the New York City Consumers' League, a society dedicated to improving conditions for the growing number of female sales clerks, while Sarah devoted her time to the anti-imperialist movement opposed to American colonization in the Philippines. But Rob was never far from his mother's thoughts, and in 1870 she sent a check for $500 to the Reverend Robert Clute, who was raising funds to rebuild St. Andrew's Episcopal Church in Darien, Georgia.

Sarah wished that she could "rebuild the whole pretty town in his memory," she wrote Clute, "for I believe during his short and happy life he never had any greater trial of his feelings than the destruction of Darien." Sarah died "very peacefully," Effie told a friend, on New Year's Eve in 1902, at the age of eighty-seven. Her last words were: "Rob, Rob, where are you? Why don't you come and get me?" Effie herself died three years later, in 1905, and while her obituary in the *New York Times* praised her labors "in the cause of charity and reform," it also devoted ample space to "her brother, Col. Robert G. Shaw," who died "at the head of his colored regiment."[6]

Effie's sister-in-law outlived her by only three years. Annie Haggerty Shaw, who had fled to Switzerland, was denied even the comfort of raising a child—unlike Wilmina Hallowell and Effie Lowell—and devoted most of her days to religious charities. Newspapers later reported that she became "an invalid" around middle age, but it was not the custom of the time to report why, and the deeply private Annie—who had once asked Rob to burn all of her letters—corresponded only sporadically with Effie. In the fall of 1904, the sixty-nine-year-old widow relocated to Boston, bought a house at 111 Commonwealth Avenue, and, according to the *Boston Herald,* "settled in it for the winter." She chose never to visit the monument erected to her husband and the Fifty-fourth—perhaps seeing his visage as he and the men marched away from Boston was simply too painful—but to residents of the city with long memories she remained "Mrs. Robert Gould Shaw." She died in her home three years later, on March 17, 1907. Her numerous obituaries all described her as "the widow of Col. Robert Gould Shaw, the young hero, who at the age of 26 commanded the Fifty-fourth regiment of Massachusetts volunteers and was buried with his Negro soldiers at Fort Wagner."[7]

Yet another young widow who never remarried was Ellen Gooding, who, like Annie Shaw, had been wedded too briefly to start a family. After her husband marched off to Readville, Ellen remained in her father's home, but by 1870 she had moved in with her younger brother, Charles Edward Allen Jr., and his wife Amelia. On April 5, 1864, less than two months after receiving news of her husband's death, Ellen applied for a pension. Later that month the government agreed, granting her an allowance of $8 each month. Evidently, Ellen never learned that James actually died at Andersonville, as her pension application listed him as "killed at the battle of

Olustee in the State of Florida on the Twentieth day of February." (In fact, Corporal Gooding was yet alive, and would be for another three months.) Ironically, since the Fifty-fourth was still refusing their lower salaries at that date, a deceased James Henry Gooding was worth more to his wife than if he had been alive. The haste with which she filed for a widow's pension reveals the hardships faced by the wives of the soldiers in the state's black regiments. The payments ceased when Ellen died at the age of sixty-six on April 24, 1903, from "mitral regurgitation [and] cardiac dilation," a disorder of the heart.[8]

Less successful in her pension application was Cynthia Downing Smith, the mother of Private John Smith. In 1890, Congress passed the Dependent Pension Act, which erased the previous link between an allowance and service-related injuries so that almost any deceased or incapacitated veteran, or their family, received a pension. Perhaps Cynthia hoped that the army would take pity on her as "a subject for charity," or that over the intervening decades they might have forgotten how her son died. "Cynthia Smith is a poor woman," her friend Ester Perkins swore, "having no property to aid in her support, and no means of support as she is too old to do any kind of labor." Cynthia was not in luck. "Rejection," scribbled a clerk in the Pension Office. "Soldier's death in no way due to his military service. Was hung for a crime."[9]

A NUMBER OF THE VETERANS OF THE MASSACHUSETTS REGIMENTS had great difficulty finding their place in civilian life after the guns fell silent, often owing to their psychological or physical wounds. After his years spent as an enslaved domestic and then as a manservant, Nicholas Said was never able to put down roots, and he continued to wander in the decades after the war. He had enlisted, he once told a journalist, "because all his folks seemed to be doing so." But he never came to feel at ease in the Fifty-fifth and, almost alone among his fellows, had no desire to advance in the ranks. He decided to resume teaching, but not in Detroit, where he had worked in 1862. Instead, he returned to the South, having found himself more comfortable among the heavily black population of the Lowcountry than in Michigan. He settled in Charleston, where he rented a room at a boardinghouse on Calhoun Street that catered to prosperous African

Americans. How long Said stayed in Charleston is unclear. In an account he elsewhere contradicted, he remembered that he "left Charleston for Savannah, Georgia, in the commencement of 1870." Said was again restless.[10]

Said remained in Savannah for just a few days, but while there he "conceived the idea of writing [his] Biography or rather adventures." He also began a speaking tour across Georgia, lecturing to black audiences on "Africa and its resources." He "soon got tired of that business" and took another teaching job in Culloden, a small town in the central part of the state. He taught there for six months, devoting his evenings and Sundays to writing his memoirs. As was customary for authors who lacked publishing connections, Said sought to defray printing expenses by obtaining subscriptions through advance sales. Yet another speaking tour carried the veteran of the Fifty-fifth back to Florida. By the time he reached Tallahassee in May 1871, he had funds enough to open an account with the Freedman's Savings and Trust. Bank managers routinely described depositors' features as a form of identification, and the clerk duly listed his age as thirty-four, noted his place of birth as "Soudan, African," and characterized him as "dark." Said gave "Teacher" as his occupation, but when asked about his residence, he replied only: "Traveler." The impressed clerk had evidently heard about Said's speaking tour, as he wrote on the bottom of the account book: "This is the wonderful Nickolas Said doubtless."[11]

Published in 1873 by the Memphis firm of Shotwell and Company, *The Autobiography of Nicholas Said; A Native of Bornou, Eastern Soudan, Central Africa* ran to 224 pages but contained not a single word about his time in the Fifty-fifth. Having decided to teach and travel in the South's black belt rather than in the relatively more welcoming but whiter North, Said evidently thought it prudent to hide his military service. Freedmen's Bureau reports were filled with stories of the violence and hostility heaped upon black soldiers. As one white doctor in Virginia threatened, "We will not allow niggers to come among us and brag about having been in the yankee army." Said's otherwise richly detailed memoir summarized eight years of his life into sixteen fraudulent words: "The succeeding seasons from 1858, to 1866, were passed alternately in Italy, Germany, France, and England." He shifted his arrival into Maine with the Rochussens ahead by seven years to the month by claiming that they "landed in Portland in December 1867." Otherwise, the *Autobiography* reveals that Said either had a nearly photographic memory for dates, details, and even the names of ships or had kept a diary or daybook over the years, as all of those specifics can be corroborated. By erasing two of the most momentous years of his extraordinary life, Said preserved his ability to live in the former Confederacy, but at the cost of denying history a private's account of everyday life in the Fifty-fifth.[12]

Said's omission, however, did little to protect him from the animosity of Southern whites, since his literary abilities put the lie to widely held theories of black inferiority. Even before his *Autobiography* was printed, critics doubted that the exotic stories he told in his public lectures were close to the truth. "A semi-civilized party of the African persuasion named Nicholas Said, who has been traveling over Georgia the past year or two," snipped the *Macon Weekly Telegraph,* "is devoting his valuable time at present to swindling the newspapers" with stories of his early years. A Savannah editor joined in, adding that "if Nicholas Said, the wandering African celebrity, does not wish to be called a humbug, he should quit drinking whiskey by the wholesale." Nor were these doubts reserved to Southern journalists. The *Columbus Daily Enquirer* scoffed that Said's inappropriately housed lecture at Temperance Hall featured a staggered rate for entry, with "admission for Democrats 50c., for Radicals 75c, [and] no charge for freedmen."[13]

For the better part of the next decade, Said vanished from view, publishing no more and delivering no further lectures. Census takers in 1880 found him living in Brownsville, Tennessee, teaching school and renting a room from twenty-nine-year-old Cincinnati Jordan and his wife Mary. As was typical of the era, the census official simply guessed at his age, placing him around forty and so shaving a few years off his age, and they misspelled his surname as "Side." Said died two years later, on August 6, 1882, at roughly the age of forty-six. He had evidently kept in touch with at least one officer from his regiment, since the only extant record of his death was the notation that Charles Fox inscribed into the brief history of the Fifty-fifth that the white officer had penned fourteen years before.[14]

In contrast to Said, Henry Jarvis soon learned where he belonged. Having escaped from a man he once described as the meanest master on Virginia's Eastern Shore, the disabled veteran—he had taken three balls at Honey Hill and lost his right leg as a result—remained in the Boston area for five years. The army fitted him with an artificial leg "made by Palmer & Co. [of] Boston," but because surgeons had sawed away the bone "at the upper third of his thigh," Jarvis found it easier to hobble about on crutches. (He was just one of 30,000 U.S. veterans to receive an artificial limb after the war.) Henry found himself among the many returning veterans who crowded into the seaport, but few Boston shippers wished to take a chance on an incapacitated former oysterman. In 1870 he returned to Virginia, living first on his pension in a soldiers' home in Hampton—quite near Fort Monroe, his destination in 1861—and then retracing his steps back across the Chesapeake Bay to the hamlet of Cheapside on the Eastern Shore. Private Augustus Brooks, who had helped drag Jarvis off the battlefield in 1864, joined his friend there.[15]

After Jarvis had reached Massachusetts in 1863, he learned that his wife had remarried. Now, upon his return to the Eastern Shore, he discovered that her new husband had died. As far as the proud veteran was concerned, she should have waited for him, and he wanted nothing more to do with her. Instead, on the day after Christmas in 1872, the thirty-six-year-old Jarvis married Mary Jane White of Elizabeth City County, age twenty-one. Still furious with his first wife, Jarvis assured the Reverend William Thornton that he was a "widower." As Mary Jane explained later, "in old *slave* times the negro men slaves lived with the Slave women, [but] they were not lawfully married and were frequently separated at the will of old or new masters," a historically accurate statement that skirted the question of why Henry did not wish to have his first wife back. Jarvis bought five acres with a small house with his pension, and Mary Jane bore him three children. Mary Jane could read, and she tried to tutor her husband, but he thought it inappropriate for "a woman to be a teachin' her husban' [as it] ain't accordin' to scripture." The devout teacher was more successful, however, in prodding Jarvis into thinking more about the hereafter. Jarvis finally "got de glory in [his] soul." But that had limits. When once asked whether he had forgiven his old master, Jarvis insisted that he had. "But," the old veteran added, "I'd gib my oder leg to meet him in battle."[16]

As time passed, Jarvis's war-related injuries grew worse. He had taken a ball in one arm as well, and that limb eventually became useless. His rheumatism became so problematic that his wife "had to turn him over in bed." Brooks's wife, Georgianna, lived nearby and helped when she could, but by 1890 Mary Jane "had to dress him [for] he is nearly totally disable [and] he Cant do Eny Work at all." Private Henry Jarvis died on March 9, 1890, around the age of fifty-eight, yet one more veteran whose military service robbed him of an old age. His youngest son, Ellison, had just turned six. Mary Jane received a widow's pension of $30 each month under the 1890 law and earned another $2 each week "by Washing, Ironing and Scrubbing." She lived to be seventy-five, dying in her son William's Norfolk house on August 23, 1926.[17]

Colonel Charles Francis Adams Jr. also found his proper place in life. Upon being discharged in early August, Adams retired to Newport to regain his health and to plan his future with fiancée Mary Elizabeth Ogden. From the moment of their first meeting in 1863, Adams had regarded Mary Elizabeth—known to her friends as Minnie—as "so charming and attractive a person" as he had ever encountered. Quite possibly, Adams also saw the courteous Minnie as his natural foil, as his father had recently reprimanded him for his chronic rudeness. It could not have hurt that her father, Edward Ogden of New York, was a man of vast inherited wealth who could open doors in the business world unknown even to the Adams family. They wed on November 8, only three months after Adams's return from the war, and spent the next eleven months on a grand tour of Europe. The young couple enjoyed Paris and Rome, but only "after a fashion!" Adams admitted. "That I failed, and failed woefully, to avail myself of my opportunities, goes without saying, for it was I!" Whatever his critics might say about him, Adams, like all of the men in his family, possessed the gift of honest self-knowledge.[18]

Armed with his father-in-law's business connections, Adams secured a seat on the Massachusetts Railroad Commission. He also maintained an interest in national politics, though he remained incurious about the concerns of American blacks and even disdainful of their efforts at political reform. Charles Sr. regarded President Ulysses Grant as an unqualified spoilsman, and in both 1872 and 1876 Charles Jr. and Henry publicly supported their father's unsuccessful bids for the Republican nomination. "Universal suffrage," the former colonel lectured in 1869, "can only mean in plain English the government of ignorance and vice:—it means a European, and especially Celtic, proletariat on the Atlantic coast, an African proletariat on the shores of the Gulf; and a Chinese proletariat on the

Pacific." A good many early free-soilers, of course, had despised the institution of slavery without ever caring much for the enslaved. But Adams
was atypical of the young Harvard men who had stepped forward to lead
black troops, the majority of whom grew to appreciate their men and remained true to the reformist tendencies of their early days. In fact, Adams
was not merely indifferent but openly hostile to Reconstruction reforms,
perhaps because he regarded the freedmen's demands for economic rights
as similar to the claims advanced by the Irish immigrants who built Northern railroads. "We cannot live forever on the dry husks of the anti-slavery
agitation, or upon the animosities of the late war," Charles wrote Henry in
1870. "That long battle is over."[19]

If nothing else, Adams's military service had earned him a measure of
independence from his imperious father. Mary Elizabeth bore him five
children, three daughters and two sons. Breaking with the family tradition of naming one son after the father, the couple instead named the
girls Mary, Elizabeth, and Louisa, after Charles's late sister, while the twin
boys were christened John and Henry. Both boys graduated from Harvard
in 1898. "Nothing tells like being contemptuous," he once remarked to
Henry while trying to explain his personal philosophy. Adams devoted
his final years to writing history, serving as president of the Massachusetts
Historical Society, and condemning the German people in 1914 as "the
common enemies of mankind." He died of pneumonia on March 20,
1915, and was buried in Quincy.[20]

Far prouder of his military service was disabled veteran William H.
Carney. The numerous wounds he had received at Wagner—one ball remained too far inside his body for safe extraction—ended his career, and he
was granted an honorable discharge on June 30, 1864. Like Henry Jarvis,
Carney had labored as an oysterman before the war, and as with Jarvis, that
profession was no longer possible for him. He had once briefly considered
a career in the ministry, but evidently his experiences in the war turned
his thoughts away from religion. Even before being mustered out, Carney had contacted Massachusetts general R. G. Pierce about "obtaining a
situation" in the state's military bureaucracy. When nothing came of that,
he tried again, inquiring as to a position as a messenger for the assembly.
But hampering his chances was the fact that the Virginia runaway was still
barely literate; his two missives were filled with misspellings, and he even

managed to mangle the general's surname into "Purse." Carney instead returned to New Bedford, where, on October 11, 1865, he wed twenty-two-year-old Susanna Williams. Census takers listed Williams, three years Carney's junior, as a mixed-race Virginia native, and so it is possible that Susanna too had somehow escaped slavery before the war and found her way to the coastal town, known in the antebellum period as the "fugitive's Gibraltar."[21]

Carney found work with the post office as a "Letter Carrier," even though he needed two crutches to move about. A daughter, Clara, was born in June 1876, even as Carney, as one doctor remarked, remained "a constant sufferer from gunshot-wounds received while in the Army." The fourth ball had damaged Carney's left hip, while the second, in his right leg, caused "nearly complete loss of knee-jerk" by the late 1880s. The troubled joint led to rheumatism, which he treated with "Alkaline and tonics." By 1900, Clara, now twenty-three, supplemented the family's income as a "Music teacher at home" in their house at 128 Mill Street.[22]

Carney's wartime heroism was never forgotten in New England. Nor was he anxious to let his countrymen forget, and he proved a popular speaker on the veterans' circuit, addressing civic organizations. The lectures and the black press kept his name before the public, as did a lengthy 1889 interview he gave about the assault on Wagner. Congressman John Simpkins continued to lobby for a fitting award. Eight African Americans had already been awarded the Congressional Medal of Honor, and in the spring of 1900 President William McKinley announced that Carney would be the ninth. (Because his bravery predated those awards already handed out for meritorious service in 1864 and 1865, Carney became, technically, the first black Medal of Honor recipient.) His medal, bestowed on May 25, was "awarded for most distinguished gallantry in action." The citation, which in fact undercounted the number of wounds he had received on July 18, 1863, read: "When the color sergeant was shot down, this soldier grasped the flag, led the way to the parapet, and planted the colors thereon. When the troops fell back he brought off the flag, under a fierce fire in which he was twice severely wounded." By the start of the twentieth century, the phrase "the old flag never touched the ground" became one of the most popular across the North, and Carney's words, one New Englander remarked, were "known by every schoolboy in the land."[23]

William Carney's heroism at Wagner
not only earned him the Medal of
Honor but inspired the patriotic song
"Boys the Old Flag Never Touched
the Ground," composed shortly after
his death by Henry Mather and
George Lothrop and published as
sheet music with Carney's face on the
cover. *Courtesy National Gallery of Art.*

The award, granted thirty-seven years after the battle, eased Carney's finances in later years but also, ironically, hastened his demise. Carney was offered the position as messenger for the Massachusetts secretary of state, and so for the next eight years he and Susanna resided in Boston. But his legs continued to trouble him, and in the fall of 1908 he was getting into a crowded elevator in the State House when he stepped aside to make room for one more. Carney's leg was somehow "crushed" by the door. He died two weeks later, on December 9, in Boston's City Hospital.[24]

His passing received more attention in the national media than that of any man in his regiment since Shaw's death—more than Ned Hallowell's even. The black press devoted banner headlines to the story, praising him as "Brave Negro Soldier" or "Noted Colored Hero," and all of them ending "with the words often quoted in Massachusetts: 'The old flag never touched the ground.'" Black Americans "have lost one of their oldest and most renowned soldiers," commented Julius Taylor, the editor of Chicago's *Broad Ax.* "A character such as William H. Carney adds more to a Negro's contribution to militarism than half of the speeches that might be made relating their exploits." The white press covered the story of Carney's tragic accident too, as did one of his old officers. Sixty-nine-year-old Pen Hallowell drafted a lengthy obituary for the *Boston Evening Transcript*. "It is fit that the last act, the act which cost his life, should be one of courtesy," Hallowell observed. "In stepping aside to make room for another his leg was caught and crushed. Sergeant William H. Carney was a gentleman. Peace to him!"[25]

Susanna moved back to her Mill Street home in New Bedford, which Clara continued to use for music lessons. Census takers found the two, then ages sixty-four and thirty-three, living quietly in 1910. Ten years later, Susanna was deceased and Clara resided alone, as she was when census takers knocked on her door in 1930. She died in 1939 at the age of sixty-three. As was the case with Charlotte and Emily Hallowell and Carlotta Lowell, Clara evidently chose never to marry.[26]

Carney's obituary was just one of many essays Pen Hallowell wrote in the years after he resigned his commission in the fall of 1863. He purchased an elegant home at 50 Mystic Street in West Medford, Massachusetts—a home large enough to encompass a family like the one in which he was raised—and began a new life as a wool merchant with his brothers. Hallowell had met Sarah Wharton Haydock in Manhattan in July 1861, and although he regarded her, seven years his junior, as a "kid," he had given her a photograph of himself, and she remained on his mind throughout his time in the war. They married on January 27, 1868, in a simple Quaker ceremony at her father's house in Manhattan, and spent their honeymoon in Antietam, where Pen had been shot six years earlier. Sarah and Pen settled into life in West Medford, where in 1866 they were joined by Ned and Richard and their wives. Six children followed, starting with Anna in 1871 and ending with Susan Morris in 1883.[27]

Shortly after Ned's death, Pen quit the wool business and went into banking, taking a senior position with the National Bank of Commerce. But Hallowells were ever activists at heart, and along with his brother Richard and sister-in-law Wilmina, he helped finance the Calhoun Colored School in Alabama. Mostly, he devoted his off hours to writing letters and editorials on the war, its memory, and the ongoing struggles of African Americans. On one occasion, Hallowell condemned segregation in Boston by noting that Shaw and his men were buried side by side in the sands of Morris Island; as he put it, "There was no segregation at Fort Wagner."

Another time he contacted the chairman of a local hospital whose institution had refused to hire a highly qualified black nurse, fuming that "the
founder of Christianity would slam the door of opportunity in the faces of
these people." When in 1909 he read that President William Howard Taft
had remarked that black bureaucrats and officials "should not be forced
on unwilling white communities," Hallowell published a lengthy piece in
the *Boston Herald* wondering if it was then fair for "white postmasters and
other officials" to be "forced upon unwilling negro communities." Why
the president thought it important "to know officially the color of a citizen" was beyond Hallowell's comprehension. "However, let us not be too
much disgusted and discouraged by William H. Taft, a type of reactionist,
and Booker T. Washington, a type of submissionist," the seventy-year-old
banker wrote. "Let us rather remember that the dark days of Slavery were
succeeded by the bright days of Liberty."[28]

Pen Hallowell reserved his utmost disdain, however, for Woodrow Wilson, the Virginia-born Democrat who taught government at Princeton
University before moving into politics. Pen was particularly incensed by the
fourth edition of Wilson's *A History of the American People,* which covered
the war years. Not content merely to pepper the *Boston Herald* with letters
on the topic—although he did that too—the well-connected Hallowell
sent two missives to publisher Henry Wilbur, complaining about what
he regarded as a book that "abounds with apologies for slavery." Wilson's
volume, Hallowell huffed, said not a single word about "Colonel Robert
Gould Shaw, and utterly ignores the arming of the blacks in the North, a
movement which contributed 186,000 men to our cause." Instead, Wilson spent several pages on Jefferson Davis's last-minute decision to use
"slaves as armed troops," an effort that raised roughly thirty-five men. (In
an aside, Hallowell added that he wished Davis had raised more, as those
regiments "would have deserted *en masse* to the Yankees.") The volume, at
least, helped explain Wilson's "present attitude toward the race problem"
and his support for segregation. For Southern reactionaries, "it would be a
toss-up whether to vote for Jefferson Davis, were he alive, or for Woodrow
Wilson."[29]

By that point, Hallowell was seventy-five and still putting in long days
at his bank. After contracting pneumonia, he died on April 11 and was
cremated after a Quaker service in his native Philadelphia. Former Massa-

chusetts governor Eugene Foss attended, and Pen's old comrade from the Twentieth, Oliver Wendell Holmes Jr., now a Supreme Court justice, wrote to say that his death laid "a great space bare for him," as Pen was his "oldest friend [and] the most generously gallant spirit and I don't know but the greatest soul I ever knew." African American historian Benjamin Griffith Brawley dedicated his *Social History of the American Negro* to "The Memory of Norwood Penrose Hallowell, Patriot." The many newspaper accounts of his life devoted considerable space to his roles in the two infantry regiments. "So gallantly did he bear himself at the head of this regiment, and so well did his colored soldiers fight in battle," observed the *Boston Herald,* "that public opinion in the North and deep-seated prejudice in the South became reconciled to Gov. John A. Andrew's move in organizing the negro soldiers." Sarah lived on until 1934, dying at the age of eighty-eight.[30]

WHILE PEN HALLOWELL SPENT HIS LATER YEARS DEFENDING THE SO-cial changes brought about by the war, a large number of black veterans threw themselves into the fray, either by becoming activists themselves or by seeking to change society through political office. Of the 1,510 identifiable men of color who held office during Reconstruction, at least 130 first served in the nation's military. Although he never sought office, James Monroe Trotter was among the most energetic of activists. Upon being mustered out, the former second lieutenant, now all of twenty-three, returned to Chillicothe, evidently to marry Virginia Isaacs, the sweetheart of his teenage years. Two months James's junior, she had been born free in Cincinnati. Trotter was anxious to relocate to Boston, where he could combine teaching with activism. The couple rented a home at 105 Kendall Street, and while Trotter applied for positions, he found work as a clerk with the post office. As was all too common in the nineteenth century, their first two children died while infants, and believing that the insalubrious urban conditions had contributed to their deaths, Virginia returned home to Ohio to give birth to their third child, who was born on April 7, 1872, and christened William Monroe. Two healthy daughters followed in 1874 and 1883. By then, the family had moved back to Massachusetts, settling in suburban Hyde Park in Boston's predominantly white South End and buying a house valued at $6,000.[31]

Trotter, who was so light in color that an 1870 census taker mistook him for white, remained active in Boston's black public life. In 1878 the onetime music student published *Music and Some Highly Musical People* as a tribute to African American accomplishments and to demonstrate, as he observed in the preface, that musical aptitude was "not in the exclusive possession of the fairer-skinned race." Trotter also remained close to writer and activist William Wells Brown, who had recruited for the two Massachusetts regiments in 1863, and in 1875 Trotter and Brown organized a commemoration at Faneuil Hall to mark the passing of Senator Charles Sumner. In 1882 a white man was promoted over Trotter to become the branch's chief clerk. Although his income was solid enough to allow him to purchase a home, the former lieutenant, who had helped persuade the men of the Fifty-fifth not to accept a racially based salary, promptly resigned in protest.[32]

Furious that he was denied a patronage position controlled in New England by Republicans, and equally angry about President Rutherford B. Hayes's withdrawal of federal troops from the South in 1877, Trotter publicly broke with his party and embraced the term "Independent." Few black Republicans followed his lead, even if the white Democrats Trotter endorsed were hardly typical of their national party. In the same year he resigned his clerkship, Trotter threw his energies into former senator Benjamin F. Butler's Massachusetts gubernatorial campaign. Having been a Democrat in the 1850s, Butler shifted to the Republicans after famously defining runaways as "contraband" at Fort Monroe. But by 1882 he was once again calling himself a Democrat. Butler won his race, and Trotter was rewarded by being appointed recorder of deeds in Washington by Democratic president Grover Cleveland, replacing Republican Frederick Douglass and becoming the first black New Englander to receive a high-ranking federal position. "The Democrats and Republicans in Congress are almost equally perturbed by it," observed the *Boston Evening Transcript*, "the former objecting to Mr. Trotter's color, and the Republicans objecting to his politics."[33]

Trotter's health suffered while in Washington, and in 1887 his employee Rosetta Douglass informed her father that "he has been lying very ill of pneumonia." The Republicans recaptured the White House the following year, and Trotter lost his position to former senator Blanche K. Bruce. He died of pneumonia at the age of fifty on February 26, 1892. As ever, obituaries listed his service in the Fifty-fifth, and the black-owned *Cleveland Gazette* forgave him for his political apostasy with a lengthy tribute. Trotter lived long enough to see his son attend Harvard University, where William Monroe became the first black student in Cambridge to earn a Phi Beta Kappa key. Had Trotter lived even into his sixties, he would have seen his son launch the Niagara Movement (with W. E. B. Du Bois), found the National Equal Rights League, edit the *Boston Guardian,* carry on an active correspondence with Pen Hallowell, and engage in a well-publicized debate on segregation with President Wilson.[34]

Lieutenant Peter Vogelsang was another veteran who balanced activism with a career that provided for his family. After being mustered out on September 2, the forty-seven-year-old Vogelsang prepared to return to the New York City area. During the war, his family had relocated to Duffield Street in Brooklyn. His eldest son, George Peter, now twenty-four and working as a clerk, lived with his siblings Maria and John and his maternal aunt, Maria Margaret DeGrasse, who had helped care for his children during Vogelsang's absence. Maria had been an elder sister to Vogelsang's wife Theodosia, who had died of tuberculosis in 1854. Still single at forty-nine, Maria had been courted by her brother-in-law prior to his enlistment, and when he returned from the South she traveled to Boston to greet his ship. Just five days later, the Reverend Havens of Boston performed the ceremony joining "Lieut. Peter Vogelsang to Maria. M. De Grasse, all of Brooklyn city."[35]

Vogelsang briefly returned to working as a hotel clerk, but in 1869 he secured a position as a messenger and doorman with the New York Customs House, a position that paid $1,000 per year. Vogelsang's antebellum jobs and the highly literate letters he posted during the war to the *Weekly Anglo-African* indicate that he probably deserved the rank of clerk with the city, which drew a higher salary of $1,400, but such positions were reserved for white men. Jobs with the Customs House were controlled by the Republicans and doled out to loyal party members and deserving veterans, and the black lieutenant was an avowed Grant man. One journalist claimed that there was "no man who knows so many distinguished public men," including "every politician, merchant, or other habitual caller" at the Customs House, as did Vogelsang. Although known for his fierce heroism on the battlefield, the reporter added, Vogelsang was as "polite as a French diplomatist," the "personification of good humor," and a man "who could say 'No' to a persistent office seeker with as much grace as another man would have said 'Yes.'"[36]

When necessary, the old soldier could be a tough doorman. In one instance during the fall of 1885, collector Edward Hedden was accosted by a businessman, much "under the influence of liquor," whose license to keep a lunch stand in the Customs House had not been renewed. The exchange grew heated, and when Hedden rang his bell to call for assistance, the salesman threatened to punch "the Collector's head." The "intruder found himself suddenly seized by Peter Vogelsang," the New York *Herald* reported, "and incontinently bounced." Although sixty-eight, Vogelsang remained a formidable adversary, a trait much in demand in postwar Manhattan, which possibly also explains why a series of collectors preferred to keep Vogelsang near to hand rather than upstairs in a clerk's office.[37]

Vogelsang reserved his evenings and weekends for politics and community activism. Just as his father had, he joined and frequently led a variety of black self-help organizations and fraternal orders. He was one of the founders of the Morning Star Lodge, the Grand Masters Council No. 27, and the Brooklyn Patriarchie No. 22. He twice served as an officer in the William Lloyd Garrison Post, was "an old member" of the African Mutual Relief Society and the Boyer Lodge (a Masonic order named for the former Haitian president), and volunteered as secretary of the Ogden B. Fund. On Sundays he and Maria attended Brooklyn's Bethel Church, where he sat in the section reserved for members of the GAR, or Grand Army of the Republic, a national fraternal organization with hundreds of branches. As the son of a native of St. Croix, Vogelsang served also as secretary of the enormous "welcome-home" ceremony staged at the Cooper Institute in 1870 to celebrate the return of American minister E. D. Bassett. Two years later, when white Republicans began to abandon the increasingly corrupt Grant administration, Vogelsang stood with other black activists who remained loyal to the president owing to his crackdown on Southern vigilantism. At a meeting of the "Colored Men of Brooklyn in Council," Vogelsang was elected a vice president of a group that pledged allegiance "to the party by which the principles of equal liberty for all were inaugurated" and promised to help coordinate the Grant campaign in "King's County and other places on Long Island."[38]

In 1884, for the first time since James Buchanan's election in 1856, the nation voted a Democrat, Grover Cleveland, into the White House. Upon taking office in March 1885, Cleveland appointed Daniel Magone, the former chairman of the Democratic state committee, as Manhattan's new collector. Wielding the Civil Service Act of 1883 as a weapon, Cleveland and Magone removed both incompetent employees and effective, longtime personnel whose chief crime was that they were Republicans. Especially hard hit were black treasury workers, who were replaced with white Democrats. Vogelsang, now sixty-nine, was probably not much surprised when he was dismissed in June 1886. For "nearly a quarter of a century [he] had been the special messenger and usher attached to the Collector's office," lamented the New York *Herald*. "Peter was one of the noted characters of the Custom House." The editor of the New York *Freeman* was blunter still. "The change of politics alone was the cause of his removal, along with other colored men who held positions in the same department." By 1888, only five black men worked for the Port of New York, and only as messengers or porters.[39]

Marie Vogelsang died that same year, and Vogelsang moved in with his son John. His old wounds had begun to bother him, and since 1879 the army had listed him as "partially disabled" and increased his pension. The loss of his wife and position hastened the end. He died of a stroke on Monday, April 4, 1887, less than ten months after being dismissed. "His death removes from our city a valiant soldier, a useful and painstaking friend, a humble Christian, a kind father, and devoted husband," the *Freeman* commented in a lengthy obituary. "He won his title before Fort Wagner, where his regiment, the 54th Massachusetts Volunteers, under Col. Shaw, took such a prominent part; and for coolness and distinguished bravery on the field he was recommended by the officers for promotion." The editor listed the many societies, charities, and lodges he had served, praised his activities as "distinguished by promptness, honesty and ability," and rightly remarked that his death "closed the eventful career of this distinguished citizen."[40]

No veteran of the three black regiments reached the political heights achieved by Lieutenant Stephen A. Swails. Nor did any of the other tens of thousands of black men who had served during the Civil War. After the war, the thirty-three-year-old Swails initially remained in Charleston, courting Susan Aspinall, the light-skinned daughter of mariner Albert Aspinall and a woman twelve years his junior. To make ends meet he took a position with the Freedmen's Bureau, created by Congress the previous March and largely staffed by officers and veterans. The couple married on April 18, 1866, in the home of an abolitionist white minister, Reverend Joseph B. Seabrook. The bride's friend Mary McKinley assured the reverend that Susan had never been married, and the groom also vowed that he was single. Although technically true, his oath to Seabrook ignored the sad reality of Sarah Thompson and their children.[41]

Within two years, the Swails family, which soon included son Florian and daughter Irene, were living in Kingstree, Williamsburg County, a district with twice as many black residents as whites. There the former waiter bought a house on the corner of Main and Brooks Streets for $800 and began to read law. Like any aspiring attorney at the time, Swails found a senior lawyer who accepted him as an apprentice, tutored him in the basics of jurisprudence, and at length recommended him to an informal board of local attorneys, who then approved his request to hang out his own shingle. Swails also began to edit a newspaper, the *Williamsburg Republican,* a banner that trumpeted his political affiliation. Swails quickly made a name for himself as a young man on the rise. After Congress passed the Military Reconstruction Act in March 1867, which required the defeated Confederate states to call conventions to craft new constitutions, Swails put his name forward as delegate. Congress demanded that delegates be chosen on the basis of universal male suffrage, and a good number of black men were elected, including Swails and Robert Smalls, whom Swails had first met in June 1863 when his regiment arrived in the low country. The light-skinned veteran was still unknown enough in Charleston, however, that the editor of the *Courier* identified him as a white man "of Northern birth."[42]

Just as Swails began to prepare for his first run at political office in 1868, the Democratic editor of the *Daily Albany Argus* dredged up his unsavory prewar reputation. In a story widely reprinted in the conservative press from Cleveland to South Carolina, the editor reminded voters of Swails's earlier days in Cooperstown and Elmira. "He was a vagabond; he was one of those mean, cunning, drunken, thieving 'niggers,' that almost every northern village has." The lengthy exposé recounted Swails being fired from his job for "habitual drunkenness and dishonesty" and told how, after getting Sarah Thompson pregnant, he abandoned her and their child for a life in the military. The *Argus* also charged that Swails had "hunted after a white man in this place, while he was on one of his drunks, with a large knife." Not content to stop there, the editor, perhaps unwisely, also dismissed the twice-injured officer as merely being "wounded in some skirmish," an absurd understatement that surely infuriated black veterans in Swails's district and made it easier for voters to disregard the other allegations as Democratic lies. Perhaps black Republicans simply could not see the dissolute youth in the tough, ambitious veteran who chaired political meetings and encouraged them to stand firm for the party of Lincoln. "After the ballots were counted, Swails won his first term in the South Carolina state senate."[43]

Along with the Reverend Benjamin Franklin Randolph, a former army chaplain and Freedmen's Bureau agent, Swails, at considerable danger to himself, attended the Republican national convention as a Grant delegate. In the elections that fall, Randolph was installed in South Carolina's state senate, only to be assassinated soon after. Swails's political visibility was such that shortly after taking his seat in the senate, his was one of the four names of black men being discussed for an open seat in Congress. "The colored voters in South Carolina have resolved to fill the places the State is entitled to with men of their own class," noted one Pennsylvania editor. In the end, fellow state senator and South Carolina native Joseph Rainey was tapped to fill the First District's congressional chair in Washington. But for a new arrival who just three years before was patrolling the streets of Charleston, Swails's rise made for heady drink.[44]

Swails quickly earned the enmity of white conservatives with his demands for equal political, social, educational, and economic rights. Swails was determined that his constituents would receive a decent education, possibly because he had never received one himself. South Carolina had been one of the four Southern states to flatly outlaw black literacy before the war, and Robert Smalls, who was also sensitive about his lack of formal schooling, had written provisions into the new state constitution for education to be free, integrated, and compulsory for all residents. By the early 1870s, thanks to elementary schools funded by the American Missionary

Association and the Freedmen's Bureau, some older pupils were ready to take the next step. The South Carolina College in Columbia had closed during the war for lack of students and briefly functioned instead as a Confederate hospital. The college reopened in late 1865 as a university, and four years later, assemblyman William J. Whipper, a black veteran from Beaufort, introduced a law banning racial discrimination in admissions. When the trustees responded by claiming that former slaves were not yet prepared for higher education, the legislature fired the directors and, as one hostile newspaper huffed, replaced them with a "mob of carpet-baggers and negroes," including Stephen Swails. As the editor added, "It is evidently the intention of the African element to capture the University after the solemn assurances given some time since that this institution should be left to the uses of whites." Despite such fights, conservative Democrats could not imagine why black Carolinians demanded antidiscrimination laws.[45]

For those whites who longed to restore the old order, the democratic reforms of the Reconstruction years had to be resisted at all costs. White vigilantes and Ku Klux Klansmen fought back, and by 1870, Swails reported, "you cannot speak without a guard if you are a Republican." In the spring of 1873, Swails journeyed to Washington with Lieutenant Governor Richard Gleaves to urge Grant to travel south and investigate conditions for himself. Two years before, the president had signed both the Ku Klux Klan Act and the Force Act into law and suspended habeas corpus in nine South Carolina counties—although not Williamsburg—but since then he had requested the resignation of his crusading attorney general, Amos Akerman, whom Grant's cabinet had come to regard as unnecessarily obsessed with the Klan. The president assured the two that he hoped to "do so at some future time [and] regretted he would not be able at present to take such a tour" of the South. "General Grant declines a carpet-bag invitation," sneered one hostile editor.[46]

Expecting no further assistance from Washington, Swails decided that black Carolinians would have to be responsible for their own protection. He had been the second-in-command of the state militia, but when former state assemblyman Robert Elliott Brown was elected to Congress, Swails was elevated into command and accepted the rank of major general. After white vigilantism worsened in Georgetown—a town Swails was familiar with from the last days of the war—he and Adjutant General H. W. Purvis called out the state national guard and marched them toward the coast. Swails also lobbied the War Department not to remove from the state any more regular troops, who were being ordered to the Mexican border and to the Indian wars in the Dakotas. "Swails, who is a brigadier of militia and a nigger," one Democratic editor scoffed, "was certain the troops could not be safely removed now."[47]

In 1872, Swails was elected president pro tem of the state senate, a position that allowed him to control the flow of bills and shape legislation, and it also gave him considerable patronage power. (His family joined him in Columbia, where Marie, a third child, was born in January 1873.) When Democrats complained about the cost of Reconstruction reforms, Swails replied that the real debate should be over priorities rather than money. Democrats from Charleston, he replied, sought funds otherwise earmarked for the militia to restore the city's Military Hall, a prewar symbol of racial control and currently a haven for white vigilantes. "It would be a Godsend if the Military Hall in Charleston was burned down," Swails snapped. Carolina Democrats quite literally fought back, turning out at one 1878 Republican rally in their old Confederate uniforms and tearing "down the United States flag with their sabres," trampling it underfoot, and tearing "it in shreds." Just days later, on October 5, several whites fired two shots at Swails as he spoke in Kingstree. The shooters perhaps intended to miss, but if they hoped to intimidate the former lieutenant, they were disappointed. Swails again boarded a train for Washington, where he and Congressman Rainey called on an unreceptive President Hayes, warning him that without federal soldiers, "the Republicans of South Carolina would not be allowed a fair opportunity to express their sentiments at the November election."[48]

"Terrorism in South Carolina" read the October 15 headline in the *Cincinnati Daily Gazette*. One week before, the state Democratic Executive Committee, accompanied by a band of Red Shirts—as the paramilitary supporters of the former Confederate cavalryman and current governor Wade Hampton styled themselves—disrupted a Republican meeting and warned Swails that he was "required to leave Williamsburg in ten days." In the resulting melee, the Red Shirts shot and killed a black Republican. Swails attempted to reach the safety of the courthouse, but riders cut him off and threatened that he would be killed if he did not abandon the county. Swails again left for Washington, after which the mob beat "the Rev. Pinckney, the colored Deputy-Postmaster." In the nation's capital, Swails cautioned one journalist that although Republicans enjoyed solid majorities in the Low-country districts, the Democrats would surely win in light of "the terrorism prevailing." It was a prescient claim. Although black voters courageously turned out on Election Day—a particularly brave act in a time when casting a ballot was a public affair—the Democrats announced that they carried Williamsburg by 600 votes. The U.S. elections supervisor, who was black, was denied "admission to the room occupied by the election managers." Only seven African Americans in the county voted Democratic, one resident assured a reporter, but whites wanted "to get [Swails] out of the way until after the election," and with him gone, stealing the election "was easier." Swails left his family behind, and three months later, in January 1879, Susan gave birth to another son, Stephen Jr.[49]

A federal district attorney issued arrest warrants for seventeen men for election fraud, but "the affidavits were mostly made by negroes," one journalist jeered, and none of the accused ever faced trial. Swails took a position in Washington as a clerk with the Treasury Department, but he continued to hope that he might return to the state that had been his home for the past sixteen years. Evidently, his family remained in South Carolina. In 1881 he decided to test the waters by announcing that he would "spend his vacation among old friends at Kingstree." The editor of the Kingstree Star, the Republican's Democratic rival, warned that if Swails "came back, it would be at his peril," adding that the "Democratic party cannot countenance such a procedure." Undaunted, Swails returned, delivering a speech in the town's AME church that conservatives denounced as a "most bitter and diabolical race harangue." Threatened once more that his presence in "our midst will not be tolerated," Swails returned to his Treasury desk. When the death of Congressman Edward Mackey in 1884 left a vacancy in the House of Representatives, Swails's old supporters advanced his name, claiming that his residence in Washington "would add greatly to his usefulness as a Congressman." Swails still qualified as a resident of the district because he continued to own his home in Kingstree. In the end, the nomination went to Robert Smalls. Four years later, despite not having lived in the state for nine years, Swails received the Republican nomination in the Third District, but being unable to campaign, he lost the election to Democrat James Cothran.[50]

The year before, in 1887, Swails had applied for a pension and been granted $7.75 each month. Although only fifty-five, the twice-shot veteran's health began to deteriorate. At some point he returned to Kingstree, and this time his enemies left him alone. He was able to see his daughter Marie graduate from Charleston's Avery Normal School in 1896, and his son Florian marry the following year. On May 12, 1900, after Swails, then sixty-eight, began to suffer from "acute dysentery" and his temperature rose to 102, Susan called on Dr. D. C. Scott, who remained at his patient's bedside until death came on May 17. The deceased, Scott recorded, had "developed symptoms of congestion of the brain [and] rapidly became worse and died in 5 or 6 hours in a comatose condition." Fearful that his grave might be desecrated, Susan had his body shipped back to Charleston, a city he had helped to liberate, where he was buried in the Humane and Friendly Society Cemetery. For a man who had faced allegations of corruption, upon his death, his Kingstree house was valued at $749—slightly less than what he had paid for it decades before—and his other "personal property" was worth only $265, for a total of $1,014. Susan Swails lived another four years, dying at the age of sixty-four in December 1903.[51]

THE WAR'S OFFICIAL END HAD FOUND FORMER SERGEANT MAJOR Lewis Douglass laboring as a sutler in the Lowcountry; with the end of the actual fighting, he returned home to Rochester by way of Talbot County, Maryland. Hoping to find his son a position with the Freedmen's Bureau, Frederick Douglass contacted Senator Charles Sumner in late April 1865, reminding the Massachusetts Republican that Lewis "took part in the memorable and disastrous, though glorious assault on Fort Wagner." Now, however, his "health having broken down in the service," Lewis desired a clerkship in Washington. But either Sumner lacked the influence he had wielded just weeks before, prior to Lincoln's assassination, or Lewis's rudimentary penmanship—his letters failed to display the elegant handwriting that graced Charles's missives—cost him the clerkship. Instead, after a brief but financially unrewarding bout with the Maryland chapter of the Equal Rights League, Lewis took a job teaching in Rochester, while he continued to press Amelia for a wedding date.[52]

Lewis found teaching dull, however, and in the spring of 1866 he and his brother Frederick Jr. fled west to Denver. They went to work selling dry goods to miners and settlers with their father's old friend Henry Waggoner, who ran the Red, White, and Blue Mining Company. Lewis promised his father that he was laboring as hard as he ever had. "In my business I am up early and late." But he thought the "business promises much, [as] it is the only kind of business paying at all in Denver." The "boys have taken hold in good Earnest," Waggoner assured their father. "Lewis, I take to be a young man of strong, clear sense." Where Frederick appeared a bit "more cautious, reflecting hesitation," the twenty-six-year-old Lewis "seems to drive right a head at the object aimed at." One year later, Lewis had been promoted to secretary of a different silver mining company.[53]

Lewis never intended to remain in the West, and having put aside some money, he returned east in search of Amelia. While ice skating with friends in New Jersey in February 1868, he was set upon by white toughs, who quickly discovered that they had picked on the wrong veteran. Lewis had been careful not to pack one skate, and donning it like a glove, he "very successfully stopped" one attacker "by splitting his head with the skates." The group attempted to circle behind Douglass, but when another lunged forward, Lewis sliced upwards and "took his thumb nearly off." The veteran who had once sprinted down the beach toward Fort Wagner was not about to be intimidated by a group of "cowards," and perhaps also in recounting the story he wished to remind his onetime fiancée that he remained a vigorous, capable man of business.[54]

At length, Amelia relented. The two were married on October 7, 1869, in the Syracuse home of her father, the Reverend Jermain W. Loguen, shortly after Lewis served as a delegate to the Washington Colored Men's Convention. Lewis's parents and brother Charles were in attendance, giving him "courage when I promise to obey *you*," he remarked, "and who will stand up with you when you promise to command *me*." After waiting for so long, Douglass little cared whether the ceremony was "conducted with the least possible display," and he reassured Amelia, telling her not to worry "that any arrangements you may make will meet with my disapprobation." The two enjoyed a happy and content life for the next thirty-nine years, their marriage ending only with Lewis's death. But of course there would be no children.[55]

The newlyweds relocated to Washington, where Lewis, his father, and activist and restaurateur George T. Downing had already announced "the publication of a first class Weekly Journal in the interest of the colored people of America." Until the group could raise the necessary funds, Lewis took a job in the Government Printing Office at $24 per week, where he was harassed by members of the Typographical Union for having never been a member. After Douglass responded that his earlier turns at setting type had been in wartime Rochester, when he "had not attained his majority," it became clear that the real problem was his race. Even as Douglass pursued legal action against the union, he found time to be elected a member of Washington's "Legislative Assembly," as the city council was then called. Finally, by the spring of 1873, Lewis had put enough money aside to start the *New National Era,* on which he served as senior editor. Constant reminders of his color complicated his daily existence, however. During the previous year, when Lewis, Charles, and "several colored veterans"—among them Swails—attended the national convention in Pittsburgh as Grant delegates, the hotel manager refused them rooms. But the veteran never forgot his fellows. Although a solid Republican, Lewis publicly endorsed Trotter's controversial appointment as recorder of deeds, despite the fact that Trotter had replaced his own father.[56]

In his final years, Lewis prospered in Washington's booming real estate market. He enjoyed spending time with Charles's large number of sons, who lived nearby. But by the time he reached his midsixties, Douglass's health took a sudden downturn, and only then, in 1907, did the proud veteran finally apply for a pension. He was granted $28 each month. Amelia and Charles were both by his bedside when he died of "chronic nephritis"— inflammation of the kidneys and urinary tract, a condition probably related to his 1863 injuries—in his Seventeenth Street home on September 19, 1908, at the age of sixty-seven. The Veterans Administration paid the undertaker's costs and bought a casket. Amelia lived until 1936, dying in the same house of a heart attack at the age of ninety-three.[57]

Charles, the youngest of the Douglass offspring to survive childhood, outlived Lewis by a dozen years. After being mustered out of the Fifth Cavalry, he had returned to Rochester, where he helped to tend the family gardens, which almost constituted a small farm. But he had enjoyed his brief time in Washington, where the black community had grown rapidly during the war. When his brothers journeyed west in 1866, Charles, the longtime army clerk, got a position with the Freedmen's Bureau. His neat, precise script earned him the praise of his superiors, especially General Oliver O. Howard, who ran the new government agency. Within a month of his arrival in Washington he became, as he bragged to his father, only "the second colored man in the Government that has been given a first-class internship." As fascinated by the political world as his father, Charles loved the partisan flavor of the city. But even more, he enjoyed the civil liberties that Washington granted to black men; New York State, by contrast, continued to deny the franchise to black men without property. "I can get along better here than in Rochester and have more rights," Charles reminded his father. "I will become a voter here." When a slate of black candidates was successful in the 1867 elections, Charles was jubilant and took part in a torchlight procession through the city.[58]

By then, Charles had married. His bride was Mary Elizabeth Murphy, or Libbie, born four years after him, in 1848. Their first child, Charles Frederick Douglass, was born in Washington in June 1867, shortly after he obtained his clerkship. Five more children followed, with the last, Edward Douglass, born in 1877. But the children were often unwell, and only the second, Joseph Douglass, would outlive his father; Edward did not even survive two years. The tragic losses put a strain on the marriage, and when Lewis stayed with his brother's family in the summer of 1869, just before his own wedding, he grumbled to Amelia that because "of a disposition of Charley's wife to be exceedingly disagreeable," he had moved into a nearby boardinghouse. During one low point in the marriage, an "all fired up" Libbie hinted to her father-in-law that Charles had been unfaithful, an allegation that he denied on the grounds that Libbie was routinely jealous of female clerks he worked with. Charles and Libbie had the ability to produce children, but their growing family did not always lead to happiness.[59]

Because the Bureau remained under a steady barrage of criticism from Democrats on Capitol Hill, Charles fretted about his job security. But if the Bureau was discontinued, he hoped at least that he might continue on with its "Educational Department." Charles was wise to plan ahead: in 1872, when Congress abruptly cut off the Bureau's funding, he took over "the supervision of two school buildings now being erected in the county, and in connection with my clerical duties." When even that began to look insecure, Charles accepted a position as clerk to a commission investigating the acquisition of the newly independent Dominican Republic. In 1875, Grant elevated him to the rank of consul. But he hated life on the island and regarded the "Dominicans [as] a savage set." After only one year, he complained to his father that it "seems that under any circumstances I am to fail at my undertakings, and my life is to be one series of blunders." Even so, he remained in his post for another year.[60]

Libbie died in September 1878, the year after they returned to Washington, and two years later, census takers found the widower running a cigar store. Later that same year, he married again, this time to Laura Antoinette Haley, and one year after that she gave birth to Haley George Douglass, a healthy child who would live until 1954. Haley would go on to attend Harvard, but Charles took particular pride in Joseph, who even as a teenager earned a reputation as one of the "finest violinists in Washington" (much to the enjoyment of Joseph's grandfather, who also played the violin). By 1887, Charles was again employed as a clerk, this time at the pension office, where he processed forms for fellow veterans—including his mentally unstable brother-in-law, Nathan Sprague—and the following year he celebrated Joseph's marriage to Atlanta's Fannie Mae Howard. Reporting on the wedding, the black-owned Washington *Bee* praised Charles's son as perhaps the best classical musician in the city. Lewis had spent his final years in the real estate business, so it was surely no accident that his admiring younger brother followed the same path, founding the Highland Beach resort on the Chesapeake Bay, a summer community, one black journalist marveled, with "over 150 beautiful cottage sites for sale to reputable members of the race."[61]

Charles Douglass died on November 23, 1920, at the age of seventy-six. The numerous obituaries all remembered his military service, with the *Boston Herald* praising his involvement in two of the Bay State's historic regiments. One journalist mistakenly promoted him in death, calling him "Major Charles R. Douglass."[62] Perhaps the most fitting epitaph for Douglass, and indeed for all of the men he had served with, was provided by Paul Laurence Dunbar. The poet had once shared a stage with Joseph Douglass, and his father, Joshua Dunbar, had served beside Charles in both the Fifty-fifth and the Fifth Cavalry. In "The Colored Soldiers," Dunbar wrote:

In the early days you scorned them,
And with many a flip and flout
Said "These battles are the white man's,
And the whites will fight them out."
Up the hills you fought and faltered,
In the vales you strove and bled,
While your ears still heard the thunder
Of the foes' advancing tread. . . .
Ah, they rallied to the standard
To uphold it by their might;
None were stronger in the labors,
None were braver in the fight.
From the blazing breach of Wagner
To the plains of Olustee,
They were foremost in the fight
Of the battles of the free. . . .
They were comrades then and brothers,
Are they more or less to-day?
They were good to stop a bullet
And to front the fearful fray.
They were citizens and soldiers,
When rebellion raised its head;
And the traits that made them worthy,—
Ah! those virtues are not dead. . . .
And their deeds shall find a record
In the registry of Fame;
For their blood has cleansed completely
Every blot of Slavery's shame.
So all honor and all glory
To those noble sons of Ham—
The gallant colored soldiers
Who fought for Uncle Sam![63]

The Legacy of the Regiments

ALTHOUGH OVERJOYED TO RETURN HOME TO FAMILY AND FRIENDS in the fall of 1865, the veterans of the three Massachusetts units soon discovered that they missed their wartime mates: the cheerful comradery, the hard-earned esprit de corps, and the friendship and support of men who understood what they had endured. They also took justifiable pride in what they had accomplished, not only at Wagner and Olustee but in their principled stand against a discriminatory pay scale and a War Department that regarded them as manual laborers unfit for command. As a black editor later remarked, "The history of the Fifty-fourth Massachusetts is the grandest heritage the Afro-American possessed and one of the brightest portions of the history of the American soldier." Even as they returned to their old lives, or built new ones, those who had survived the war refused to lose touch with their comrades. And they demanded that the nation they had helped preserve remember their sacrifices.[1]

Of course, other veterans, both white and black, felt the same. What was remarkable was that many white veterans not only accepted but embraced their black comrades. Just one year after the war, veterans in Decatur, Illinois, founded the Grand Army of the Republic (GAR), a fraternal organization and advocacy group that quickly branched into hundreds of posts across the North. A handful of these remained as racially segregated as the army had been, but the GAR leadership—Republicans all—lobbied for black voting rights and back pay for former slaves who had been denied signing bonuses. Most white officers joined posts that commemorated the black regiments they had been mustered out of rather than those they had originally joined. Black veterans returned the favor. Black Pennsylvanians who had journeyed to Readville formed the Shaw Post, designed to "perpetuate his Memory and to cherish his bravery and loyalty to his country and flag." And especially in New England, even predominantly white GAR posts were proud to accept members from black regiments, particularly if they had been wounded in action. When William Carney tried to join New Bedford's largely white Rodman Post, the group's president declared: "We have Ft. Wagner's hero here, who round his body wound the flag he bore when wounded and 'it never touched the ground.'" Veterans from the Fifth Cavalry joined Hartford's Taylor Post, as did several soldiers from the Fifty-fourth.[2]

As the first black regiments to be raised in the free states, as well as the first to enjoy any visibility among the press and Northern politicians, the Massachusetts units justifiably believed that had they faltered in their first test, the tens of thousands of black recruits who followed would have been barred from service. By the war's end, 178,975 African Americans, constituting one-twelfth of all the soldiers who fought for the United States, had filled 145 infantry regiments, seven cavalry units, 13 artillery groups, and one engineering battalion. An astonishing 74 percent of Northern black men of military age enlisted to fight for a nation that denied them citizenship. Of the total number of enlistees, however, 140,313 were black Southerners recruited either in the loyal slave states or from the Confederacy. James Henry Gooding was among the 2,751 blacks killed in action; far more, 65,427, died of disease or went missing. "Only two short years have elapsed since stern, hard necessity, and the loyalty of the colored man, have led hundreds of thousands to strike hands with us, and bid us God-speed," remarked one soldier from the Fifty-fifth. "When I look back to the years '61 and '62, it makes me stronger in my belief that time brings all things right."[3]

Fort Wagner "was their Bunker Hill," Senator Charles Sumner remarked in December 1865. "Though defeated" in that July battle, "they were yet victorious," as "the cause was advanced." Northern whites who had scoffed at the notion that black men could make effective combatants "learned to know colored troops, and they learned to know themselves," and from that day on, "nobody doubted their capacity or courage as soldiers." Pen Hallowell also dedicated many of his later writings to the proposition that the courage of the Massachusetts regiments had not merely opened the doors to thousands more black recruits but turned the tide against the Confederacy. "When we remember that Grant lost 60,000 men in 60 days, a number equal to Lee's effective army at that time, it well becomes a question worthy [of] the serious attention of the historian" what might have happened had not black soldiers been permitted to enlist. Thomas Wentworth Higginson expressed similar thoughts when asked to comment on the view, so prevalent among Democratic officers, that "the chief obstacle" to black soldiers came from common soldiers. Rather than point a finger at Washington, as well he might have done, Higginson instead blamed "civilians at home." But after the summer of 1863, he believed, nothing was "more remarkable than the facility with which the expected aversion of the army everywhere vanished before the admirable behavior of the colored troops."[4]

Officers and decorated soldiers from elite units were in great demand as speakers after the war, and both white and black men associated with the Massachusetts regiments sought to remind the public of their valor. Henry Monroe, a New Bedford musician who had become a minister after returning to civilian life, delivered a series of lectures on "Camp Fires of the Fifty-Fourth Massachusetts." Reverend Monroe's talks featured a stereopticon—a slide show of projected photographs on glass—to illustrate "the charge on Wagner" and "the pathos of brave deeds and heroic deaths." Virginia congressman John Mercer Langston, once a recruiter for the Fifty-fourth, spoke about black soldiers at an 1891 Emancipation Day rally in Rochester, accompanied by the surviving musicians from the regiment's band. Former captain Luis Emilio announced that he planned to write a history of the Fifty-fourth and urged former comrades to forward him stories and photographs. Published in 1891 as *A Brave Black Regiment,* the memoir was expanded three years later as *A History of the Fifty-Fourth.* Advertisements quoted the late Governor Andrew, who had died shortly after leaving office in 1867: "To any given thousand men in arms there never has been committed a work so full of glory as was carried out by the Massachusetts Fifty-fourth."[5]

The black press wasted few opportunities to mention the regiments, no matter how tangential they were to the story at hand. When forty-eight-year-old George Haynes, a North Carolina–born carpenter, had the misfortune to lose "$58 of his pension money from his pocket," the editor of the *Cleveland Gazette* played to the sympathy of his readers by noting that Haynes had "lost both eyes and one arm in the war" to a "premature explosion" while serving in "the old Fifty-fourth." In 1869, Charles Lewis became one of the first two black men to win election to the Massachusetts assembly, and the faraway editor of the San Francisco *Elevator* crowed that his election was his just due as "a member of the Massachusetts Fifty-Fourth Regiment, who lost a leg in service." And in one of those curious human interest stories treasured by Victorian readers, two black Kansas newspapers reported that Jonathan Moore, a white veteran from Michigan, had bequeathed $5,000 to Daniel Prime. Moore had been wounded in the leg while fighting on the Carolina coast, and Prime, a sergeant with the Fifty-fourth, tore off his shirt, tied it into a tourniquet "to stop the flow of blood, and carried the lieutenant to the rear." Moore spent decades trying to learn "the name of the man who had saved his life" so that he might reward him in his will.[6]

Obituaries unfailingly noted which deceased veterans had served in one of the three regiments, especially as Jim Crow segregation set in during the 1890s. Joseph T. Wilson, a pioneering journalist and historian who in 1888 wrote *The Black Phalanx: A History of the Negro Soldiers of the United States,* was memorialized as a veteran of the Fifty-fourth and "in its best sense an agitator." Reverend Monroe died in 1891, still delivering lectures on the conflict, and editors praised his service "with that historic regiment until mustered out after the war." Frank Welch, a Connecticut barber who finished his term as a first lieutenant, was remembered in 1893 as one of just "thirty-nine [black] officers" to rise into commissioned ranks in the army. Three years hence saw the death of the Reverend J. R. B. Smith, who, like Emilio, had lied his way into the Fifty-fourth at age sixteen before being ordained in the AME Church and becoming "prominent in the G.A.R. and the Republican party." Charles Potter had endured Wagner only to be injured in the July 1865 riot in Charleston, and his 1916 obituary paid homage not only to his years in the Fifty-fourth but also to his participation in commemorative events staged by the regiment's survivors. When Pennsylvania postmaster S. Clay Miller died in 1915, a black editor in Wilkes-Barre took care to note his "brilliant Civil War record and [that he] was decorated for gallantry in the attack on Fort Wagner."[7]

LONG BEFORE WHITE AMERICANS ON EITHER SIDE OF THE MASON-Dixon Line began to memorialize battlefields and town squares with statues and markers, soldiers in the Fifty-fourth and their abolitionist allies began to discuss a fitting memorial for Rob Shaw. On September 15, 1863, just two months after Shaw's death, Charles Russell Lowell dined with John Andrew, who promised the young officer that he "meant to live long enough to see erected in Charleston a monument to honor Shaw." Lydia Maria Child's 1863 "Tribute to Colonel Shaw" inspired others to consider the creation of some sort of permanent memorial, as did sculptor Edmonia Lewis's bust of Shaw. When the bust was displayed in Boston's Mercantile Hall for the benefit of black veterans, it stood before "a three-quarters length portrait of the lamented Colonel Shaw, the hero-martyr of the assault on Fort Wagner." At about the same time, Charles Sumner contacted Frank and Sarah Shaw, suggesting a work of art to commemorate Rob and "the cause in which he fell & the companions by whom he was surrounded." The necessity of winning the war intervened, but in the fall of 1865, his memory on the matter jogged by the return of the Fifty-fourth and Fifty-fifth to Boston, Sumner returned to the idea. Placing an advertisement in the *Daily Advertiser,* he proposed this time that the monument be erected in Boston, near the steps that led up to the State House from Beacon Street, as "it was in the State House that the regiment was equipped," while from that street "the devoted commander rode to death." Sumner decided that "no common stone or shaft will be sufficient. It must be of bronze. It must be an equestrian statue." Although he mentioned the men of the Fifty-fourth as well in a December speech, he clearly envisioned a statue of Shaw only, "there riding always."[8]

While prosperous and influential Northern whites debated the proposition, Shaw's black comrades began to raise funds for a monument. Although they had not yet received their promised wages, the survivors of Wagner pooled their meager resources, amassing $2,832. The newly arriving recruits of the Fifty-fifth added another $1,000. Black refugees and freedpeople in Port Royal passed the collection plate one Sunday and raised $27. "Think of it!" one congregant marveled. "I have seen larger and far more wealthy congregations give less when pressed," yet "most of our congregation were women." In September 1863, a black Baptist church in Beaufort collected $60 more. "The colored people seem to take a great interest in this effort to honor Col. Shaw's memory," a black journalist with the *Beaufort Free South* reported, "and we learn that a large sum has already been promised by the different colored regiments." Higginson's First South Carolina Volunteers added $583.50 to the fund, and black Floridians shipped $144.95 up the coast to the account's treasurer. By the end of 1863, the committee had raised an impressive $4,647.45, all of it from unpaid soldiers or underpaid black laborers.[9]

The death of Governor Andrew in 1867 stalled the drive for a larger monument, although by that year the memorial's fund had grown to $7,000, about one-third of what the monument's backers guessed to be necessary. The Shaw family proposed an executive committee chaired by entrepreneur John Murray Forbes, who had also run the Black Committee that initially raised funds for the Fifty-fourth in 1863. But the project was again delayed as the family disagreed with the committee over the proposed design. The original proposal called for a freestanding equestrian statue, but to Sarah Shaw, Rob "had not been a great commander" on the order of a Grant or Sherman, "and only men of the highest rank should be so honored." The thought was extraordinary, coming from Rob's own mother, but then, even in 1863 she had wanted her son to lead black troops in the antislavery cause, not for his own personal glory. Consequently, Sarah also hoped that any memorial would pay equal tribute to the soldiers who fought beside him. "I want very much to have the names of all the men of the 54th killed at Fort Wagner & afterwards, put on the base at the back—it seems to me due the privates," she confided to one committee member. It would be wrong "that it is only men with rich relations and friends who can have monuments."[10]

The project stalled yet again in 1874 with Sumner's death. Thirteen years later, in August 1887, the three black regiments held a reunion in Boston's Tremont Temple. The veterans donned their carefully preserved uniforms and staged a parade in front of the State House, after which James Monroe Trotter delivered the main address. "His speech was a masterpiece of oratory," reported one black editor, and although Trotter evidently said nothing about a proposed monument, former governor John David Long, who then spoke at Andrew's grave, urged that it be completed. "There were flags and handkerchiefs out of every window in town," a journalist observed of the reunited veterans, as "everybody seemed to wish them welcome."[11]

A Boston GAR rally four years later kept up the drumbeat, with the editor of the black-run *New York Age* remarking that while "there are few of us who may not know who Robt. G. Shaw was and what interest he had to our race," the Fifty-fourth yet lacked proper memorialization. The final prod, ironically, came from the South. In 1895, residents of Fort Mill, South Carolina—roughly 100 miles from where Wagner once stood—erected a monument to the "faith and loyalty" of the Southern slave during the conflict. A journalist with the *Charleston News and Courier* praised the simple granite shaft placed within the town square as a "most significant and unique" war memorial. For the handful of runaway slaves, such as William Carney, who had served with the Fifty-fourth, an honest monument dedicated to black warriors to counter a Southern fantasy about content, passive bondmen took on a new urgency—particularly since fewer and fewer veterans remained alive to see it erected.[12]

The final design placed a mounted Shaw amid his men in a huge bronze relief. "I think the change from a statue to a bas-relief permits us to make it a memento for those who fell at Fort Wagner," Forbes acknowledged. The contract went to Augustus Saint-Gaudens, who was paid $22,000, a sum that drained the treasury of all but a few hundred dollars. The artist, curiously, chose not to use the visages of any real veterans, despite the fact that Carney, delivering mail just down the road in New Bedford, was a

New England celebrity and popular GAR speaker. The monument was completed in time for its proposed May 31, 1897, unveiling.[13]

The remaining members of the three regiments prepared to celebrate a memorial that they understood was as much for themselves as it was for their fallen commander. Many also probably guessed that it would be their final major reunion. "To the surviving officers of the Fifty-Fourth and Fifty-Fifth Mass. Infantry, and the Fifth Mass. Cavalry Regiments," read the elegantly printed circular mailed out by Stephen Swails and Pen Hallowell. Hallowell directed those who planned to attend to "wear uniforms, with sash, belt, and sword, but not side-arms." Aware that some veterans had fared better in life than others, he added that "all survivors, however, will be welcome, whether with or without uniforms." Frank Shaw had died in 1882, but Sarah Shaw and Rob's sisters—Anna, Susanna, Ellen, and Josephine Shaw Lowell, all of whom had seen their brother march away in 1863—planned to attend. The elderly Forbes was by this time too weak to appear, but the committee invited Booker T. Washington to serve as the day's principal speaker, with William James—brother of Garth Wilkinson James, who had died in 1883—as a secondary orator. "The monument is really superb, certainly one of the finest things of this century," William's brother Henry gushed. Black newspapers as far west as Wichita retold Shaw's story, glorying in the fact that the "memory of the first commander of an Afro-American regiment is about to be honored."[14]

The march by the unveiled monument began just after noon. Although the bas-relief commemorated only the men of the Fifty-fourth, the parade "of colored heroes and their white commanders," as the *Boston Herald* observed, included roughly 200 veterans representing all three regiments. The marchers snaked through the city streets, past the memorial, and concluded at Faneuil Hall, where the fifty-eight-year-old "Col. Hallowell and his staff reviewed them" as they marched into the building. Charles Francis Adams Jr. put aside his disdain for his men long enough to ride before the veterans of the Fifth Cavalry. William Carney was given the honor of bearing the flag, and behind him marched Lewis Douglass and Stephen Swails. Farther back yet walked George Garrison and the Reverend William Jackson. At Faneuil, Washington delivered an address that one editor described as "unremarkable," an overly charitable assess-

Surviving members of the three black regiments returned to Boston in 1897 for the unveiling of the Robert Gould Shaw Memorial. Lewis Douglass, Stephen Swails, and William Carney—carrying the tattered American flag—marched in the procession; Pen Hallowell reviewed the troops. The rear of the relief bears the words of Charles Eliot: "The Black rank and file volunteered when disaster clouded the Union Cause. Served without pay for eighteen months till given that of white troops. Faced threatened enslavement if captured. Were brave in action. Patient under heavy and dangerous labors. Cheerful amid hardships. Together they gave to the Nation and the World undying proof that Americans of African descent possess the pride, courage and devotion of the patriot soldier." *Courtesy Massachusetts Historical Society.*

ment given Washington's patronizing observation that the "full measure of the fruit of Fort Wagner and all that this monument stands for will not be realized until every man covered with black skin shall by patient and natural effort, grow to that height in industry, property, intelligence and moral responsibility" where no white American "could deny him his rights." But George T. Downing, an activist and in-law of the late Peter Vogelsang, saved the evening by denouncing "the bigotry and injustice which he said were shown toward colored people at the present time, notwithstanding their heroism and bravery during the war." As the evening's speeches drew to a close a grateful Sarah Shaw turned to Saint-Gaudens: "You have immortalized my native city, you have immortalized my dear son, you have immortalized yourself."[15]

IN THE DAYS SURROUNDING THE EVENT, BOSTON NEWSPAPERS AGAIN recounted the details of the assault on Wagner. But within one year, after Congress declared war with Spain over Cuba, it was as almost as if white Americans had to be reminded once more of black valor during the previous conflict. In a replay of 1863, only Massachusetts and Ohio urged black men to enlist, while New York State, fumed one black journalist, took the position that "its Afro-Americans have no place in the national guard, or in politics, or in almost anything else." In Mobile, Alabama, white soldiers "tried to lynch a Negro in their camp." As the editor of the black-owned *Cleveland Gazette* wondered, why must the nation be crippled by these old divisions when it should be fighting as a united country? "In our civil war 186,000 colored troops were enlisted," the editor wrote, "and the conduct of the Fifty-fourth Massachusetts at the assault upon Fort Wagner, July 18, 1863, proved that the Negro, well led, makes a heroic soldier."[16]

The need to remind the nation that black soldiers fought to end slavery—and indeed, that slavery had caused the bloody conflict in the first place—became more pressing still in 1913 as the fiftieth anniversary of both Gettysburg and Wagner arrived. Aged white veterans from both sides gathered at Gettysburg, symbolically shaking hands across the low stone wall that marked the furthest point of the Confederate advance on the battle's third day. Black soldiers, by comparison, had little interest in gestures that erased the abolitionist nature of the Massachusetts regiments or ignored Confederate atrocities. Banner headlines in black newspapers repeated that Shaw was "Buried with His Niggers," and blacks in Indianapolis named a public school in Shaw's honor, placing a large tablet above the main door "showing in relief the intrepid colonel leading America's dusky sons against the bonds of humankind." While only a small number of veterans of the three units remained alive in 1913, those who could do so again met that August in Faneuil Hall, where they heard former state attorney general Albert Pillsbury recount for the audience that during the war black soldiers had not waited for whites to grant them their rights but had seized the opportunity to assert their manhood and citizenship. "When you are fit to have your rights you will take them," Pillsbury shouted, "and until you take them you are not fit to have them."[17]

Within the year, the Great War was upon Europe, and even as Americans hoped to stay out of the conflict they once more debated the proper role of black men in the military. In 1863, some conservatives had argued that African Americans would not make for proficient combatants, while others worried, correctly, that black veterans would leverage their service into demands for political rights. By 1915, any white politician who questioned the former was sure to be reminded of Wagner, but few Democrats anywhere in the nation—and certainly not President Woodrow Wilson—cared to advance the cause of civil rights. The sons of deceased veterans, such as Salem Whitney, whose father had died during the siege at Wagner, gave interviews in which they expressed their willingness to serve. One speaker at Savannah's "Emancipation Celebration" noted that when Abraham Lincoln had finally turned to "the young men of our race," black soldiers had "flocked to the Fifty-fourth," even from those states that refused them the vote. Boston activists, including William Monroe Trotter, attempted to ban showings of D. W. Griffith's *The Birth of a Nation* by pointing out the problem of showing a film that demeaned black soldiers in the city that had erected a memorial to "a white officer who lost his life while leading a Negro regiment."[18]

After a German U-boat sank the RMS *Lusitania* off the southern coast of Ireland in May 1915, Americans assumed that a congressional declaration of war would be imminent. The War Department worked to discourage black enlistments, and one governor announced it folly to train black men at Southern camps. Black editors responded by wondering how the army could reach its stated quota if "the sign is up, 'No colored man wanted.'" When the "Fifty-fourth Massachusetts stormed Fort Wagner in '63 it established for all time the fact that the colored soldier could fight and fight well," the Washington *Bee* and the *Trenton Evening Times* editorialized. A black regiment "planted its blood-stained banner on the ramparts of Fort Wagner," observed another editor.[19]

After Congress declared war in April 1917, there were roughly 10,000 black regulars in the army, including two cavalry regiments and two infantry units, all of them led by white officers. The newly created Selective Service system drafted more than 370,000 African Americans. But when it became clear that the Wilson administration intended to employ them only in labor battalions or as cooks and stevedores, black activists returned to the legacy of the Fifty-fourth. In view of the policy that "white soldiers and negroes in the National Army cannot mingle" with one another, Cyrus

Adams, the editor of the St. Paul *Western Appeal*, reminded his readers that "the gallant Colonel Rob Shaw" was buried beside his men. Black soldiers were good for more than working with picks and shovels, Benjamin Turner insisted in a New Jersey newspaper, adding: "I will only need to remind you of his actions around such places at Fort Wagner." As in the past, most of the editorials that alluded to Wagner were printed in the Northern press, but a handful of courageous black editors in Georgia and Mississippi bluntly noted that during a time when white Southerners fought against the United States, "black soldiers fought and died for the Union at Fort Wagner." The Omaha *World Herald* published an essay on "Traditions of Our Negro Soldiers," recounting the history from "Peter Salem at Bunker Hill [to] Carney at Fort Wagner," while the *Cleveland Plain Dealer* claimed that the assault on Wagner "set the standard for the new negro division—or divisions." Chicago's *Broad Ax* guessed that half a million black men would serve "before this world's war is over [and] will outshine his glory at Fort Wagner." Hoping to drive home the point about black courage, the GAR post in New Bedford changed its name to the Sergt. William H. Carney Camp. In the end, roughly 380,000 black men served in the war, a higher number than during the Civil War, although only 42,000 saw combat.[20]

As always, white conservatives feared that black veterans would expect political rights in exchange for their sacrifice, as had men like Swails and Vogelsang in earlier years, and they responded to the modest gains registered by black activists during the war years with race riots in Omaha, Chicago, and Tulsa. At the same time, Southern whites increasingly lost interest in festivities honoring national reconciliation, such as the anniversary celebration in Gettysburg in 1913, and instead began to emphasize their Civil War–era victories over those black soldiers who had stood with the United States. In August 1917, white Floridians celebrated the "Battle of Ocean Pond," as they called the battle at Olustee Junction. During the previous month, whites from Georgia and South Carolina converged on Morris Island to commemorate the "Repulse of the Federal troops in their assault on Fort Wagner."[21]

Black journalists and their progressive white allies were quick to respond. On the 115th anniversary of Frederick Douglass's birth, William Monroe Trotter, together with a Shaw descendant and the National Equal Rights League, called for a "nation-wide observance" dedicated to the "spirit of Douglass' efforts for his race and rights." Designed to advance

Black Americans never forgot the heroism of the Fifty-fourth. In this photograph, "Black Family by Fireplace," from his 1920 series "Southern Negroes," photographer Lewis Hine captured the image of a well-dressed, middle-class Georgia couple reading to their daughters. Above the mantelpiece is a Curtis and Cameron print of the Robert Gould Shaw Memorial. *Courtesy National Gallery of Art.*

specific reform measures, the group suggested that three days be set aside to mark the history of the struggle, with one of them being "Fort Wagner [Day] July 18." Each July, black-owned newspapers retold the story of how the Fifty-fourth "stood like heroes in the midst of carnage and evoked from their superiors the heartiest thanks for their courage." In 1925, the year when as many as 60,000 members of the Ku Klux Klan marched from the White House to the Capitol, veterans in Norfolk erected a large granite column topped by a statue of the young William Carney, Virginia's most decorated black soldier. Placed in the black section of the segregated West Point Cemetery, the monument's base contained a number of marble plates bearing the names of black Virginians who had perished on behalf of their country.[22]

After the bombing of Pearl Harbor, black Americans once more prepared to fight for a country that refused them equal rights or decent housing and that, in some parts of the nation, restricted their right to register and vote. Correctly worried that once again Washington intended black men for little more than service regiments, black editors as far west as Los Angeles reminded readers of the now-thirty-one black Congressional Medal of Honor recipients, starting with "Sgt. William H. Carney." At this point, no veterans of the regiments remained alive. The last two survivors were Eli Biddle and Ira Waterman. Biddle had been a seventeen-year-old painter when he signed on in Boston. Wounded at Wagner, he became a Methodist preacher after the war and died in Boston in 1940 at ninety-four. Waterman was a nineteen-year-old Sheffield farmer when he enlisted in the fall after Wagner. He died at the age of ninety-seven on July 31, five months before America's entrance into World War II.[23]

With more than 125,000 African Americans serving overseas in that war, the old question—which white Americans seemingly wished to revisit with every conflict—of whether blacks would make effective combatants appeared at last resolved. But they had fought in segregated units, as they had in every campaign since the spring of 1863. The promotions of Swails and Vogelsang into the ranks of commissioned officers, as controversial as that had been, had not signaled an end to racial barriers in the U.S. Army, since nobody in the War Department ever expected them to lead white troops—with one exception. General William Birney, the son of slaveholder-turned-abolitionist James G. Birney, had published a lengthy editorial in the *Liberator* in early 1865 insisting that the "best way to put an end to [racism] is to unite men of different colors in the same grand emotions of patriotism." Having seen action at Chancellorsville, Birney had transferred to the Twenty-second USCT in South Carolina. To employ black officers only in black regiments, Birney concluded, would merely "deepen and strengthen the guilty prejudice now existing." The white officers who had served with him in the Twenty-second, he observed, had learned to put aside "their former bitter prejudice." At the very least, Birney hoped, if the army had to remain segregated, "let there be a black regiment in each brigade," so that soldiers might learn to fight alongside those of a different race. Although Birney was admittedly a man of solid antislavery credentials, his editorial was an indication of how rapidly Northern opinion had shifted on black soldiers. But two months later the war ended, and with it any possible move toward military desegregation.[24]

If none of the soldiers of the three pioneering black regiments lived long enough to see an integrated military, that did not stop activists from invoking their memory. In 1943 the previously all-white Marine Corps began accepting black recruits, and during that same year the War Department mandated that black officers be trained in integrated facilities. The black press continued to push for more. "Between the years 1863 and 1926," observed the black-owned *Los Angeles Tribune,* "soldiers serving in all-Negro outfits were awarded 31 Congressional Medals of Honor," dating back to the "54th Massachusetts Colored Infantry" and their "gallantry at Fort Wagner." At the war's end, labor leader A. Philip Randolph urged President Harry Truman to issue an executive order desegregating the U.S. armed forces, as a draft bill for military integration had stalled in Congress. Eighty-three years after Birney's editorial, Truman at last decided the time had arrived. In Executive Order 9981, he observed that it was "essential that there be maintained in the armed services of the United States the highest standards of democracy, with equality of treatment and opportunity for all those who serve in our country's defense." The black soldiers who had refused racially based pay and demanded the right to rise in the officer corps could not have said it better.[25]

A CENTURY AND A HALF AFTER THE THREE REGIMENTS WERE MUS-tered out, the meaning of the war remains disputed, at least among the general public. So too does the legacy of the black units. In 2014, during the bicentennial of the February 1864 Battle of Olustee, the Florida chapter of the Sons of Union Veterans requested that the National Park Service (NPS) permit a monument to soldiers from the Fifty-fourth to stand beside the 1912 obelisk erected by the Daughters of the Confederacy. NPS officials agreed and began to conduct hearings. The idea was condemned by the Sons of the Confederacy, and especially by Republican state assemblyman Dennis Baxley, who fretted that a marker honoring those black soldiers who fought in Florida to preserve the United States constituted "revisionist history." Michael Givens, the commander-in-chief of the Sons of Confederate Veterans, added that a second marker "will disrupt the hallowed grown [*sic*] where Southern blood was spilled in defense of Florida," a statement that ignored the complicated truth that North Carolina native James Henry Gooding, who was shot at Olustee, also shed "Southern blood" on that landscape. The issue remains unresolved.[26]

Just over a year later, on June 17, 2015, a white vigilante opened fire in Charleston's historic Emanuel AME Church, killing nine congregants who had gathered for bible study and prayer. The killer had photographed himself holding a Confederate flag, and the murders set off another round of debates about the banner's meaning. As Confederate flags began to come down across the South, Bostonians awoke on Monday, June 29, to find a Confederate battle flag hanging from the tip of Rob Shaw's sword on the Saint-Gaudens memorial. Passersby attempted to pull down the flag but only managed to shred it; a visitor from Lowell succeeded in untying it just before police arrived. "Such an expression of hate is not acceptable," one Bostonian complained. "Obviously it's pretty upsetting to see," observed another. "When somebody puts something in a spot like that, obviously they are trying to send a message, and it's an upsetting message."[27]

Silent and resolute, the bronze soldiers and the young colonel on horseback take no notice. They have seen worse, from the racism of the antebellum home front through the hard fighting of the war and into the dark days of Reconstruction-era Klan vigilantism. They stare straight ahead and continue their long march into history.

Acknowledgments

Writing a book is often a tough grind, but some aspects of the process never get old, and my favorite part of wrapping one up is getting to express my gratitude to friends and colleagues who helped along the way. I am absurdly lucky to count so many kind, supportive, and wonderful people as my pals.

Andrew Cohen read Chapter 1 and helped me sort out Peter Vogelsang's confusing marriages and genealogy; his *Contraband,* as good fortune would have it, came out at just the right moment. Other exceptional scholars—Patrick Rael, Leslie Gordon, and Matt Mason—read some of the early sections and saved me from several errors, as did Thomas J. Brown, whose knowledge of the Fifty-fourth is encyclopedic. Tom's co-edited volume *Hope and Glory* appears often enough in my notes to indicate what an immense help it was in crafting this book. Two more longtime pals, John Quist and John Belohlavek, put aside their own projects long enough to comment on portions of the manuscript; the tradition of Friday martinis with John B. at SHEAR conferences is now nearly three decades old and remains for me a highlight of the meeting.

Three very clever friends read Chapter 6 and provided me with detailed comments and suggestions. If in the end I did not accept Gary Kornblith's suggestion that I rename that section "Hospital Sketches" in a nod to Louisa May Alcott, I did incorporate all of his other shrewd recommendations. (It is always wise, of course, to listen to a man who wears a Frederick Douglass tie, as Gary does on occasion.) Carol Faulkner also gave the chapter a good, close reading and brought several books to my attention that had escaped notice, as did Stacey Robertson, who bluntly told me what parts of the chapter didn't work. Only a dear pal will do that.

During the spring semester of 2015, I was invited to be the Merrill Family Visiting Professor at Cornell University, which gave me the opportunity to try out portions of this material on a group of marvelous students and the time to write it up into some of these chapters. I am deeply grateful to Ed Baptist, Barry Strauss, and especially the wonderful Amy Kohout for making those months a terrific experience.

Two dear friends of many years, Alan Gallay and Don Wright, read every page of the manuscript, as they have for other projects in earlier years. Come to that, Alan has been reading my pages now for thirty-six years, since our long-ago days in graduate school, and it's hard to imagine finishing a book without their insightful comments, tough criticism, and Don's hilarious doodles in the margins. But both know, I hope, that that's not why I so value their friendship. Their only flaws are that they both now live so far away. My pal Graham Hodges, at least, remains nearby at Colgate University, and Clarence Taylor and Carol Berkin—to whom I owe so much—are not too terribly far off in Manhattan.

At Basic Books, Dan Gerstle has been an absolutely superb and attentive editor, and this is a much better volume for his multiple readings and thoughtful editorial pen. Cindy Buck and Sandra Beris helped to transform the manuscript into a book. Thanks especially to my extraordinary agent, Dan Green, who supported this project from the first and who reads every page I send him and responds with wise and discerning comments. I am also grateful to Peter Ginna for his advice and support. And as luck would have it, I have generous cousins—Martha Ware and Steve Cole, and Frank Schroth and Annie Davis—who opened up their homes (and wine cellars) to me in Washington and Boston long enough for me to conduct much of the research in this book. Plus, they are just lovely people to talk books and music and politics with. Jeanann Wieners helped me with some of the images without laughing at my Luddite sensibilities (well, actually she did). At Le Moyne College, I am again indebted to research librarian Wayne Stevens, who can track down the most obscure monograph or document, and to the college's Committee on Research and Development for its generous funding for the images and maps reproduced here.

Thunder at the Gates would not be the book it is without Leigh Fought's advice, support, and editorial suggestions, and not merely because she is one of the nation's leading experts on Frederick Douglass and his family. She tells me when pages work, makes perceptive recommendations on how to fix paragraphs that need help, and was genuinely heartbroken by the murder of James Henry Gooding at the hands of Andersonville guards. Most of all, Leigh listened patiently to my endless stories about the men and women who fill these pages and just generally puts up with me, which is no small feat, and so to her I dedicate this book. Final thanks, of course, go to my brilliant, gorgeous, and industrious daughters, Kearney and Hannah, who are perfect in every way. To quote the great philosopher Pete Townshend, they make me laugh and sing, now that I'm old and gray.

Notes

ABBREVIATIONS USED IN THE NOTES

CFA	Charles Francis Adams Jr.
CWH	*Civil War History*
ENH	Edward Needles "Ned" Hallowell
GTG	George T. Garrison
JAA	John A. Andrew
JHG	James Henry Gooding
LC	Library of Congress
LHD	Lewis Henry Douglass
MHS	Massachusetts Historical Society
NA	National Archives, Washington
NBPL	New Bedford Public Library
NPH	Norwood Penrose "Pen" Hallowell
NYHS	New-York Historical Society
NYPL	New York Public Library
OR	*The War of the Rebellion: A Compilation of the Official Records of the Union and Confederate Armies*
RGS	Robert Gould Shaw
WAA	New York *Weekly Anglo-African*

PROLOGUE

1. Charles B. Fox, *Record of the Service of the Fifty-Fifth Regiment of Massachusetts Volunteer Infantry* (Cambridge, MA, 1868), 68–72.

2. *Liberator,* March 31, 1865; Harriet Alonso, *Growing Up Abolitionist: The Story of the Garrison Children* (Amherst: University of Massachusetts Press, 2002), 176.

3. Douglas R. Egerton, *Death or Liberty: African Americans and Revolutionary America* (New York: Oxford University Press, 2009), 94–95.

4. *New York Journal of Commerce,* August 24, 1864; Cleveland *Plain Dealer,* March 6, 1863.

5. *Congressional Globe,* 37th Cong., 3rd Sess., 74.

6. Louis P. Masur, *Lincoln's Hundred Days: The Emancipation Proclamation and the War for the Union* (Cambridge, MA: Harvard University Press, 2012), 223; *New York Journal of Commerce,* August 24, 1864; Earl Mulderink, *New Bedford's Civil War* (New York: Fordham University Press, 2012), 103; Bruce Levine, *The Fall of the House of Dixie: The Civil War and the Social Revolution That Transformed the South* (New York: Random House, 2013), 161.

7. *Congressional Globe,* 37th Cong., 3rd Sess., 85; Henry Pearson, *The Life of John A. Andrew* (Boston, 1904), 2:79.

8. Chandra Manning, *What This Cruel War Was Over: Soldiers, Slavery, and the Civil War* (New York: Knopf, 2007), 90, 95; *Congressional Globe,* 37th Cong., 2nd Sess., 242–243.

9. *Chicago Times,* in Augusta *Daily Constitutionalist,* April 4, 1863; Richard Abbott, "Massachusetts and the Recruitment of Southern Negroes, 1863–1865," *CWH* 16 (1968): 206; *Detroit Free Press,* in New Haven *Columbian Register,* February 21, 1863.

10. JHG to *New Bedford Mercury,* April 18, 1863, in *On the Altar of Freedom: A Black Soldier's Civil War Letters from the Front,* ed. Virginia Adams (Amherst: University of Massachusetts Press, 1991), 13.

CHAPTER ONE

1. Charles B. Fox to Feroline Fox, August 7, 1863, Fox Papers, MHS; GTG to Helen Garrison, August 3, 1863, Garrison Family Papers, Smith College; Declaration for Invalid Pension, April 17, 1882, Henry Jarvis File, Pension Office, NA; John Smith, Regimental Descriptive Book, 1863, 55th Massachusetts Infantry, NA.

2. JHG to *New Bedford Mercury,* August 9, 1863, in Adams, *On the Altar of Freedom,* 47.

3. Nicholas Said, Register of Signatures of Depositors in Branches of the Freedman's Savings and Trust Company, May 23, 1871, Tallahassee, Florida, NA; "A Native of Bornoo," *Atlantic Monthly* (October 1867): 487; Nicholas Said, *The*

Autobiography of Nicholas Said, A Native of Bournou, Eastern Soudan, Central Africa (Memphis, 1873), 9, 35–37.

4. J. F. Ade Ajayi and Michael Crowder, *A History of West Africa* (New York: Columbia University Press, 1970), 217; Louis Brenner, *The Shehus of Kukawa: A History of the al-Kanemi Dynasty of Bornu* (Oxford: Clarendon Press, 1973), 12–13, 60–61; Richmond Palmer, *The Bornu Sahara and Sudan* (London, 1936), 270; John Wright, *Libya, Chad, and the Central Sahara* (Lanham, MD: Rowman & Littlefield, 1989), 97; Said, *Autobiography,* 39–43; in "Native of Bornoo" (488), either Said or the interviewer spelled the town name as "Kashna." It may today be Katsina, Nigeria.

5. Said, *Autobiography,* 44–57; "Native of Bornoo," 488–490.

6. "Native of Bornoo," 490–491; Said, *Autobiography,* 65–73, 111–112, 121–122; Caroline Finkel, *Osman's Dream: The History of the Ottoman Empire* (New York: Basic Books, 2006), 441, 452–453; Said, *Autobiography,* 122–123.

7. "Native of Bornoo," 485, 491–492; Edward Crankshaw, *The Shadow of the Winter Palace: Russia's Drift to Revolution* (New York: Da Capo Press, 1976), 131–132; Said, *Autobiography,* 124. Said's military papers list his height as five feet, seven inches, and note his "dark" complexion and hair color. See Nicholas Said, Regimental Descriptive Book, 1863, 55th Massachusetts Infantry, NA. His colonel during the war, Norwood Penrose Hallowell, described Said's tattoos in his book *The Negro as a Soldier in the War of the Rebellion* (Boston, 1897), 3.

8. "Native of Bornoo," 491–492; Said, *Autobiography,* 125–146; Pennsylvania *Washington Reporter,* December 30, 1863; NPH (*The Negro as a Soldier,* 3) reported that "his linguistic ability was very marked."

9. "Native of Bornoo," 492–494.

10. Said, *Autobiography,* 185–186. Said misidentified the owner of the hotel as "Marshall Hughes, a model Christian." On proprietor Robert Marsh Hughes, see *The Whole Proceedings on the Queen's Commission of Oyer and Terminer and Gaol Delivery* (London, 1861), 748.

11. "Native of Bornoo," 494; Said, *Autobiography,* 186–189; Copies of Lists of Passengers Arriving at Ports on the Atlantic and Gulf Coasts, 1820–1873, Series M575, Record Group 85, NA. Although Said's travels sound almost too fantastic to be true, where it is possible to check the stories he presented prove to be accurate. The ship's passenger list included not only Said but Isaac Jacob Rochussen, age twenty-seven, and his wife Catherine.

12. *New Albany Daily Ledger,* January 6, 1860; New York *Commercial Advertiser,* January 5, 1860; Washington *Constitution,* January 6, 1860; Said, *Autobiography,* 189; *WAA,* February 25, 1860.

13. New York *Commercial Advertiser,* January 9, 1860, May 16, 1860; Said, *Autobiography,* 189–197; *Providence Evening Press,* January 7, 1860; "Native of Bornoo," 494; Said, *Autobiography,* 197–200.

14. "Native of Bornoo," 495; Said, *Autobiography*, 200–202. The Washington *National Intelligencer* (December 11, 1852) noted that "the brig Concord" sailed between Buffalo and Detroit; the *Trenton State Gazette* (April 24, 1860) placed a "Rev. George Duffield" at a Constitutional Union Party rally; the New York *Herald* (January 15, 1853) listed the "Steamer Egitto" as sailing from Constantinople to Trieste; and in Nicholas Said, Regimental Descriptive Book (1863, 55th Massachusetts Infantry, NA), it is confirmed that at the time of his enlistment Said was living in Detroit. On voting restrictions in Michigan, see Dana Weiner, *Race and Rights: Fighting Slavery and Prejudice in the Old Northwest, 1830–1870* (DeKalb: Northern Illinois University Press, 2013), 45–46.

15. Petition of Cynthia Ann Downing Smith, April 15, 1882, and General Affidavit of Ester A. Perkins, May 14, 1892, both in John M. Smith File, Pension Office, NA; John Smith, 1850 Federal Census, Brunswick, Cumberland, Maine, Roll M432–251, Page 236B, Image 172, NA; Cynthia Ann Smith, 1850 Federal Census, Roll M432–251, Page 209B, Image 118, NA; John Smith, Consolidated List of Civil War Draft Registration Records, Record Group 110, NA; John Smith, Regimental Descriptive Book, 1863, 55th Massachusetts Infantry, NA. John M. Smith's father never appeared in state or federal census records.

16. *New York Gazette*, April 1, 1811; *Frederick Douglass' Paper*, February 16, 1855; New York *Herald*, May 12, 1854; Peter Vogelsang, Regimental Descriptive Book, 1864, 54th Massachusetts Infantry, NA; Peter Vogelsang, 1840 Federal Census, New York City, Roll 306, Page 229, NA; Peter Vogelsang, U.S. Civil War Draft Registration Records, Record Group 110, NA; Carla Peterson, *Black Gotham: A Family History of African Americans in Nineteenth-Century New York City* (New Haven, CT: Yale University Press, 2011), 166–168; Julie Winch, *A Gentleman of Color: The Life of James Forten* (New York: Oxford University Press, 2002), 277.

17. Peter Swails, 1860 Federal Census, Elmira, New York, Roll M653–730, Page 457, Image 79, NA; Stephen A. Swails, 1860 Federal Census, Cooperstown, New York, Roll M653–841, Page 665, NA. On Keyes's hotel, see *Albany Evening Journal*, July 11, 1862.

18. In Daniel M. Morse, 1860 Federal Census, Cooperstown, New York (Roll M653–841, Page 657, Image 654, NA), Morse is identified as a "merchant" and Sarah Thompson is listed as a "servant" and "mulatto," the same descriptions used for Kate Swails, Stephen's sister; Joseph Husbands, 1850 Federal Census, Otsego County, New York, Roll M432–579, Page 272B, Image 552, NA; Joseph Husbands, 1855 New York State Census, New York State Archives, Albany; *Daily Albany Argus*, September 28, 1868. The *Charleston Courier* (December 8, 1867) identified Swails as "white," and the San Francisco *Bulletin* (February 24, 1870) called him "a light quadroon."

19. *Elmira City Directory*, Elmira, 1863, 144. Although the allegations published in the *Daily Albany Argus* on September 28, 1868, were both partisan and racist, the charge that he impregnated and "abandoned" a "colored girl . . . by the name of Thompson, by whom he had a child," was essentially sustained by the New York *Weekly Anglo-African*, which reported on May 7, 1864, that "Mrs. Lieut. Swails" of "Cooperstown" was living in "her mother's house in Elmira" during the war. Stephen Swails Jr., age thirty (and so born in 1862), appeared in the 1892 New York State Census as living in Buffalo and working as a "Hosteler." In Minnie Swails, 1880 Federal Census, Elmira, New York (Roll 817, Page 446A, Image 471), Minnie, age seventeen, is listed as living in Elmira with her mother, here named Sarah Jackson, a forty-two-year-old black "laundress," and her brother Stephen A. Swails Jr. On December 1, 1900, Mary McKinley testified that Sergeant Stephen Swails had never been married before his 1866 marriage to Susan Swails, but as a lifetime resident of Charleston, McKinley was hardly in a position to know about Swails's New York years. See her deposition in Stephen Swails File, Pension Office, NA.

20. Stephen Fox, *The Guardian of Boston: William Monroe Trotter* (Boston: Atheneum, 1970), 3–4; James Monroe Trotter, Regimental Descriptive Book, 1863, 55th Massachusetts Infantry, NA; *Cleveland Gazette*, March 5, 1892; Robert Thomas, 1860 Federal Census, Athens, Ohio, Roll M653–934, Page 237, Image 478, NA. On Reverend Gilmore's school, see Washington *National Era*, April 27, 1848.

21. James M. Gooding, 1850 Federal Census, New Bern, North Carolina, Roll M432–626, Page 299B, NA; James Henry Gooding, Admissions, 1837–1866, Association for the Benefit of Colored Orphans, NYHS, 78; An Index to Marriage Bonds Filed in the North Carolina State Archives, Raleigh, 1977, no page; Marriage Certificate, September 28, 1862, in JHG File, Pension Office, NA.

22. William Seraile, *Angels of Mercy: White Women and the History of New York's Colored Orphan Asylum* (New York: Fordham University Press, 2011), 32–33.

23. *Newark Daily Advertiser*, January 13, 1846; Winch, *A Gentleman of Color*, 277; Boston *Emancipator and Republican*, September 15, 1847.

24. James Henry Gooding, Admissions, 1837–1866, Association for the Benefit of Colored Orphans, NYHS, 78; Albert Westlake, 1850 Federal Census, Woodbridge, New Jersey, Roll M432–455, Page 52B, NA; *New Bedford Directory*, 10th ed. (New Bedford, 1865), 70.

25. Kathryn Grover, *The Fugitive's Gibraltar: Escaping Slaves and Abolitionism in New Bedford, Massachusetts* (Amherst: University of Massachusetts Press, 2001), 265–272; Eric Dolin, *Leviathan: The History of Whaling in America* (New York: Norton, 2007), 213–215.

26. W. Jeffrey Bolster, *Black Jacks: African American Seamen in the Age of Sail* (Cambridge, MA: Harvard University Press, 1997), 5, 178; Dolin, *Leviathan,* 224; JHG, Seamen's Protection Papers, July 18, 1856, NBPL.

27. Bark *Sunbeam,* Crew List, NBPL; New Bedford *Whaleman's Shipping List and Merchants' Transcript,* July 22, 1856; Dolin, *Leviathan,* 223; Herman Melville, *Moby Dick, or, The Whale* (Norwalk, CT: Easton Press, 1977), 34.

28. Bolster, *Black Jacks,* 177; New Bedford *Whaleman's Shipping List and Merchants' Transcript,* June 17, 1856, June 24, 1856.

29. Bark *Sunbeam,* Log, June 17, 1859, August 7, 1856, August 5, 1856, August 10, 1856, August 27, 1859, NBPL; Bark *Sunbeam,* Accounts, NBPL; Adams, *On the Altar of Freedom,* 128.

30. Bark *Sunbeam,* Log, June 18, 1857, October 18, 1856, August 7, 1858, NBPL; New Bedford *Whaleman's Shipping List and Merchants' Transcript,* November 11, 1856, December 2, 1856, July 28, 1857, January 5, 1858, July 13, 1858, November 1, 1859, November 29, 1859, February 14, 1860, February 21, 1860, May 8, 1860; Boston *Daily Evening Traveler,* March 8, 1860; *Boston Courier,* March 16, 1860; Bark *Sunbeam,* Crew List, NBPL.

31. *Boston Courier,* December 22, 1859; New Bedford *Whaleman's Shipping List and Merchants' Transcript,* December 27, 1859, June 12, 1860, December 4, 1860; New York *Commercial Advertiser,* May 24, 1860; New York *Herald,* October 19, 1860; *New London* (Connecticut) *Daily Chronicle,* December 1, 1860; *Black Eagle,* Log, December 10, 1860, December 14, 1860, January 4, 1861, February 12, 1861, March 20, 1861, New Bedford Whaling Museum; *Black Eagle,* Log, April 29, 1861, November 3, 1861. Historian W. Jeffrey Bolster (communication to author, September 16, 2014) notes that not only was "it possible that a man of color commanded a whaleship in 1861" but "twenty years or so later, it would have been unremarkable."

32. Ellen Allen Gooding, Death Record, April 24, 1903, Massachusetts Vital Records, 1840–1911, New England Genealogical Society, Boston; Charlotte Pierce Adams, Death Record, August 18, 1867, ibid.; JHG, Massachusetts Marriage Records, 1840–1911, ibid.; *Rhode Island Vital Extracts, 1836–1850* (Providence, 1912), 241; Charles Edward Allen, 1850 Federal Census, Roll M432–309, Page 222A, Image 26, NA; New Bedford *Whaleman's Shipping List and Merchants' Transcript,* June 2, 1857, October 29, 1861; *New Bedford Directory,* 10th ed. (New Bedford, 1865), 26; Crew List, *Richard Mitchell,* February 1862, NBPL; Boston *Daily Evening Traveler,* February 3, 1862, May 7, 1862, June 23, 1862; *Salem Register,* July 17, 1862; *Boston Daily Advertiser,* August 16, 1862, September 16, 1862.

33. Case of Ellen Gooding, April 22, 1864, in JHG File, Pension Office, NA; Marriage Certificate, September 28, 1862, ibid. On Reverend James D. Butler, see *The Sailor's Magazine for the Year Ending 1859* (New York, 1859), 114.

34. William Carney, Registry of Death, March 24, 1909, New Bedford, William Carney File, Pension Office, NA; *Boston Evening Transcript,* October 30, 1863; *Liberator,* November 6, 1863; William Still, *The Underground Railroad* (Philadelphia, 1872), 315–316.

35. Grover, *Fugitive's Gibraltar,* 253–254; 329, note 120; *Liberator,* November 6, 1863; Philadelphia *Press,* November 4, 1863; Edwin B. Jourdain, Affidavit, August 11, 1909, William Carney File, Pension Office, NA.

36. *Albany Evening Journal,* August 23, 1862; Dudley Cornish, *The Sable Arm: Black Troops in the Union Army, 1861–1865* (Lawrence: University Press of Kansas, 1987 [1956]), 6; James Horton, "Defending the Manhood of the Race: The Crisis of Citizenship in Black Boston at Midcentury," in *Hope and Glory: Essays on the Legacy of the 54th Massachusetts Regiment,* ed. Martin Blatt, Thomas J. Brown, and Donald Yacovone (Amherst: University of Massachusetts Press, 2001), 18–19; *Newark Daily Advertiser,* September 11, 1861.

CHAPTER TWO

1. New York *Herald,* July 28, 1871.

2. ENH to NPH, March 31, 1858, Hallowell Family Papers, Haverford College.

3. William Penrose Hallowell, *Record of a Branch of the Hallowell Family, Including the Longstreet, Penrose, and Norwood Branches* (Philadelphia, 1893), 64; Richard Miller, *Harvard's Civil War: The History of the Twentieth Massachusetts Volunteer Infantry* (Lebanon, NH: University Press of New England, 2005), 14; NPH, *Selected Letters and Papers of N. P. Hallowell* (Peterborough, 1896), 84–85.

4. Hallowell, *Hallowell Family,* 64; NPH, *The Negro as a Soldier,* 3; Carol Faulkner, *Lucretia Mott's Heresy: Abolition and Women's Rights in Nineteenth-Century America* (Philadelphia: University of Pennsylvania Press, 2011), 175; *Boston Herald,* April 12, 1914; Miller, *Harvard's Civil War,* 14; Russell Duncan, *Where Death and Glory Meet: Colonel Robert Gould Shaw and the 54th Massachusetts Infantry* (Athens: University of Georgia Press, 1999), 53.

5. James Brewer Stewart, *Wendell Phillips: Liberty's Hero* (Baton Rouge: Louisiana State University Press, 1986), 214; Miller, *Harvard's Civil War,* 13; NPH, *Selected Letters,* 67.

6. Joan Waugh, *Unsentimental Reformer: The Life of Josephine Shaw Lowell* (Cambridge, MA: Harvard University Press, 1998), 23–26; Duncan, *Death and Glory,* 4; Peter Burchard, *One Gallant Rush: Robert Gould Shaw and His Brave Black Regiment* (New York: St. Martin's Press, 1965), 4–5.

7. Joan Waugh, "The Shaw Family and the Fifty-Fourth Massachusetts Regiment," in *Hope and Glory,* ed. Blatt et al., 56–57; Lorien Foote, *Seeking the One Great Remedy: Francis George Shaw and Nineteenth-Century Reform* (Athens: University Press of Georgia, 2000), 40; Burchard, *One Gallant Rush,* 4–5.

8. Burchard, *One Gallant Rush,* 6–7, 10–11; Duncan, *Death and Glory,* 10–11, 14, 18–19; Waugh, "Shaw Family," 61–63; *New York Age,* June 6, 1891.

9. Burchard, *One Gallant Rush,* 24–25; *Liberator,* November 9, 1860; On John Shaw's hotel in Nassau, see New York *Herald,* January 28, 1860.

10. RGS to Susanna Shaw, April 5, 1861, in *Blue-Eyed Child of Fortune: The Civil War Letters of Colonel Robert Gould Shaw,* ed. Russell Duncan (Athens: University of Georgia Press, 1994), 71.

11. Alonso, *Growing Up Abolitionist,* 156; Miller, *Harvard's Civil War,* 16–17.

12. Francis Brown, *Harvard University in the War of 1861–1865* (Boston, 1886), 149; New York *Evening Post,* July 24, 1863; RGS to Sarah Shaw, April 18, 1861, in *Blue-Eyed Child,* ed. Duncan, 73; RGS to Sarah Shaw, April 20, 1861, in *Letters: RGS* (no editor) (Cambridge, 1864), 10.

13. RGS to Susanna Shaw, April 28, 1861, in *Letters: RGS,* 20; RGS to Frank Shaw, April 23, 1861, in *Blue-Eyed Child,* ed. Duncan, 77; RGS to Sarah Shaw, April 26, April 27, and April 29, 1861, ibid., 82–85; RGS to Josephine Shaw, April 30, 1861, ibid., 88.

14. Walter Stahr, *Seward: Lincoln's Indispensable Man* (New York: Simon & Schuster, 2012), 298; RGS to Sarah Shaw, May 2, 1861, in *Blue-Eyed Child,* ed. Duncan, 90–91.

15. Burchard, *One Gallant Rush,* 37; Duncan, *Death and Glory,* 30; RGS to Sarah Shaw, May 19, 1861, in *Blue-Eyed Child,* ed. Duncan, 101.

16. Duncan, *Death and Glory,* 44; RGS to Sarah Shaw, June 9, 1861, in *Blue-Eyed Child,* ed. Duncan, 106–107; RGS to Sarah Shaw, July 13, 1861, ibid., 113; RGS to Susanna Shaw, August 15, 1861, ibid., 128.

17. Hallowell, *Hallowell Family,* 70–72; Brown, *Harvard University in the War,* 167; RGS to Sarah Shaw, June 9, 1861, in *Blue-Eyed Child,* ed. Duncan, 106–107; George A. Bruce, *The Twentieth Regiment of Volunteer Infantry* (Boston, 1906), 10–11.

18. Alfred Roe, *The Twenty-Fourth Massachusetts Regiment* (Worcester, 1907), 21; NPH, *Selected Letters,* 23; Bruce, *Twentieth Regiment,* 6–13.

19. Baltimore *The South,* October 25, 1861; Stephen Sears, *George B. McClellan: The Young Napoleon* (New York: Ticknor and Fields, 1988), 121.

20. Miller, *Harvard's Civil War,* 66–67; New York *Commercial Advertiser,* October 24, 1861.

21. Miller, *Harvard's Civil War,* 71–72; Report, Colonel Edward Hinks, October 23, 1861, *OR,* Series I, Vol. 5, 312–313; Sears, *McClellan,* 121.

22. NPH, *Selected Letters,* 3–4, 11.

23. Sears, *McClellan,* 121; Report, Colonel Edward Hinks, October 23, 1861, *OR,* Series I, Vol. 5, 314; NPH, *Selected Letters,* 10; *Philadelphia Inquirer,* October 24, 1861; Boston *Daily Evening Traveler,* October 26, 1861.

24. Eric Foner, *The Fiery Trial: Abraham Lincoln and American Slavery* (New York: Norton, 2010), 169–170; Hans Trefousse, *Ben Butler: The South Called Him Beast!* (New York: Octagon Books, 1957), 79; Benjamin Butler to Simon Cameron, July 30, 1861, in *Private and Official Correspondence of Gen. Benjamin Butler,* ed. Benjamin Butler and Jesse Marshall (Norwood, 1917), 1:185–188.

25. General Affidavit, Peter Drummond, April 3, 1894, Henry Jarvis File, Pension Office, NA; Henry and Mary Jane Jarvis, Marriage License, December 26, 1872, ibid.; Henry Jarvis to State of Massachusetts, September 15, 1868, ibid.; Henry Jarvis interview, in M. F. Armstrong and Helen Ludlow, *Hampton and Its Students* (New York, 1874), 110–111. Although the interviewers transcribed Jarvis's language in what appears to be stereotypical slave dialect, the young Hampton students were black. Their transcription perhaps reflects their class status or urban background.

26. Adam Goodheart, *1861: The Civil War Awakening* (New York: Vintage Books, 2011), 335; Jarvis interview, in Armstrong and Ludlow, *Hampton and Its Students,* 111–113.

27. Miller, *Harvard's Civil War,* 96–97; Amherst *Farmer's Cabinet,* December 19, 1861.

28. Miller, *Harvard's Civil War,* 98; Fox, *Fifty-Fifth Regiment,* 98; James Oakes, *The Radical and the Republican: Frederick Douglass, Abraham Lincoln, and the Triumph of Antislavery Politics* (New York: Norton, 2007), 147.

29. Edward Kirkland, *Charles Francis Adams Jr.: The Patrician at Bay* (Cambridge, MA: Harvard University Press, 1965), 8–10; Martin Duberman, *Charles Francis Adams* (New York, 1961), 214–215; CFA to Abigail Brooks Adams, July 9, 1861, in *A Cycle of Adams Letters,* ed. Worthington Ford (Boston, 1920), 1:18–19.

30. CFA to Charles Francis Adams Sr., June 10, 1861, in *Adams Letters,* ed. Ford, 1:9–10; CFA, *An Autobiography* (Cambridge, 1916), 11, 123–124.

31. Kirkland, *Adams,* 24–25; CFA to Charles Francis Adams Sr., November 26, 1861, in *Adams Letters,* ed. Ford, 1:72–73; Henry Adams to CFA, December 28, 1861, ibid., 94.

32. CFA to Henry Adams, December 19, 1861, in *Adams Letters,* ed. Ford, 1:86–87; CFA to Charles Francis Adams Sr., November 26, 1861, ibid., 1:72; Brown, *Harvard in the War,* 87; CFA, *Autobiography,* 125–126, 137–138.

33. CFA to Henry Adams, January 3, 1862, in *Adams Letters,* ed. Ford, 1:97–98; CFA to Henry Adams, January [10?], ibid., 103.

34. CFA to Abigail Brooks Adams, February 2, 1862, in *Adams Letters,* ed. Ford, 1:111–112; CFA to Charles Francis Adams Sr., March 11, 1862, ibid., 1:117–118; CFA to Henry Adams, April 6, 1862, ibid., 1:126–127.

35. CFA to Henry Adams, April 2, 1862, in *Adams Letters,* ed. Ford, 1:129–130.

36. Stephen Ash, *Firebrand of Liberty: The Story of Two Black Regiments That Changed the Course of the Civil War* (New York: Norton, 2008), 22; CFA to Charles

Francis Adams Sr., July 28, 1862, in *Adams Letters,* ed. Ford, 1:169–170; CFA to Charles Francis Adams Sr., August 10, 1862, ibid., 1:174–175.

37. Stephen Sears, *To the Gates of Richmond: The Peninsula Campaign* (New York: Ticknor and Fields, 1992), 305; New York *Herald,* July 28, 1871; NPH, *Selected Letters,* 13–14.

38. Walter Poor to George Fox, September 9, 1861, Walter Poor Papers, NYHS; Amelia Holmes to Emily Hallowell, February 1, 1863, Hallowell Family Papers, Haverford College; Lydia Maria Child to Sarah Shaw, June 9, 1862, Shaw Family Papers, NYPL.

39. CFA, *Autobiography,* 142–143; CFA to Charles Francis Adams Sr., July 16, 1862, in *Adams Letters,* ed. Ford, 1:164–165.

40. John David Smith, "Let Us All Be Grateful That We Have Colored Troops That Will Fight," in *Black Soldiers in Blue: African American Troops in the Civil War Era,* ed. John David Smith (Chapel Hill: University of North Carolina Press, 2002), 9; Glenn Brasher, *The Peninsula Campaign and the Necessity of Emancipation: African Americans and the Fight for Freedom* (Chapel Hill: University of North Carolina Press, 2012), 73–74; Foner, *Fiery Trial,* 214.

41. Amherst *Farmer's Cabinet,* July 17, 1862; *Barre* (Massachusetts) *Gazette,* July 18, 1862; "An Act to Suppress Insurrection," July 17, 1862, in *U.S. Statutes at Large* (Washington, 1863), 12:589–592; Masur, *Lincoln's Hundred Days,* 75.

42. Philip Paludan, *The Presidency of Abraham Lincoln* (Lawrence: University Press of Kansas, 1994), 146–147; W. E. B. Du Bois, *Black Reconstruction in America* (New York, 1935), 96; "An Act to Define the Pay of Certain Officers," in *U.S. Statutes at Large,* 12:594–600; Herman Belz, "Law, Politics, and Race in the Struggle for Equal Pay During the Civil War," *CWH* 22 (1976): 210–211.

43. Scott Reynolds and Carol Sheriff, *A People at War: Civilians and Soldiers in America's Civil War* (New York: Oxford University Press, 2007), 192; John David Smith, *Lincoln and the U.S. Colored Troops* (Carbondale: Southern Illinois University Press, 2013), 20.

44. James McPherson, *Crossroads of Freedom: Antietam* (New York: Oxford University Press, 2002), 70; RGS to Frank Shaw, August 11, 1862, in *Blue-Eyed Child,* ed. Duncan, 228; Miller, *Harvard's Civil War,* 165.

45. Stephen Sears, *Landscape Turned Red: The Battle of Antietam* (New York: Ticknor and Fields, 1983), 176–177; RGS to Frank Shaw, September 21, 1862, in *Blue-Eyed Child,* ed. Duncan, 241–242.

46. NPH, *Selected Letters,* 16.

47. CFA, *Autobiography,* 152–153; CFA to Abigail Brooks Adams, September 25, 1862, in *Adams Letters,* ed. Ford, 1:189.

48. Sears, *Landscape Turned Red,* 228; Charles Russell Lowell to Anna Lowell,

September 19, 1862, in *Life and Letters of Charles Russell Lowell,* ed. Edward Emerson (Boston, 1907), 224–225; Brown, *Harvard in the War,* 168, NPH, *Selected Letters,* 15; Miller, *Harvard's Civil War,* 174–177.

49. NPH, *Selected Letters,* 16–19.

50. Ibid., 19; Miller, *Harvard's Civil War,* 179.

51. *Boston Evening Transcript,* September 22, 1862; *Philadelphia Inquirer,* September 25, 1862; *Salem Register,* September 22, 1862; Report, Norman Hall, September 20, 1862, *OR,* Series 1, Vol. 19, 321–322; Report, Napoleon Dana, September 30, 1862, ibid., 319–320.

52. Duncan, *Death and Glory,* 40; Burchard, *One Gallant Rush,* 65; RGS to Susanna Shaw, September 28, 1862, in *Blue-Eyed Child,* ed. Duncan, 249.

53. RGS to Annie Haggerty, November 23, 1862, in *Blue-Eyed Child,* ed. Duncan, 261; RGS to Sarah Shaw, November 21, 1862, ibid., 259; RGS to Josephine Shaw, October 13, 1862, Shaw Family Papers, NYPL.

54. McPherson, *Crossroads of Freedom,* 138–139; John Hope Franklin, *The Emancipation Proclamation* (New York: Doubleday, 1963), 46–47; Vitor Izeckson, *Slavery and War in the Americas: Race, Citizenship, and State Building in the United States and Brazil, 1861–1870* (Charlottesville: University of Virginia Press, 2014), 106–107.

55. Ronald White, *A. Lincoln: A Biography* (New York: Random House, 2009), 542; Walter Poor to George Fox, September 9, 1861, Walter Poor Papers, NYHS; RGS to Sydney Gay, August 6, 1861, in *Blue-Eyed Child,* ed. Duncan, 122–123; RGS to Frank Shaw, August 3, 1862, ibid., 224.

56. Brasher, *Peninsula Campaign,* 55–56; *London Spectator,* December 13, 1862, reprinted in the *Liberator,* January 9, 1863.

57. *Barre* (Massachusetts) *Gazette,* October 11, 1861; Masur, *Lincoln's Hundred Days,* 117–118; Izeckson, *Slavery and War,* 108.

58. *Liberator,* March 6, 1863; Weiner, *Race and Rights,* 219.

59. Margot Minardi, *Making Slavery History: Abolitionism and the Politics of Memory in Massachusetts* (New York: Oxford University Press, 2010), 167.

60. Foner, *Fiery Trial,* 230; Cornish, *Sable Arm,* 78 Noah Trudeau, *Like Men of War: Black Troops in the Civil War, 1862–1865* (Edison: Castle Books, 1998), 13–14; Amherst *Farmer's Cabinet,* August 27, 1863. Although the First Kansas today claims to be the earliest regiment of black soldiers, it was raised without federal authorization. In 1864 the unit became the Seventy-Ninth Infantry USCT.

61. CFA, *Autobiography,* 147; RGS to Frank Shaw, December 30, 1862, in *Blue-Eyed Child,* ed. Duncan, 272.

62. P. J. Staudenraus, *The African Colonization Movement, 1816–1865* (New York: Octagon Books, 1961), 247; *Liberator,* December 26, 1862; *Salem Observer,* December 20, 1862; Atchison (Kansas) *Freedom's Champion,* September 20, 1862.

CHAPTER THREE

1. Oakes, *The Radical and the Republican*, 175–176; Masur, *Lincoln's Hundred Days*, 245; Franklin, *Emancipation Proclamation*, 101.

2. Cornish, *Sable Arm*, 161; Manning, *What This Cruel War*, 108; Jefferson Davis, General Order No. 111, December 24, 1862, *OR*, Series II, Vol. 5, 797.

3. *Liberator*, January 16, 1863; *WAA*, January 17, 1863; "Bill to Authorize Black Soldiers," in *The Papers of Thaddeus Stevens*, ed. Beverly Palmer (Pittsburgh: University of Pittsburgh Press, 1997), 1:354–355; Hans Trefousse, *Thaddeus Stevens: Nineteenth-Century Egalitarian* (Chapel Hill: University of North Carolina Press, 1997), 130; Masur, *Lincoln's Hundred Days*, 222.

4. New Haven *Columbian Register*, February 21, 1863; Masur, *Lincoln's Hundred Days*, 222–223; Allen Bogue, "William Parker Cutler's Congressional Diary," *CWH* 33 (1987): 329; Alexander Stevens, Speech of February 2, 1863, in *Papers of Stevens*, ed. Palmer, 1:357.

5. Cornish, *Sable Arm*, 99; *Liberator*, February 13, 1863; Foner, *Fiery Trial*, 250.

6. John Forbes to JAA, January 22, 1863, Andrew Papers, MHS; *Liberator*, January 30, 1863, May 6, 1864; JAA to Edwin Stanton, February 3, 1863, in *Freedom: Series II: The Black Military Experience: A Documentary History of Emancipation, 1861–1867*, ed. Ira Berlin, Joseph P. Reidy, and Leslie S. Rowland (Cambridge: Cambridge University Press, 1982), 336.

7. John Forbes to JAA, February 2, 1863, Andrew Papers, MHS; John Forbes to JAA, January 30, 1863, NPH Papers, MHS.

8. JAA to Francis Shaw, January 30, 1863, Andrew Papers, MHS.

9. Ibid.; JAA to RGS, January 30, 1863, Andrew Papers, MHS.

10. RGS to Annie Haggerty, February 4, 1863, in *Blue-Eyed Child*, ed. Duncan, 283.

11. Ibid., 285–286; RGS to Francis Shaw, February 8, 1863, in *Blue-Eyed Child*, ed. Duncan, 286–287.

12. RGS to Annie Haggerty, February 8, 1863, in *Blue-Eyed Child*, ed. Duncan, 285–286; Waugh, "Shaw Family," 67; Duncan, *Death and Glory*, 56.

13. William Struthers to Morris Hallowell, March 17, 1863, NPH Papers, MHS; JAA to Francis Shaw, February 6, 1863 (two letters of that date), ibid.; JAA to RGS, February 7, 1863, Andrew Papers, MHS.

14. JAA to Edwin Stanton, February 9, 1863, Andrew Papers, MHS; ENH and RGS, Regimental Descriptive Book, 1863, 54th Massachusetts Infantry, NA; Special Order, William Schouler, April 15, 1863, 54th Massachusetts Infantry Papers, NA; *Liberator*, February 20, 1863, June 5, 1863; *Douglass' Monthly*, March 1863,

815; Jane Maher, *Biography of Broken Fortunes: Wilkie and Bob, Brothers of William, Henry, and Alice James* (New York: Archon, 1986), 31, 35.

15. RGS to Sarah Shaw, February 20, 1863, in *Blue-Eyed Child*, ed. Duncan, 289–290; RGS to Annie Haggerty, February 16, 1863, ibid., 287; Charles Russell Lowell to Anna Lowell, February 4, 1863, in *Letters of Lowell*, ed. Emerson, 233–234; RGS to Elizabeth Lyman, February 20, 1863, Lyman Family Papers, MHS.

16. Richard Abbott, "Massachusetts and the Recruitment of Southern Negroes," *CWH* 14 (1968): 198; Cornish, *Sable Arm*, 107; Joseph E. Stevens, *1863: The Rebirth of a Nation* (New York: Bantam, 1999), 113.

17. *Liberator*, May 1, 1863; David Blight, *Frederick Douglass' Civil War: Keeping Faith in Jubilee* (Baton Rouge: Louisiana State University Press, 1989), 158; Pearson, *Andrew*, 2:82; Luis Emilio, *History of the Fifty-Fourth Regiment* (Boston, 1894), 11; Charles Russell Lowell to H. L. Higginson, February 15, 1863, in *Letters of Lowell*, ed. Emerson, 235.

18. RGS to Sarah Shaw, February 20, 1863, in *Blue-Eyed Child*, ed. Duncan, 290; Duncan, *Death and Glory*, 62; Gary Collison, *Shadrach Minkins: From Fugitive Slave to Citizen* (Cambridge, MA: Harvard University Press, 1997), 130–133.

19. John Mercer Langston, *From the Plantation to the Capitol* (Hartford, 1894), 201.

20. William Cheek and Aimee Cheek, *John Mercer Langston and the Fight for Black Freedom, 1829–65* (Urbana: University of Illinois Press, 1989), 391; David Gerber, *Black Ohio and the Color Line, 1860–1915* (Urbana: University of Illinois Press, 1976), 33–34; David Tod to John Mercer Langston, May 16, 1863, in *Freedom: Series II*, ed. Berlin et al., 336.

21. George Stearns to Frederick Douglass, August 8, 1863, Douglass Papers, LC; *Douglass' Monthly*, April 1863, 820; Frederick Douglass to Gerrit Smith, June 19, 1863, Smith Papers, Syracuse University.

22. New Bedford *Republican Standard*, February 19, 1863; Ezra Greenspan, *William Wells Brown: An African American Life* (New York: Norton, 2014), 397; *WAA*, February 28, 1863; Mulderink, *New Bedford's Civil War*, 102.

23. *WAA*, April 18, 1863; *Philadelphia Inquirer*, March 31, 1863; *Liberator*, April 17, 1863, April 24, 1863.

24. Blight, *Douglass' Civil War*, 160; *Camden Democrat*, March 28, 1863; Boston *Daily Evening Traveler*, January 1, 1863; *Boston Herald*, January 2, 1863.

25. *New-York Tribune*, February 6, 1863; *Boston Herald*, February 8, 1863; *Lowell Daily Citizen and News*, February 10, 1863, February 16, 1863; *Washington* (Pennsylvania) *Reporter*, February 18, 1863.

26. *Douglass' Monthly*, March 1863, 808, April 1863, 818; *Liberator*, March 13, 1863; *WAA*, March 7, 1863; Hartford *Courant*, March 7, 1863; New York *Evening*

Post, March 5, 1863; *New-York Tribune,* March 5, 1863; Baltimore *Sun,* March 6, 1863.

27. Portland *Daily Eastern Argus,* March 6, 1863; Harrisburg *Weekly Patriot and Union,* March 26, 1863, April 2, 1863; Cleveland *Plain Dealer,* February 24, 1863.

28. Duncan, *Death and Glory,* 60; *Liberator,* June 26, 1863; *WAA,* April 4, 1863; JHG to *New Bedford Mercury,* March 3, 1863, in *On the Altar of Freedom,* ed. Adams, 4.

29. Cornish, *Sable Arm,* 235; Julie Griffiths Crofts to Frederick Douglass, April 13, 1863, Douglass Papers, LC.

30. George L. Stearns to Frederick Douglass, March 24, 1863, Smith Papers, Syracuse University; Frederick Douglass to Gerrit Smith, March 6, 1863, ibid.; Charles Remond Douglass, Birth Record, *Vital Records of Lynn, Massachusetts, to the Year 1850* (Boston, 1904), 131; Charles Douglass, Regimental Descriptive Book, April 1863, 54th Massachusetts Infantry, NA; *Cleveland Gazette,* October 11, 1902; *WAA,* May 16, 1863, erroneously listed Charles Douglass as a sergeant and Stephen Swails as a corporal; the elder man held the higher rank.

31. *Rochester City Directory* (Rochester, 1861), 123; LHD to Amelia Loguen, March 31, 1863, Walter O. Evans Collection, Savannah; *WAA,* April 11, 1863; LHD, Regimental Descriptive Book, March 1863, 54th Massachusetts Infantry, NA: Frederick Douglass, 1860 Federal Census, Rochester, NY, Roll M653–784, Page 300, Image 299, NA. In his biography, McFeely writes that Charles and Lewis "found themselves vulnerable to their father's newest great cause," a statement that erases all agency from these two adult men; William S. McFeely *Frederick Douglass* (New York: Norton, 1991), 223.

32. William Carney and JHG, Regimental Descriptive Book, March 1863, 54th Massachusetts Infantry, NA; JHG, Consolidated Lists of Civil War Draft Registration Records, Record Group 110, NA; Emilio, *Fifty-Fourth,* 19; *WAA,* May 9, 1863; NPH, *The Negro as a Soldier,* 9; JHG to *New Bedford Mercury,* March 7, 1863, in *On the Altar of Freedom,* ed. Adams, 5. Stevens, *1863,* 112–114, remarks that the New Bedford men were "disillusioned by what they saw," as there "was nothing to eat, and no one seemed to have any idea of where they should go," a statement flatly contradicted by Gooding's March 7 letter. Diedrich erroneously claims that for "months, the Massachusetts 54th remained without uniforms or proper shoes," a fiction she evidently learned from the film *Glory;* Maria Diedrich, *Love Across Color Lines: Ottilie Assing and Frederick Douglass* (New York: Hill and Wang, 1999), 248.

33. Stephen Swails, Regimental Descriptive Book, 1863, 54th Massachusetts Infantry, NA; Duncan, *Death and Glory,* 68; Margaret Washington, *Sojourner Truth's America* (Urbana: University of Illinois Press, 2009), 305; Peter Vogelsang, Regimental Descriptive Book, 1863, 54th Massachusetts Infantry, NA; RGS to Francis Shaw, April 24, 1863, in *Blue-Eyed Child,* ed. Duncan, 325.

34. George Alexander, Regimental Descriptive Book, 1863, 54th Massachusetts Infantry, NA; *WAA,* May 2, 1863, May 9, 1863; Joseph Barge to Blanche K. Bruce, February 17, 1876, Bruce Papers, Howard University Library.

35. *Liberator,* March 20, 1863, April 3, 1863; RGS to Charles Morse, March 12, 1863, Shaw Collection, MHS; RGS to Sarah Shaw, March 12, 1863, in *Letters: RGS,* 271; *Boston Daily Evening Traveler,* March 11, 1863; New Haven *Columbian Register,* March 14, 1863; LHD to Amelia Loguen, April 8, 1863, Douglass Papers, LC; RGS to Sarah Shaw, March 17, 1863, in *Blue-Eyed Child,* ed. Duncan, 309.

36. Lincoln Stone, *Report of the Surgeon-General, Fifty-Fourth Regiment,* NPH Papers, MHS; LHD to Amelia Loguen, April 8, 1863, Douglass Papers, LC.

37. Pearson, *Andrew,* 2:84; Edwin Redkey, "A Profile of the Fifty-Fourth Massachusetts Regiment," in *Hope and Glory,* ed. Blatt et al., 22–24.

38. *WAA,* March 28, 1863, May 9, 1863; JHG to *New Bedford Mercury,* April 6, 1863, in *On the Altar of Freedom,* ed. Adams, 9; RGS to Charles Morse, February 24, 1863, Shaw Collection, MHS.

39. RGS to Charles Morse, February 21, 1863, Shaw Collection, MHS; RGS to Francis Shaw, February 25, 1863, in *Blue-Eyed Child,* ed. Duncan, 300; NPH, *The Negro as a Soldier,* 2, 10; RGS to Amos Lawrence, March 25, 1863, Lawrence Papers, MHS.

40. Boston *Daily Evening Traveler,* March 11, 1863; LHD to Amelia Loguen, April 8, 1863, Douglass Papers, LC; RGS to Annie Haggerty, February 23, 1863, in *Blue-Eyed Child,* ed. Duncan, 296; JHG to *New Bedford Mercury,* March 18, 1863, in *On the Altar of Freedom,* ed. Adams, 6.

41. *WAA,* May 9, 1863; Stevens, *1863,* 114; *Liberator,* February 13, 1863, June 5, 1863. Diedrich, *Love Across Color Lines,* 248, incorrectly insists that the Fifty-fourth's "weapons were ridiculously outmoded."

42. NPH, *The Negro as a Soldier,* 9; Smith, *Lincoln and the U.S. Colored Troops,* 50; Duncan, *Death and Glory,* 73–74; *WAA,* March 28, 1863.

43. JHG to *New Bedford Mercury,* March 24, 1863, April 3, 1863, in *On the Altar of Freedom,* ed. Adams, 7, 10.

44. Ira Berlin, *Generations of Captivity: A History of African American Slaves* (Cambridge, MA: Belknap Press of Harvard University Press, 2003), 257; *WAA,* May 2, 1863; William Jackson to R. G. Pierce, May 28, 1863, Massachusetts 54th Infantry Papers, NA; LHD to Amelia Loguen, April 8, 1863, Douglass Papers, LC; JHG to *New Bedford Mercury,* March 18, 1863, in *On the Altar of Freedom,* ed. Adams, 6.

45. JHG to *New Bedford Mercury,* August 16, 1863, in *On the Altar of Freedom,* ed. Adams, 50. Although Gooding wrote these sentiments after Shaw's death, they correspond with his earlier assessment of his colonel's ability and political courage.

46. RGS to Francis Shaw, March 30, 1863, in *Blue-Eyed Child,* ed. Duncan, 316; Charles Russell Lowell to RGS, May 23, 1863, in *Letters of Lowell,* ed. Emerson, 242.

47. Emilio, *Fifty-Fourth,* 23; Maher, *Broken Fortunes,* 32; LHD to Amelia Loguen, April 15, 1863, Evans Collection, Savannah.

48. LHD to Amelia Loguen, March 3, 1863, May 9, 1863, May 20, 1863, Evans Collection, Savannah; *WAA,* May 20, 1863.

49. Foote, *One Great Remedy,* 98; RGS to Elizabeth Lyman, February 20, 1863, Lyman Family Papers, MHS; RGS to Francis Shaw, April 5, 1863, in *Blue-Eyed Child,* ed. Duncan, 321; RGS to Sarah Shaw, April 14, 1863, ibid., 323; RGS to Sarah Shaw, April 17, 1863, ibid., 324; Waugh, *Unsentimental Reformer,* 71; RGS to Henry James, May 4, 1863, Shaw Family Telegrams, NYHS; RGS to Annie Haggerty Shaw, May 9, 1863, ibid.; RGS to Ogden Haggerty, May 8, 1863, ibid.; RGS to Charles Morse, July 3, 1863, Shaw Collection, MHS.

50. Emilio, *Fifty-Fourth,* 24; William Schouler, Special Order No. 267, May 27, 1863, and Special Order No. 336, June 24, 1863, 54th Massachusetts Infantry Papers, NA; NPH, 1863, 55th Massachusetts Infantry, NA; RGS to Susanna Shaw, May 7, 1863, in *Blue-Eyed Child,* ed Duncan, 329; RGS to Francis Shaw, May 11, 1863, ibid., 329; RGS to John Murray Forbes, June 3, 1863, ibid., 338.

51. ENH, Regimental Descriptive Book, April 1863, 54th Massachusetts Infantry, NA; Fox, *Fifty-Fifth,* 1; William Lloyd Garrison to Fanny Garrison, September 18, 1862, Anti-Slavery Collection, Boston Public Library; William Lloyd Garrison to GTG, June 11, 1863, in *Letters of William Lloyd Garrison,* ed. Walter Merrill (Cambridge, MA: Harvard University Press, 1979), 5:160; Donald Williams, *Prudence Crandall's Legacy: The Fight for Equality* (Middletown, CT: Wesleyan University Press, 2014), 273; Lucy McKim to Wendell Phillips Garrison, April 27, 1863, Garrison Family Papers, Smith College.

52. Michael Meier, "Lorenzo Thomas and the Recruitment of Blacks," in *Black Soldiers in Blue,* ed. Smith, 259; Smith, "Let Us All Be Grateful," in ibid., 28; Abbott, "Recruitment of Southern Negroes," 200; Izeckson, *Slavery and War,* 110; Weiner, *Race and Rights,* 221; Ian Spurgeon, *Soldiers in the Army of Freedom: The 1st Kansas Colored* (Norman: University of Oklahoma Press, 2014), 248; Cornish, *Sable Arm,* 130–131.

53. Grover, *Fugitive's Gibraltar,* 279; Cornish, *Sable Arm,* 161–162; NPH, *The Negro as a Soldier,* 6.

54. *Douglass' Monthly,* April 1863, 844; Joseph Glatthaar, *Forged in Battle: The Civil War Alliance of Black Soldiers and White Officers* (New York: Free Press, 1989), 203; *Liberator,* May 15, 1863; RGS to Sarah Shaw, April 7, 1863, in *Blue-Eyed Child,* ed. Duncan, 321; *WAA,* March 28, 1863.

55. Worcester *National Aegis,* May 2, 1863; *Albany Evening Journal,* April 28,

1863; Emilio, *Fifty-Fourth,* 31; Charles Russell Lowell to Josephine Shaw, May 24, 1863, in *Letters of Lowell,* ed. Emerson, 246; RGS to JAA, April 6, 1863, Andrew Papers, MHS; JAA to Edwin Stanton, April 1, 1863, in *Freedom: Series II,* ed. Berlin et al., 131.

56. RGS to Charles Morse, July 3, 1863, Shaw Collection, MHS; LHD to Amelia Loguen, May 20, 1863, and May 27, 1863, Evans Collection, Savannah.

57. Duncan, *Death and Glory,* 84; RGS to Sarah Shaw, May 18, 1863, in *Blue-Eyed Child,* ed. Duncan, 332; JHG to *New Bedford Mercury,* May 20, 1863, and May 24, 1863, in *On the Altar of Freedom,* ed. Adams, 21–24; Pearson, *Andrew,* 2:86–87.

58. *WAA,* May 23, 1863; *Liberator,* May 22, 1863; JHG to *New Bedford Mercury,* May 18, 1863, in *On the Altar of Freedom,* ed. Adams, 23; RGS to Francis Shaw, May 22, 1863, in *Letters: RGS,* 289; RGS to Sarah Shaw, May 18, 1863, in *Blue-Eyed Child,* ed. Duncan, 332.

59. Pearson, *Andrew,* 2:88; Jacqueline Jones, *Saving Savannah: The City and the Civil War* (New York: Knopf, 2008), 176.

60. *Liberator,* June 5, 1863, June 26, 1863, July 31, 1863; *WAA,* June 6, 1863; Emilio, *Fifty-Fourth,* 31.

61. *WAA,* June 13, 1863; NPH, *The Negro as a Soldier,* 7; Emilio, *Fifty-Fourth,* 32; Lydia Maria Child to Francis Shaw, March 21, 1876, Shaw Family Papers, NYPL; Maher, *Broken Fortunes,* 37–38.

62. Pearson, *Andrew,* 2:89; *Liberator,* June 5, 1863, December 22, 1865; *Douglass' Monthly,* May 1863, 838.

63. Frederick Douglass to Gerrit Smith, June 19, 1863, Smith Papers, Syracuse University; RGS to Charles Morse, July 3, 1863, Shaw Collection, MHS; RGS to Annie Haggerty Shaw, June 1, 1863, in *Blue-Eyed Child,* ed. Duncan, 335.

CHAPTER FOUR

1. RGS to Annie Haggerty Shaw, June 1, 1863, in *Blue-Eyed Child,* ed. Duncan, 335; Emilio, *Fifty-Fourth,* 35; LHD to Amelia Loguen, June 18, 1863, Evans Collection, Savannah; McFeely, *Douglass,* 225, describes the *DeMolay* as "an unpromising transport ship," a characterization at odds with that given by Shaw and Emilio.

2. RGS to Annie Haggerty Shaw, June 1, 1863, in *Blue-Eyed Child,* ed. Duncan, 335; Telegraph, David Hunter to W. W. Davis, June 6, 1863, in Letters Sent, Department of the South, Record Group 393, NA; David Hunter to John Moore, June 6, 1863, ibid.

3. Emilio, *Fifty-Fourth,* 37–38; JHG to *New Bedford Mercury,* June 8, 1863, in *On the Altar of Freedom,* ed. Adams, 26–27. Gooding erred on the date in noting that they debarked the *DeMolay* on the morning of June 5. Both Shaw and Emilio indicate that it was the previous day.

4. A. D. Smith to JAA, June 18, 1863, Andrew Papers, MHS; Kate Clifford Larson, *Bound for the Promised Land: Harriet Tubman* (New York: Ballantine, 2004), 203; LHD to Amelia Loguen, June 18, 1863, Evans Collection, Savannah.

5. Emilio, *Fifty-Fourth*, 38; RGS to Sarah Shaw, June 6, 1863, in *Blue-Eyed Child*, ed. Duncan, 339; Thomas Wentworth Higginson to Louisa Higginson, June 5, 1863, in *The Complete Civil War Journal and Selected Letters of Thomas Wentworth Higginson*, ed. Christopher Looby (Chicago: University of Chicago Press, 1999), 283; Thomas Wentworth Higginson, *Cheerful Yesterdays* (Boston, 1900), 257; Thomas Wentworth Higginson, *Army Life in a Black Regiment* (Cambridge, 1900), 304–305.

6. Walter Fraser, *Charleston! Charleston! The History of a Southern City* (Columbia: University of South Carolina Press, 1989), 262; Edward Ball, *Slaves in the Family* (New York: Farrar, Straus & Giroux, 1998), 338; Report on the Attacks on Forts Sumter, Moultrie, and Wagner, 1863, Henry Wilson Hubbell Collection, NYHS.

7. *Liberator,* February 6, 1863; RGS to Sarah Shaw, June 6, 1863, in *Blue-Eyed Child*, ed. Duncan, 339; NPH, *The Negro as a Soldier*, 4–5; Ash, *Firebrand of Liberty*, 53; Edward Pierce to JAA, July 3, 1863, Andrew Papers, MHS.

8. Thomas Wentworth Higginson to Louisa Higginson, June 5, 1863, in *Civil War Journal*, ed. Looby, 283; Thomas Wentworth Higginson to Mary Higginson, June 10, 1863, ibid., 284; Trudeau, *Men of War*, 122–123; RGS to Clemence Haggerty, June 17, 1863, in *Blue-Eyed Child*, ed. Duncan, 350.

9. Emilio, *Fifty-Fourth*, 38.

10. RGS to Clemence Haggerty, June 17, 1863, in *Blue-Eyed Child*, ed. Duncan, 350; JHG to *New Bedford Mercury*, April 18, 1863, in *On the Altar of Freedom*, ed. Adams, 13; A. D. Smith to JAA, June 11, 1863, Andrew Papers, MHS.

11. RGS to Charles Morse, July 3, 1863, Shaw Collection, MHS; RGS to Sarah Shaw, June 6, 1863, in *Blue-Eyed Child*, ed. Duncan, 339; RGS to Francis Barlow, June 20, 1863, Shaw Family Papers, NYHS.

12. *WAA,* June 27, 1863; Emilio, *Fifty-Fourth*, 41; JHG to *New Bedford Mercury*, June 14, 1863, in *On the Altar of Freedom*, ed. Adams, 29; RGS to Annie Haggerty Shaw, June 12, 1863, in *Blue-Eyed Child*, ed. Duncan, 342.

13. RGS to Annie Haggerty Shaw, June 12, 1863, in *Blue-Eyed Child*, ed. Duncan, 342–343; E. Merton Coulter, "Robert Gould Shaw and the Burning of Darien, Georgia," *CWH* 5 (1959): 370; Amherst *Farmer's Cabinet*, June 25, 1863; RGS to Charles Morse, July 3, 1863, Shaw Collection, MHS; JHG to *New Bedford Mercury,* June 14, 1863, in *On the Altar of Freedom,* ed. Adams, 29.

14. RGS to Annie Haggerty Shaw, June 12, 1863, in *Blue-Eyed Child*, ed. Duncan, 342–343; RGS to Francis Barlow, June 20, 1863, Shaw Family Papers, NYPL; Keith Wilson, "In the Shadow of John Brown," in *Black Soldiers in Blue*, ed. Smith, 324.

15. Wilson, "In the Shadow of John Brown," 323; George Stephens to *WAA,* July 4, 1863; Larson, *Bound for the Promised Land,* 217.

16. JHG to *New Bedford Mercury,* June 22, 1863, and June 26, 1863, in *On the Altar of Freedom,* ed. Adams, 31, 64; LHD to Amelia Loguen, June 18, 1863, Evans Collection, Savannah.

17. Emilio, *Fifty-Fourth,* 44; *Lowell Daily Citizen and News,* July 2, 1863; Worcester *National Aegis,* July 4, 1863; Brenda Wineapple suggests that Hunter was relieved as commander of the Department of the South because of Shaw's protests of Montgomery's tactics, which Hunter did in fact endorse. The decision to replace Hunter with Gillmore was made on June 3, however, eight days before the raid at Darien; Wineapple, *White Heat: The Friendship of Emily Dickinson and Thomas Wentworth Higginson* (New York: Knopf, 2008), 136.

18. Emilio, *Fifty-Fourth,* 45; JHG to *New Bedford Mercury,* June 14, 1863, in *On the Altar of Freedom,* ed. Adams, 30; Catherine Clinton, *Fanny Kemble's Civil Wars* (New York: Simon & Schuster, 2000), 183; RGS to Charles Morse, July 3, 1863, Shaw Collection, MHS; LHD to Amelia Loguen, September 28, 1864, Evans Collection, Savannah.

19. Washington *National Intelligencer,* July 8, 1863; RGS to Francis Shaw, June 22, 1863, in *Blue-Eyed Child,* ed. Duncan, 357; RGS to Sarah Shaw, June 25, 1863, ibid., 359; Edward Pierce to JAA, July 3, 1863, Andrew Papers, MHS; RGS to Charles Russell Lowell, June 20, 1863, Shaw Family Papers, NYPL. Frederick Douglass was also confused as to the exact location of St. Simons Island, telling Gerrit Smith that "Lewis my son is now in Florida"; see his letter of June 19, 1863, Smith Papers, Syracuse University.

20. RGS to JAA, July 2, 1863, in Emilio, *Fifty-Fourth,* 47–48; *Liberator,* April 8, 1864; RGS to Francis Shaw, July 1, 1863, in *Blue-Eyed Child,* ed. Duncan, 366; RGS to Clemence Haggerty, July 1, 1863, ibid., 367–368.

21. Pearson, *Andrew,* 2:98–99; Glatthaar, *Forged in Battle,* 170; Cornish, *Sable Arm,* 185; Herman Belz, "Law, Politics, and Race," *CWH* 22 (1976): 199; JAA to William Schouler, April 25, 1863, 54th Massachusetts Infantry Papers, NA; *Liberator,* May 6, 1864; Cornish, *Sable Arm,* 187.

22. *Journals of Charlotte Forten Grimké,* ed. Brenda Stevenson (New York: Oxford University Press, 1988), 490–491; RGS to Sarah Shaw, July 3, 1863, in *Blue-Eyed Child,* ed. Duncan, 372; Ash, *Firebrand of Liberty,* 91–92.

23. RGS to Sarah Shaw, July 4, 1863, in *Blue-Eyed Child,* ed. Duncan, 373; Laura Towne, *Letters and Diary of Laura Towne* (Cambridge, 1912), 114; *Journals of Grimké,* ed. Stevenson, 492–493. Duncan, *Death and Glory,* 102–103, 169 suggests an "affair" between Shaw and Charlotte Forten. Duncan writes: "Shaw spent nearly a week in her company, often seeing her day and night. His four-day letter to his mother dated July 3–6 indicates his infatuation." Apart from Forten's ongoing

relationship with Seth Rogers, her journals indicate that she and Shaw met only three times, always in the company of numerous other people. As Thomas Brown observed in a perceptive book review of *Death and Glory,* Duncan's hints of an affair are "highly sensational," and Brown correctly notes that far from being evidence of "his infatuation," the letter of July 3–6 that Shaw wrote to his mother was one he asked her to forward to Annie; Thomas Brown, *South Carolina Historical Magazine* 101 (2000): 77.

24. James Bowen, *Massachusetts in the War, 1861–1865* (Springfield, 1889), 354; RGS to Annie Haggerty Shaw, July 13, 1863, in *Blue-Eyed Child,* ed. Duncan, 383.

25. RGS to George Strong, July 6, 1863, in Emilio, *Fifty-Fourth,* 49.

26. Emilio, *Fifty-Fourth,* 50; Stephen Wise, *Gate of Hell: Campaign for Charleston Harbor, 1863* (Columbia: University of South Carolina Press, 1994), 53.

27. Report, Quincy Adams Gillmore, February 26, 1864, Department of the South, Record Group 393, NA; Wise, *Gate of Hell,* 9; Emilio, *Fifty-Fourth,* 52.

28. Emilio, *Fifty-Fourth,* 52. With the lowlands somewhat drained, what was known as Legare Island is no longer as recognizable. Terry's main camp stood near what is now aptly named Yankee Drive, and its southern edge is now State Road 10-432.

29. E. Milby Burton, *The Siege of Charleston, 1861–1865* (Columbia: University of South Carolina Press, 1970), 155–156; Stevens, *1863,* 307; *Springfield* (Massachusetts) *Republican,* January 10, 1887; *Janesville* (Wisconsin) *Daily Gazette,* July 20, 1863; Wise, *Gate of Hell,* 72; R. S. Ripley to W. F. Nance, July 10, 1863, *OR,* Series I, Vol. 28, 368; Emilio, *Fifty-Fourth,* 53.

30. Lorenzo Lyon to father, July 14, 1863, Lyon Family Papers, NYHS; Burton, *Siege of Charleston,* 157–158; Report, Joseph Abbott, August 16, 1863, *OR,* Series I, Vol. 28, 364; Wise, *Gate of Hell,* 78; Emilio, *Fifty-Fourth,* 54.

31. Emilio, *Fifty-Fourth,* 55–56.

32. Cornish, *Sable Arm,* 151; JHG to *New Bedford Mercury,* July 20, 1863, in *On the Altar of Freedom,* ed. Adams, 36; Emilio, *Fifty-Fourth,* 58.

33. LHD to Frederick and Anna Douglass, July 20, 1863, Douglass Papers, LC; Peter Vogelsang to *WAA,* August 22, 1863; *WAA,* August 1, 1863.

34. George Stephens to *WAA,* July 21, 1863; Peter Vogelsang to *WAA,* August 22, 1863; Surgeon's Affidavit, November 10, 1879, Peter Vogelsang File, Pension Office, NA; Peter Vogelsang, Regimental Descriptive Book, Company Muster Roll, July and August 1863, 54th Massachusetts Infantry, NA.

35. Peter Vogelsang to *WAA,* August 22, 1863; LHD to Frederick and Anna Douglass, July 20, 1863, Douglass Papers, LC; George Stephens to *WAA,* July 21, 1863; JHG to *New Bedford Mercury,* July 20, 1863, in *On the Altar of Freedom,* ed. Adams, 37.

36. Peter Vogelsang to *WAA,* August 22, 1863; *WAA,* November 14, 1863; JHG to *New Bedford Mercury,* July 20, 1863, in *On the Altar of Freedom,* ed. Adams, 37; Redkey, "Profile of the Fifty-Fourth," 27; George Stephens to *WAA,* July 21, 1863.

37. *WAA,* August 1, 1863; Emilio, *Fifty-Fourth,* 62; Trudeau, *Men of War,* 76; P. G. T. Beauregard to Samuel Cooper, July 17, 1863, *OR,* Series II, Vol. 6, 125.

38. Emilio, *Fifty-Fourth,* 63; *Liberator,* August 7, 1863; RGS to Annie Haggerty Shaw, July 15, 1863, in *Blue-Eyed Child,* ed. Duncan, 385; Maher, *Broken Fortunes,* 40; LHD to Frederick and Anna Douglass, July 20, 1863, Douglass Papers, LC.

39. Maher, *Broken Fortunes,* 40–41; Glatthaar, *Forged in Battle,* 136.

40. Emilio, *Fifty-Fourth,* 64–65; Worcester *Massachusetts Spy,* August 5, 1863; RGS to Annie Haggerty Shaw, July 17, 1863, in *Blue-Eyed Child,* ed. Duncan, 386; LHD to Frederick and Anna Douglass, July 20, 1863, Douglass Papers, LC.

41. RGS to Annie Haggerty Shaw, July 17, 1863, in *Blue-Eyed Child,* ed. Duncan, 386; Emilio, *Fifty-Fourth,* 62.

42. Seraile, *Angels of Mercy,* 70; Manning, *What This Cruel War,* 116–117; Benjamin Quarles, *The Negro in the Civil War* (Boston: Little, Brown, 1953), 242–243; Martin Blatt, "Glory: Hollywood History and Popular Culture," in *Hope and Glory,* ed. Blatt et al., 223; Stevens, *1863,* 308; Foote, *One Great Remedy,* 116.

43. George Stephens and Peter Vogelsang to *WAA,* August 22, 1863.

44. Emilio, *Fifty-Fourth,* 65–68; Stevens, *1863,* 308.

CHAPTER FIVE

1. Emilio, *Fifty-Fourth,* 70–71; *Springfield* (Massachusetts) *Republican,* January 10, 1887; Wise, *Gate of Hell,* 16–17.

2. Wise, *Gate of Hell,* 59–61; NPH, *The Negro as a Soldier,* 11; Amherst *Farmer's Cabinet,* August 6, 1863; Emilio, *Fifty-Fourth,* 67, 70.

3. Trudeau, *Men of War,* 74; Report, Quincy Adams Gillmore, February 26, 1864, Department of the South, Record Group 393, NA.

4. Amherst *Farmer's Cabinet,* July 23, 1863; *New York Times,* July 18, 1863; Lorenzo Lyon to father, July 13, 1863, Lyon Family Papers, NYHS.

5. Emilio, *Fifty-Fourth,* 68; Burchard, *One Gallant Rush,* 132; Eon Smith to Truman Seymour, July 17, 1863, Department of the South, Letters Sent, Record Group 393, NA; George Washington Williams, *A History of the Negro Troops in the War of the Rebellion* (New York, 1888), 194; Iredell Jones to father, July 20, 1863, in *Southern Historical Society Papers,* ed. J. William Jones (Richmond, 1884), 12:37.

6. Glatthaar, *Forged in Battle,* 137; Emilio, *Fifty-Fourth,* 68; Report, Quincy Adams Gillmore, February 26, 1864, Department of the South, Record Group 393, NA.

7. Emilio, *Fifty-Fourth,* 72; Worcester *Massachusetts Spy,* August 5, 1863.

8. Emilio, *Fifty-Fourth,* 72; JHG to *New Bedford Mercury,* July 20, 1863, in *On the Altar of Freedom,* ed. Adams, 38; Iredell Jones to father, July 20, 1863, in *Southern Historical Society Papers,* ed. Jones, 12:37; Worcester *Massachusetts Spy,* August 5, 1863.

9. Alec Johnson to Burt Wilder, July 25, 1813, Burt Wilder Papers, Cornell University; RGS to Francis Shaw, July 18, 1863, in *Blue-Eyed Child,* ed. Duncan, 387; Larson, *Bound for the Promised Land,* 220; Emilio, *Fifty-Fourth,* 73, 77.

10. Emilio, *Fifty-Fourth,* 76–77; Catherine Clinton, *Harriet Tubman: The Road to Freedom* (New York: Little, Brown, 2004), 176; Trudeau, *Men of War,* 81.

11. Emilio, *Fifty-Fourth,* 77; JHG to *New Bedford Mercury,* July 20, 1863, in *On the Altar of Freedom,* ed. Adams, 38; Maher, *Broken Fortunes,* 43, incorrectly attributes this speech to Truman Seymour.

12. JHG to *New Bedford Mercury,* July 20, 1863, in *On the Altar of Freedom,* ed. Adams, 38; *Liberator,* September 11, 1863.

13. Emilio, *Fifty-Fourth,* 68–70; Report, ENH, November 7, 1863, *OR,* Series II, Vol. 28, 362.

14. Report, Joseph Abbott, August 16, 1863, *OR,* Series I, Vol. 28, 365; Emilio, *Fifty-Fourth,* 70. JHG to *New Bedford Mercury,* July 20, 1863, in *On the Altar of Freedom,* ed. Adams, 38, wrote that Shaw picked up the state flag, but he was not in a position to do so. John Wall and then William Carney carried the national flag, so Shaw must have briefly advanced the regimental colors.

15. NPH, *The Negro as a Soldier,* 11; Report, Quincy Adams Gillmore, February 26, 1864, Department of the South, Record Group 393, NA; LHD to Frederick and Anna Douglass, July 20, 1863, Douglass Papers, LC; LHD to Amelia Loguen, July 20, 1863, Carter G. Woodson Papers, LC; *Liberator,* August 28, 1863.

16. Emilio, *Fifty-Fourth,* 81; Maher, *Broken Fortunes,* 44; Worcester *Massachusetts Spy,* August 5, 1863; NPH, *The Negro as a Soldier,* 13–14.

17. Worcester *Massachusetts Spy,* August 5, 1863; JHG to *New Bedford Mercury,* July 20, 1863, in *On the Altar of Freedom,* ed. Adams, 38; *Liberator,* August 28, 1863.

18. Wise, *Gate of Hell,* 106; Lorenzo Lyon to father, July 20, 1863, Lyon Family Papers, NYHS.

19. Quarles, *The Negro in the Civil War,* 16; Emilio, *Fifty-Fourth,* 83; *WAA,* August 1, 1863; Report, ENH, November 7, 1863, *OR,* Series II, Vol. 28, 362.

20. Wise, *Gate of Hell,* 107; Report, Quincy Adams Gillmore, February 26, 1864, Department of the South, Record Group 393, NA; LHD to Frederick and Anna Douglass, July 20, 1863, Douglass Papers, LC; NPH, *The Negro as a Soldier,* 11–13; Emilio, *Fifty-Fourth,* 84, 91.

21. *Boston Journal,* December 29, 1892; NPH, *The Negro as a Soldier,* 13–14; *Liberator,* August 28, 1863; George Washington Williams, *A History of Negro Troops*

in the War of the Rebellion (New York, 1888), 199; William Carney to State of Massachusetts, December 6, 1864, William Carney File, Pension Office, NA.

22. *Liberator,* August 7, 1863, August 28, 1863; Amherst *Farmer's Cabinet,* August 6, 1863.

23. Maher, *Broken Fortunes,* 46; Lorenzo Lyon to father, July 20, 1863, Lyon Family Papers, NYHS; George Stephens to *WAA,* August 8, 1863.

24. Larson, *Bound for the Promised Land,* 220.

25. Burton, *Siege of Charleston,* 168; Howard Westwood, *Black Troops, White Commanders, and Freedmen During the Civil War* (Carbondale: Southern Illinois University Press, 1992), 92; Quincy Adams Gillmore to Commanding Officer, Confederate Force, July 19, 1863, Department of the South, Letters Sent, Record Group 393, NA; *Washington* (Pennsylvania) *Reporter,* August 19, 1863.

26. James Guthrie, *Camp-Fires of the Afro-American* (Philadelphia, 1899), 467; NPH, *The Negro as a Soldier,* 15; Emilio, *Fifty-Fourth,* 98. The Morris Island–based correspondent for the *New-York Tribune* was evidently the first to report the "nigger" comment, in the July 30 edition. See *Liberator,* August 7, 1863.

27. Burton, *Siege of Charleston,* 114; Emilio, *Fifty-Fourth,* 101; NPH, *The Negro as a Soldier,* 15. On burial pits, see Drew Gilpin Faust, *This Republic of Suffering: Death and the American Civil War* (New York: Knopf, 2009), 70–74.

28. William Scott to Margaret Scott, July 24, 1863, Margaret Scott Collection, NYHS; Worcester *Massachusetts Spy,* August 5, 1863; Quincy Adams Gillmore to James Dahlgren, July 19, 1863, Department of the South, Letters Sent, Record Group 393, NA. General Hagood later placed the conference two days earlier, on July 22, and he also claimed that Putnam's body was returned. In fact, it was never recovered. See Emilio, *Fifty-Fourth,* 101.

29. JHG to *New Bedford Mercury,* July 24, 1863, in *On the Altar of Freedom,* ed. Adams, 41; JAA to Edwin Stanton, September 26, 1863, Department of the South, Letters Received, Record Group 393, NA; LHD to Frederick and Anna Douglass, July 20, 1863, Douglass Papers, LC; Charles Russell Lowell to Anna Lowell, July 26, 1863, in *Letters of Lowell,* ed. Emerson, 284–285; Amherst *Farmer's Cabinet,* July 30, 1863; *Journals of Grimké,* ed. Stevenson, 494, 497.

30. Ogden Haggerty to Charles Haggerty, July 24, 1863, and Ogden Haggerty to JAA, July 29, 1863, Shaw Telegrams, NYHS; JAA to Mrs. Ogden Haggerty, July 30, 1863, ibid.; *WAA,* July 26, 1863; Casualty Sheet, RGS, Regimental Descriptive Book, 1863, 54th Massachusetts Infantry, NA.

31. Worcester *Massachusetts Spy,* July 29, 1863; *Boston Transcript,* reprinted in *Liberator,* July 31, 1863; *Liberator,* August 7, 1863; Report, Quincy Adams Gillmore, February 26, 1864, Department of the South, Record Group 393, NA; NPH, *The Negro as a Soldier,* 16.

32. JHG to *New Bedford Mercury,* July 24, 1863, in *On the Altar of Freedom,* ed. Adams, 42; *New Orleans Tribune,* November 5, 1865.

33. *Liberator,* October 9, 1863.

34. *WAA,* August 1, 1863, February 6, 1864; Report, ENH, November 7, 1863, *OR,* Series II, Vol. 28, 362; *Liberator,* July 31, 1863, August 28, 1863.

35. Wise, *Gate of Hell,* 232–233; Abraham Palmer, *The History of the Forty-Eighth Regiment, New York State Volunteers* (Brooklyn, 1885), 17.

36. *WAA,* August 1, 1863; *Washington* (Pennsylvania) *Reporter,* August 19, 1863; Glatthaar, *Forged in Battle,* 140; *New Haven Palladium,* July 27, 1863.

37. Quarles, *The Negro in the Civil War,* 16–17; Report, R. S. Ripley, July 22, 1863, *OR,* Series I, Vol. 28, 373.

38. *Liberator,* August 7, 1863; Westwood, *Black Troops,* 92; *Liberator,* August 7, 1863.

39. Ball, *Slaves in the Family,* 338–339; William Scott to Margaret Scott, July 24, 1863, Margaret Scott Collection, NYHS; Iredell Jones to father, July 20, 1863, in *Southern Historical Society Papers,* ed. Jones, 12:37; Burton, *Siege of Charleston,* 167.

40. *Liberator,* July 31, 1863; *Manchester Daily Mirror,* July 27, 1863; Paul Escott, *Lincoln's Dilemma: Blair, Sumner, and the Republican Struggle over Racism and Equality in the Civil War Era* (Charlottesville: University of Virginia Press, 2014), 158; *Boston Transcript,* reprinted in *Liberator,* August 7, 1863; Clinton, *Tubman,* 178.

41. *Washington* (Pennsylvania) *Reporter,* August 19, 1863.

42. New York *Herald,* reprinted in *WAA,* August 1, 1863; *Cleveland Gazette,* March 19, 1892; Escott, *Lincoln's Dilemma,* 158; Masur, *Lincoln's Hundred Days,* 227.

43. *Liberator,* July 31, 1863; *Boston Daily Advertiser,* August 21, 1863.

44. Charles Russell Lowell to John Forbes, August 4, 1863, in *Letters of Lowell,* ed. Emerson, 293–294; Charles Russell Lowell to Henry Higginson, September 14, 1863, ibid., 304; CFA Jr. to Charles Francis Adams, July 22, 1863, in *Adams Letters,* ed. Ford, 2:52–53.

45. Manning, *What This Cruel War,* 122.

46. *Liberator,* September 4, 1863; Ulysses Grant to Abraham Lincoln, August 23, 1863, Lincoln Papers, LC.

47. Foner, *Fiery Trial,* 251; *Liberator,* August 21, 1863; Cornish, *Sable Arm,* 156; Martin Delany to Edwin Stanton, December 15, 1863, in *Freedom: Series II,* ed. Berlin et al., 101.

48. Blight, *Douglass's Civil War,* 160; Amherst *Farmer's Cabinet,* February 25, 1864; *Liberator,* July 1, 1864.

49. Frederick Douglass, *Life and Times* (New York: Scribner's, 1962), 342; Trudeau, *Men of War,* 87.

CHAPTER SIX

1. Alexia Helsley, *Beaufort* (Charleston, SC: History Press, 2005), 112; J. M. Woodward, Surgeon General's Office, June 14, 1881, Peter Vogelsang File, Pension Office, NA; *Journals of Grimké,* ed. Stevenson, 495. No. 6 General Hospital still stands and is now numbered 411 Craven Street.

2. Peter Vogelsang to *WAA,* August 22, 1863.

3. S. J. Plympton to H. Gordon, September 8, 1863, Department of the South, Letters Sent, Record Group 393, NA; Helsley, *Beaufort,* 112; *A Woman Doctor's Civil War: Esther Hill Hawks' Diary,* ed. Gerald Schwartz (Columbia: University of South Carolina Press, 1984), 50; Peter Vogelsang to *WAA,* August 22, 1863.

4. *Esther Hill Hawks' Diary,* ed. Schwartz, 50; *Liberator,* August 7, 1863; LHD to Amelia Loguen, August 15, 1863, Evans Collection, Savannah; Larson, *Bound for the Promised Land,* 221.

5. *Esther Hill Hawks' Diary,* ed. Schwartz, 51; *Liberator,* July 31, 1863, August 7, 1863.

6. William Carney to State of Massachusetts, December 6, 1864, William Carney File, Pension Office, NA; *Journals of Grimké,* ed. Stevenson, 495–497.

7. William Carney to State of Massachusetts, December 6, 1864, William Carney File, Pension Office, NA; William Carney, Regimental Descriptive Book, Company Muster Roll, September 1863 to June 1864, 54th Massachusetts Infantry, NA; Certificate of Disability for Discharge, July 21, 1864, ibid.; J. H. Hoadley to ENH, December 6, 1863, Massachusetts 54th Papers, NA; Horatio Bates to JAA, April 25, 1863, ibid.

8. *Esther Hill Hawks' Diary,* ed. Schwartz, 54; Worcester *Massachusetts Spy,* August 5, 1863. Hawks provided only the rank and surname of the man who spoke these words, but of the five men named Morgan in the regiment, only John Morgan held the rank of sergeant.

9. Asa Tyler, 1860 Federal Census, Onondaga County, New York State, Roll M653–829, Page 535, Image 326, NA; *Esther Hill Hawks' Diary,* ed. Schwartz, 50–51. Reason, the only black person on the Tyler farm, lived with Asa, age seventy-eight, Asa's wife, and their three grandchildren.

10. *Esther Hill Hawks' Diary,* ed. Schwartz, 52–53. Hawks mistakenly believed that Cyrus was killed at Wagner, but Emilio, *Fifty-Fourth,* 385, lists him as dying on July 16 on James Island. On William's fate, see U.S. Register of Colored Troop Deaths During the Civil War, 122–123, Record Group 94, NA. For Henry Krunkleton, see Federal Census of 1860 and 1870 (where his surname is spelled Crunkleton), Franklin, Pennsylvania, Roll M653–1112, Page 626, Image 91, and Allegheny Ward 2, Allegheny, Pennsylvania, Roll M593–1290, Page 125B, Image 252.

11. Emilio, *Fifty-Fourth,* 83, 329; Glatthaar, *Forged in Battle,* 164.

12. Emilio, *Fifty-Fourth,* 333; Maher, *Broken Fortunes,* 48–49.

13. *Journals of Grimké,* ed. Stevenson, 498; William Davis to Commanding Officer, August 6, 1863, Massachusetts 54th Papers, NA.

14. ENH, Regimental Descriptive Book, August 1, 1863, 54th Massachusetts Infantry, NA; Morris Hallowell to General Thomas, August 1, 1863, Massachusetts 54th Papers, NA; ENH, Medical Certificate, August 1, 1863, ibid.

15. Amelia Holmes to Emily Hallowell, August 5, 1863, Hallowell Family Papers, Haverford College; *Journals of Grimké,* ed. Stevenson, 503.

16. ENH, Regimental Descriptive Book, August 1, 1863, 54th Massachusetts Infantry, NA; Morris Hallowell to General Thomas, August 1, 1863, Massachusetts 54th Papers, NA; ENH, Medical Certificate, August 1, 1863, ibid.; ENH to John Forbes, August 6, 1863, Hallowell Family Papers, Haverford College.

17. LHD to Amelia Loguen, August 15, 1863, and August 27, 1862, Evans Collection, Savannah.

18. Charles Douglass to Frederick Douglass, September 18, 1863, Douglass Papers, LC; James McCune Smith, Certification, October 6, 1863, in Massachusetts 54th Papers, NA; *WAA,* September 26, 1863. On the residents of the Brooks House, see *WAA,* March 7, 1863. "New arrivals" included abolitionist "William Wells Brown of Massachusetts, Leo Lloyd of Liberia, [and] the Reverend W. T. Catto of New Haven."

19. Frederick Douglass to Gerrit Smith, October 10, 1863, Gerrit Smith Papers, Syracuse University Library. Diedrich, *Love Across Color Lines,* 254, in an unconvincing attempt to invent an affair between Frederick Douglass and German journalist Ottilie Assing, imagines a scenario in which Anna remained in Rochester, while "it was Ottilie who often accompanied Douglass on his daily trips to the army hospital [*sic*]; to her he returned in the evenings," despite the fact that Frederick surely took a room at the Brooks House. Diedrich's creative fiction includes this passage: "For Assing, these weeks of care and fear were an invaluable chance to prove to Douglass that her love was not limited to him alone, was not purely self-centered, but extended to his family. For three precious weeks of extreme emotional challenge, in which his son's life was at stake, Assing could slip into the role of mother and nurse, adviser and listener, friend and lover." Astonishingly, Diedrich's sole citation for this scenario is the above letter to Gerrit Smith, which never once mentions Assing.

20. *WAA,* November 13, 1863, December 5, 1863; LHD, Certificate of Disability for Discharge, March 2, 1864, Lewis Douglass, Regimental Descriptive Book, 54th Massachusetts Infantry, NA. The surgeon's report found "Scrotal Abscess gangrenous in its character. There is now a fistulous opening in Perineum with discharge of pus."

21. Nathan Sprague, General Affidavit, June 28, 1905, Sprague File, Pension Office, NA; Rosetta Douglass-Sprague, General Affidavit, February 20, 1905, ibid.;

LHD, General Affidavit, September 13, 1906, ibid.; Charles Douglass, General Affidavit, September 17, 1906, ibid.; Charles Douglass to Frederick Douglass, December 20, 1863, Douglass Papers, LC; Julie Griffiths Crofts to Frederick Douglass, February 19, 1864, ibid.

22. LHD to Amelia Loguen, January 31, 1864, Evans Collection, Savannah.

23. LHD to Amelia Loguen, May 20, 1864, September 28, 1864, and March 26, 1865, Evans Collection, Savannah.

24. Foote, *One Great Remedy,* 90–91.

25. Ibid., 130; Joan Waugh, "'It Was a Sacrifice We Owed': The Shaw Family," in *Hope and Glory,* ed. Blatt et al., 68–70.

26. Carol Bundy, *The Nature of Sacrifice: A Biography of Charles Russell Lowell Jr.* (New York: Farrar, Straus & Giroux, 2005), 345, 456–472; *Letters of Lowell,* ed. Emerson, 36–37, 68; Waugh, *Unsentimental Reformer,* 83; Alec Johnson to Burt Wilder, July 25, 1913, Burt Wilder Papers, Cornell University.

27. *Boston Herald,* November 27, 1904; *Cleveland Gazette,* March 23, 1907.

28. Westwood, *Black Troops,* 11, 87.

29. Charles Sumner to Abraham Lincoln, May 20, 1863, Lincoln Papers, LC; *Richmond Whig,* April 3, 1863; Massachusetts Citizens to JAA, June 18, 1863, Lincoln Papers, LC; JAA to Abraham Lincoln, June 18, 1863, ibid.; *WAA,* July 4, 1863; *Liberator,* May 22, 1863.

30. Johnson Hagood to William Nance, July 16, 1863, *OR,* Series II, Vol. 6, 123; Forwarded, William Nance, July 16, 1863, ibid., 124; P. G. T. Beauregard to Samuel Cooper, July 17, 1863, ibid., 125; P. G. T. Beauregard to Samuel Cooper, July 21, 1863, ibid., 134.

31. Westwood, *Black Troops,* 89; Emilio, *Fifty-Fourth,* 405; Ira Berlin, *Slaves Without Masters: The Free Negro in the Antebellum South* (New York: Pantheon, 1974), 137.

32. ENH to E. W. Smith, December 13, 1863, *OR,* Series II, Vol. 6, 775; Emilio, *Fifty-Fourth,* 397–401.

33. Milledge Bonham to P. G. T. Beauregard, July 22, 1863, *OR,* Series II, Vol. 6, 139–140; James Seddon to P. G. T. Beauregard, July 22, 1863, ibid., 139.

34. P. G. T. Beauregard to James Seddon, July 23, 1863, *OR,* Series II, Vol. 6, 145; P. G. T. Beauregard to Milledge Bonham, July 29, 1863, ibid., 159; Emilio, *Fifty-Fourth,* 403; JAA to Abraham Lincoln, July 27, 1863, Lincoln Papers, LC; Francis Shaw to Abraham Lincoln, July 31, 1863, ibid.

35. Hannah Johnson to Abraham Lincoln, July 31, 1863, in *Freedom: Series II,* ed. Berlin et al., 582–583. Johnson never identified her son, and no soldier with that surname listed his residence as Buffalo, which was the home of sixteen soldiers. Three Johnsons were from New York State. Alexander Johnson lived in Elmira, B. S. Johnson was from Mount Morris, and James Johnson was from Owego,

near Binghamton. All three survived Wagner. In 1860 a fifty-year-old black woman named Hannah Johnson was working as a servant in Buffalo's Hotel Continental. See Federal Census of 1860, Niagara, New York State, Roll M653–822, Page 143, Image 152.

36. Abraham Lincoln, General Order No. 252, *OR,* Series II, Vol. 6, 163.

37. Roger Pickenpaugh, *Captives in Blue: The Civil War Prisoners of the Confederacy* (Tuscaloosa: University of Alabama Press, 2013), 192; Milledge Bonham to James Seddon, August 8, 1863, in *OR,* Series II, Vol. 6, 190; James Seddon to Milledge Bonham, August 9, August 14, 1863, ibid., 191, 202; James Seddon to Jefferson Davis, August 23, 1863, ibid., 194; Jefferson Davis to James Seddon, August 25, 1863, ibid., 194.

38. Raleigh *Daily Progress,* July 24, 1863; *Richmond Dispatch,* August 5, 1864; Westwood, *Black Troops,* 92; Wise, *Gate of Hell,* 126.

39. Westwood, *Black Troops,* 96; Henry Worthington, 1860 Federal Census, Defiance, Ohio, Roll M653–947, Page 306, Image 63, NA. Archibald Worthington appeared in the 1850 census, at which time he was thirty and Henry was three, but not in the 1840 census. Kirk, Counsel, and Harrison do not appear in the federal census for any year.

40. *Liberator,* May 4, 1865; Emilio, *Fifty-Fourth,* 405–406.

41. *Liberator,* May 4, 1865; *The Private Journal of Henry William Ravenel,* ed. Arney Childs (Columbia: University of South Carolina Press, 1947), 182; *Savannah Republican,* September 25, 1863; Wise, *Gates of Hell,* 126.

42. Gideon Welles to Edwin Stanton, August 3, 1863, in *OR,* Series II, Vol. 6, 171; Ethan Hitchcock to Edwin Stanton, August 3, 1863, ibid.; *Liberator,* March 11, 1864; Charles Russell Lowell to Aunt Ellen, September 16, 1863, in *Letters of Lowell,* ed. Emerson, 305.

43. McFeely, *Douglass,* 228.

44. *Douglass's Monthly,* August 1863; Douglass, *Life and Times,* 347; Foner, *Fiery Trial,* 255.

45. *Liberator,* November 27, 1863; Westwood, *Black Troops,* 100.

46. Amelia Nelson, Claim, Daniel Nelson File, Pension Office, NA; Sarah Vorhies, Claim, Isaac Vorhies File, ibid.

47. Sarah Dorsey, Claim, Isaac Dorsey Jr. File, Pension Office, NA; John Mackey, Claim, Wesley Ryal File, ibid.

48. Jarvis interview, in Armstrong and Ludlow, *Hampton and Its Students,* 111–113.

49. Trudeau, *Men of War,* 275.

50. Jesse Swails, Consolidated Lists of Civil War Draft Registrations, 1863–1865, NM-65, Entry 172, Records of the Provost Marshal General's Bureau, Record Group 110, NA; *Boyd's Elmira and Corning City Directory* (Elmira, 1874),

236; Stephen Swails, Quartermaster's Office, September 22, 1863, Regimental Descriptive Book, 1863, 54th Massachusetts Infantry, NA; Stephen Swails, Company Muster Roll, November-December 1863, ibid.; *Liberator,* April 8, 1864; *WAA,* May 7, 1864. Minnie Swails, 1880 Federal Census, Elmira, New York, Roll 817, Page 446A, Image 0471, lists Minnie as being seventeen, placing her birth sometime in 1863.

51. Nina Silber, *Daughters of the Union: Northern Women Fight the Civil War* (Cambridge, MA: Harvard University Press, 2005), 64; David Demus, 1870 Federal Census, Montgomery, Franklin, Pennsylvania, Roll M593–1346, Page 418A, Image 196; Edwin Jourdain, Affidavit, William Carney File, Pension Office, NA; Maria Margaret Vogelsang, April 15, 1872, Register of Signatures of Depositors in the Freedman's Savings and Trust Company, NA; William Dupree, Affidavit, James Trotter File, Pension Office, NA; CFA, *Autobiography,* 164.

52. Faust, *This Republic of Suffering,* 103–104; Lydia Maria Child to Sarah Shaw, June 9, 1862, and May 1, 1863, Shaw Family Papers, NYHS; LHD to Amelia Loguen, April 8, 1863, Douglass Papers, LC.

53. *WAA,* April 30, 1864; *Liberator,* May 6, 1864.

54. Judith Giesberg, *Army at Home: Women and the Civil War on the Northern Home Front* (Chapel Hill: University of North Carolina Press, 2009), 185; *Liberator,* April 8, 1864; *WAA,* August 27, 1864; Trudeau, *Men of War,* 253; ENH to JAA, November 3, 1863, Regimental and Company Books, Massachusetts 54th, NA; Morris Hallowell to JAA, November 4, 1863, Andrew Papers, MHS; Cornish, *Sable Arm,* 188.

55. Mulderink, *New Bedford's Civil War,* 113–114; *WAA,* August 6, 1864, August 13, 1864; Grover, *Fugitive's Gibraltar,* 278.

56. Fox, *Fifty-Fifth,* 28; *WAA,* April 2, 1864.

CHAPTER SEVEN

1. Bowen, *Massachusetts in the War,* 684; Fox, *Fifty-Fifth,* 108; Burt Wilder to W.N., May 24, 1863, Burt Wilder Papers, Cornell University; Joshua Dunbar, Nicholas Said, John Smith, and Henry Jarvis, Regimental Descriptive Book, June 1863, 55th Massachusetts Infantry, NA; Jarvis interview, in Armstrong and Ludlow, *Hampton and Its Students,* 109–110.

2. Langston, *From the Plantation,* 204; *WAA,* June 13, 1863, July 6, 1863; Mulderink, *New Bedford's Civil War,* 112–113; *Liberator,* August 7, 1863.

3. NPH, Regimental Descriptive Book, 1863, 55th Massachusetts Infantry, NA; Fox, *Fifty-Fifth,* 98–100; *Liberator,* July 3, 1863; *WAA,* June 20, 1863.

4. Maher, *Broken Fortunes,* 60; Donald Yacovone, "The Fifty-Fourth Massachusetts Regiment, the Pay Crisis, and the 'Lincoln Despotism,'" in *Hope and Glory,* ed. Blatt et al., 42; Fox, *Guardian of Boston,* 5.

5. NPH, *The Negro as a Soldier,* 7–8; Fox, *Fifty-Fifth,* 110–112.

6. Samuel Flora, John Brown, Donald Cardoron, and Joseph Crooks, Regimental Descriptive Book, 1863, 55th Massachusetts Infantry, NA.

7. Fox, *Fifty-Fifth,* 110; Alonso, *Growing Up Abolitionist,* 164; William Jackson to Edward Pierce, July 18, 1863, Massachusetts 55th Papers, NA.

8. Fox, *Fifty-Fifth,* 2.

9. *Boston Evening Transcript,* July 15, 1863; *Boston Recorder,* July 17, *Washington* (Pennsylvania) *Reporter,* December 30, 1863; *WAA,* November 12, 1864; Nicholas Said, Regimental Descriptive Book, 1863 Massachusetts 55th Infantry, NA.

10. John Smith, Consolidated Lists of Civil War Draft Registration Records, Record Group 110, NA; Edward Wild to Headquarters, October 15, 1863, John M. Smith, Regimental Descriptive Book, 1863, 55th Massachusetts Infantry, NA; John M. Smith File, Pension Office, NA.

11. Edward Wild to Headquarters, October 15, 1863, John M. Smith, Regimental Descriptive Book, 1863, 55th Massachusetts Infantry, NA; James Thurber to Alfred Hartwell, October 15, 1863, ibid.

12. Charles R. Douglass, Regimental Descriptive Book, 1863, 54th Massachusetts Infantry, NA; Henry Littlefield to Edward Smith, September 13, 1863, Massachusetts 54th Papers, NA.

13. Charles Douglass to Frederick Douglass, September 8, 1863, and September 18, 1863, Douglass Papers, LC; Frederick Douglass to Gerrit Smith, June 19, 1863, Smith Papers, Syracuse University.

14. Charles Douglass to Frederick Douglass, July 6, 1863, Douglass Papers, LC.

15. Redkey, "Profile of the Fifty-Fourth," 22–23; Unknown to Adjutant General Schoular, August 19, 1863, Shaw Telegrams, NYHS; Warren Freeman, William Freeman, Charles Bateman, William Henry Morris, Evan Carrington, Charles Cassell, Jerome Cross, Samuel Flora, Joseph Crooks, Luke Foutz, and James Hamilton, Regimental Descriptive Book, 1863, 54th Massachusetts Infantry, NA.

16. *WAA,* June 12, 1863.

17. Fox, *Fifty-Fifth,* 7; Cornish, *Sable Arm,* 253.

18. Fox, *Fifty-Fifth,* 7; Alonso, *Growing Up Abolitionist,* 164–165; William Lloyd Garrison to GTG, August 6, 1863, in *Letters,* ed. Merrill, 5:167; GTG to Helen Garrison, August 3, 1863, Garrison Family Papers, Smith College; *WAA,* August 22, 1863.

19. *WAA,* August 22, 1863; Charles Fox to Feroline Fox, July 23, 1863, Fox Papers, MHS; GTG to Helen Garrison, August 3, 1863, Garrison Family Papers, Smith College.

20. Charles Fox to Feroline Fox, July 29, 1863, and July 30, 1863, Fox Papers, MHS; Fox, *Fifty-Fifth,* 9–10. On New Bern during the war years, see Catherine

Bishir, *Crafting Lives: African American Artisans in New Bern, North Carolina* (Chapel Hill: University of North Carolina Press, 2013), chap. 4.

21. Charles Fox to Feroline Fox, July 30, 1863, July 31, 1863, August 10, 1863, and August 2, 1863, Fox Papers, MHS; *WAA,* January 30, 1864; JHG to *New Bedford Mercury,* August 9, 1863, in *On the Altar of Freedom,* ed. Adams, 47.

22. Report, Bernard Beust, August 25, 1863, Department of the South, Letters Received, Record Group 393, NA; NPH, Regimental Descriptive Book, 1863, 55th Massachusetts Infantry, NA; GTG to William Garrison, December 10, 1863, Garrison Family Papers, Smith College; *Boston Daily Advertiser,* August 21, 1863.

23. Charles Fox to Feroline Fox, August 16, 1863, and August 19, 1863, Fox Papers, MHS; *WAA,* August 22, 1863.

24. GTG to Wendell Garrison, August 12, 1864, Garrison Family Papers, Smith College; GTG to William Garrison, February 10, 1864, ibid.

25. JHG to *New Bedford Mercury,* October 17, 1863, in *On the Altar of Freedom,* ed. Adams, 72; JHG, Regimental Descriptive Book, 1863, 54th Massachusetts Infantry, NA; Peter Vogelsang, Field and Staff Muster Rolls, 54th Massachusetts Infantry, NA; General Order No. 66, ENH, December 1, 1863, ibid.; Emilio, *Fifty-Fourth,* 135.

26. *Liberator,* August 21, 1863, October 2, 1863; Charles Fox to Feroline Fox, September 3, 1863, and September 26, 1863, Fox Papers, MHS; JHG to *New Bedford Mercury,* August 30, 1863, in *On the Altar of Freedom,* ed. Adams, 54.

27. J. A. Burns to M. S. Littlefield, September 5, 1863, Regimental and Company Books, 54th Massachusetts Infantry, Vol. 1, NA; Henry Hooper to J. A. Burns, October 23, 1863, ibid.

28. Charles Fox to Feroline Fox, January 26, 1864, Fox Papers, MHS; GTG to William Garrison, January 29, 1864, Garrison Family Papers, Smith College.

29. William Scott to Margaret Scott, July 30, 1863, and August 11, 1863, Margaret Scott Collection, NYHS; Cornish, *Sable Arm,* 245; JHG to *New Bedford Mercury,* July 24, 1863, in *On the Altar of Freedom,* ed. Adams, 40.

30. Burton, *Siege of Charleston,* 172; Charles Fox to Feroline Fox, September 8, 1863, Fox Papers, MHS; JHG to *New Bedford Mercury,* August 23, 1863, in *On the Altar of Freedom,* ed, Adams, 51–52.

31. Charles Fox to Feroline Fox, August 12, 1863, and August 20, 1863, Fox Papers, MHS; Washington *National Intelligencer,* August 26, 1863; Amherst *Farmer's Cabinet,* August 27, 1863; GTG to Helen Garrison, August 7, 1863, Garrison Family Papers, Smith College.

32. *Liberator,* September 18, 1863, July 15, 1864; Charles Hill to unknown, August 29, 1863, Thomas William Faulds Collection, NYHS.

33. Stevens, *1863,* 316; Fraser, *Charleston,* 264–265; Earl Hess, *Field Armies and Fortifications in the Civil War: The Eastern Campaigns, 1861–1864* (Chapel Hill:

University of North Carolina Press, 2005), 270; Fox, *Fifty-Fifth*, 11; Gustavas Fox to Virginia Fox, August 21, 1863, Gustavas Fox Collection, NYHS; *Journal of Ravenel*, ed. Childs, 181.

34. Wise, *Gate of Hell*, 140; Report, John McConihe, August 18, 1863, *OR*, Series I, Vol. 28, 366; Emilio, *Fifty-Fourth*, 110.

35. Emilio, *Fifty-Fourth*, 111; Fox, *Fifty-Fifth*, 11–12; Alonso, *Growing Up Abolitionist*, 166; *Liberator*, September 18, 1863.

36. NPH, *The Negro as a Soldier*, 19–20; Amherst *Farmer's Cabinet*, August 6, 1863, August 20, 1863.

37. *Liberator*, September 18, 1863; *WAA*, November 14, 1863; Mulderink, *New Bedford's Civil War*, 112.

38. GTG to William Garrison, January 29, 1864, Garrison Family Papers, Smith Library; *Liberator*, September 18, 1863.

39. Wise, *Gate of Hell*, 202; *Liberator*, September 18, 1863; *Richmond Enquirer*, September 8, 1863; *Richmond Whig*, September 8, 1863.

40. Maher, *Broken Fortunes*, 66; Wise, *Gate of Hell*, 203; *WAA*, October 10, 1863; Report, James Ashcroft, September 13, 1863, Department of the South, Letters Received, Record Group 393, NA; *Liberator*, September 18, 1863.

41. Stevens, *1863*, 317; *Liberator*, September 18, 1863; *Augusta Chronicle*, September 10, 1863; *Charleston Mercury*, September 10, 1863.

42. JHG to *New Bedford Mercury*, September 9, 1863, and October 24, 1863, in *On the Altar of Freedom*, ed. Adams, 56, 71; *Richmond Dispatch*, September 8, 1863; Charles Fox to Feroline Fox, September 25, 1863, and October 15, 1863, Fox Papers, MHS.

43. Charles Fox to Feroline Fox, September 7, 1863, Fox Papers, MHS; Jesse Frémont to John Greenleaf Whittier, February 14, 1864, in *The Letters of Jesse Benton Frémont*, ed. Pamela Herr (Champaign: University of Illinois Press, 1991), 372; *Liberator*, September 18, 1863, October 2, 1863; JHG to *New Bedford Mercury*, September 9, 1863, in *On the Altar of Freedom*, ed. Adams, 56; *WAA*, January 30, 1864.

44. Request, Parkers Brown, December 17, 1863, Department of the South, Letters Received, Record Group 393, NA; Foote, *One Great Remedy*, 120; Susie King Taylor, *Reminiscences of My Life in Camp* (Boston, 1902), 31.

45. *Liberator*, September 18, 1863; JHG to *New Bedford Mercury*, November 21, 1863, and December 12, 1863, in *On the Altar of Freedom*, ed. Adams, 82, 90.

46. Quincy Adams Gillmore to Alfred Terry, August 2, 1863, Department of the South, Letters Sent, Record Group 393, NA; *Liberator*, September 18, 1863; Report, James Beecher, September 13, 1863, Department of the South, Letters Received, Record Group 393, NA; *WAA*, August 22, 1863.

47. *Liberator*, September 16, 1864; Smith, *Lincoln and the U.S. Colored Troops*, 56.

48. Report, James Beecher, September 13, 1863, Department of the South, Letters Received, Record Group 393, NA; S. L. McHenry to Edward Wild, August 19, 1863, Massachusetts 54th Papers, NA; Special Order No. 28, Edward Wild, September 1, 1863, ibid.

49. JHG to Abraham Lincoln, September 28, 1863, in *On the Altar of Freedom,* ed. Adams, 118–120.

50. *Houston Tri-Weekly Telegraph,* November 25, 1863; *Philadelphia Inquirer,* October 1, 1863; Washington *Daily National Republican,* October 2, 1863; *Lancaster Daily Inquirer,* October 6, 1863; General Order No. 105, Quincy Adams Gillmore, November 25, 1863, NPH Papers, MHS; *WAA,* January 23, 1864.

51. *WAA,* August 22, 1863; JHG to *New Bedford Mercury,* August 9, 1863, in *On the Altar of Freedom,* ed. Adams, 48–49.

52. Cornish, *Sable Arm,* 187; H. N. Sheldon to Burt Wilder, February 23, 1913, Burt Wilder Papers, Cornell University; Pearson, *Andrew,* 2:100–102; *Liberator,* November 20, 1863; *WAA,* December 12, 1863.

53. Pearson, *Andrew,* 2:103–104; Yacovone, "The Pay Crisis," 41; William Dupree to Burt Wilder, February 23, 1910, Burt Wilder Papers, Cornell University; Theodore Tilton to *Boston Journal,* December 15, 1863, in *A Grand Army of Black Men: Letters from African American Soldiers in the Union Army,* ed. Edwin Redkey (Cambridge: Cambridge University Press, 1992), 235; ENH to NPH, November 23, 1863, NPH Papers, MHS.

54. *Liberator,* April 8, 1864; *WAA,* January 30, 1864; NPH, *The Negro as a Soldier,* 17; GTG to William Garrison, December 10, 1863, Garrison Family Papers, Smith College.

55. *Liberator,* January 29, 1864; *WAA,* January 12, 1864; Philadelphia *Christian Recorder,* January 2, 1864, in *Grand Army of Black Men,* ed. Redkey, 46.

56. JHG to *New Bedford Mercury,* November 21, 1863, in *On the Altar of Freedom,* ed. Adams, 82–83.

57. JAA to James Congdon, December 20, 1863, in *On the Altar of Freedom,* ed. Adams, 122–123; ENH to JAA, November 23, 1863, Hallowell Family Papers, Haverford College.

58. Fox, *Fifty-Fifth,* 17; GTG to William Garrison, January 21, 1864, Garrison Family Papers, Smith College; Maher, *Broken Fortunes,* 64; Charles Fox to Feroline Fox, August 14, 1863, Fox Papers, MHS.

59. Trefousse, *Stevens,* 140; Pearson, *Andrew,* 2: 104; *Congressional Globe,* 38th Cong., 1st Sess., 466, 481; *Liberator,* February 12, 1864.

60. Stephen Swails to E. D. Townsend, January 14, 1864, in *Freedom: Series II,* ed. Berlin et al., 377.

61. Special Order No. 408, E. D. Townsend, September 11, 1863, Massachusetts 54th Papers, NA; NPH to E. D. Townsend, October 25, 1863, ibid.; NPH,

Medical Certificate, October 9, 1863, ibid.; NPH, Regimental Descriptive Book, 1863, 55th Massachusetts Infantry, NA.

62. JAA to NPH, November 9, 1863, NPH Papers, MHS; *Liberator,* November 27, 1863; Fox, *Fifty-Fifth,* 14; GTG to William Garrison, June 14, 1864, and to Helen Garrison, June 7, 1864, Garrison Family Papers, Smith College; *Practicing Medicine in a Black Regiment: The Civil War Diary of Burt G. Wilder,* ed. Richard Reid (Amherst: University of Massachusetts Press, 2010), 97.

63. Fox, *Fifty-Fifth,* 20; *Civil War Diary of Wilder,* ed. Reid, 99; Emilio, *Fifty-Fourth,* 143; ENH to NPH, December 10, 1863, Hallowell Family Papers, Haverford College; John Posey to Mathias Embry, December 27, 1863, in *Voices of the 55th: Letters from the Massachusetts 55th Volunteers,* ed. Noah Trudeau (Dayton: Morningside, 1996), 55.

64. Manning, *What This Cruel War,* 147; Stevens, *1863,* 412; Request, A. G. Bennett, December 18, 1863, Department of the South, Letters Received, Record Group 393, NA; JHG to *New Bedford Mercury,* January 2, 1864, in *On the Altar of Freedom,* ed. Adams, 96–97.

65. JHG to *New Bedford Mercury,* January 2, 1864, in *On the Altar of Freedom,* ed., Adams, 96–97; Emilio, *Fifty-Fourth,* 148.

CHAPTER EIGHT

1. Report, ENH, February 3, 1864, Department of the South, Letters Received, Record Group 393, NA; ENH to JAA, February 5, 1864, Massachusetts 54th Papers, NA; Emilio, *Fifty-Fourth,* 150; Quincy Adams Gillmore to Henry Halleck, March 7, 1864, *OR,* Series I, Vol. 5, 276.

2. Emilio, *Fifty-Fourth,* 151–152; C. M. Duren, "The Occupation of Jacksonville, February 1864, and the Battle of Olustee: Letters of C. M. Duren," *Florida Historical Quarterly* 32 (1954): 262; JHG to *New Bedford Mercury,* February 28, 1864, in *On the Altar of Freedom,* ed. Adams, 112–113.

3. JHG to *New Bedford Mercury,* February 28, 1864, in *On the Altar of Freedom,* ed. Adams, 113; *Norwich Aurora,* February 26, 1864.

4. William Burger to ENH, February 11, 1864, Department of the South, Letters Sent, Record Group 393, NA; Quincy Adams Gillmore to ENH, February 9, 1864, ibid.; JHG to *New Bedford Mercury,* February 28, 1864, in *On the Altar of Freedom,* ed. Adams, 113; *WAA,* March 5, 1864.

5. Fox, *Fifty-Fifth,* 22; William Burger to James Montgomery, February 11, 1864, *OR,* Series I, Vol. 35, 474; Duren, "Occupation of Jacksonville," 264; *WAA,* April 9, 1864; Trudeau, *Men of War,* 135.

6. GTG to William Garrison, February 10, 1864, Garrison Family Papers, Smith College.

7. Richard White to Philadelphia *Christian Recorder,* April 2, 1864, in *Voices,* ed.

Trudeau, 73; *WAA,* April 9, 1864; Charles Fox to Feroline Fox, February 16, 1864, Fox Papers, MHS.

8. John M. Smith File, Pension Office, NA; John Smith, Regimental Descriptive Book, 1863, 55th Massachusetts Infantry, NA; Edward Wild to Headquarters, October 15, 1863, ibid.; James Thurber to Alfred Hartwell, October 15, 1863, ibid.; Charles Fox to Feroline Fox, February 18, 1864, Fox Papers, MHS.

9. Fox, *Fifty-Fifth,* 116, 118; John Wesley Cork, Regimental Descriptive Book, 1863, 55th Massachusetts Infantry, NA; Spencer Lloyd, Regimental Descriptive Book, 1863, ibid.

10. Charges and Specifications, John Wesley Cork, Spencer Lloyd, and John M. Smith, Regimental Descriptive Book, 1864, 55th Massachusetts Infantry, NA. John M. Smith File, Pension Office, NA, identified Hammond as "a widow woman."

11. Statement of J. D. Hodges, February 18, 1864, John Wesley Cork, Regimental Descriptive Book, 1864, 55th Massachusetts Infantry, NA.

12. Charges and Specifications, John Wesley Cork, Spencer Lloyd, and John M. Smith, Regimental Descriptive Book, 1864, 55th Massachusetts Infantry, NA; Charles Fox to Feroline Fox, February 18, 1864, Fox Papers, MHS.

13. *Boston Post,* March 7, 1864; Charles Fox to Feroline Fox, February 18, 1864, Fox Papers, MHS.

14. Charles Fox to Feroline Fox, February 19, 1864, Fox Papers, MHS; *Boston Herald,* March 4, 1864; *Boston Traveler,* March 2, 1864; *Boston Post,* March 3, 1864, March 7, 1864; John Smith, Casualty Sheet, February 18, 1864, in Massachusetts 55th Papers, NA; Spencer Lloyd, Casualty Sheet, February 18, 1864, ibid.

15. *New York Herald,* March 2, 1864; *Boston Post,* March 7, 1864; Portland *Daily Eastern Argus,* March 4, 1864; *WAA,* March 26, 1864; *Milwaukee Sentinel,* March 14, 1864; *Esther Hill Hawks' Diary,* ed. Schwartz, 61.

16. Glatthaar, *Forged in Battle,* 118; Diane Miller Sommerville, *Rape and Race in the Nineteenth-Century South* (Chapel Hill: University of North Carolina Press, 2004), 148; Faye E. Dudden, *Fighting Chance: The Struggle over Woman Suffrage and Black Suffrage in Reconstruction America* (New York: Oxford University Press, 2011), 3.

17. Quincy Adams Gillmore to Henry Halleck, March 7, 1864, *OR,* Series I, Vol. 5, 276; Arthur Bergeron, "The Battle of Olustee," in *Black Soldiers in Blue,* ed. Smith, 137.

18. Emilio, *Fifty-Fourth,* 157; Levine, *House of Dixie,* 170.

19. Report, ENH, March 1, 1864, *OR,* Series I, Vol. 35, 315; New York *Evening Post,* February 29, 1864; Philadelphia *Christian Recorder,* April 9, 1864; Joseph Wilson, *The Black Phalanx* (Hartford, 1890), 266.

20. *Hartford Daily Courant,* March 2, 1864; Report, ENH, March 1, 1864, *OR,* Series I, Vol. 35, 315; Emilio, *Fifty-Fourth,* 157.

21. Report, ENH, March 1, 1864, *OR,* Series I, Vol. 35, 315; Emilio, *Fifty-Fourth,* 163; *Liberator,* March 4, 1864; Amherst *Farmer's Cabinet,* March 10, 1864. The Baltimore *Sun,* February 29, 1864, erroneously reported that Seymour's troops faced 15,000 Confederates.

22. Report, ENH, March 1, 1864, *OR,* Series I, Vol. 35, 315; Amherst *Farmer's Cabinet,* March 10, 1864; *Liberator,* March 18, 1864; Bergeron, "The Battle of Olustee," 141–142; Robert Broadwater, *The Battle of Olustee, 1864: The Final Union Attempt to Seize Florida* (Jefferson, NC: McFarland, 2006), 121.

23. Broadwater, *Battle of Olustee,* 121–122; Emilio, *Fifty-Fourth,* 165; Trudeau, *Men of War,* 150; Amherst *Farmer's Cabinet,* March 10, 1864.

24. Report, Loomis Langdon, March 25, 1864, *OR,* Series I, Vol. 35, 317; Broadwater, *Battle of Olustee,* 126; Trudeau, *Men of War,* 148; Emilio, *Fifty-Fourth,* 168; Report, ENH, March 1, 1864, *OR,* Series I, Vol. 35, 315; *WAA,* April 2, 1864.

25. Bergeron, "Battle of Olustee," 143; *WAA,* March 26, 1864.

26. Emilio, *Fifty-Fourth,* 169; Stephen Swails File, Pension Office, NA; Stephen Swails, Casualty Sheet, February 20, 1864, Regimental Descriptive Book, 1864, Massachusetts 54th Infantry, NA; Report, ENH, March 1, 1864, *OR,* Series I, Vol. 35, 315.

27. Emilio, *Fifty-Fourth,* 172–173; Amherst *Farmer's Cabinet,* March 10, 1864; Charles Fox to Feroline Fox, February 22, 1864, Fox Papers, MHS; *WAA,* April 2, 1864.

28. Report, ENH, March 1, 1864, *OR,* Series I, Vol. 35, 315; *WAA,* March 26, 1864, May 28, 1864; Maher, *Broken Fortunes,* 68; Duren, "Occupation of Jacksonville," 270; NPH, *The Negro as a Soldier,* 24; *Hartford Daily Courant,* March 2, 1864; *Liberator,* March 4, 1864.

29. Philadelphia *Christian Recorder,* April 9, 1864; *WAA,* March 26, 1864; *Richmond Whig,* February 20, 1864; Smith, *Lincoln and the U.S. Colored Troops,* 79; Trudeau, *Men of War,* 151.

30. Baltimore *Sun,* February 29, 1864; Washington *National Intelligencer,* March 1, 1864; Charleston *Courier,* February 23, 1864; Hartford *Connecticut Courant,* March 5, 1864.

31. Cornish, *Sable Arm,* 268–239; *Liberator,* March 18, 1864; Worcester *National Aegis,* March 19, 1864; Amherst *Farmer's Cabinet,* March 10, 1864; Hartford *Connecticut Courant,* March 4, 1864; *Salem Observer,* March 5, 1864.

32. *WAA,* April 16, 1864.

33. *Esther Hill Hawks' Diary,* ed. Schwartz, 63.

34. Stephen Swails, Casualty Sheet, February 20, 1864, Regimental Descriptive Book, 1864, Massachusetts 54th Infantry, NA; Reports, Quartermaster's Office, March 13, 1864, and April 15, 1864, Regimental Descriptive Book, 1864, Massachusetts 54th Infantry, NA.

35. *WAA,* May 7, 1864, April 23, 1863; Stephen Swails, Company Muster Roll, 1864, Regimental Descriptive Book, 1864, Massachusetts 54th Infantry, NA; Richard Allison to Stewart Taylor, October 1864, ibid.; War Department Memorandum, January 1883, in *Freedom: Series II,* ed. Berlin et al., 582–583.

36. War Department Memorandum, January 1883, in *Freedom: Series II,* ed. Berlin et al., 582–583; Duren, "Occupation of Jacksonville," 282.

37. New Bedford *Republican Standard,* April 28, 1864; *WAA,* April 23, 1864; James Henry Gooding, Casualty Sheet, February 20, 1864, Regimental Descriptive Book, 1864, Massachusetts 54th Infantry, NA.

38. William Marvel, *Andersonville: The Last Depot* (Chapel Hill: University of North Carolina Press, 1994), 41–43.

39. Pickenpaugh, *Captives in Blue,* 126; Williams, *History of Negro Troops,* 305; *Liberator,* December 30, 1864.

40. U.S. Congress, *Trial of Henry Wirz: Letter from the Secretary of War* (Washington, 1867), 174, 178, 280, 408, 526. Benjamin Quarles, *The Negro in the Civil War,* 207, erroneously suggested that black prisoners were generally better off than whites, as they "would not be penned up in such a notorious prison slaughterhouse as Andersonville."

41. U.S. Congress, *Trial of Henry Wirz,* 408; James Henry Gooding, Casualty Sheet, July 19, 1864, in Regimental Descriptive Book, 1864, Massachusetts 54th Infantry, NA. William Marvel, *Andersonville,* 155, without mentioning Gooding by name, says that he was the only officer from the Fifty-fourth captured at Olustee.

42. Emilio, *Fifty-Fourth,* 179; *Liberator,* March 8, 1864; Charles Fox to Feroline Fox, February 1, 1864, Fox Papers, MHS; GTG to Helen Garrison, June 7, 1864, and to William Garrison, June 14, 1864, Garrison Family Papers, Smith College.

43. Yacovone, "Pay Crisis," 44, 48; Special Order No. 234, John Foster, June 7, 1864, Department of the South, Letters Sent, Record Group 393, NA.

44. GTG to Helen Garrison, June 7, 1864, Garrison Family Papers, Smith College.

45. ENH to E. D. Judd, March 23, 1864, Regimental and Company Books, Massachusetts 54th Infantry, Vol. 1, NA; John Foster to Henry Halleck, July 7, 1864, *OR,* Series I, Vol. 35, 168; John Anderson to Alfred Hartwell, June 17, 1864, Department of the South, Letters Sent, Record Group 393, NA; "Private letter," April 8, 1864, endorsed by JAA, Lincoln Papers, LC; *WAA,* February 13, 1864, April 23, 1864.

46. *WAA,* April 16, 1864, April 27, 1864; James Monroe Trotter to Edward Kinsey, March 13, 1864, in *Voices,* ed. Trudeau, 71.

47. C. F. Atkinson, *Grant's Campaigns of 1864 and 1865* (London, 1908), 362.

48. *WAA,* July 9, 1864; Charge of Mutiny, June 16, 1864, Wallace Baker, Regimental Descriptive Book, 1864, Massachusetts 55th Infantry, NA. Baker's induction papers list him as "5 feet 4½ inches high."

49. Glatthaar, *Forged in Battle,* 115–118; *Boston Herald,* June 28, 1864; *WAA,* July 9, 1864.

50. Fox, *Fifty-Fifth,* 139; *WAA,* July 9, 1864, July 30, 1864; *Boston Daily Advertiser,* June 27, 1864; Indianapolis *Freeman,* June 24, 1911; NPH, *The Negro as a Soldier,* 18; *Liberator,* July 29, 1864.

51. Fox, *Fifty-Fifth,* 86–89; *Liberator,* May 27, 1864; Abraham Lincoln to JAA, February 18, 1864, Lincoln Papers, LC; JAA to Abraham Lincoln, May 27, 1864, ibid.; Alonso, *Growing Up Abolitionist,* 168; ENH to JAA, June 4, 1864, Regimental and Company Books, Massachusetts 54th Infantry, Vol. 1, NA.

52. Edward Bates to Abraham Lincoln, April 23, 1864, Lincoln Papers, LC; Belz, "Law, Politics, and Race," 207; *Liberator,* May 6, 1864, May 13, 1864, May 27, 1864.

53. Glatthaar, *Forged in Battle,* 174; Quarles, *The Negro in the Civil War,* 202; Edwin Stanton to Abraham Lincoln, June 17, 1864, Lincoln Papers, LC; *Cincinnati Daily Gazette,* August 7, 1871; *New Orleans Tribune,* August 23, 1864, October 19, 1864; *Liberator,* February 26, 1864, May 13, 1864.

54. *Liberator,* August 12, 1864; Abraham Lincoln to Edward Bates, June 24, 1864, Lincoln Papers, LC; Edward Bates to Edwin Stanton, June 20, 1864, ibid.; Pearson, *Andrew,* 119; NPH, *The Negro as a Soldier,* 18–19.

55. James Monroe Trotter to Edward Kinsey, July 18, 1864, in *Voices,* ed. Trudeau, 123; *WAA,* April 30, 1864, August 6, 1864; *Liberator,* October 4, 1864, July 8, 1864.

56. Alonso, *Growing Up Abolitionist,* 171; GTG to William Garrison, June 14, 1864, Garrison Family Papers, Smith College.

57. Trudeau, *Men of War,* 257; Report, ENH, June 11, 1864, Department of the South, Letters Received, Record Group 393, NA.

58. Fox, *Fifty-Fifth,* 30; George Walker to Burt Wilder, October 1914, Burt Wilder Papers, Cornell University; James Monroe Trotter to Edward Kinsey, July 18, 1864, in *Voices,* ed. Trudeau, 122.

59. W. S. Brown to Burt Wilder, March 25, 1895, Burt Wilder Papers, Cornell University; Trudeau, *Men of War,* 262–263.

60. George Walker to Burt Wilder, October 1914, Burt Wilder Papers, Cornell University; *Liberator,* July 22, 1864, July 26, 1864; *WAA,* August 13, 1864.

61. Emilio, *Fifty-Fourth,* 227–228; Fox, *Fifty-Fifth,* 34; *Liberator,* November 25, 1864; ENH, Regimental Descriptive Book, 1864, Massachusetts 54th Infantry, NA; LHD to Amelia Loguen, September 28, 1864, Evans Collection, Savannah; LHD to Frederick Douglass, August 22, 1864, Douglass Papers, LC.

62. Fox, *Fifty-Fifth,* 37; James Monroe Trotter to Edward Kinsey, November 21, 1864, in *Voices,* ed. Trudeau, 156; *WAA,* November 12, 1864; *Liberator,* November 11, 1864.

63. Emilio, *Fifty-Fourth,* 227–228; Thomas Robinson to ENH, November 2,

1864, *OR,* Series I, Vol. 35, 323; Rufus Saxton to John Foster, September 8, 1864, ibid., 278; ENH to Stuart Taylor, October 5, 1864, Regimental and Company Books, Massachusetts 54th Infantry, Vol. 1, NA; Stephen Swails, Regimental Descriptive Book, 1864, Massachusetts 54th Infantry, NA; Manning, *What This Cruel War,* 185; ENH to Morris Hallowell, December 2, 1864, Hallowell Family Papers, Haverford College.

64. Emilio, *Fifty-Fourth,* 236; Alonso, *Growing Up Abolitionist,* 172.

65. ENH to Hannah Hallowell, November 28, 1864, Hallowell Family Papers, Haverford College.

66. Emilio, *Fifty-Fourth,* 238; Trudeau, *Men of War,* 320.

67. Fox, *Fifty-Fifth,* 41; Alonso, *Growing Up Abolitionist,* 173; *Savannah Republican,* December 3, 1864; Philadelphia *Weekly Times,* May 10, 1884.

68. *Savannah Republican,* December 3, 1864; Philadelphia *Weekly Times,* May 10, 1884; Emilio, *Fifty-Fourth,* 243; James Monroe Trotter to Edward Kinsey, December 18, 1864, in *Voices,* ed. Trudeau, 165.

69. Andrew Smith, autobiographical sketch, June 1913, Burt Wilder Papers, Cornell University; Jordon Bobson to Burt Wilder, May 14, 1917, ibid.; Emilio, *Fifty-Fourth,* 244; Fox, *Fifty-Fifth,* 43; *Savannah Republican,* December 3, 1864; *Liberator,* December 16, 1864, December 30, 1864.

70. Trudeau, *Men of War,* 326; James Monroe Trotter to Edward Kinsey, December 18, 1864, in *Voices,* ed. Trudeau, 165; *Savannah Republican,* December 3, 1864.

71. George Walker to Burt Wilder, October 1914, Burt Wilder Papers, Cornell University; Jarvis interview, in Armstrong and Ludlow, *Hampton and Its Students,* 109–110; Henry Jarvis File, Pension Office, NA; Henry Jarvis, Regimental Descriptive Book, 1864, Massachusetts 55th Infantry, NA; *WAA,* December 24, 1864.

72. Fox, *Fifty-Fifth,* 45; Trudeau, *Men of War,* 329–330; *WAA,* December 24, 1864, February 4, 1865; Henry Jarvis, Regimental Descriptive Book, 1864, Massachusetts 55th Infantry, NA; Jarvis interview, in Armstrong and Ludlow, *Hampton and Its Students,* 109–110; James Monroe Trotter to Edward Kinsey, December 18, 1864, in *Voices,* ed. Trudeau, 165.

73. William Scott to Burt Wilder, November 21, 1914, Burt Wilder Papers, Cornell University; NPH, *The Negro as a Soldier,* 24; Trudeau, *Men of War,* 329; ENH to Hannah Hallowell, December 4, 1864, Hallowell Family Papers, Haverford College.

74. *Liberator,* December 16, 1864; Alonso, *Growing Up Abolitionist,* 174; Emilio, *Fifty-Fourth,* 262.

CHAPTER NINE

1. *WAA,* January 9, 1864.

2. Pearson, *Andrew,* 2:91; Stevens, *1863,* 255.

3. Noah Trudeau, "Proven Themselves in Every Respect to Be Men: Black Cavalry in the Civil War," in *Black Soldiers in Blue,* ed. Smith, 277.

4. *WAA,* December 19, 1863; GTG to William Garrison, January 21, 1864, Garrison Family Papers, Smith College; *Massachusetts in the Rebellion* (Boston, 1866), 488; *Liberator,* May 13, 1864.

5. CFA, *Autobiography,* 163–164; CFA to Charles Francis Adams Sr., January 16, 1864, in *Adams Letters,* ed. Ford, 2:117–118; CFA to Charles Francis Adams Sr., October 31, 1863, ibid., 2:99–100; CFA to Abigail Brooks Adams, August 27, 1864, ibid., 2:186; CFA to William Wardell, January 8, 1864, CFA, Regimental Descriptive Book, 1864, 1st Massachusetts Cavalry, NA; Special Order No. 26, E. D. Townsend, January 18, 1864, ibid.

6. Charles R. Douglass, Regimental Descriptive Book, 1864, 5th Massachusetts Cavalry, NA; Frederick Douglass Jr., Scrapbook, Evans Collection, Savannah.

7. *Liberator,* May 13, 1864; *WAA,* May 7; Trudeau, "Black Cavalry," 283, 287.

8. Trudeau, "Black Cavalry," 298; Kirkland, *Adams,* 29; CFA to Charles Francis Adams Sr., November 2, 1864, in *Adams Letters,* ed. Ford, 2:215; *WAA,* June 4, 1864.

9. CFA to Charles Francis Adams Sr., November 2, 1864, in *Adams Letters,* ed. Ford, 2:215.

10. Edward Bartlett to father, November 26, 1864, Bartlett Papers, MHS; Charles Douglass to Frederick Douglass, May 31, 1864, Douglass Papers, LC; Nick Salvatore, *We All Got History: The Memory Books of Amos Webber* (New York: Crown, 1996), 133; *WAA,* July 30, 1864.

11. McPherson, *Battle Cry of Freedom,* 740; Trudeau, *Men of War,* 221; New York *Herald,* June 29, 1864.

12. Edward Bartlett to Martha, November 30, 1864, Bartlett Papers, MHS; Charles Douglass to Frederick Douglass, May 31, 1864, Douglass Papers, LC.

13. Smith, "Let Us All Be Grateful," 56; *New York Times,* June 26, 1864; *WAA,* June 25, 1864.

14. Smith, "Let Us All Be Grateful," 56; *New York Times,* June 26, 1864; *WAA,* June 25, 1864, July 9, 1864, July 23, 1864; New York *Herald,* June 29, 1864; *Boston Herald,* June 21, 1864.

15. *WAA,* June 25, 1864; *New York Times,* June 26, 1864.

16. Smith, "Let Us All Be Grateful," 56.

17. CFA to Charles Francis Adams Sr., December 31, 1864, in *Adams Letters,* ed. Ford, 2:240; CFA to Abigail Brooks Adams, August 12, 1864, ibid., 2:175; CFA to S. E. Chamberlain, September 1, 1864, CFA, Regimental Descriptive Book, 1864, 5th Massachusetts Cavalry, NA.

18. CFA to Charles Francis Adams Sr., November 2, 1864, in *Adams Letters,* ed. Ford, 2:217–219; CFA to Henry Adams, September 18, 1864, ibid., 2:194; CFA, *Autobiography,* 166.

19. Edward Bartlett to father, November 26, 1864, Bartlett Papers, MHS; *WAA,* July 16, 1864.

20. CFA to Charles Francis Adams Sr., August 5, 1864, in *Adams Letters,* ed. Ford, 2:172–173; CFA to Henry Adams, July 22, 1864, ibid., 2:168.

21. CFA to Abigail Brooks Adams, August 27, 1864, in *Adams Letters,* ed. Ford, 2:186–187; CFA to Charles Francis Adams Sr., August 20, 1864, ibid., 2:182; CFA to Henry Adams, September 18, 1864, ibid., 2:196.

22. CFA to Abigail Brooks Adams, August 27, 1864, in *Adams Letters,* ed. Ford, 2:186–187; CFA to Charles Francis Adams Sr., November 2, 1864, ibid., 2:219; CFA to Henry Adams, September 23, 1864, ibid., 2:199.

23. CFA, Regimental Descriptive Book, 1864, 5th Massachusetts Cavalry, NA; Charles Douglass, Regimental Descriptive Book, 1864, 5th Massachusetts Cavalry, NA; Charles Douglass to Frederick Douglass, September 15, 1864, and October 17, 1864, Douglass Papers, LC. William McFeely, *Douglass,* 235, writes that "Douglass was in Lincoln's debt for Charles's discharge," but there is no evidence that Frederick asked for his son to be sent home, or that Lincoln intervened with the War Department in Charles's behalf.

24. *Boston Traveler,* March 14, 1864; *Liberator,* April 15, 1864; Emilio, *Fifty-Fourth,* 193–194, 233; John Foster to JAA, November 18, 1864, in *Freedom: Series II,* ed. Berlin et al., 343.

25. ENH to William Burger, June 1, 1864, Massachusetts 54th Paper, NA; Fox, *Fifty-Fifth,* 33; James Monroe Trotter to Francis Garrison, August 2, 1864, in *Voices,* ed. Trudeau, 141; *WAA,* July 24, 1864.

26. ENH to JAA, February 24, 1864, Regimental and Company Books, 54th Massachusetts, Vol. I, NA; *WAA,* June 4, 1864.

27. Edward Bates to Abraham Lincoln, April 23, 1864, Lincoln Papers, LC; *Liberator,* May 13, 1864; James Monroe Trotter to Francis Garrison, August 2, 1864, in *Voices,* ed. Trudeau, 141; *WAA,* July 30, 1864.

28. William Burger to Alexander Schimmelfennig, December 7, 1864, Department of the South, Letters Sent, Record Group 393, NA; Special Orders No. 4 and 11, Leonard Perry, December 10, 1864, December 19, 1864, *OR,* Series I, Vol. 44, 682, 765; Report, Charles Trowbridge, December 21, 1864, ibid., 451.

29. Report, ENH, December 21, 1864, *OR,* Series I, Vol. 44, 450; Report, Charles Trowbridge, December 21, 1864, ibid., 451; Report, P. G. T. Beauregard, December 22, 1864, ibid., 449.

30. ENH to Hannah Hallowell, December 26, 1864, and ENH to Emily Hallowell, December 31, 1864, Hallowell Family Papers, Haverford College; Maher, *Broken Fortunes,* 52.

31. Organization of Troops in the Department of the South, December 31, 1864, *OR,* Series I, Vol. 44, 855; *WAA,* January 4, 1865.

32. Special Order No. 44, Leonard Perry, January 27, 1865, *OR,* Series I, Vol. 47, 141; John Marszalek, *Sherman: A Soldier's Passion for Order* (New York: Free Press, 1992), 334; Whittington Johnson, *Black Savannah, 1788–1864* (Fayetteville: University of Arkansas Press, 1996), 172–173.

33. *Salem Register,* January 26, 1865; James Monroe Trotter to Edward Kinsey, January 29, 1865, in *Voices,* ed. Trudeau, 180.

34. *Boston Traveler,* January 23, 1865; *Salem Register,* January 26, 1865; *Boston Evening Transcript,* January 23, 1865; *Liberator,* January 27, 1865; Stephen Swails, Regimental Descriptive Book, 1865, 54th Massachusetts Infantry, NA; Special Order, William Burger, January 15, 1865, ibid.

35. Leonard Perry to ENH, February 1, 1865, *OR,* Series I, Vol. 47, 203; *Liberator,* February 24, 1865; Leonard Perry to ENH, February 6, 1865, ibid., 325; Emilio, *Fifty-Fourth,* 273.

36. Emilio, *Fifty-Fourth,* 273–275; ENH to Emily Hallowell, February 17, 1865, Hallowell Family Papers, Haverford College.

37. *Liberator,* February 24, 1865; Fraser, *Charleston,* 268; McPherson, *Battle Cry of Freedom,* 829.

38. Emilio, *Fifty-Fourth,* 277–279.

39. Fraser, *Charleston,* 269; Fox, *Fifty-Fifth,* 56.

40. Bernard Powers, *Black Charlestonians: A Social History, 1822–1885* (Fayetteville: University of Arkansas Press, 1994), 68; Levine, *House of Dixie,* 262; *Liberator,* April 14, 1865; *New Orleans Tribune,* March 19, 1865; *Salem Register,* March 9, 1865; Fox, *Fifty-Fifth,* 56–57.

41. Trudeau, *Men of War,* 357–358; Emilio, *Fifty-Fourth,* 284–285.

42. *Liberator,* April 7, 1865; *Salem Register,* March 9, 1865.

43. Unsigned letter to William Burger, June 22, 1865, Regimental and Company Books, 54th Massachusetts, Vol. 1, NA.

44. Leonard Perry to ENH, February 28, 1865, March 2, 1865, March 4, 1865, *OR,* Series I, Vol. 47, 618, 658–659; George Hodges to C. H. Thomas, March 1, 1865, Department of the South, Letters Sent, Record Group 393, NA; George Hodges to John Hatch, February 28, 1865, ibid.; ENH to Emily Hallowell, March 26, 1865, Hallowell Family Papers, Haverford College; *Journal of Ravenel,* ed. Childs, 212–215, 220.

45. Special Orders, No. 74, William Burger, March 24, 1865, *OR,* Series I, Vol. 47, 17; Special Orders, No. 74, Quincy Adams Gillmore, March 24, 1865, Department of the South, Letters Sent, Record Group 393, NA; Robert Gourdine to Burt Wilder, December 30, 1918, Wilder Papers, Cornell University; George Garrison Diary (extract), March 2, 1865, ibid.; *Liberator,* March 31, 1865; *WAA,* March 25, 1865; Fox, *Fifty-Fifth,* 61, 66–67.

46. Edward Bartlett to family, December 25, 1864, Bartlett Papers, MSH; CFA

to Henry Adams, January 1, 1865, in *Adams Letters,* ed. Ford, 2:243; *WAA,* February 18, 1865.

47. Foner, *Fiery Trial,* 328; Nelson Lankford, *Richmond Burning: The Last Days of the Confederate Capital* (New York: Penguin, 2002), 144; Edward Bartlett to R. S. Ripley, March 29, 1865, Bartlett Papers, MHS; Trudeau, *Men of War,* 419.

48. Trudeau, *Men of War,* 420–421; Manning, *What This Cruel War,* 213; *WAA,* April 22, 1865.

49. *WAA,* April 22, 1865; Trudeau, *Men of War,* 423; Quarles, *The Negro in the Civil War,* 331; Edward Bartlett to brother, April 3, 1865, Bartlett Papers, MHS; *Liberator,* April 14, 1865.

50. *Liberator,* April 14, 1865; Rembert Patrick, *The Fall of Richmond* (Baton Rouge: Louisiana State University Press, 1960), 68; Ernest Furgurson, *Ashes of Glory: Richmond at War* (New York: Knopf, 1996), 337; CFA, *Autobiography,* 166; CFA to Charles Francis Adams Sr., April 10, 1865, in *Adams Letters,* ed. Ford, 2:261–262; Charles Francis Adams Sr. to CFA, April 28, 1865, ibid., 265.

51. *Liberator,* April 14, 1865; Quarles, *The Negro in the Civil War,* 332; Lankford, *Richmond Burning,* 122.

52. Trudeau, *Men of War,* 412; John Boles, *Black Southerners, 1619–1869* (Lexington: University Press of Kentucky, 1983), 197; Samuel Clayton to Jefferson Davis, January 10, 1865, *OR,* Series IV, Vol. 3, 1010; *Charleston Mercury,* January 13, 1865; Bruce Levine, *Confederate Emancipation: South Plans to Free and Arm Slaves During the Civil War* (New York: Oxford University Press, 2005), 126–127.

53. CFA to Charles Francis Adams Sr., April 10, 1865, in *Adams Letters,* ed. Ford, 2:263–264; LHD to Amelia Loguen, March 26, 1865, Evans Collection, Savannah; *Liberator,* January 20, 1865; *WAA,* June 17, 1865.

CHAPTER TEN

1. Richmond *Enquirer,* February 11, 1865; Emory Thomas, *The Confederate Nation, 1861–1865* (New York: Harper & Row, 1979), 304; William Davis, *Jefferson Davis: The Man and His Hour—A Biography* (New York: HarperCollins, 1991), 625.

2. ENH to NPH, April 3, 1865, Hallowell Family Papers, Haverford College; ENH to Hannah Hallowell, April 3, 1865, ibid.

3. *Liberator,* March 31, 1865; Alonso, *Growing Up Abolitionist,* 175; William Lloyd Garrison to Helen Garrison, April 15, 1865, in *Letters,* ed. Merrill, 270.

4. *New-York Tribune,* April 18, 1865; Henry Mayer, *All on Fire: William Lloyd Garrison and the Abolition of Slavery* (New York: St. Martin's, 1998), 578; *New York Times,* April 17, 1865; *Esther Hill Hawks' Diary,* ed. Schwartz, 130; *Liberator,* April 28, 1865.

5. *Liberator,* May 5, 1865; Fox, *Fifty-Fifth,* 74; Fraser, *Charleston,* 273.

6. Report, ENH, April 26, 1865, *OR,* Series I, Vol. 47, 1036; Emilio, *Fifty-Fourth,* 294.

7. Report, ENH, April 26, 1865, *OR,* Series I, Vol. 47, 1036; Emilio, *Fifty-Fourth,* 296–298; *Boston Traveler,* May 17, 1865. Dr. Charles Briggs characterized Swails's injury as "a flesh wound in the right arm, missile minié ball." See Physician's Affidavit, February 4, 1887, Stephen Swails File, Pension Office, NA.

8. Report, ENH, April 26, 1865, *OR,* Series I, Vol. 47, 1036; Emilio, *Fifty-Fourth,* 301–302.

9. Emilio, *Fifty-Fourth,* 302–303; Edward Stevens, Regimental Descriptive Book, 1865, 54th Massachusetts Infantry, NA.

10. Report, ENH, April 26, 1865, *OR,* Series I, Vol. 47, 1037; Emilio, *Fifty-Fourth,* 303–304; Trudeau, *Men of War,* 394.

11. Report, ENH, April 26, 1865, *OR,* Series I, Vol. 47, 1037; Emilio, *Fifty-Fourth,* 308; Report, Edward Potter, May 6, 1865, ibid., 1028; Report, Frank Goodwin, April 29, 1865, ibid., 1038; *Boston Traveler,* May 17, 1865; ENH to Hannah Hallowell, April 27, 1865, Hallowell Family Papers, Haverford College.

12. ENH to unknown, April 29, 1865, Hallowell Family Papers, Haverford College; Report, Edward Potter, May 6, 1865, *OR,* Series I, Vol. 47, 1031; General Orders, Leonard Perry, May 5, 1865, ibid., 408; Special Orders, E. Harris Jewett, May 5, 1865, ibid., 408.

13. Petitioners to Edwin Stanton, January 1865, in *Freedom: Series II,* ed. Berlin et al., 340–341.

14. *Boston Herald,* May 15, 1865; Stephen A. Swails, Regimental Descriptive Book, 1865, 54th Massachusetts Infantry, NA; Peter Vogelsang, Regimental Descriptive Book, 1865, 54th Massachusetts Infantry, NA; *WAA,* February 4, 1865.

15. James Monroe Trotter, Regimental Descriptive Book, 1865, 55th Massachusetts Infantry, NA; Peter Vogelsang, Regimental Descriptive Book, 1865, 54th Massachusetts Infantry, NA; *Civil War Diary of Wilder,* ed. Reid, 251; *New Orleans Tribune,* July 15, 1865; *WAA,* July 22, 1865, September 5, 1865.

16. Glatthaar, *Forged in Battle,* 209–210; Emilio, *Fifty-Fourth,* 311; ENH to sister, May 15, 1865, Hallowell Family Papers, Haverford College.

17. *Liberator,* July 25, 1865; Augusta *Daily Constitutionalist,* March 26, 1865; Emilio, *Fifty-Fourth,* 312–313. When the college moved to its present location in 1922, the square was renamed in honor of Francis Marion.

18. Robert Zalimas, "A Disturbance in the City: Black and White Soldiers in Postwar Charleston," in *Black Soldiers in Blue,* ed. Smith, 368; *Liberator,* May 5, 1865; *WAA,* April 29, 1865; ENH to sister, May 6, 1865, Hallowell Family Papers, Haverford College.

19. Zalimas, "Disturbance in the City," 363; Fraser, *Charleston,* 274–275; *Liberator,* June 24, 1865, July 25, 1865.

20. *Providence Evening Press,* March 3, 1865; *WAA,* April 29, 1865.

21. John McKivigan, *Forgotten Firebrand: James Redpath and the Making of Nineteenth-Century America* (Ithaca, NY: Cornell University Press, 2008), 108; *WAA,* April 29, 1865.

22. Special Orders, George Pope, July 1, 1865, Stephen Swails, Regimental Descriptive Book, 1865, 54th Massachusetts Infantry, NA; Susan Swails, June 13, 1871, Registers of Signatures of Depositors in Branches of the Freedmen's Savings and Trust Company, NA; Albert Aspinall, 1860 Federal Census, Ward 5, Charleston, South Carolina, Roll M653–1216, Page 379, Image 392, NA.

23. JHG, Regimental Descriptive Book, 1865, 54th Massachusetts Infantry, NA; ENH to William Dale, May 1, 1865, Regimental and Company Books, Massachusetts 54th, Vol. 1, NA; Charles Hill to William Thomas, August 3, 1865, William Thomas Collection, NYHS; Fox, *Fifty-Fifth,* 120–121.

24. *Liberator,* April 4, 1865; *WAA,* May 27, 1865. In 1989 the remains of nineteen soldiers from the Fifty-fifth, who had died during the fall 1863 siege, were discovered buried on Folly Island and reinterred at Beaufort's National Cemetery with full military honors.

25. *Journal of Ravenel,* ed. Childs, 246; *Liberator,* July 28, 1865; Charges and Specifications Preferred Against Private Alfred Lee, July 29, 1865, Compiled Military Service Records of Volunteer Union Soldiers Who Served with the U.S. Colored Troops, 54th Massachusetts Infantry, NA.

26. Andrew Smith, Autobiographical Sketch, June 1913, Burt Wilder Papers, Cornell University. Writing almost fifty years after the event, Smith spelled the deserter's name as Peleit, but Alfred Pelette was the only soldier in the Fifty-fifth to have a surname close to Peleit.

27. Samuel Benton, Regimental Descriptive Book, 1865, 54th Massachusetts Infantry, NA; ENH to L. B. Perry, June 19, 1865, 54th Massachusetts Papers, NA; Fox, *Fifty-Fifth,* 77, 134, 142.

28. Zalimas, "Disturbance in the City," 369; McKivigan, *Forgotten Firebrand,* 110.

29. Melinda Hennessey, "Racial Violence During Reconstruction," *South Carolina Historical Magazine* 86 (1985): 102; Report, W. T. Bennett, July 15, 1865, in 54th Massachusetts Papers, NA.

30. Zalimas, "Disturbance in the City," 376; *New Orleans Tribune,* July 28, 1865; Report, W. T. Bennett, July 15, 1865, in 54th Massachusetts Papers, NA; *WAA,* July 29, 1865.

31. Zalimas, "Disturbance in the City," 377–378.

32. Fox, *Fifty-Fifth,* 79–80.

33. Alonso, *Growing Up Abolitionist,* 175; Julie Saville, *The Work of Reconstruction: From Slave to Wage Laborer in South Carolina, 1860–1870* (Cambridge:

Cambridge University Press, 1994), 27; James Monroe Trotter to Edward Kinsey, July 1, 1865, in *Voices,* ed. Trudeau, 183.

34. Fox, *Fifty-Fifth,* 81; *Liberator,* June 9, 1865, June 16, 1865, July 28, 1865.

35. *Liberator,* June 9, 1865, June 16, 1865, July 21, 1865, July 28, 1865; George Nye to Charles Fillebrown, August 19, 1865, Department of the South, Letters Received, Record Group 393, NA.

36. *Journal of Ravenel,* ed. Childs, 247; Isaac Dyer to Charles Fillebrown, August 1, 1865, Department of the South, Letters Received, Record Group 393, NA; John McGould to Charles Fillebrown, October 5, 1865, ibid.; *WAA,* May 27, 1865.

37. James Monroe Trotter to Edward Kinsey, July 1, 1865, in *Voices,* ed. Trudeau, 183; GTG to William Garrison, July 12, 1865, Garrison Family Papers, Smith College; A. J. Williams to George Hooker, December 5, 1865, Department of the South, Letters Received, Record Group 393, NA; Fox, *Fifty-Fifth,* 82.

38. *Journal of Ravenel,* ed. Childs, 245.

39. James Bucher to L. B. Perry, July 25, 1865, Department of the South, Letters Received, Record Group 393, NA; Saville, *Work of Reconstruction,* 144, 148. There were six men with the surname of Johnson in the Fifty-fifth. This may have been Colonel John J. Johnson, the only officer of that name.

40. *Liberator,* June 16, 1865; Patrick, *Fall of Richmond,* 124–125.

41. Salvatore, *We All Got History,* 145; Charles Francis Adams Jr., Regimental Descriptive Book, 1865, 5th Massachusetts Cavalry, NA.

42. CFA to Charles Francis Adams Sr., May 2, 1865, in *Adams Letters,* ed. Ford, 2:267–269; CFA, Regimental Descriptive Book, 1865, 5th Massachusetts Cavalry, NA.

43. Salvatore, *We All Got History,* 149; Postscript, in *Adams Letters,* ed. Ford, 2:270; CFA, Regimental Descriptive Book, 1865, 5th Massachusetts Cavalry, NA; CFA, *Autobiography,* 166–167.

44. Ebenezer Woodward to John Q. Adams, June 28, 1865, CFA, Regimental Descriptive Book, 1865, 5th Massachusetts Cavalry, NA; Report, Aaron Hooker, July 30, 1865, ibid.; CFA to Edwin Stanton, July 21, 1865, ibid.; Special Order No. 413, E. D. Townsend, August 1, 1865, ibid.; Postscript, in *Adams Letters,* ed. Ford, 2:270; Charles Francis Adams Sr. to CFA, March 24, 1865, ibid., 259.

45. *Liberator,* June 2, 1865, December 1, 1865; William Lloyd Garrison to Wendell Phillips Garrison, May 25, 1865, in *Letters,* ed. Merrill, 5:276; ENH to Morris Hallowell, August 12, 1865, Hallowell Family Papers, Haverford College.

46. *Liberator,* June 25, 1865; ENH to Morris Hallowell, July 10, 1865, Hallowell Family Papers, Haverford College; *WAA,* July 22, 1865; Peter Vogelsang, Regimental Descriptive Book, 1865, 54th Massachusetts Infantry, NA.

47. ENH to sister, July 11, 1865, Hallowell Family Papers, Haverford College; Emilio, *Fifty-Fourth,* 317–318; Stephen A. Swails, Regimental Descriptive

Book, 1865, 54th Massachusetts Infantry, NA; Stephen A. Swails File, Pension Office, NA.

48. Emilio, *Fifty-Fourth,* 318–320.

49. Ibid., 320–321; Thomas Wentworth Higginson, *Massachusetts in the Army and Navy During the War of 1861–65* (Boston, 1895), 298–299. Redkey, "Profile of the Fifty-fourth," 21, placed the total number of those serving in the Fifty-fourth at a slightly lower 1,357.

50. P. F. Oliver to Burt Wilder, August 16, 1915, Burt Wilder Papers, Cornell University; Fox, *Fifty-Fifth,* 83; *Liberator,* September 15, 1865; *Newark Daily Advertiser,* September 20, 1865.

51. Fox, *Fifty-Fifth,* 84; *Liberator,* September 29, 1865; *Boston Evening Transcript,* September 25, 1865; William Lloyd Garrison to Edwin Stanton, September 15, 1865, in *Letters,* ed. Merrill, 5:296; Higginson, *Massachusetts in the Army,* 300–301.

52. Salvatore, *We All Got History,* 149; Higginson, *Massachusetts in the Army,* 166–167.

53. *New Orleans Tribune,* October 4, 1865, October 19, 1865; *Liberator,* November 24, 1865.

CHAPTER ELEVEN

1. Donald Shaffer, *After the Glory: The Struggles of Black Civil War Veterans* (Lawrence: University Press of Kansas, 2004), 45–49.

2. ENH, Regimental Descriptive Book, 1865–1867, 54th Massachusetts Infantry, NA.

3. Hallowell, *Record of a Branch of the Hallowell Family,* 65; Voter Records, Medford, Massachusetts, Town and Vital Records, 1620–1988, MHS.

4. ENH, 1870 Federal Census, Medford, Middlesex, Massachusetts, Roll M593–629; Page 598B, Image 481, NA; *Philadelphia Inquirer,* July 28, 1871; *Lowell Daily Citizen and News,* July 28, 1871; *Alexandria Gazette,* July 28, 1871; *Portland Daily Press,* July 28, 1871; *Boston Journal,* July 28, 1871; *Boston Daily Advertiser,* July 28, 1871.

5. Amelia Holmes to Emily Hallowell, August 16, [1884?], Hallowell Family Papers, Haverford College; Charlotte Hallowell, 1900 Federal Census, Medford Ward 3, Middlesex, Massachusetts, Roll 663, Page 5A, NA; Charlotte and Emily Hallowell, Passport Applicants, 1795–1905, Roll 309, NA; Charlotte Hallowell, 1910 Federal Census, Medford Ward 3, Middlesex, Massachusetts, Roll T624–602, Page 6A, NA; Charlotte and Emily Hallowell, 1930 Federal Census, Medford, Middlesex, Massachusetts, Roll 924, Page 4A, Enumeration District 0316, Image 743.0, NA.

6. Lydia Maria Child to Frank Shaw, December 6, 1870, Shaw Family Papers, NYHS; Foote, *One Great Remedy,* 168–179; Waugh, "Shaw Family," 74–75;

Coulter, "Shaw and the Burning of Darien," 372; *New York Times,* October 13, 1905, October 7, 1924.

7. *Boston Herald,* November 27, 1904, March 19, 1907, March 21, 1907, March 27, 1907; *Cleveland Gazette,* March 23, 1907.

8. Ellen Gooding, 1870 Federal Census, New Bedford Ward 6, Bristol, Massachusetts, Roll M593–605, Page 258A, NA; Alan Borden, Power of Attorney, April 22, 1864, James Henry Gooding File, Pension Office, NA; Widow's Declaration for Army Pension, April 5, 1864, ibid.; Ellen Gooding, Death Record, Massachusetts Vital Records, 1840–1911, New England Historic Genealogical Society, Boston.

9. Shaffer, *After the Glory,* 122; Petition of Cynthia Ann Downing Smith, April 15, 1882, and Affidavit of Ester A. Perkins, May 14, 1892, John M. Smith File, Pension Office, NA.

10. *Boston Evening Transcript,* July 15, 1863; Said, *Autobiography,* 202–203.

11. Said, *Autobiography,* 203–205; Nicholas Said, Register of Signatures of Depositors in Branches of the Freedman's Savings and Trust Company, May 23, 1871, Tallahassee, Florida, NA.

12. Schaffer, *After the Glory,* 31; Said, *Autobiography,* 185, 189. As noted in Chapter 1, notes 11 and 14, where verifiable—including the names and sailing routes of ships mentioned in his memoirs—Said's account proves to be accurate.

13. *Macon Weekly Telegraph,* May 23, 1871; *Savannah Daily Advertiser,* July 1, 1871; *Columbus Daily Enquirer,* January 18, 1871.

14. Nicholas Said, 1880 Federal Census, Haywood County, Tennessee, Roll 1262, Page 232B, NA; Allan Austin, "Mohammed Ali Ben Said: Travels on Five Continents," *Contributions in Black Studies* 12 (1994): 24, note 1. Fox's copy of *Fifty-Fifth,* which contains the note about Said's death, is in the MHS.

15. William Capelle, Affidavit, June 7, 1871, Henry Jarvis File, Pension Office, NA; James Williamson, Surgeon's Certificate, August 24, 1867, ibid.; Henry Jarvis, Declaration for Original Invalid Pension, April 17, 1882, ibid.; George Smith, Affidavit, May 19, 1890, ibid.; Henry Jarvis to the State of Massachusetts, September 15, 1868, ibid. Jarvis's leg was made by a company founded in 1846 by Benjamin Palmer, himself an amputee. The firm was one of five that provided artificial legs to Union veterans. See Guy Hasegawa, *Mending Broken Bones: The Union and Confederate Programs to Supply Artificial Limbs* (Carbondale: Southern Illinois University Press, 2012), 88–89.

16. Mary Jane Jarvis, Affidavit, April 30, 1894, Henry Jarvis File, Pension Office, NA; Henry and Mary Jane Jarvis, Marriage License, December 26, 1872, ibid.; Jarvis interview, in Armstrong and Ludlow, *Hampton and Its Students,* 113–114.

17. Mary Jane Jarvis, Affidavit, May 19, 1890, Henry Jarvis File, Pension Office,

NA; Georgianna Brooks, Affidavits, March 26, 1894, April 3, 1894, ibid.; Mary Jane Jarvis, Widow's Claim for Pension, June 16, 190, ibid.; George Johnson, Affidavit, May 1, 1894, ibid.; American Red Cross, Finance Division, November 31, 1926, ibid.; Board of Health, Record of Deaths, March 12, 1894, ibid.; Mary Jane Jarvis, Application for Accrued Pension, Widows, March 30, 1894, ibid.

18. Kirkland, *Adams,* 32; CFA, *Autobiography,* 168.

19. Eric Foner, *Reconstruction: America's Unfinished Revolution, 1863–1877* (New York: Oxford University Press, 1988), 497; Duberman, *Adams,* 391; Mark Wahlgren Summers, *The Ordeal of the Reunion: A New History of Reconstruction* (Chapel Hill: University of North Carolina Press, 2014), 305.

20. Kirkland, *Adams,* 221; Paul C. Nagel, *Descent from Glory: Four Generations of the John Adams Family* (Cambridge, MA: Harvard University Press, 1983), 301.

21. William H. Carney to R. G. Pierce, October 23, 1863, May 22, 1865, William Carney Papers, Camp Meigs Records, NBPL; Susanna Carney, Pension Request, January 15, 1908, William H. Carney File, Pension Office, NA; William H. Carney, 1870 Federal Census, New Bedford Ward 3, Bristol, Massachusetts, Roll M593–605, Page 110B, Image 225, NA.

22. Amos Webber, Physician's Affidavit, July 28, 1893, and F. H. Hooper, Surgeon's Certificate, June 12, 1888, William H. Carney File, Pension Office, NA; William H. Carney, 1900 Federal Census, New Bedford Ward 3, Bristol, Massachusetts, Roll 637, Page 15B, Enumeration District 0187. On the number of Massachusetts soldiers who did not survive the war, see William Schouler, *A History of Massachusetts in the Civil War* (Boston, 1868), 613.

23. Topeka *Colored Citizen,* April 7, 1898; William Carney, Regimental Descriptive Book, 1900, 54th Massachusetts Infantry, NA; Grover, *Fugitive's Gibraltar,* 279.

24. *Pawtucket* (Rhode Island) *Times,* December 9, 1908; NPH, *Selected Letters,* 94; Registry of Death, New Bedford, Massachusetts, December 24, 1908, and Susanna Carney, Pension Request, January 15, 1909, William Carney File, Pension Office, NA.

25. *Pawtucket* (Rhode Island) *Times,* December 9, 1908; *Augusta* (Georgia) *Chronicle,* December 10, 1908; *Topeka Plaindealer,* January 1, 1909; *Boston Herald,* December 9, 1908; Chicago *Broad Ax,* December 17, 1908; NPH, *Selected Letters,* 94.

26. Susanna Carney, 1910 Federal Census, New Bedford Ward 4, Bristol, Massachusetts, Roll T624–579, Page 19B, Enumeration District 0199, NA; Clara Carney, U.S., Social Security Applications and Claims Index, 1936–2007, NA; Clara Carney, 1920 Federal Census, New Bedford Ward 4, Bristol, Massachusetts, Roll T625–686, Page 7A, Enumeration District 139, Image 366; Clara Carney, 1930

Federal Census, New Bedford, Bristol, Massachusetts, Roll 891, Page 2A, Enumeration District 0126, Image 840.0.

27. Hallowell, *Record of a Branch of the Hallowell Family,* 70; NPH, *Selected Letters,* 21; NPH, 1870 Federal Census, Medford, Middlesex, Massachusetts, Roll M593–629, Page 631A, Image 548, NA.

28. *Boston Herald,* April 12, 1914; NPH, *Selected Letters,* 73–74, 78.

29. NPH, *Selected Letters,* 74–77, 83.

30. Edward White, *Justice Oliver Wendell Holmes: Law and the Inner Self* (New York: Oxford University Press, 1993), 33, 589; Benjamin Griffith Brawley, *Social History of the American Negro* (New York: Collier-Macmillian, 1921); *Boston Journal,* April 14, 1914; *Springfield* (Massachusetts) *Republican,* April 13, 1914, April 16, 1914; *Boston Herald,* April 12, 1914, April 13, 1914, April 15, 1914.

31. John Bowles, Affidavit, December 30, 1908, and William Dupree, Affidavit, August 20, 1908, James Trotter File, Pension Office, NA; Fox, *Guardian of Boston,* 9.

32. James Monroe Trotter, 1870 Federal Census, Boston, Ward 11, Suffolk, Massachusetts, Roll M93–647, Page 169B, Image 345, NA; James Monroe Trotter, *Music and Some Highly Musical People* (Boston, 1878), 4; Greenspan, *Brown,* 471; Fox, *Guardian of Boston,* 10.

33. Fox, *Guardian of Boston,* 11–12; Stephen Kantrowitz, *More Than Freedom: Fighting for Black Citizenship in a White Republic, 1829–1889* (New York: Penguin, 2012), 416–417.

34. Amelia Loguen to Frederick Douglass, April 14, 1887, Douglass Papers, LC; *Cleveland Gazette,* March 5, 1892; Certificate of Death, February 26, 1892, James Monroe Trotter File, Pension Office, NA; NPH to William Monroe Trotter, March 1, 1910, in NPH, *Selected Letters,* 85–86; Douglas R. Egerton, *The Wars of Reconstruction: The Brief, Violent History of America's Most Progressive Era* (New York: Bloomsbury, 2014), 332.

35. San Francisco *Elevator,* October 27, 1865. Peter Vogelsang, 1880 Federal Census, Brooklyn, New York (Roll 586, Page 504C, NA), listed Maria as approximately seventy, making her birth year 1810, but census takers were notoriously inaccurate in their guesses. When Maria opened an account with the Freedman's Bank in 1872, she gave her birth year as 1816, making her two years younger than her husband. See Maria Margaret Vogelsang, April 15, 1872, Register of Signatures of Depositors in Branches of the Freedman's Savings and Trust Company, NA.

36. Andrew Wender Cohen, *Contraband: Smuggling and the Birth of the American Century* (New York: Norton, 2015), 141–142.

37. New York *Herald,* November 10, 1885.

38. Lydia Maria Child to Francis Shaw, April 13, 1873, Shaw Family Papers, NYPL; New York *Freeman,* April 9, 1887; New York *World,* September 22, 1870, September 23, 1870; New York *Herald,* May 3, 1872.

39. Cohen, *Contraband,* 256; *New-York Tribune,* July 4, 1885; New York *Herald,* June 11, 1886; New York *Freeman,* April 9, 1887.

40. New York *Freeman,* April 9, 1887; Peter Vogelsang, Affidavit, November 10, 1879, Peter Vogelsang File, Pension Office, NA.

41. Susan Swails, Declaration for Widow's Pension, June 4, 1900, Susan Swails, Deposition, November 7, 1900, Mary McKinley, December 1, 1900, and Harriet Aspinall, Deposition, August 11, 1900, Stephen Swails File, Pension Office, NA. On Seabrook, see Bernard E. Powers Jr., *Black Charlestonians: A Social History, 1822–1885* (Fayetteville: University of Arkansas Press, 1994), 211.

42. Steven Swails, 1870 Federal Census, Williamsburg, South Carolina, Roll M593–1511, Page 78B, Image 160, NA; Gordon Jenkinson, *Williamsburg District: A History of Its People and Places* (Charleston: History Press, 2007), 88; Charleston *Courier,* December 8, 1867.

43. *Daily Albany Argus,* September 28, 1868; Cleveland *Plain Dealer,* October 12, 1868.

44. *New-York Tribune,* October 27, 1868; Harrisburg *Weekly Patriot and Union,* October 15, 1868.

45. Egerton, *Wars of Reconstruction,* 162; John Reynolds, *Reconstruction in South Carolina, 1865–1877* (Columbia, 1903), 233; Chicago *Pomeroy's Democrat,* March 8, 1873.

46. Walter Edgar, *South Carolina: A History* (Columbia: University of South Carolina Press, 1998), 399; William S. McFeely, *Grant: A Biography* (New York: Norton, 1981), 370–373; *Boston Journal,* March 28, 1873; Cleveland *Plain Dealer,* August 27, 1872; *Augusta Chronicle,* August 28, 1872; *Auburn Daily Bulletin,* March 28, 1873; New York *Herald,* March 28, 1873.

47. Charleston *Courier,* September 13, 1873, December 11, 1873; *New-York Tribune,* August 21, 1874; *Alexandria Gazette,* August 21, 1874; Chicago *Pomeroy's Democrat,* March 8, 1873.

48. Thomas Holt, *Black over White: Negro Political Leadership in South Carolina During Reconstruction* (Urbana: University of Illinois Press, 1977), 109; Chicago *Daily Inter-Ocean,* April 12, 1876; Cleveland *Plain Dealer,* April 12, 1876; *Albany Evening Journal,* April 12, 1876; *Augusta Chronicle,* April 13, 1876; New York *Irish American Weekly,* April 22, 1876; *Charleston News and Courier,* March 4, 1874; *St. Albans* (Vermont) *Daily Messenger,* October 14, 1878; Baltimore *Sun,* October 16, 1878.

49. *New-York Tribune,* October 30, 1878, November 20, 1878; Madison *Wisconsin State Journal,* November 26, 1878; Chicago *Daily Inter-Ocean,* October 23, 1878; *Cincinnati Daily Gazette,* October 15, 1878; *Cincinnati Commercial Tribune,* October 23, 1878. Stephen A. Swails Jr.'s birth and death dates are found in *South Carolina Death Records,* Columbia, South Carolina Department of Archives and History.

50. Troy *Times,* October 20, 1881; Concord *New Hampshire Patriot and State Gazette,* July 17, 1789; *Boston Journal,* July 16, 1879; Madison *Wisconsin State Journal,* July 22, 1879; *Portland Daily Press,* July 12, 1879; *New-York Tribune,* July 11, 1879; *New York Globe,* February 16, 1884; St. Paul *Western Appeal,* September 29, 1888.

51. Columbia *The State,* June 17, 1896, December 25, 1897, May 18, 1900; *Charleston Courier,* May 18, 1900, May 19, 1900; Surgeon's Certificate, January 18, 1887; D. C. Scott, Affidavit, December 1, 1900; U.S. Pension Agency, October 31, 1900; R. D. Rollins, Report, County Treasurer, August 2, 1900, Stephen Swails File, Pension Office, NA. Summers, *Ordeal of the Reunion,* 320, remarks that Swails had a "stained reputation" without noting how partisan and often racist the charges were.

52. Frederick Douglass to Charles Sumner, April 29, 1865, in *The Life and Writings of Frederick Douglass,* ed. Philip S. Foner (New York: International, 1975), 4:165; LHD to Amelia Loguen, January 7, 1866, Evans Collection, Savannah; Charles Douglass to Frederick Douglass, February 10, 1866, Douglass Papers, LC. McFeely, *Douglass,* 235, mistakenly observes that Lewis encountered his cousin after being "stationed briefly, with a detachment of the Fifty-fourth," in Maryland. The regiment was never stationed in Maryland, and Douglass had been mustered out because of his wounds two years before.

53. LHD to Frederick Douglass, October 29, 1866; Henry Waggoner to Frederick Douglass, August 27, 1866; Charles Douglass to Frederick Douglass, May 25, 1867; Charles Douglass to Frederick Douglass, February 24, 1868, Douglass Papers, LC.

54. LHD to Amelia Loguen, February 10, 1868, Evans Collection, Savannah.

55. *Wilmington Daily Commercial,* January 19, 1869; Lewis Douglass to Amelia Loguen, July 5, 1869, Evans Collection, Savannah; Charles Douglass, Deposition, October 20, 1908, LHD File, Pension Office, NA. The Loguen house at 293 East Genesee Street is no longer standing; the site is now occupied by a Rite Aid pharmacy.

56. Broadside, February 1869, Gerrit Smith Papers, Syracuse University; San Francisco *Elevator,* June 11, 1869, May 24, 1873; Washington *Daily National Intelligencer,* June 3, 1869; *Jackson* (Michigan) *Daily Citizen,* January 27, 1871; *New-York Tribune,* May 20, 1871; *Washington Notes and News,* December 12, 1871; *Providence Evening Press,* September 21, 1872; Washington *Daily National Republican,* September 19, 1872; Washington *Bee,* March 5, 1887.

57. Charles Douglass to Frederick Douglass, February 24, 1868, Douglass Papers, LC; LHD to Amelia Loguen Douglass, January 30, 1895, Evans Collection, Savannah; Charles Douglass, Deposition, October 20, 1908, Lewis Douglass File, Pension Office, NA; LHD, Declaration for Pension, February 11, 1907, ibid.; E. L. Bailey to Fannie Douglass, July 6, 1937, ibid.; Amelia Loguen Douglass, Certifi-

cation of Death, August 8, 1936, ibid.; LHD, Certificate of Death, September 19, 1908, Washington Public Library.

58. Charles Douglass to Frederick Douglass, June 6, 1867, April 19, 1867, April 30, 1867, May 9, 1867, Douglass Papers, LC.

59. LHD to Amelia Loguen, July 17, 1869, Evans Collection, Savannah; Charles Douglass, 1870 Federal Census, Washington, Roll 593–127, Page 694B, Image 388, NA; Charles Douglass to Frederick Douglass, September 7, 1868, May 13, 1873, Douglass Papers, LC.

60. Egerton, *Wars of Reconstruction,* 147; Charles Douglass to Frederick Douglass, July 14, 1868, January 20, 1872, August 5, 1876, August 18, 1877, Douglass Papers, LC.

61. Charles Douglass to Frederick Douglass, April 26, 1887, Douglass Papers, LC; Charles Douglass, 1880 Federal Census, Washington, D.C., Roll 123, Page 379A, Image 0762, NA; *Cleveland Gazette,* October 11, 1902, June 13, 1908; Washington *Bee,* July 8, 1905, October 6, 1906.

62. Washington *Bee,* December 4, 1920; *Boston Herald,* November 25, 1920; *St. Louis Clarion,* December 18, 1920; Washington *Colored American,* December 19, 1903.

63. Paul Laurence Dunbar, *Complete Poems* (New York, 1922), 50–51.

EPILOGUE

1. Richard Reid, "USCT Veterans in Post–Civil War North Carolina," in *Black Soldiers in Blue,* ed. Smith, 393; *Cleveland Gazette,* April 2, 1892.

2. Charleston *Missionary Record,* July 5, 1873; Barbara Gannon, *The Won Cause: Black and White Comradeship in the Grand Army of the Republic* (Chapel Hill: University of North Carolina Press, 2011), 60, 89, 104–105.

3. Cornish, *Sable Arm,* 288; Steven Hahn, *A Nation Under Their Feet: Black Political Struggles in the Rural South from Slavery to the Great Migration* (Cambridge, MA: Harvard University Press, 2003), 92; Duncan, *Death and Glory,* 50; Smith, "Let Us All Be Grateful," 8; *Liberator,* January 20, 1865; *WAA,* June 18, 1864.

4. *Liberator,* September 16, 1864, December 22, 1865; NPH, *The Negro as a Soldier,* 28.

5. *New York Age,* August 15, 1891, November 21, 1891; *Cleveland Gazette,* May 16, 1891, March 19, 1892.

6. *Cleveland Gazette,* March 28, 1891; San Francisco *Elevator,* May 7, 1869; Kansas City *Rising Son,* September 4, 1903; Wichita *Colored Citizen,* September 5, 1903.

7. *Cleveland Gazette,* October 17, 1891, December 5, 1891, May 6, 1893, August 22, 1896; *Springfield* (Massachusetts) *Republican,* January 18, 1916; *Wilkes-Barre Times Leader,* June 18, 1915.

8. Lydia Maria Child to Sarah Shaw, April 8, 1866, Shaw Family Papers, NYPL; *Liberator,* January 22, 1864, December 9, 1864; *New Orleans Tribune,* November 1, 1864; Charles Russell Lowell to Josephine Shaw, September 15, 1863, in *Letters of Lowell,* ed. Emerson, 304; Kathryn Greenthal, "Augustus Saint-Gaudens and the Shaw Memorial," in *Hope and Glory,* ed. Blatt et al., 116; *Liberator,* August 21, 1863, December 22, 1865; Stephen Puleo, *A City So Grand: The Rise of an American Metropolis, 1850–1900* (Boston: Beacon Press, 2010), 150; Thomas J. Brown, "The Peaceable War Memorial," in *The Civil War in Art and Memory,* ed. Kirk Savage (Washington, DC: National Gallery of Art, 2016), 249.

9. Marilyn Richardson, "Taken from Life: Edward Bannister, Edmonia Lewis, and the Memorialization of the Fifty-Fourth Massachusetts Regiment," in *Hope and Glory,* ed. Blatt et al., 94; Katie Kresser, "Power and Glory: Brahmin Identity and the Shaw Memorial," *American Art* 20 (2006): 41; *Liberator,* October 9, 1863, September 4, 1863, November 20, 1863.

10. Greenthal, "Augustus Saint-Gaudens," 117–118, 127; Thomas J. Brown, "Civic Monuments of the Civil War," in *Hope and Glory,* ed. Blatt et al., 146; Kresser, "Power and Glory," 42; Brown, "Peaceable War Memorial," in *Civil War in Art,* ed. Savage, 249; *Liberator,* October 20, 1865, January 13, 1865.

11. Invitation to Luis Emilio, July 1, 1887, NPH Papers, MHS; Washington *Bee,* August 6, 1887.

12. *New York Age,* June 6, 1891; David Blight, "The Shaw Memorial," in *Hope and Glory,* ed. Blatt et al., 90.

13. Kresser, "Power and Glory," 47; Kirk Savage, "Race, Art, and the Shaw Memorial," in *Hope and Glory,* ed. Blatt et al.,158, 164–165; Stephen T. Riley, "A Monument to Colonel Robert Gould Shaw," *Proceedings of the Massachusetts Historical Society* 75 (1963): 36.

14. Circular, May 20, 1897, NPH Papers, MHS; Circular, April 1, 1897, ibid.; Circular, May 26, 1897, ibid.; Waugh, "Shaw Family," 53; Brown, "Civic Monuments of the War," 152–153; Wichita *National Reflector,* May 15, 1897.

15. *Boston Herald,* June 1, 1897; Trudeau, *Men of War,* 467; Allen Flint, "Black Response to Colonel Shaw," *Phylon* 45 (1984): 218; Waugh, "Shaw Family," 53.

16. *Cleveland Gazette,* August 6, 1898.

17. *Topeka Plaindealer,* October 15, 1915; *Cleveland Gazette,* December 25, 1915; *Springfield* (Massachusetts) *Republican,* January 18, 1916; St. Paul *Western Appeal,* December 4, 1915.

18. *Savannah Tribune,* October 2, 1915; *Topeka Plaindealer,* January 15, 1915; *Springfield* (Massachusetts) *Republican,* April 20, 1915; Indianapolis *Freeman,* July 26, 1913, October 2, 1915, December 25, 1915.

19. Washington *Bee,* April 1, 1916, May 6, 1916; *Trenton Evening Times,* April 4, 1916; *Boston Herald,* July 16, 1916, July 19, 1916; *Boston Journal,* July 19, 1916.

20. St. Paul *Western Appeal,* January 25, 1919; *Trenton Evening Times,* January 19, 1917, August 19, 1917; *Savannah Tribune,* January 19, 1918; Gulfport *Daily Herald,* April 17, 1917; Omaha *World Herald,* May 29, 1918; Cleveland *Plain Dealer,* December 14, 1917; Chicago *Broad Ax,* April 6, 1918; *Boston Herald,* July 18, 1918; Arthur Barbeau and Florette Henri, *The Unknown Soldiers: Black American Troops in World War I* (Philadelphia: Temple University Press, 1974), 38.

21. Columbia *The State,* July 8, 1917; *Augusta Chronicle,* July 18, 1917; *Charleston Courier,* July 8, 1917.

22. Chicago *Broad Ax,* January 28, 1922, May 29, 1926; Gannon, *The Won Cause,* 76–77; *Topeka Plaindealer,* February 5, 1926; *Springfield* (Massachusetts) *Republican,* October 21, 1928.

23. *Los Angeles Tribune,* December 6, 1943; Trudeau, *Men of War,* 468; Redkey, "Profile of the Fifty-Fourth," 33; *Springfield* (Massachusetts) *Republican,* August 1, 1941.

24. *Liberator,* February 16, 1865; Rawn James Jr., *The Double V: How Wars, Protest, and Harry Truman Desegregated America's Military* (New York: Bloomsbury, 2013), 228.

25. *Los Angeles Tribune,* December 6, 1943; *For Jobs and Freedom: Selected Speeches and Writings of A. Philip Randolph,* ed. Andrew Kersten (Amherst: University of Massachusetts Press, 2015), 295.

26. Eric Lach, "Confederates Look to Win 'Second Battle of Olustee' in Florida," *TPM Muckraker,* December 5, 2013; Lizette Alvarez, "Blue and Gray Still in Conflict at a Battle Site," *New York Times,* January 16, 2014.

27. Niko Emack-Bazelais and Jennifer Smith, "Confederate Flag Hung from Boston Memorial for Black Soldiers," *Boston Globe,* June 29, 2015.

Index

Douglas R. Egerton is a professor of history at Le Moyne College. The award-winning author of seven previous books, he lives with his wife, historian Leigh Fought, in Fayetteville, New York.